Party Change in Southern Europe

It has been argued that political parties are weakening. In Southern Europe, however, political parties have shown remarkable pragmatism. Not only have they played a crucial role in the installation and consolidation of democracy, mostly in the 1970s and 1980s, but they have also adapted to the aftermaths of severe political crises during the 1990s.

Party Change in Southern Europe addresses a basic issue: have parties in Southern Europe weakened over the decade 1995–2005? Or have they rather changed? And if so, how have they changed? To answer these questions the authors analyse the transformations undergone by the two main parties in Italy, Spain, Greece, Portugal, Turkey and Cyprus (North and South) focusing on several dimensions of change. For each political group, systematic analysis is offered on:

- party organization (have party rules and power relationships changed since the mid-1990s? What has happened to party membership and leadership?);
- electoral politics (have parties turned into campaign machines committed to meeting the requirements of communication consultants?);
- competitive strategies (have parties changed their competitive strategies? If so, on what basis?); and
- party values and programmes (on which occasions have parties softened their ideology and modified their electoral programmes? Did these changes affect the policies implemented once in government?)

This book was previously published as a special issue of *South European Society & Politics*.

Anna Bosco is Associate Professor of Political Parties and Interest Groups at the University of Trieste. She is Assistant Editor of *South European Society & Politics*.

Leonardo Morlino is Professor of Political Science at the Istituto Italiano di Scienze Umane (Florence) and Director of the Research Centre on Southern Europe (Florence).

Party Change in Southern Europe

Edited by
Anna Bosco and Leonardo Morlino

Routledge
Taylor & Francis Group

LONDON AND NEW YORK

First published 2007 by Routledge

711 Third Avenue, New York, NY 10017, USA
2 Park Square, Milton Park, Abingdon, Oxon OX14 4RN

Routledge is an imprint of the Taylor & Francis Group, an informa business

First issued in paperback 2016

Typeset in Minion 10.5/13pt by the Alden Group, Oxfordshire

British Library Cataloguing in Publication Data
A catalogue record for this book is available from the British Library

Library of Congress Cataloging in Publication Data
A catalog record for this book has been requested

ISBN 978-1-138-97796-9 (pbk)
ISBN 978-0-415-37355-5 (hbk)

CONTENTS

What Changes in South European Parties? A Comparative Introduction

Anna Bosco & Leonardo Morlino

Party changes are a traditional topic of research and a major political issue within European democracies. Country-based studies and cross-national projects have explored the transformation of political parties and resulted in a number of empirical and theoretical contributions.[1] In Southern Europe, however, political party changes have not gone hand in hand with comparative research. Hence, whereas during the last 15 years parties in Portugal, Spain, Italy, Greece, Cyprus and Turkey have undergone a wide range of changes and innovations, these processes have not been the subject of systematic cross-national investigation. On the one hand, there are works that focus on single parties or countries, neglecting the comparative perspective. On the other hand, the small number of publications that have adopted a cross-national perspective (for example, Ignazi & Ysmal 1998; Morlino 1998; Bosco 2000; Diamandouros & Gunther 2001) cover in depth no more than the first half of the 1990s, with the sole exception of the most recent work by Van Biezen (2003) and Evans (2005) concerning Spain, Portugal and the Italian right-wing parties.

This research project has been set up to investigate whether and how political parties in Southern Europe changed between 1995 and 2005. The decade starting in the mid-1990s seems particularly relevant for the study of party change in Southern Europe, as shown by events such as the crossing of the government threshold by the right-wing Popular Party in Spain, the development of a system of coalitional bipolarism in Italy, the long opposition role played by the Portuguese and Greek conservative parties, the transformation of political Islam in Turkey and the consolidation of two different party systems in Cyprus.

For each country we decided to focus only on the two main parties. This decision is justified by the fact that we are not interested in small elite parties, where the role and choice of leaders are the prominent features, but in political parties with large electoral support that address the issues of membership, organization, identity, incumbency, as well as all the other aspects that are at the core of the present debate in the party literature (Krouwel 2006). As a consequence, we chose the two parties that by the mid-1990s were the main government and opposition forces in the South European countries.[2] We were lucky enough to involve in the project a group of distinguished scholars who agreed to research the evolution of the selected parties. The articles that follow are the result of such an effort.[3]

As our interest is fundamentally empirical and comparative, we asked the authors to follow a common framework of analysis based on four dimensions of party change: the values and programme, the organization, competitive strategy and campaign politics. The reason why we selected those aspects and not others (Gunther & Diamond 2003; Krouwel 2006) was that they represent the main dimensions (values, actors, rules and structures) along which a system can change. We were—and are—aware that each of these features could have become the subject of a whole book rather than a section of an article. However, by including all four dimensions, we chose to offer a broader picture of party developments. The authors of this special issue, in their contributions, analyse those aspects systematically in each party, so that the reader may trace the same dimension across all the parties.

At the end of the field research, with the written papers in our hands, the main empirical results to emphasize concern the survival of party membership, the role of party leaders, the current content of South European left- and right-wing parties in terms of values and programmes, and the balance of organizational power. These topics will be addressed in the next four sections, to be followed by a fifth concluding section on overall party changes (competitive strategy and campaign politics included).

Do Parties Still Enrol Members?

The data on party members collected by Mair and Van Biezen (2001) make clear that a lot has changed across Europe since the 1980s, as party membership has declined in almost every country.[4] This decline has been explained by a variety of arguments, ranging from the insufficient 'supply' of members—due to political dealignment, generalized welfare state provisions and expanded education and leisure opportunities—to the weak 'demand' of party leaders and organizers, who seem to have found more efficient and less time-consuming ways to raise financial revenues, connect with the voters and mobilize electoral support (Scarrow 1996; Katz 2002).

How do South European parties fit into this picture of declining membership? Before answering the question, it is important to stress that the data we present here need to be viewed with caution. The articles in this issue report aggregate figures that refer to the total number of individual members claimed by each party. More often than not these data are inflated. As party leaders and officials consider the level of membership an indicator of legitimation to be used both outside (with the media) and inside the party (in internal battles), the tendency to 'adjust' the rolls is very common.

Any researcher who has ever tried to get membership data from party officials, however, knows only too well that there is no way of checking the reliability of these figures. It is only when party leaders themselves decide to clean up the files that we can get more truthful information on the extent of their membership. In this context, two examples are in order. In Portugal the decision made by the new PSD leader, Marcelo Rebelo de Sousa, to clean up the membership files in 1996 resulted in a decrease of almost 60 per cent in the number of members. In Turkey the clientelistic tradition of the parties, the habit of local party officials of increasing the number of delegates they control by enrolling friends and relatives and the absence of any obligation on members to pay dues result in exceptionally large party memberships. As a consequence, when in 2000 CHP members were asked to reregister, the membership figure plummeted from almost two million to a meagre 170,000 (see Jalali et al., this issue). Notwithstanding these problems, we believe that membership data provided by parties may still be a reliable source to identify trends and a useful tool for comparative purposes.

Table 1 presents the total number of members of the two main parties in each South European country over the 1976–2005 period and reports the same data as a percentage of the overall electorate (M/E or rate of organization), a measure that makes it possible to compare party memberships across nations and over time. The table also illustrates membership variation in each of the last three decades.

The trends in party membership show that today, in all but two countries, the main parties have more affiliates than ten years ago (Table 1[a]). Only in Portugal and Italy is this not the case, while in northern Cyprus the number of party members has not changed. As for Turkey and northern Cyprus, however, we should stress that the data refer to only one of the two main parties: the AKP is a recent political force for which only the 2005 membership figure is available, while the northern Cypriot UBP does not have a register of party members (see Christophorou, this issue).

Such a picture of stability and growth with minor patches of decline is confirmed when we shift from raw numbers to the analysis of the rate of organization. The last column of Table 1(b) clearly shows that between 1996 and 2005 most of the party memberships not only kept pace with the growth of the electorate, but in four cases (Spain, Greece, the Republic of Cyprus and Turkey) even managed to grow at a higher rate than the national electorates. Only in Portugal and northern Cyprus is the M/E ratio negative, while in Italy the decrease in party affiliation was matched by that in the overall electorate, resulting in a zero rate. Therefore, a first conclusion that can be drawn from these data is that in Southern Europe there is no party membership decline as in the rest of Europe. In the 1996–2005 decade such a decline was limited to two countries, while even Italy seems to have stopped the haemorrhage of members that had characterized the general crisis of the early 1990s. Actually, if we compare the changes in the M/E ratio registered by the two main parties in a number of European polities between 1990 and 2000 with those recorded in Southern Europe, we identify different tendencies (Table 2).

When the rates of change registered in 1996–2005 are compared with those of the preceding 20 years another important aspect emerges very neatly, since this period

Table 1 Party Membership of the Two Main Parties in Southern Europe (1976–2005)

(a) Party members: absolute numbers and rate of change[*]

	Party membership				Rate of change (%) [†]		
	1976	1986	1996	2005	1976–86	1986–96	1996–2005
Portugal	116,573	148,109	262,748	190,949	+27.1	+77.4	−27.3
Spain	75,860	421,497	911,817	1,127,073	+455.6	+116.3	+23.6
Italy	2,889,516[‡]	3,320,341[‡]	802,713[§]	732,466[§]	+14.9	−75.8[¶]	−8.8
Greece	47,000	520,000	539,070	600,000	+1,006.4	+3.7	+11.3
Cyprus	24,958	26,000	38,515	49,443	+4.2	+48.1	+28.4
N. Cyprus CTP	—	—	3,000	3,000	—	—	0
Turkey CHP	—	—	163,540	561,041	—	—	+243.1
Turkey AKP				2,362,857			

(b) Party members: M/E ratios

	M/E ratio				Change in M/E ratio		
	1976	1986	1996	2005[**]	1976–86	1986–96	1996–2005
Portugal	1.8	1.9	3.1	2.2	+0.1	+1.2	−0.9
Spain	0.3	1.4	2.8	3.2	+1.1	+1.4	+0.4
Italy	7.1	7.3	1.6	1.6	+0.2	−5.7	0
Greece	0.7	5.9	5.9	6.1	+5.2	0	+0.2
Cyprus	8.1	7.5	9.4	9.9	+0.6	+1.9	+0.5
N. Cyprus CTP	—	—	2.8	2.0	—	—	−0.8
Turkey CHP	—	—	0.8	1.4	—	—	+0.6
Turkey AKP				5.5			

[*] Portugal (1976–87–95–2005); Spain (1982–86–96–2004); Italy (1976–87–96–2004); Greece (1977–85–96–2005); Republic of Cyprus (1981–86–96–2004); northern Cyprus (1993–2003); Turkey (1995–2005).

[†] Change in party membership as a percentage of the membership at the beginning of the selected period.

[‡] The two main parties are the Christian Democracy and the Communist Party.

[§] The two main parties are Forza Italia and the DS.

[¶] The rate is of course based on two different groups of parties.

[**] The 2005 M/E ratio is calculated on the electorate of the last available elections, that is, 2002 in Turkey, 2004 in Spain and Greece, 2005 in Portugal and northern Cyprus and 2006 in Italy and the Republic of Cyprus.

Sources: Data provided by the contributors to this issue and Katz and Mair (1992) for Italy 1976–86.

Table 2 Change in M/E Ratio of the Two Main Parties

Austria 1990–99	− 6.1
Norway 1990–97	− 4.9
Finland 1989–98	− 2.3
Ireland 1990–98	− 1.3
Sweden 1989–98	− 1.3
Germany 1989–99	− 1
Portugal 1995–2005	**− 0.9**
The Netherlands 1989–2000	− 0.8
United Kingdom 1989–98	− 0.7
Denmark 1989–98	− 0.3
Italy 1996–2005	**0**
Greece 1996–2004	**+ 0.2**
Spain 1996–2004	**+ 0.4**
Cyprus 1996–2005	**+ 0.5**

Source: Own calculations based on data provided by Mair and Van Biezen (2001).

evinces a different trend in relation to the past. The last three columns of Table 1(a) and (b) show that four of the five countries for which data are available for the whole time span recorded a spectacular increase in the numbers of party members between the mid-1970s and the mid-1990s. Such an upward trend, however, becomes more moderate (in Spain, Greece and the Republic of Cyprus) or stops abruptly (in Portugal) by 1995–96. The dramatic growth of rank and file, related to the need to build party organization from scratch after the democratic transition, may have concentrated in the first decade, as in Greece and Spain, or in the second, as in Portugal, but since the mid-1990s it has slowed down or stopped altogether.

Italy, on the other hand, has followed the opposite pattern. After the sweeping changes of the parties and the party system in the first half of the 1990s (Morlino 1996), the main parties that emerged from that 'political big bang'—both new, as in the case of Berlusconi's FI, and old, as with the former communists renamed DS—have managed to keep the decrease in their rank and file below the threshold of ten per cent, putting an end to the deep membership decline of the preceding decade (Table 1[a]). A second conclusion, therefore, is that between 1996 and 2005 party memberships in Southern Europe have all distanced from their own past of exceptional growth or decline, becoming more similar to their other European counterparts.

The data presented up to this point show whether political parties are successful in retaining their membership, but do not tell us anything about the quality of their efforts to enrol members. To complete the picture of the party rank and file we therefore now turn to the trends in membership density (M/V), a ratio calculated by dividing a party's membership by its own voters. Such a measure indicates 'a party's ability to penetrate its own electorate organizationally' (Poguntke 2002, 52) and can be used to gauge the different capabilities of the South European parties in encapsulating their electoral support.

When we consider the M/V ratio (Table 3), the picture of stability and moderate growth shown by the analysis of the rate of organization is not confirmed. On the

Table 3 Membership Density (1976–2005)

	M/V ratio				Change in M/V ratio		
	1976	1986	1996	2005	1976–86	1986–96	**1996–2005**
Portugal	3.6	3.6	5.7	4.5	0	+2.1	**−1.2**
Spain	1.1	3.0	4.8	5.4	+1.9	+1.8	**+ 0.6**
Italy	10.8	14.1	5.1	4.5	+3.3	−9.0	**−0.6**
Greece	1.4	9.4	10.0	9.4	+8.0	+0.6	**−0.6**
Cyprus	13.3	13.3	15.4	19.1	0	+2.1	**+ 3.7**
N. Cyprus CTP	—	—	12.0	6.0	—	—	**−6.0**
Turkey CHP	—	—	5.4	9.2	—	—	**+ 3.8**
Turkey AKP				21.9			

Sources and notes: See Table 1.

contrary, the South European main parties seem to have had difficulty in organizing the support of their voters: in four cases out of seven, a negative ratio is recorded for the 1996–2005 period.

Moreover, the data in the last column of Table 3 reinforce our contention that between 1996 and 2005 political parties in Southern Europe entered a different phase. On the one hand, Portugal, Spain, Greece and northern Cyprus record a membership density much lower than in the previous decades, signalling that parties are probably less motivated—and less able—to convert voters into members than in the past. On the other hand, again, the Italian case evinces a different pattern, as the political parties that consolidated their presence after the mid-1990s show a moderately negative membership density, similar to that displayed by the Greek parties—which did not have to face a political earthquake like the Italian one—a sign that the worst times are over. Overall, Table 3 sheds light on our third conclusion: parties are gradually losing their capacity to offer lukewarm supporters a more permanent organizational shelter, a trend shared with other Western European political forces (Poguntke 2002, 54–56).

Taken together, the data on party membership display a number of differences between the national cases, as well as among the parties. This leads us to the last question to be addressed: which parties are more able to build up and keep stable their membership over time? And, in particular, does the left–right divide make any difference in terms of membership organization? Table 4, which reorganizes, along the left–right split, the data on party membership presented in the previous tables, reveals an unexpected picture.

If we look at the organization rate and the membership density, it is evident that in 2005 the right-wing parties fare better than those positioned on the left of the political continuum, since the former seem more able both to attract affiliates and to organize their supporters than the latter. As expected, the only exception is the Italian FI, a party that was born as a 'light' organization with no interest whatsoever in enrolling members (see Raniolo, this issue). However, if the evolution over the 1996–2005 period is taken into account, a mixed picture emerges, since only the Italian FI, the Spanish PP and the Cypriot DISY show an increase in the raw number of members

Table 4 Party Membership Change: Left- and Right-Wing Parties

	M/E ratio 2005		Change in M/E ratio 1996–2005		Change rate in number of members (%) 1996–2005		M/V ratio 2005		Change in M/V ratio 1996–2005	
	L	R	L	R	L	R	L	R	L	R
Portugal	0.9	1.3	−0.2	−0.8	−7.9	−36.0	2.9	7.1	−0.8	−2.0
Spain	1.3	1.9	+0.2	+0.2	+23.8	+30.9	4.2	6.8	+0.3	+1.2
Italy	1.2	0.4	−0.6	+0.1	−18.3	+47.6	7.6	1.9	−1.1	+0.4
Greece	2.5	3.5	+0.8	−0.7	+60.6	−8.7	8.3	10.4	+2.8	−4.4
Cyprus	2.8	7.1	−0.6	+1.1	−0.4	+44.8	10.6	27.8	−0.9	+8.6
Turkey	1.4	5.5	+0.6	—	+243.1	—	9.2	21.9	+3.8	—

Sources: See Table 1.

coupled with the growth of both the M/E and the M/V ratios. Conversely, over the decade, the Portuguese PSD and the Greek ND lose members and face negative M/E and M/V ratios. In the same vein, by 2005, the party membership of the left-wing organizations fare worse than their centre-right counterparts, but—again—show a mixed picture of positive (in the case of CHP and the Greek and Spanish socialist parties) and negative developments over the 1996-2005 decade (PS, DS and AKEL).

The reasons behind these different features will become clearer when we assess the role of incumbency on party change in the concluding section. Here we would like to develop another consideration related to the role played by party members in the internal balance of power. Recent studies have argued that the shrinking of party membership is one of the symptoms of the 'ascendancy of the party in public office' (Katz & Mair 2002, p. 126). From such a perspective the presence and consistency of party affiliates has to do with the party's internal balance of power. It has also been argued that where party members have been empowered with 'internal process incentives' (Ignazi 2002), such as the opportunity to elect the party leader or to choose the candidates to public offices, this may have the consequence of strengthening the party leadership at the expense of the activists and the middle-level elites (Mair 1994, Katz 2001). In short, according to these works, exploring the 'ground floor' of the party building helps us to understand better the organization of the higher floors of power.

From this point of view, what is the evidence offered by the South European parties? Here we want to stress two points. First, not only is there no shrinking of party memberships—as we have already pointed out—but also party organizers are introducing new forms of affiliation. As a matter of fact, our cases reveal the birth of a new kind of party affiliate, the sympathizer. Sympathizers are affiliates who do not pay dues. They share with regular members a number of rights, which differ from party to party, and—most importantly—their names are included in a separate roll. Since 2000 all the main left-wing parties—PS, PSOE, DS, PASOK and AKEL (albeit in a less formalized way)—have enrolled sympathizers.

How can such a blurring of the distinction between members and non-members (Scarrow 2005) be explained? We argue that this new category of members has been introduced because it represents an asset for parties. It is true that sympathizers do not pay dues and this can be considered a cost for the organization. In times of public funding, however, dues are not so important and parties can do without them fairly well. What is really important is that sympathizers constitute an additional source of supporters. Thanks to their inscription in a specific roll, sympathizers can be contacted and mobilized when necessary (before elections, but also in special political contingencies)—a task made easy by the new technologies. In other words, by transforming members that have stopped paying their dues into sympathizers and opening their doors to new sympathizers, parties have gained a larger base of supporters who do not object to getting political messages and petitions from time to time.

The relevance of this new figure has been confirmed by a senior PSOE party officer who explained to one of the authors of this introduction that preparing the sympathizers' roll had been an opportunity to get important information, such as their email addresses and mobile phone numbers. Today, PSOE's sympathizers account for 48.7 per cent of the whole membership (Bosco 2005, 75). In addition, the fact that the last congress of the Spanish PP, held in 2004, decided to enrol sympathizers for the first time proves that also the right-wing parties are beginning to recognize their importance. Overall, for most South European parties affiliates are an asset, even if they do not pay dues.

The second point we want to stress relates to membership empowerment through internal incentives. On this issue, the picture offered by our parties is varied. In the next section we show that members elect the leader in a number of parties. Other parties give their membership the possibility of choosing candidates for public office at both national and local levels. Thus the PSOE membership is called to elect the candidate for prime minister; the members of AKEL, DISY and, again, PSOE vote for different municipal and local candidates; and the DS, PASOK and DISY can consult their affiliates through internal referenda and consultations. On the basis of our research it is not possible to make an assessment of the marginalization of party activists and the empowerment of the leaders. Scarrow (1999) has already shown that this kind of democratic incentive may be intended to revitalize the base and make the party more attractive to potential voters rather than to weaken activists and cadres. We can only emphasize that the most powerful leaders in Southern Europe, such as those of the PP, FI, the AKP, the CHP and the UBP (see next section), are elected by party congress and that their memberships are among those that have not been empowered in any way. On the other hand, parties whose members have benefited from the new participative incentives do not seem to have more autonomous and powerful leaders than in the past. On this issue, however, more focused empirical research is needed.

How Important Are Party Leaders?

When looking at recent organizational developments of parties, also in other, non-South European democracies, it is inevitable that we should assess the role of

Table 5 How Party Leadership Is Selected

Mode	Portugal	Spain	Italy	Greece	Cyprus	Turkey
Acclamation			FI			
Open primary			Union*	PASOK		
Member vote	PS PSD		DS		DISY	
Party congress		PP PSOE		ND	CTP UBP	AKP CHP
Party assembly					AKEL	

* Centre-left coalition, named Union in the 2006 elections, formed by the DS, Democracy and Freedom, Communist Refoundation Party and other minor political forces.

leadership in the parties we are analysing. More precisely, we can select three problems to address the topic: how the leaders are selected; how their powers are concentrated within the party; what the key mechanisms of turnover are.

As can be easily seen in Table 5, most of the main parties still choose their leaders in the traditional delegative way, through election by party congress (PP, PSOE, ND, CTP, UBP, AKP, and CHP) and the party assembly, that is, the central committee in the case of AKEL. However, more recently, mainly in reaction to the weakening of party links at territorial level, new forms of selection have emerged: open primaries were held among the Greek socialists (2004) and the Italian centre left (2005); while systems of internal voting by party members, similar to closed primaries, were set up by the Portuguese socialists (1998) and social democrats (2006), by the Italian DS (2000) and by the Cypriot DISY (2003). In addition, acclamation by party delegates became the way to elect the leader of the Italian FI.

In these innovations, the main South European parties are not too different from the other well-established Western European democracies, where the election in the party congress remains the dominant mode of selection, accounting for twice as many cases of primaries and party member elections added together (Scarrow et al. 2000, pp. 142– 144). Thus, an immediate first conclusion is that there is innovation and adaptation in leadership selection to strengthen the links with the rank and file, and this phenomenon is consistent with what is happening in the other European countries.

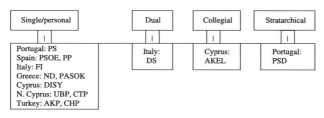

Figure 1 Alternatives in Concentration of Leadership Powers.

On the power of leaders, the evidence points to the following conclusions (see Figure 1). There is almost no innovation: parties maintain a single leadership as a dominant feature, since it appears at least a better-suited tool to develop a more efficient electoral competition within the party system. De-ideologization and other developments that have undermined the grassroots level have brought about an additional strengthening of the single leadership and, more specifically, of a highly personalized leadership, such as in the Italian FI and the northern Cypriot UBP. So, if there is a trend, this seems to be the strengthening of personal leadership, an already dominant phenomenon in Southern Europe (see below).

This trend is so marked that different arrangements, such as that of the Italian DS or the Portuguese PSD, or even the collective leadership of the Cypriot AKEL, have to be considered exceptions related to the specific traditions and histories of those parties. The dual leadership in the DS may only be a temporary arrangement due to the strong personality of the present president of the party, Massimo D'Alema. It is difficult to think that such a dualism will survive and the traditional prominence of the secretary will not be re-established once D'Alema has left that position or has accepted a governmental office. The situation of AKEL is more ambiguous. On the one hand, it is a rather traditional communist party, whose secretary-general is a *primus inter pares* with limited prominence. On the other hand, the present leader enjoys a more significant role than in the past, due mainly to his personal influence. Finally, the stratarchical structure of the Portuguese PSD is more seriously grounded in the history and tradition of that party since its beginning, due to the local notables who were the key leading actors in the party's foundation.

On the whole, a comparison with other Western European cases supports a second conclusion: the important role of single leadership in some South European parties. This is also confirmed by a sort of litmus test we can add, once we consider the reasons of leadership turnover in these cases. One of the prevailing reasons why there is turnover in single, but not personalized, leadership is electoral fiasco. If there is such a failure, but no turnover follows, then we can affirm that the party is a 'personal party', in which the leader is *legibus solutus*, not constrained by organizational or political internal rules, and other leaders are always in a subordinate position (see also Calise 2000 and Gunther & Diamond 2003). This is what we can see clearly in the Italian FI, the northern Cypriot UBP and the Turkish CHP. For the other Turkish party, AKP, which had its first electoral contest in 2002, the test of electoral defeat cannot be

Figure 2 Single and Personal Leadership.

applied, but a general assessment also identifies it as a party characterized by personal leadership (Figure 2).

For the other cases a single, less clearly personalized leadership seems the rule. The two Greek parties, for example, show an important trend. Both PASOK and the ND had a strong personalized charismatic leadership in the first decade of their existence and later (Morlino 1998). Their institutionalization, however, brought about the change into parties with a strong leadership, but no longer personalized. Thus, this litmus test is revealing in the sense of clarifying the characteristics of parties with single leadership. Furthermore, in some cases, such as the Spanish PP, the turnover is characterized by strong continuity, rather than change: a new leader is proposed and imposed by the predecessor. That is, there is a cooptative mode of leader recruitment. In addition, in the specific case of the PP, there is a relevant problem: the new PP leader, Mariano Rajoy, was supported by the defeated previous prime minister, José María Aznar. Actually, Aznar was able to impose his successor at a moment when an electoral victory was expected, but Rajoy was confirmed after the PP lost the 2004 elections. Thus, in spite of having lost the elections, Aznar seems to have been able to retain the control of the party. From this perspective this seems a mixed case of single/personal leadership.

On the whole, the most interesting result of this overview—and our third conclusion—is that the notion of a high or higher personalization of party politics during the last 15 years (1990–2005) is not supported by our research. There is some personalization of party politics. Also Calise (2005), Van Biezen and Hopkin (2005) and Costa Lobo (2005) note aspects of 'presidentialization' of politics in Italy, Spain and Portugal, respectively. But Costa Lobo provides the most balanced assessment: 'there are trends that indicate presidentialization is at work, although the evidence is not unequivocal', and this is also consistent with our results. More precisely, it seems that the personalization that characterized the 1970s and the 1980s in some South European countries was rather the result of the first years of transition, installation and consolidation (Morlino 1998), rather than a stable and recurrent characteristic in these countries.

Why were the expectations not met, and how do we account for the exceptions in Italy, northern Cyprus and Turkey? On the whole, personalization of politics has been a prevailing feature of South European politics because a political culture characterized by cynicism, passivity and clientelism in some areas was complemented by the phases of transition and democratic consolidation, where a few leaders played a key role, and by a consistent trend of de-ideologization since the 1970s. Subsequent developments have been characterized by the institutionalization of parties and party systems, inevitable leadership turnover, and the weakening of clientelism—partly because of the role played by European Union policies. Thus, while within political contexts such as those of Central and Northern European democracies—well established for a long time and with little, if any, clientelism—de-ideologization and development of TV political communication are at the origin of a trend of party personalization, in Southern Europe party institutionalization and the undermining of clientelism played against the other two factors. This explains why a trend towards higher personalization does not appear in the South European cases and eventually all European cases will come closer on this feature.

Such an explanation, which in the end stresses a sort of equifinality, is also useful to account for the three exceptions: in Italy, since the early 1990s, there has been a long transitional phase (see also Calise 2005) and FI is a party born at the beginning of that phase and thanks to it; in northern Cyprus, the UBP is totally controlled by a leader who had the advantage of a long incumbency within a very unusual context; in Turkey there remains a long, gradual process of democratic transition and consolidation which affects both parties, the AKP and the CHP.

What Is Left? And What Is Right?

In the context of South European politics is the left–right cleavage still relevant? A consistent number of research results have confirmed this proposition at both mass and elite levels (Morlino 1998). The research by Benoit and Laver (2006) also shows this very effectively (Table 6). On a 1 to 10 scale the most radical leftist party is the communist Cypriot AKEL, but the Italian DS is also considered to be much more to the left than all other leftist parties: the communist legacy seems to be still present despite the elapsed years and the other more radical heirs of the old Communist Party, such as the Party of Communist Refoundation (PRC) and the Party of Italian Communists (PdCI). At the other end of the spectrum, the Cypriot conservative DISY is again the most rightist, closely followed by the Spanish PP. For the latter the authoritarian legacy seems totally forgotten, but after 2000 Aznar adopted a confrontational style of government with polarizing consequences.

Another interesting aspect is the distance between the two main parties. As expected, Cyprus is the most radicalized country, but Italy and Spain follow. Here there is something new and surprising: Spain, which has been characterized for years by moderate politics, is now more polarized (see above) than Greece, which has long

Table 6 Assessment on a Left–Right Scale and Mutual Distance

Country	Party	L/R	Party	L/R	L/R distance
Portugal	PS	4.3	PSD	6.9	2.6
Spain	PSOE	4.1	PP	8.5	4.4
Italy	DS	3.0	FI	7.8	4.8
Greece	PASOK	5.2	ND	7.8	2.6
Cyprus	AKEL	1.5	DISY	8.7	7.2
N. Cyprus	CTP	—	UBP	—	—
Turkey	CHP	3.7	AKP	7.1	3.4

Note: For simplicity's sake we recalculated the left—right positions, assessed by country experts, on a 1—10 scale.
Source: Benoit and Laver (2006, Appendix B).

been a highly polarized polity. Our research confirms these opposite trends in the two countries (see Table 6).

This analysis suggests that a more detailed investigation is necessary for the understanding of what kind of left and what kind of right we have in those countries. Tables 7 and 8 suggest a picture where values, programmes and an overall assessment of left and right are provided. To begin with the left, the only party with persisting reference to Marxism is AKEL; all other parties have abandoned this classical point of reference in their values and ideology. The Greek PASOK under Simitis is the party that during recent years has covered more ground in moderating its values and programmes up to the point of creating uncertainty and indecision inside the party. We can safely say that this is so, since the other socialist parties, such as the PS, the PSOE and the DS, made those changes much earlier (Table 7). No doubt the Turkish CHP with its autarchic positions is an original kind of left in this picture: rejection of the market and competition are complemented by protection of small business and strong secularism. In addition, the left-wing parties of Portugal, Spain, Italy and Greece are inside the European Socialist Party and their relationships are fairly continuous at EU level (this is not the case for AKEL, a member of United European Left/North European Green Left). Thus, they have been influencing each other for years, even if at a slow pace. On the whole, our first conclusion is that the centrist drive of socialism in Southern Europe is consistent with the transformations within the leftist parties of all the other Western European countries: no longer do they recall the glorious old values and programmes of their predecessors, despite the recurrent reference to solidarity and social justice.

Finding a common definition for the right-wing parties is much more difficult, since nothing similar to the common origins of the left exists. In terms of values, however, the various ways of combining and conjugating the liberal tenets of freedom and the market seem common ground for all of them (Table 8).

A few peculiarities are worth recalling. First of all, the Portuguese Social Democrat notion of 'third way' for a conservative party: 'there is no ideology, but only good or bad management' (see Jalali, this issue). Second, the broad renovation carried out by the Spanish PP, the only party with some authoritarian legacy abandoned both at the programmatic and leadership level. The old Francoist minister Fraga Iribarne is still the honorary president of the party, but the leadership has almost completely changed. Then there is the modernization and broad reorganization of ND in recent years in terms of both leadership and programmes. Of course, economic problems are at the forefront for the northern Cypriot left and right. The support for moderate secularism by the Turkish AKP, which is complemented by the stronger secularism of the CHP, may guarantee Turkey a safer path towards a viable democratic regime.

We know that party values and programmes can be translated into policies. Here, again, Benoit and Laver (2006) with their data on the expert survey on policy importance and positions of parties can help us to complete the picture sketched out above.[5] When considering the degree of importance of the main policy issues for the parties we have mentioned, it is immediately clear (Table 9) that the same policies

Table 7 The South European Left

Country	Party	Values, programmes, overall assessment[*]
Portugal	PS	• no references to Marxism in party statute (since 1986); stress on solidarity and social justice • pragmatic liberalism, implementation of new social policies and economic orthodoxy; stress on education, information society, welfare state (esp. health care and the social security system) • moderate orientation
Spain	PSOE	• equality and social justice, solidarity, freedom and pluralism • orthodox economic policy, stress on civil rights, education and housing, but also on dialogue and consensus building • innovation within moderate leftism
Italy	DS	• detachment from the old Marxist tradition and full acceptance of liberal democracy at least since 1991; appreciation of economic institutions of capitalism, market-oriented economic ideas and rethinking of the role of the state in the economy • stress on women's rights, civil rights and environmental policy increased salience of institutional reform issue since early 1990s • moderate leftist posture, with left-wing hardliners
Greece	PASOK	• since 2000 genuine political liberalism • exclusion of references to social classes in the party programme and reference to civil society; stress on economic accumulation structures and processes, drastic control of inflation and deficits, and strong currency; extensive privatization programmes (esp. Simitis 1998); later, 'post-materialist' agenda and the promotion of liberal values • party's uncertainty and indecision, but moderate posture
Cyprus	AKEL	• Marxist identity, but since 1990 road to socialism pursued by democratic means, with respect for pluralism and freedoms • stress on the modernization of the state and private institutions and changes in the relationship between the administration and the citizens • radical positions
Northern Cyprus	CTP	• former communist identity modified since 1990–92 • liberal socialist formation accepting free market and privatization • more moderate posture
Turkey	CHP	• statist ideology; opposition to the privatization of state enterprises reservations about the market system; defender of secularism • rhetoric pronouncements rather than focus on policies; criticisms of IMF[†]-approved economic stabilization and restructuring programmes; protection of small businesses against 'unfair' competition; state subsidies to agriculture • distrust of external economic actors seen as always ready to exploit Turkey; approval of the relationship with Europe, but harsh criticism of the government for subservience to the EU on specific issues such as Cyprus • autarchic bent

[*] The assessment refers to the first years of the 21st century.
[†] International Monetary Fund.

Table 8 The South European Right

Country	Party	Values, programmes, overall assessment[*]
Portugal	PSD	• 'third way' notion that 'there is no ideology, only good or bad management' • pattern of programmatic indefinition; in 2002 programme of deep tax cuts, a 'fiscal shock' designed to jolt the economy into greater growth (abandoned once in office); main goal being maximization of votes and winning of elections • conservative, moderate party
Spain	PP	• conservative liberalism • policy mix of liberal economic policies and sustainable welfare social policies; weakening of the trade unions • conservative posture
Italy	FI	• stress on economic free enterprise, the breaking-up of the state and market centrality with an authoritarian vision of society; anti-communist position • consequent policy positions; pro-American stand complemented by Eurosceptic attitudes • moderate, conservative party with radical position on occasions
Greece	ND	• recently ideas and policies traditionally identified with the social-democratic left, such as the amelioration and increase of social security schemes • new political programme focused on non-ideological issues (such as education, health, social order and state efficiency, culture and the environment), as well as on problems related to the management of the state and the economy (for example, bad administration and state inefficiency, tax evasion, corruption) • moderate, centrist party
Cyprus	DISY	• democracy and democratic principles given a prominent place • moderate positions complemented by often expressed nationalist stands • moderate, right-wing party
Northern Cyprus	UBP	• liberal democrat ideology in favor of market economy • necessity of development of various sectors of the economy; emphasis on political issues and the EU supporting a European course for Turkish Cypriots • moderate party
Turkey	AKP	• emphasis on democracy, freedom of expression, human rights, and the rule of law; moderate secularism envisaged as a *sine qua non* condition for democracy • recognizing the role of the state in the free market economy only with a regulatory and supervisory capacity; in foreign policy close ties with the United States, European countries and the European Union • moderate, conservative centre-right party

[*] The assessment refers to the first years of the 21st century.

attract the attention of leftist and rightist parties. And this is evident, as party elites of a given country have to cope with the problems of that country at any particular time. Thus, on the one hand, we have a clue to one of the reasons why some authors argue that the left–right divide is blurred: the fact that parties cover the same issues will confuse anyone who is not well aware of the different, or even radically different,

Table 9 Importance of Main Policy Issues for Left and Right

Dimension	Portugal		Spain		Italy		Greece		Cyprus		Turkey	
	PS	PSD	PSOE	PP	DS	FI	PASOK	ND	AKEL	DISY	CHP	AKP
Taxes vs. spending	12.29	**14.33**	**14.59**	**15.35**	**15.02**	**16.82**	13.81	**14.47**	**17.0**	14.5	12.77	13.22
Social policies	11.63	11.52	13.29	12.32	13.13	11.09	10.06	8.38	10.75	9.5	9.04	10.44
Decentralization	**13.57**	**12.81**	13.87	14.82	14.12	10.68	13.31	10.5	15.0	12.25	13.89	15.43
Environment	12.24	10.9	11.51	8.97	12.98	9.23	12.06	10.13	10.0	10.25	12.07	8.36
Deregulation			**14.64**	**16.65**	13.49	**16.07**	**14.56**	**16.38**	**17.25**	**16.75**	13.31	13.7
Nationalism											13.56	13.1
Religion											**17.7**	**17.96**
Immigration	**13.4**	11.8	13.97	14.69	14.96	13.25	**13.88**	13.31	11.0	13.0	8.32	9.15
EU joining									15.75	**18.0**	**15.26**	**17.68**

Note: These figures were kindly made available by Kenneth Benoit and Michael Laver and are part of a data set for their new book (2006). We would like to acknowledge here their generosity and thank them.

positions that parties have on those same issues. The other recurring reason to support the hypothesis of the blurring border is the centrist drive of leftist parties and of some rightist ones, which has already been emphasized. Besides, we know that the same issues can become relevant for different parties as a systemic-competitive effect.

There are, however, some relative exceptions. In Portugal the PSD pays more attention to economic aspects such as 'taxes versus spending' than the socialists; in Italy, deregulation seems more important for FI than for the DS and, conversely, immigration is more important for the DS than for FI; and in Greece the problems of immigration are relatively more important for PASOK, while aspects of economic policy are more relevant for the ND. Behind the varying importance paid to different policy issues there are also different political analyses and policy intentions: the Cypriot AKEL envisages the solution to the economic problems of its country through a domestic political economy related to the dimension 'taxes versus spending', whereas clearly for DISY the possible solution to Cypriot problems will come from the economic help that the country is going to receive from the EU.

In giving additional empirical support to our previous analysis, the presence or absence of a dimension is also helpful. In this way we can see how joining the EU is a particularly relevant dimension in Cyprus before 2004 and, above all, how religion versus secularism and nationalism are specific elements of the Turkish parties, as already stressed above. The Spanish and Italian distances between the two main parties along the left–right division (Table 6) are also evident when policies are considered. Table 10 is useful in adding meaningful details to our conclusions on the different positions of the parties. The economic policy dimension on the choice between higher public spending and lower taxes is the classical dividing policy between left and right, and in fact on this dimension we have the greater distance among the left and the right in Portugal, Spain, Italy and Cyprus. At the same time the very moderate path undertaken by PASOK in Greece is indirectly confirmed by the fact that this dimension is not among the most divisive ones: social policies and civil rights, state involvement in economic regulation, and immigration policy are more divisive. In Turkey the fact that religious issues are the most important, as well as divisive, is also confirmed by these data (see figures in bold in Table 10).

In sum, the left–right cleavage is alive and important; the differences between leftist and rightist parties are still strong despite the centrist drives on the left and the political emptying of the right; Turkey presents a partially different profile, where religion and nationalism play a key role in political life. The empirical evidence provided by the data gathered by Benoit and Laver (2006) concurs with these conclusions and gives further detail on various issues.

Who's the Boss?

Who rules inside South European parties? Is it possible to discern a common pattern in the internal balance of power, or do some specific features and dissimilarities prevail? The relevance of the intra-party centre–periphery cleavage and the identity of

Table 10 Positions of Left and Right on the Main Policy Issues

Dimension	Portugal		Spain		Italy		Greece		Cyprus		Turkey	
	PS	PSD	PSOE	PP	DS	FI	PASOK	ND	AKEL	DISY	CHP	AKP
Taxes vs. spending	**8.6**	**14.5**	**7.4**	**16.7**	**6.7**	**17.5**	10.9	14.8	**6.0**	**15.0**	6.3	8.2
Social policies	**8.1**	**14.9**	**5.6**	**17.2**	5.0	12.9	**7.8**	**14.0**	12.8	10.5	**9.8**	**17.1**
Decentralization	7.3	10.8	8.5	14.7	7.4	8.9	8.8	10.6	14.0	6.5	11.5	6.4
Environment	8.8	13.6	9.1	16.6	7.3	17.2	11.4	13.8	7.8	13.0	8.6	15.7
Deregulation			9.3	17.3	7.5	16.6	**11.4**	**16.7**	**3.0**	**16.8**	7.4	13.4
Nationalism											11.0	11.2
Religion											**18.7**	**4.7**
Immigration	7.7	12.2	7.4	16.6	**4.4**	**14.4**	**9.3**	**14.6**	7.5	11.5	8.4	10.4
EU joining									12.8	19.0	15.0	17.4
Distance (mean)	5.1		8.6		8.2		4.1		6.8		5.1	

Note: See Table 9.

the 'top decision makers' are the two main issues that should be considered to answer the questions above.

On the relevance of the centre–periphery cleavage within parties, the articles in this issue show that in a number of parties the leaders at the sub-national level may be crucial decision makers. These local 'notables' or 'barons', as they are known in political jargon across Southern Europe, are party leaders at a relevant local level (a region, a province or an important municipality), who frequently hold an elective public office. The presidents of the Spanish autonomous communities or the presidents of the Portuguese municipalities are examples. Local notables can mobilize votes, patronage and territorial organization, resources that enable them to retain control over delegates to national congresses and over the selection of parliamentary candidatures, as well as to rise to important positions in the party's national executive. The role played by local notables varies from party to party, as well as over time, and depends on different factors, such as the institutional features of the country and the specific characteristics and timing of the party building.[6] However, what emerges neatly from our research is the salience of incumbency. When the party, at the national level, is in opposition the influence of the local notables within the party tends to increase, redefining the political weight of other main actors, such as the party leader. In the Spanish PSOE, for instance, the regional barons played an important role for most of the 1990s, when the party was in opposition, and it is only with the socialists' return to government under the consolidated leadership of Rodríguez Zapatero (2004) that their role has been reshaped (see Méndez Lago, this issue). In the same vein, the Portuguese PSD's absence from government for most of the 1995–2005 decade strengthened the local notables vis-à-vis the party's central leadership (see Jalali, this issue).

The second issue we address relates to the internal balance of power. Table 11 summarizes some of the main features of the decisional process within South European parties. Rather than a systematic comparison, the table offers a rough picture of who has the power to rule within the parties and has to be read in the light of the personal leadership of some of the parties emphasized above (see Figure 2).

Here, three points need to be stressed. First, our research reveals that between 1995 and 2005 the party leaders and the top executives are the most important decision makers in the parties of Southern Europe. Party leaders are elected along with their executives (PP) or have the possibility to choose the party officials who will sit in the executive; in this way they can build strong loyalty linkages with their executives (PSD, PS, DS, PSOE). In any case party leaders are very influential within the party executives, up to the point at which they are completely predominant (FI, UBP, CHP, AKP). Second, the parliamentary groups are not characterized by political autonomy. On the contrary, they tend to abide by the decisions made by the party executives or directly by the party leader (FI, CHP). The lack of political autonomy of the parliamentary group is evident in the process of selection of parliamentary candidates, where the central executives and the party leaders play the most important role, possibly bargaining with the party executives at the local level. On the whole, our research confirms for the rest of Southern Europe the findings of Van Biezen (2000; 2003) for the Spanish and

Table 11 Power Relationships in South European Parties

Party	Party executive	Parliamentary group and related candidate selection	
PSD	The top executive is elected on the party leader proposal. The president of the parliamentary group also participates	Subordinate to the party executive	Role of the local level
PS	The top executive is chosen by the party leader	Subordinate to the party executive	Centralized process
PP	The executive committee is elected through a closed and blocked list along with the party leader. The party presidency has strong powers	Subordinate to the party executive. Since 1993 the party president has the ex officio leadership of the parliamentary groups	Centralized process
PSOE	Strong power of the national executive	Subordinate to the party executive and leader	Role of the regional level
DS	The top executive is elected on the party leader proposal	Subordinate to the party executive	Role of the regional level
FI	Dependent on the party leader	Dependent on the party leader	Dependent on the party leader
PASOK	Prominence of the party leader	Progressive strengthening of the parliamentary group	Centralized process with strong influence of the party leader
ND	The party leader is in control of the executive committee (since 2004)	The weakest component of the party	Dependent on the party leader
AKP	The leader exercises a paramount influence within the executive committee	Works together with the party executive and both are dominated by the party leader	Centralized process with strong influence of the party leader
CHP	The executive is dominated by the party leader who often is the sole decision maker	Dependent on the party leader	Dependent on the party leader
AKEL	Strong power of the top executive and the party leader	It must abide by the decisions made by the party executive. No autonomous role	Members choose candidates at the constituency level, but the candidates are approved and 'ranked' by the party executive.

(*continued*)

DISY	Power of the central organs; prominence of the party leader	It must abide by the decisions made by the party executive. No autonomous role	Members choose candidates at the constituency level, but the lists have to be approved by the party executive
UBP	Strong power of the leader, sustained by a network of loyal party officials	It must abide by the decisions made by the party executive. No autonomous role	Strong power of the party leader, who has the power to veto and nominate candidates
CTP	Democratic centralism with prominence of the leader	It must abide by the decisions made by the party executive. No autonomous role	Centralized process. There are rules that decentralize the process, but these have not been implemented so far

Portuguese parties. The internal balance of power in these parties does not show any particular predominance of the party in public office. On the contrary, evidence supports the existence of strong party executives. One last question, then, needs to be addressed: what happens when parties reach office and play a governmental role? Does the internal balance of power sketched above change abruptly?

Incumbency, Change and Overall Assessment

To draw together the threads of the previous analysis, in this final section we address a key issue that emerged from the authors' investigation, as well as from the considerations we have developed in the preceding pages: the overall impact of incumbency on parties. Moreover, we present two final tables which show, respectively, the dimensions along which South European political parties changed most during the last decade and an overall assessment of the positions of parties with regard to the dimensions we took into account in our research.

The analysis of the impact of incumbency is useful in understanding the links among the different dimensions discussed above. More precisely, the trend of membership in the right-wing parties is affected by incumbency. As Table 12 shows, the PP, DISY and FI, which were in office for the whole, or part, of the past decade, increased their membership. The rate of organization (M/E), the membership density (M/V) and the rate of change in the number of members for these parties were all growing. On the other hand, the PSD and the ND, which were in opposition for most of that time, declined on all three measures. At the same time the left-wing parties do not show any relationship between membership growth and incumbency. In fact, the incumbent PASOK and the opposing PSOE and CHP have experienced a growth in their membership, while a decline can be detected in the incumbent PS and DS, as well as in AKEL, which was in opposition for most of the 1995–2005 period. On the basis of our knowledge of the countries and previous research (Morlino 1998), the most reasonable explanation for these opposite results is that South European right-wing

Table 12 Party Membership and Incumbency in Right-Wing Parties (1996–2005)

	Growth of party membership	Decline of party membership
Incumbency most or part of the time	PP	
	DISY	
	FI	
Opposition most of the time		PSD
		ND

Note: The growth/decline of the party membership refers to the change registered in the 1996–2005 period by parties in M/E, M/V and the rate of change in the number of members. When all the measures are positive we consider this a growth; when all the measures are negative we consider this an indication of decline.

parties tend to rely on resources related to incumbency, allocated through patronage mechanisms, whereas left-wing parties rely relatively more on ideological incentives.

Being left-wing or right-wing is not relevant for change in the internal balance of power: in either case, incumbency has strong influence. The authors in this issue show that national party leaders increase their power when in office. An additional related consequence is the strengthening of the centre vis-à-vis the party local notables or, by and large, the territorial party units. The different impact of incumbency on membership and on internal power relationships can be accounted for by the fact that in the growth of membership the behaviour of people is a key element, whereas it is the elites that are at core of the second domain.

Still on the internal balance of power, another important aspect deserves to be stressed. It concerns the change of role of those leaders who are active in the party executive and become ministers or undersecretaries. On the basis of the evidence we have, we contend that when this occurs the expected atrophy or weakening of party executives does not take place. On the contrary, those leaders who keep both positions, inside the party and in the cabinet, further reinforce their own power. From the perspective of the relative power of the party executive, the presence of cabinet members possibly strengthens it, or at least does not undermine it. But it makes the leaders at the crossroads of the party executive and the cabinet the key actors inside the party (see also van Biezen 2000, p. 412 and Costa Lobo 2005, p. 278).

Table 13 sums up the most evident changes that took place inside the parties during the past decade. Table 14 compares the parties along the dimensions considered by our research. We believe that they provide a good map for future empirical and comparative research, as well as a good introduction to the articles in this special issue.

Before concluding, however, a final consideration deserves to be made with regard to electoral campaigns and competition. Up to now these aspects have been overlooked as they resulted in homogeneous, albeit important development taking place during the time span considered here. More precisely, as can be seen in the fifth column of Table 14, we classified the parties according to two dimensions. The first is the established presence of an in-house office or team of professionals permanently working on party communication and, when necessary, on electoral campaigns. Thus, we have the possibility of an internal group of professionals or alternatively the reliance on external consultants and agencies. The main strong result is that in most of our cases the external professionals are preferred, we assume, because of the difficulties and costs of establishing such an organized branch that is really needed only during the electoral campaign. Two important exceptions are the Spanish PP and the Greek ND. In both cases new leaders at the beginning of their mandates, Aznar and Karamanlis, respectively, set up these offices as a more effective tool in their strategy to bring their parties back to power. Furthermore, there are other cases such as AKEL, the UBP and the CTP where professionalization is incipient or non-existent.

The centripetal or hybrid modes of competition, which constitute the second dimension, are split almost precisely in half across countries. The centripetal strategy is recurrent in parties in Portugal, Italy and Greece. The hybrid strategy characterizes the

Table 13 What Changed Most

Country	Party	Change	Party	Change
Portugal	PS	Incentives for members and supporters; direct election of party leader; reintroduction of party congress after the 'convention *intermezzo*'	PSD	Election of party leader; more stratarchical structure
Spain	PSOE	Change of leadership brought about changes in ideology and organization	PP	No basic party changes
Italy	DS	Direct election of party leader; dual leadership (even if temporary); consolidation of organized factions; party decentralization	FI	Attempt at territorial rooting, but basic resilience of the personal party
Greece	PASOK	Incentives for members and sympathizers; leader election in primaries; greater ideological moderation; more professionalized campaigning	ND	Stronger leadership; change of leadership brought about changes in ideology and organization; strengthening of professionalized cadres; new centripetal strategy and campaigning
Cyprus	AKEL	Slow ideological revision and leadership renewal	DISY	Direct election of the leader; programme moderation; development of professionalized party bureaucracy; more internal democracy
N. Cyprus	CTP	Moderation of ideology and programmes	UBP	Minor changes because of long incumbency
Turkey	CHP	Stricter domination of party leader	AKP	Stronger secularization in values and programmes

Table 14 Relevant Party Dimensions in Southern Europe

Party	Membership	Selection and power of leadership	Organization	Competition	Left–right
PS	Decline	Member selection/single	Leader and top executive prominence	External professionals/centripetal	Moderate liberal-socialism
PSD	Decline	Member selection/stratarchical	Leader and top executive conditioned by local notables	External professionals/centripetal	Conservative pragmatism
PSOE	Growth	Congress selection/single	Leader and top executive prominence	External professionals/hybrid (2004)	Innovative liberal-socialism
PP	Growth	Congress selection/single	Leader and top executive prominence	Internal professionals/centripetal	Conservative liberalism
DS	Decline	Member selection/dual	Leader and top executive prominence	Internal professionals/centripetal	Moderate liberal-socialism (fragmented)
FI	Growth	Acclamation/personal	Leader strong prominence	External professionals/centripetal	Conservative liberalism (radical on occasion)
PASOK	Growth	Primary/single	Leader and top executive prominence	External professionals/centripetal	Moderate liberalism (uncertainties)
ND	Decline	Congress selection/single	Leader prominence	Internal professionals/centripetal	Moderate liberalism with social attention
AKEL	Decline	Executive/collegial	Leader and top executive prominence	Partly professionals/hybrid	Traditional communist left (in slow change)
DISY	Growth	Member selection/single	Leader and top executive prominence	External professionals/hybrid	Conservative nationalism
CTP	Decline	Congress selection/single	Leader and top executive prominence	Non-professionals/hybrid	Moderate liberal-socialism
UBP	—	Congress selection/personal	Leader strong prominence	Non-professionals/hybrid	Moderate liberalism
CHP	Growth	Congress selection/personal	Leader strong prominence	External professionals/hybrid	Secularism nationalism
AKP	—	Congress selection/personal	Leader strong prominence	External professionals/hybrid	Conservative liberalism

parties in Turkey and the two parts of Cyprus. We should specify that this latter mode of competition is distinguished by party tactics designed to maintain the party's previous voters, acquire other electors who voted for a party within the same ideological block and regain the party voters who abstained in the previous election. By and large, the competitive strategy is a systemic feature. Thus, we do not need to specify the party and information on the country is sufficient. The Spanish PSOE, however, broke this usual rule in the 2004 election. The socialist leadership consciously prioritized the 'capture' of socialist voters who had abstained in 2000 and left-wing voters, ignoring the centripetal drive. Post-electoral analysis showed that such a strategy had achieved its target.

Notes

[1] The 'renaissance' of comparative studies on party change starts with the important project directed by Katz and Mair (1992; 1994) and follows on with a number of other relevant contributions, such as Harmel et al. (1995), Scarrow (1996), Dalton and Wattenberg (2000), Diamond and Gunther (2001), Gunther et al. (2002), Luther and Müller-Rommel (2002), Mair et al. (2004).

[2] The selected parties are the Portuguese Socialist Party (PS) and Social Democratic Party (PSD), the Spanish Workers' Socialist Party (PSOE) and Popular Party (PP), the Italian Democrats of the Left (DS) and Forza Italia (Go Italy!; FI), the Greek Panhellenic Socialist Movement (PASOK) and Nea Demokratia (ND), the Cypriot Progressive Party of the Working People (AKEL) and Democratic Rally (DISY), the northern Cyprus Republican Turkish Party (CTP) and National Unity Party (UBP), and the Turkish Justice and Development Party (AKP) and Republican People's Party (CHP).

[3] The reports were first debated at a conference on 'Party Change in Southern Europe', held in Florence in September 2005. The whole project has been financed by the Italian Education and University Ministry, the Department of Political Sciences of the University of Trieste, the Istituto Italiano di Scienze Umane and the Osservatorio italiano sulle Transformazioni dei partiti politici, which we want to thank here for their support.

[4] Scarrow (2000) also found widespread party membership decline since the 1960s.

[5] With regard to their importance and to the assessed position of each party on them, we chose the following relevant dimensions: 'taxes versus spending' (trade-off between higher public spending and lower taxes), 'social' (for/against policies on abortion, gay rights and euthanasia), 'decentralization' (for/against decentralization of decision making), 'environment' (trade-off between environmental protection and economic growth), 'deregulation' (favouring high levels of market regulation versus deregulation), 'nationalism' (as versus cosmopolitanism in the approach to history, culture and national consciousness), 'religion' (promotion of religious versus secular principles in politics), 'immigration' (support for integration of immigrants versus support for returning immigrants to their countries of origin), 'EU joining' (support or opposition to it). The scale of expert assessment goes from 1 to 20 (Benoit & Laver 2006, pp. 98–99).

[6] This is an important topic on which there are a number of noteworthy recent contributions. See, among others, Van Biezen and Hopkin (2004) and Deschouwer (2006).

References

Benoit, K. & Laver, M. (2006) *Party Policy in Modern Democracies*, Routledge, London.

Bosco, A. (2000) *Comunisti. Trasformazioni di partito in Italia, Spagna e Portogallo*, Il Mulino, Bologna.

Bosco, A. (2005) *Da Franco a Zapatero. La Spagna dalla periferia al cuore dell'Europa*, Il Mulino, Bologna.

Calise, M. (2000) *Il partito personale*, Laterza, Roma and Bari.

Calise, M. (2005) 'Presidentialization, Italian style', in *The Presidentialization of Politics. A Comparative Study of Modern Democracies*, eds T. Poguntke & P. Webb, Oxford University Press, Oxford, pp. 88–106.

Costa Lobo, M. (2005) 'The presidentialization of Portuguese democracy?', in *The Presidentialization of Politics. A Comparative Study of Modern Democracies*, eds T. Poguntke & P. Webb, Oxford University Press, Oxford, pp. 269–288.

Dalton, R. J. & Wattenberg, M. P. (eds) (2000) *Parties without Partisans: Political Change in Advanced Industrial Democracies*, Oxford University Press, Oxford.

Deschouwer, K. (2006) 'Political parties as multi-level organizations', in *Handbook of Party Politics*, eds R. S. Katz & W. Crotty, Sage, London, pp. 291–300.

Diamond, L. & Gunther, R. (eds) (2001) *Political Parties and Democracy*, Johns Hopkins University Press, Baltimore.

Diamandouros, P. N. & Gunther, R. (eds) (2001) *Parties, Politics and Democracy in the New Southern Europe*, Johns Hopkins University Press, Baltimore.

Evans, J. A. (2005) *The South European Right in the 21st Century: Italy, France and Spain*, special issue of *South European Society & Politics*, vol. 10, no. 2.

Gunther, R. & Diamond, L. (2003) 'Species of political parties: a new typology', *Party Politics*, vol. 9, no. 2, pp. 167–199.

Gunther, R., Montero, J. R. & Linz, J. (eds) (2002) *Political Parties: Old Concepts and New Challenges*, Oxford University Press, Oxford.

Harmel, R., Heo, U., Tan, A. & Janda, K. (1995) 'Performance, leadership, factions and party change: an empirical analysis', *West European Politics*, vol. 18, no. 1, pp. 1–33.

Ignazi, P. & Ysmal, C. (eds) (1998) *The Organization of Political Parties in Southern Europe*, Praeger, Westport, CT.

Ignazi, P. (2002) 'Evoluzione organizzativa dei partiti in Europa', paper presented at the conference of the Italian Association of Sociology, Università della Calabria, Arcavacata, Italy, 26–27 September.

Katz, R. S. (2001) 'The problem of candidate selection and models of party democracy', *Party Politics*, vol. 7, no. 3, pp. 277–296.

Katz, R. S. (2002) 'The internal life of parties', in *Political Parties in the New Europe. Political and Analytical Challenges*, eds K. R. Luther & F. Müller-Rommel, Oxford University Press, Oxford, pp. 87–118.

Katz, R. S. & Mair, P. (eds) (1992) *Party Organizations. A Data Handbook*, Sage, London.

Katz, R. S. & Mair, P. (eds) (1994) *How Parties Organize. Change and Adaptation in Party Organizations in Western Democracies*, Sage, London.

Katz, R. S. & Mair, P. (2002) 'The ascendancy of the party in public office. Party organizational change in twentieth-century democracies', in *Political Parties: Old Concepts and New Challenges*, eds R. Gunther, J. R. Montero & J. J. Linz, Oxford University Press, Oxford, pp. 113–135.

Krouwel, A. (2006) 'Party models', in *Handbook of Party Politics*, eds R. S. Katz & W. Crotty, Sage, London, pp. 249–269.

Luther, K. R. & Müller-Rommel, F. (eds) (2002) *Political Parties in the New Europe. Political and Analytical Challenges*, Oxford University Press, Oxford.

Mair, P. (1994) 'Party organizations: from civil society to the state', in *How Parties Organize. Change and Adaptation in Party Organizations in Western Democracies*, eds R. S. Katz & P. Mair, Sage, London, pp. 2–22.

Mair, P. & Van Biezen, I. (2001) 'Party membership in twenty European democracies, 1980–2000', *Party Politics*, vol. 7, no. 1, pp. 5–21.

Mair, P., Müller, W. C. & Plasser, F. (eds) (2004) *Political Parties and Electoral Change. Party Responses to Electoral Markets*, Sage, London.

Morlino, L. (1996) 'Crisis of parties and change of party system in Italy', *Party Politics*, vol. 2, no. 1, pp. 5–30.

Morlino, L. (1998) *Democracy between Consolidation and Crisis: Parties, Groups and Citizens in Southern Europe*, Oxford University Press, Oxford.

Poguntke, T. (2002) 'Party organizational linkage: parties without firm social roots?', in *Political Parties in the New Europe. Political and Analytical Challenges*, eds K. R. Luther & F. Müller-Rommel, Oxford University Press, Oxford, pp. 43–62.

Scarrow, S. E. (1996) *Parties and Their Members. Organizing for Victory in Britain and Germany*, Oxford University Press, Oxford.

Scarrow, S. E. (1999) 'Parties and the expansion of direct democracy. Who benefits?', *Party Politics*, vol. 5, no. 3, pp. 341–362.

Scarrow, S. E. (2000) 'Parties without members? Party organization in a changing electoral environment', in *Parties without Partisans: Political Change in Advanced Industrial Democracies*, eds R. J. Dalton & M. P. Wattenberg, Oxford University Press, Oxford, pp. 79–101.

Scarrow, S. E. (2005) *Political Parties and Democracy in Theoretical and Practical Perspectives. Implementing Intra-party Democracy*, National Democratic Institute for International Affairs, Washington.

Scarrow, S. E., Webb, P. & Farrell, D. M. (2000) 'From social integration to electoral contestation. The changing distribution of power within political parties', in *Parties without Partisans: Political Change in Advanced Industrial Democracies*, eds R. J. Dalton & M. P. Wattenberg, Oxford University Press, Oxford, pp. 129–150.

Van Biezen, I. (2000) 'On the internal balance of party power. Party organizations in new democracies', *Party Politics*, vol. 6, no. 4, pp. 395–417.

Van Biezen, I. (2003) *Political Parties in New Democracies*, Palgrave Macmillan, New York.

Van Biezen, I. & Hopkin, J. (2004) 'Party organization in multi-level contests: theory and some comparative evidence', paper presented at the Annual Meeting of the American Political Science Association, Chicago, September, pp. 2–5.

Van Biezen, I. & Hopkin, J. (2005) 'The presidentialization of Spanish democracy: sources of prime ministerial power in post-Franco Spain', in *The Presidentialization of Politics. A Comparative Study of Modern Democracies*, eds T. Poguntke & P. Webb, Oxford University Press, Oxford, pp. 107–127.

The Woes of Being in Opposition: The PSD since 1995*

Carlos Jalali

Introduction

The reversal of fortunes of the centre-right Partido Social Democrata (Social Democratic Party, PSD)[1] over the past decade could scarcely be more striking. It was almost exactly ten years ago, in October 1995, that the PSD exited Portuguese government, after some 16 years in power, alone or in coalition. Over the ensuing decade, the PSD was to govern only briefly, in coalition with the right-wing Centro Democrático Social—Partido Popular (Democratic Social Centre—Popular Party, CDS–PP), from 2002 till 2005, and its term in office was capped by a heavy defeat in the 2005 legislative elections.

This work evaluates the dimensions of change in the PSD since 1995. In particular, the case of the PSD will be considered against the backdrop of the burgeoning party decline debate. This notion of party decline—emphasizing the declining capacity of parties to act as intermediaries between the state and the citizens—has led some

*I would like to thank the participants of the 'Party Change in Southern Europe' conference of September 2005 for their suggestions and insight. I am also indebted to Patrícia Silva for assistance with data collection for this research. Any remaining errors are, of course, entirely my own.

authors to ask provocatively if we must begin to 'think the unthinkable': modern democracy without political parties (Dalton & Wattenberg 2000). At the same time, some of the recent literature has called into question this notion of decline—viz. Katz and Mair (1995) and Montero and Gunther (2002), who have argued that conclusions of decline are overstated and largely caused by a poor selection of dimensions of change. Given the PSD's apparent decline over the past ten years, after 16 years in power, it offers an interesting case to examine within this broader debate.

The analysis of party change within the PSD over the past decade will centre on the following four key dimensions. First, on patterns of change in party values and programmes. To the extent that parties in democracy represent alternative public policy options and preferences, any change along this dimension constitutes a significant element of party transformation (Ware 1996, p. 111). Second, on party organization, resources and intra-party dynamics. To the extent that this dimension underpins much of the current debate on party decline, it constitutes a central aspect of the analysis here. Third, the PSD's competitive strategies will be considered, notably vis-à-vis its main competitor for power, the Socialist Party (PS). Finally, the paper will consider the evolution in the party's electoral campaigns, which, as Gillespie and Gallagher (1989, p. 170) point out, traditionally constitute the peak of activity and social penetration of parties in Portugal. The analysis of these key dimensions will be preceded by an overview of the PSD's electoral and political performance over the past ten years.

As will be shown, the past decade has been one of major soul-searching for the PSD, a party that appears to remain unaccustomed to the rigours of life in opposition. This is perhaps most visibly reflected in the number of leadership changes since 1995, with five different party leaders over the past decade (out of the 12 the PSD has had since democratization). Yet it is also perceptible on at least three other dimensions. The first is an acute strategic indefinition. Second, and related, the party has witnessed increasing internal factionalization, with PSD leaders in opposition having to devote as much time to holding on to their job as to challenging incumbent prime ministers for theirs. Finally, there has been a growing assertion of the sub-national party levels, suggesting a more stratarchical pattern of internal relations.

At the same time, the party's absence from power does not reflect a change in the PSD's position within the Portuguese party system. Thus, competition for government remains a contest between Socialists and Social Democrats, the two parties that have alternated at the helm of the Portuguese administration since the first legislative elections of 1976.[2] This is also reflected in the PSD's maintenance of power at the local level during the last decade—an important dimension in Portuguese party organization, as shall be seen below.

The PSD since 1995: The Rigours of Opposition

In 1995, a wholesale alternation in the Portuguese government occurred, when the PSD lost the October legislative elections. The extent of this defeat could hardly be minimized: the PSD had governed alone for the previous ten years (eight of which with an obedient single-party majority in parliament); and had been in coalition governments for six years before that. The presidential election of January 1996 was to cap the PSD's *annus horribilis*, as the outgoing PSD prime minister Cavaco Silva's belated presidential bid was defeated by the Socialist candidate, Jorge Sampaio. For the first time since 1979, the PSD now found itself entirely excluded from power at the national level.

While dramatic, the PSD's electoral defeats were not entirely unexpected. The Cavaco-Silva-led government that emerged from the 1991 elections was not only weakened by a profound economic downturn, but also dogged by successive scandals. If any doubts remained of the PSD's fate, these were quickly dispelled when Cavaco Silva announced his decision not to lead the party in the 1995 legislative elections. That role fell to Fernando Nogueira (1995–96), Cavaco Silva's heir apparent, who narrowly defeated José Manuel Durão Barroso for the leadership at a hotly contested congress in February 1995.

Following these electoral defeats, Nogueira resigned as party leader, being replaced by Marcelo Rebelo de Sousa, a Lisbon law professor and political commentator. Despite his widely perceived tactical nous, Marcelo was unable to control the party and challenge the Socialist government's popularity. His undoing was a proposed electoral alliance with the CDS–PP, the Democratic Alternative (AD). While the initial scope of the AD was the European elections of June 1999, the idea was that it could then be prolonged to the 1999 legislative elections in order more effectively to challenge the socialists for power.

However, the new AD[3] was to prove short-lived. It was an unpopular alliance within the PSD, which had neither forgotten nor forgiven the role played by the then CDS–PP party leader, Paulo Portas, in its defeat of 1995. Portas was editor of the *Independente* weekly newspaper for much of the final PSD term, and his paper had taken a leading role in eroding popular support for the PSD, reporting on (and occasionally exaggerating) successive scandals of the PSD government. At the same time, opinion polls suggested the AD electoral alliance was worth less than the sum of its parts ('Alternativa Democrática fecha Portas', *Expresso online*, 27 March 1999). Unable to dent the Socialist Party's popularity ratings, Marcelo faced growing internal opposition, and was unable to impose the alliance or quell factional opposition to his leadership. The eruption of the Universidade Moderna scandal, allegedly involving the CDS–PP leader, was to trigger the end of the AD, little more than a month after it was officially ratified. The demise of the AD also marked the end of Marcelo Rebelo de Sousa's term as party president. Having staked the success of his leadership on the coalition, he promptly resigned as PSD leader in the aftermath of the Moderna scandal.

His replacement was José Manuel Durão Barroso, who had been narrowly defeated for the leadership in 1995, and was at this stage seen as the party's prodigal son, able to lead it to victory. While Barroso had positioned himself as the main opponent of the coalition with the CDS during Marcelo's administration, he also carefully avoided overt public exposure, which could have brought against him charges of betraying the party. But the hopes that Barroso could rapidly bring the party back to national power were ultimately little more than wishful thinking by the PSD faithful. Barroso was installed as the new party leader only five months before the October 1999 legislative elections, and faced a very popular incumbent Socialist government. As such, a Socialist victory in the 1999 elections was never in any doubt, after four years of buoyant economic growth (with real GDP growth consistently exceeding that of the EU-15, and peaking at 4.7 per cent in 1998), and Portugal's admission into the euro currency zone, against all odds.

However, Barroso's inability to make inroads on the Socialist Party's lead in the run-up to the legislative elections of October 1999 was to cause rapid erosion of his internal capital of support. In the end, the PSD was to shed yet more votes, dropping to a 32.3 per cent share of the vote—its lowest total in ten years. Having lost the lustre of being the party's saviour and guiding light, Barroso now had to face growing internal dissent. Like his predecessor, Marcelo Rebelo de Sousa, Barroso was to learn that a PSD leader who is unable rapidly to deliver power (or the promise of power, through consistently strong opinion poll showings) will be unable to avoid internal factionalism.

Barroso's fortunes began to turn in the December 2001 municipal elections, in which the Social Democrats became the largest party of local government and most importantly won over important cities such as Lisbon, Porto and Coimbra, previously led by the Socialists. The election results were to provoke António Guterres' resignation as both prime minister and leader of the Socialist Party, leading President Jorge Sampaio to dissolve parliament and call general elections for three months later.

After the December elections—and the disarray within the PS to find a successor for Guterres—these 2002 legislative elections favoured the centre-right PSD most. The PSD was thus to claim victory with 40.1 per cent of the vote, but it was unable to outdistance the Socialists by as much as it had previously hoped. More significantly, the PSD fell short of the parliamentary majority it had quietly sought, with 105 of the 230 deputies in the Portuguese Assembly of the Republic.

While a minority government is not an unusual governing formula in democratic Portugal, the instability that beset the last PS government of Guterres had inoculated the PSD against this option. Facing a slowing economy, and having to push through unpopular reforms and public expenditure cuts, given the eurozone stability pact criteria, Barroso opted to form a coalition government with the CDS–PP. On the one hand, the CDS's 14 deputies were enough to provide a comfortable majority in parliament; on the other, the CDS–PP was happy to return to national government after a 20-year absence.

However, the new government was unable to avert a heavy recession, as its public expenditure cuts badly dented investor confidence in an economy heavily dependent on public sector investment. The economy registered negative growth in 2003, and the unemployment rate increased rapidly, reaching 6.7 per cent by early 2004. While this is relatively low by European standards, it marked a substantial increase for Portugal, where unemployment stood at little over four per cent at the end of 2001. Yet despite this adverse context the coalition remained relatively stable and cohesive, against historical predictions (no coalition government since democratization in 1974 having lasted a full term) and despite the residue of animosity within the PSD towards its junior coalition partner.

However, an unexpected turn of events in 2004 was to trigger the untimely demise of the PSD–CDS coalition government. On 25 June 2004 it became clear that Barroso would resign as prime minister in order to run for the presidency of the European Commission. In the aftermath, and after much hesitation, President Jorge Sampaio opted to maintain parliament, and a new PSD–CDS government was appointed, with Santana Lopes as prime minister. But the Lopes administration was to prove short-lived, and on 30 November 2004 Sampaio's intention to dissolve parliament was announced. Lopes's 168 days in office until the dissolution was announced were deeply unpopular, marked by a succession of scandals and few signs of economic recovery. Some 55 per cent of respondents in a poll in late November for *Público-RTP-Antena Um* considered the government's performance to be 'bad' or 'very bad', and over half of the respondents considered that, in hindsight, the President had been wrong to nominate Santana Lopes as prime minister ('Portugueses "chumbam" todos os ministros', *Portugal Diário*, 29 November 2004).

The PSD's unpopularity thus facilitated alternation in government in the February 2005 legislative elections, with the return of the Socialists to power after three years of a centre-right coalition administration. Not only was the Socialists' 45 per cent share of the vote sufficient to gain them their first ever parliamentary majority, but the elections were to result in a historic rout for the PSD, which obtained only 28.7 per cent of the vote, its lowest share since 1983. Lopes's position at the helm of the party was naturally untenable after this result, and he promptly resigned soon after the elections, being succeeded by former Cavaco Silva minister (and defeated candidate in the February 2000 party congress) Luís Marques Mendes.

Marques Mendes's first major test was the October 2005 local elections. Given the Socialists' unprecedented victory and the PSD's heavy defeat only eight months earlier, the local elections were seen as a potentially poisoned chalice. Yet the continuing economic recession quickly eroded the honeymoon effect for the Socialist Party, and the PSD was able to win mayoral elections in a little over half of the 308 town halls of Portugal, thus giving Mendes—who many saw as a stop-gap leader—a little more breathing space at the helm of the PSD.

If You're in a Bad Situation, Wait for it to Change: PSD Values and Programme Since 1995

As Panebianco (1988, pp. 243–244) highlights, electoral defeats exert strong pressure for change within parties, notably in terms of the party's programme and values. Yet what is remarkable in the last decade is the degree of continuity in the PSD's goals and ultimate ends. As such, the PSD experience contrasts with the prediction of Panebianco (1988, pp. 244–245) that leadership changes are likely to produce a redefinition of a party's official goals, necessary to show that 'the change of leadership was effected for profound and noble reasons related to the destiny of the organization itself', rather than 'banal rivalry or personal ambition'. Despite five leadership changes, the PSD's programmatic values underwent little redefinition, rather preserving a pattern of programmatic *indefinition*.

This continuity largely derives from the PSD's historical antecedents. The revolutionary context of 1974–75 under which democratization took place was to impact directly—and strongly—on party values and programmatic goals. The PSD emerged as a legal political organization seeking societal support for electoral purposes within the revolutionary context. As for the other political parties, 1974–75 was 'Year Zero' for political organization for the PSD (Morlino 1998, pp. 209–210; Jalali 2002, p. 19).

In particular, the shift leftwards of the revolutionary period was to skew significantly the party's ideological positioning, at least nominally. This helps explain, for instance, why the main centre-right party is called the Social Democratic Party. Indeed, the PSD initially attempted to join the Socialist International, and claimed to aim at developing a socialist society (Sousa 2000a; 2000b). For the parties of the right—including the PSD—such skewing was a crucial form of defence against the radical leftist coalition and threats of disbandment. It protected them from accusations of being reactionary counter-revolutionaries, and thus from the fate of projected parties of the right, such as the Portuguese Nationalist Party, the Progress Party, the Liberal Party and the Christian Democratic Party, all disbanded by the radical wings of the military during the revolutionary years of 1974–75.

At the same time, with weak and unconsolidated organizations, the parties in favour of liberal democracy (and chiefly here the PS and PSD) had one trump card to play against the organizational solidity and Leninist strategy of the Portuguese Communist Party (PCP): that of demonstrating wide social support, signalling to the PCP and orbiting (but not always friendly) *groupuscules* the real risks of a forced takeover.[4] Thus, in the context of 1974–75, a broad and shallow support base was preferable to a deep but narrow one, and programmatic consistency a luxury the PSD could ill afford.

After 1974–75 and the resolution of the regime-choice conflict, the PSD—along with the PS—continued to avoid the consolidation of well-defined policy platforms and programmes. The endurance of this pattern is not solely explainable by path dependencies. A coordination game also emerged between the two centrist parties, the equilibrium being a catch-all strategy for both PS and PSD. As in any coordination game, the alternative strategy—in this case, clearer ideological demarcations—would prove costly, most likely resulting in the shedding of electorate, at least in the short run. Neither party has been willing to take that risk: as Kirchheimer (1966) had predicted a decade earlier, shallow but wide support could win elections; deep but narrow could not.

As such, the impact of the revolution on the PSD's programme and values goes considerably beyond the misleading party title. It helped generate an ideologically heterogeneous party membership within the PSD, which still persists. Indeed, one of the leadership candidates at the recent April 2005 party congress stated that if elected he would reposition the PSD in the centre-left of the ideological spectrum—and managed to obtain some 43 per cent of the congress vote. In addition, it set a pattern of relative unimportance of party programmes, largely disregarded and clearly subordinated to pragmatic considerations. Certainly, in opposition the PSD has ventured little beyond vague promises of greater economic growth and well-being for the nation. That programmatic promises hold little sway is exemplified by the PSD stint in government after 2002. While the PSD centred its 2002 electoral campaign on a programme of deep tax cuts, a 'fiscal shock' designed to jolt the economy into greater growth, the proposed tax cuts were rapidly abandoned once in office.

Overall, the PSD appears to have embraced *avant la lettre* Third Way notions that 'there is no ideology, only good or bad management', party goals being scantily defined beyond the need for development in order to catch up with Europe. In terms of Gunther and Diamond's (2003) recent typologization of political parties, the PSD unequivocally falls within the purview of the electoralist catch-all category. The party is thus characterized by a 'superficial and vague ideology', the main goal being the maximization of votes and the winning of elections. As Gunther and Diamond (2003, p. 185) put it, the electoralist catch-all party is

> primarily distinguished by the party's shallow organization, superficial and vague ideology, and overwhelmingly electoral orientation, as well as by the prominent leadership and electoral roles of the party's top-ranked national-level candidates. The overriding (if not sole) purpose of catch-all parties is to maximize votes, win elections and govern.

What the last decade suggests is that party programme and values can be strongly resistant to change, in spite of the incentives generated by electoral defeats and leadership changes. As such, the PSD experience tends to confirm the old dictum: 'If you're in a bad situation, don't worry—it'll change'.

PSD Organization: A Hollowed-out and Stratarchical Party?

Given this context, the PSD inevitably presents a hybrid party organization. Whilst formally presenting a mass-type organizational form, in practice this constitutes little more than an outward façade. In a sense, then, the PSD is a 'hollowed-out' mass party, with the formal structure of a mass party coexisting in practice with patterns more commonly associated with modern cadre (Koole 1994) and cartel party typologies, and their older patronage machine predecessors.

Within this context, party leaders have played a decisive role in the PSD, and can by and large rely on the obedience of the party central office and the party's parliamentary group. Thus, party leaders have not faced generalized open rebellions in either the central office or the parliamentary group over the past decade, even if this obedience can at times be grudging. Indeed, no PSD leader has ever been ousted from the party's presidency (or defeated in a party congress), all leadership changes since the party's creation occurring due to incumbents' resignation or death.

Yet at the same time, the past ten years have revealed increasingly stratarchical internal dynamics within the PSD, which also reflect limits to a party leader's internal power. While strong party leaders are able to impose their own preferences, weaker leaders must tread more carefully. This pattern has led some authors to characterize the PSD as a party dependent on the leader's charisma (Lopes 1989; Frain 1997). Yet what the past ten years illustrate is that this 'charisma' is by no means an intrinsic personal trait, appearing rather to be strongly related to the electoral success a leader can bring than to his personality.

PSD Organizational Structure

The PSD's organizational setup follows the administrative configuration of the Portuguese state. In keeping with the formal structure of a mass party, the key bodies of political direction are the political commissions, which exist at nucleus (parish), section (municipality), district and national levels, elected by assemblies at the sub-national levels and by the party congress at the national one.[5] These political commissions provide the 'permanent political direction' of the party's activities at their level. Above the municipal level, permanent political commissions also exist, statutorily designed to provide more immediate action.

The highest figure in the party is the president of the national political commission (generally known as the president of the party), who also heads the national permanent political commission. Political oversight of these political commissions devolves to the assemblies; and to a national council at the national level, elected at congress and including district political commission presidents. Internal elections use both d'Hondt proportional representation (PR) and plurality voting, with the former used solely for the election of the national council, delegates to congress and district assemblies, and jurisdictional councils. The use of PR for the national council tends to make this the most factionalized body at national level.

The major recent innovation in the party's organization was the approval of the direct election of the party president in the March 2006 congress. A measure promised by Marques Mendes in the previous party congress, this reform served to quell the increasingly vocal appeals for greater member participation in leader elections within the PSD. A popular measure within the party rank and file, it became increasingly difficult to resist after the adoption by both PS and CDS–PP of this procedure. In the end, it was overwhelmingly approved, with almost 80 per cent of the party delegates voting in favour. The first direct elections took place in May 2006, with Marques Mendes—the only candidate in the end—obtaining 91 per cent of the vote, with a 36 per cent turnout of party militants. The implications of this change for party functioning are still unclear. The experience of the PS—see the article by Marco Lisi in this volume—suggests it may produce a greater concentration of power in the party president. That the new statutes stipulate the election of the members of the national political commission by the party congress on the proposal of the directly elected party president is consistent with this prediction.

The PSD statutes also delineate powers regarding choice of candidates, yet these provisions are vague and unclear. This is most obvious in the selection of candidates to parliament: article 41 states these are proposed by the district political commission to the national political commission; but article 21 only states that the national political commission must present its list of candidates to the national council, making no reference to the district political commission's proposal. In practice, the choice of candidates will depend on the balance of power within districts, at the national level, and between districts and national level, resulting in the need to accommodate different factions and local interests. Leaders with high internal power—notably Cavaco Silva—were largely able to impose their own preferences. Weaker leaders must proceed more carefully, and in particular cannot afford to alienate district and section bosses, on whose support they rely if challenged at congress, and whose increasing penetration of national bodies in any case grants them greater leverage over candidate selection.

Prevalence of the Party Leader within the Party

As Burton et al. (1992) stress, in a convoluted situation such as that of Portugal in 1974–75, party leaders play a necessarily critical role. The PSD was to be part of the first provisional government of the Second Republic, installed on 16 May 1974, a mere nine days after the party's public formation, when it had barely any organizational structures. A clear pattern of prevalence of the party in public office—and notably of the party leader—over the party at the grassroots thus emerges. The PSD became virtually synonymous with its party leader, Sá Carneiro, who had great visibility as a government minister. In a context of widespread mass media, this presence in government took on additional importance.

This pattern has contributed to the characterization of the PSD as a party dependent on the leader's charisma (Lopes 1989; Frain 1997). Yet what the past ten years illustrate is that this 'charisma' is by no means an intrinsic personal trait. The various party leaders that have mediated the leaderships of Nogueira and Mendes were invariably characterized as being strongly charismatic prior to reaching the party presidency. As the case of Marcelo Rebelo de Sousa—a hugely popular and mediatic figure—demonstrates, personal charisma is not enough to silence the PSD and its notables.

Rather, this charisma appears more strongly related to success (electoral and in opinion polls) than to a leader's personality. Nothing succeeds like success in a party where the key parameter for action, particularly since democratic consolidation, has been the exercise of power. This is perhaps best exemplified by the Barroso leadership. Fêted as the great saviour of the party prior to his election to the PSD presidency in 1999, Barroso quickly fell from favour after the poor legislative election results of that year, and had to direct most of his attention for the next two years to controlling the party and its notables.

Barroso's break came with the PSD's success in the 2001 municipal elections—more a reflection of socialist unpopularity than PSD support. While the PSD's success was hardly a personal victory for Barroso, the resignation of Guterres—and the real prospect of national power it brought—gave Barroso the internal power that he had been previously denied. This effect is most strongly visible in the drawing up of the PSD lists for the 2002 legislative elections, in which the PSD leader was able to stand his ground against local notables ('PSD de Beja mantém lista de candidatos', *Público online*, 30 January 2002).

The effect of power in quelling internal conflict is also apparent at the three party congresses Barroso contested as party leader. In 2000, Barroso maintained the party leadership at a closely fought and occasionally vitriolic party congress, against Santana Lopes and current party leader Marques Mendes. The two subsequent party congresses, in July 2002 and May 2004—with the PSD now back in power—were in contrast placid affairs, with Barroso unopposed for the party presidency.

Local and National Party Relations: Towards a Stratarchical Party?

At the same time, the PSD's absence from power for most of the past ten years cannot be dissociated from the increasingly stratarchical internal relations within the PSD. Cavaco Silva's electoral success until 1995 allowed him to impose his will over the various internal party networks, winning over most local notables (and exiling those he was unable to win over) and to concentrate resources at the central state level (Portugal being one of the most centralized countries in Europe: Le Galés 2002, p. 285), acting as a powerful dissuader of internal dissension.

The party's loss of national government altered the internal balance of power towards local notables, notably local office-holders, who retained access to local state resources and consequently also to patronage power. Local and district party structures—generally dominated by the party in local power—thus began to gain greater autonomy within the PSD. Since local office is often dependent on local reputation and position, mayors can dig themselves in, particularly outside the major metropolitan centres. As in France, they may be re-elected almost in perpetuity, and several date from the first local elections of December 1976.

While these are in general loyal to the national party leader, the leader is not entirely unconstrained. While he is largely given free rein in national policy and strategy choices, decisions that affect local and district bosses' interests are fiercely resisted. An equilibrium arrangement thus emerges, with local bosses providing local organization rooted in local power or a share of it, and a capacity for mobilization for the national leaders, in exchange for lack of interference in their parochial interests. In terms of intra-party patterns, the hierarchical view of national–local party relations appears to give way to a more stratarchical one, defined as where 'local office holders and national party elite act relatively independently of each other; [there is] "mutual autonomy"; local office-holders [are] ready to accept this influence by the elite in national affairs, as long as they are given a free hand to manage their own local affairs' (Koole 1996, p. 518).

Here, the 'franchise party' metaphor developed by Carty (2004) appears to be useful in illustrating the internal interactions between the local and national levels of the PSD. As Sousa (2000b, p. 1132) puts it, the PSD can be described as 'a federation of local mini-parties, with diverse styles and discourses', grouped around barons. The PSD's factionalization (particularly after the ideological clarification of the early years) has thus traditionally centred essentially on personal rivalry rather than ideological and policy differences, reflecting the party's personalist character. Up until the early 1990s, these factions were grouped around national party barons, who generally benefited from the visibility of national public office, though necessarily able to count on the support of local and sub-national party structures that they were able to mobilize. This pattern appears to have changed over the past decade, resulting in a more stratarchical party organization, as local party bosses have gradually risen to important positions in the national party that reinforce their local autonomy (Pereira 2001). This is reflected in the composition of the party's national council, the number of its members who were also incumbent mayors increasing by some 50 per cent between the 1995 and 2005 party congresses.

Sub-national and national parties cooperate but largely do not interfere in each other's sphere. Thus, the sub-national party level (both at local and district levels) is vital for party campaigning, organizing local rallies and meetings, bussing sympathizers and members to rallies, but also providing campaign finance—not least for local elections. In exchange, it does not expect influence in the national party's policy formation, but rather the protection of its local interests—most notably, unhindered choice of candidates, especially for local elections.

This is not to say that conflict does not occur. This was evident in late 2000/early 2001, when a new statute was approved in order to end 'mayor-deputies', in effect obliging mayors elected to the Assembly from the next election onwards (either legislative or local) to choose between the two mandates within 180 days of their accumulation.[6] The previous accumulation of mayoral and (suspended) parliamentary mandates served as insurance for mayors against electoral defeat in their fiefdoms. While the previous statute defined the functions of deputy and mayor as incompatible—hence barring the simultaneous assumption of functions as mayor and deputy—it did allow mayors elected to parliament then to suspend their parliamentary mandates. While their mandate was suspended, their place was taken up by the next (unelected) candidate on the party list, but they could resume functions in parliament once this incompatibility ended.

Formerly largely ignored, this became politically relevant in November 2000 when CDS–PP mayor-deputy Daniel Campelo briefly suspended his mandate as mayor of Ponte de Lima and took up his parliamentary seat in order to permit the approval of the Socialist government's 2001 budget, which his party rejected. The ensuing public furore led Socialists and Social Democrats to agree to a change to the rules—only for the PSD leadership to be forced by its local notables to abstain after initially supporting the proposed change ('A semana—Durão Barroso', *Público online*, 18 November 2000; 'Alberto Martins exclui limitação de mandatos', *Público online*, 8 February 2001).

The difficulty for party leaders in asserting their power over the local party structure is highlighted in the recent experience of Marques Mendes. While Mendes was able to veto two local notables, Valentim Loureiro and Isaltino Morais, as party candidates in the 2005 local elections, he was only able to do so after they had been formally indicted for corruption. Moreover, the local party structures were to remain loyal to Loureiro and Morais, despite indications to the contrary from the party's central office.

Conflict intensifies over local issues, for example, when the national party seeks to impose a local mayoral candidate disliked by segments of the local party. This was evident in the selection of the 2001 mayoral candidate for Trofa, when the national party-backed candidate faced resistance within the *concelho* party and particularly from the then district party boss, Luís Filipe Menezes. Despite having publicly announced João Sá as candidate, the national party was ultimately forced to yield to the 'local' candidate, Bernardino Vasconcelos. Vasconcelos and Sá were then to work on a local deal, which placed Sá second on the Vasconcelos list for Trofa.

Overall, the experience of the past ten years indicates the need to reformulate earlier descriptions of national–local party relations, as dominated by the national party and its leadership (Bruneau & MacLeod 1986, p. 200). At the same time, the current pattern of stratarchical party organization cannot be seen as an isolated development, and its seeds can be traced to the genetic imprint of the revolution on the PSD's organization.

As a result of its, to some extent, ahistorical formation, the PSD began in 1974 with very few resources—be they material, ideological or human. Developing such resources from a societal basis is a costly and slow process; given the pressing needs of the revolutionary context, it was easier to absorb existing networks. With the CDS weakened by its closer links to the old regime and the flight of many of its potential supporters (and contributors) to Brazil and Europe, the PSD became the obvious choice for the centre-right and right-wing local elites and networks in the crucial initial period of the revolution.

Yet this absorption of figures and networks associated with or close to the old regime—particularly the church and local notables in rural and northern areas—was by no means directed or even entirely controlled by the party at the centre. With an incipient organization, needing to rapidly develop its own organizational structure yet without the time or resources to do so, the PSD was happy to take support from wherever it came. Local and regional party organizations were thus largely coopted into the PSD (the most notable case being the PSD in Madeira: Frain 1997, p. 39), and thus tended to develop with a certain degree of autonomy vis-à-vis the party at the centre. What the last decade suggests is that this stratarchy becomes more evident when the party is out of national office. Local power thus serves to compensate for the weak societal role of the PSD, acting as a key transmission belt, particularly when it is excluded from national power. Local party bosses are also reinforced internally by the evident degree of rank-and-file member demobilization, making for a low effective electorate in local contests that can be further biased by the relatively easy and inexpensive practice of 'buying' party memberships ('"Ninhos" de militantes no PSD da Trofa', *Público online*, 22 December 2001).

PSD Membership

The inapplicability of the mass party model to the PSD is confirmed by the evolution of the party's membership rates. Table 1 presents the PSD's membership. While party member figures in Portugal are notoriously unreliable (for an interesting comparison of different sources, see Martins 2004, pp. 582–588), these figures make it clear that party membership has never been particularly high for the PSD, at least when compared with the traditional mass parties of older liberal democracies.

As Morlino (1998, p. 177) puts it, a mass-membership base is not 'a key element for electoral success'. Rather, the pattern for the PSD appears to be of party membership growth following rather than preceding electoral victories (Morlino 1998, p. 178), a reflection of the attractive pull of patronage power for party membership.

Table 1 PSD Membership, and Ratio of Party Membership to Party Voters and Total Electorate, 1974–2005

Year	PSD membership	PSD members as percentage of PSD voters	PSD members as percentage of electorate
1974	10,875	—	—
1975	20,445	1.4	0.3
1976	25,011	1.9	0.4
1979	32,687	—	—
1983	—	2.1	0.5
1984	67,324	—	—
1985	—	3.9	0.9
1986	89,899	—	—
1987	101,454	3.6	1.3
1988	—	—	—
1990	125,386	—	—
1991	139,253	4.9	1.7
1992	143,075	—	—
1993	162,496	—	—
1994	171,931	—	—
1995	181,390	9.1	2.1
1996	183,630	—	—
1999	77,055	4.4	0.9
2000	87,290	—	—
2002	—	4.0	1
2004	121,420	—	—
2005	116,000	7.1	1.3

Sources: Party membership, 1974–92: Morlino (1995, p. 337); 1993–96: Frain (1997, p. 94); 1999–2000: Martins (2004, p. 583); 2004: 'Mais de 121 mil militantes "laranja"', *Diário de Notícias*, 11 November 2004; 2005: 'Militantes do PSD têm pela primeira vez oportunidade de eleger directamente o líder', *Público online*, 5 May 2006. Party membership/voters ratio: own calculations (when data for the election year are unavailable, the last known membership figure prior to the election is used). Party membership/total electorate ratio: own calculations (when data for the election year are unavailable, the last known membership figure prior to the election is used).

The one notable feature of the past ten years was the clean-up of the party membership files under Marcelo's first term as party leader, which reveals the overestimation of party membership in the PSD. Thus the PSD 'lost' over 100,000 members after the clean-up undertaken in 1996 by the then PSD secretary-general Rui Rio, which provoked considerable internal resistance. However, party membership is gradually returning to previous levels. While some increase as a result of the party's return to power in 2002 cannot be excluded, sources within the PSD accept that much of this rise is artificial, with some of it due to 'buying' of party memberships. Indeed, the 2006 direct election of the party's president confirms that the party's true level of party membership is much lower than generally announced. Thus, while the party's secretary-general announced a figure of 116,000 members,[7] less than half—55,486 affiliates—were eligible to vote, eligibility being restricted to members who had joined the party at least six months prior to the election and—crucially—had paid their dues.

PSD Finances

While the PSD's financial data in Portugal must be viewed with some caution (the Portuguese Constitutional Court stated that in its judgment the declared party accounts 'do not include the totality of the financial operations and functioning' of the main political parties—Constitutional Court Resolution No. 647/2004), it appears the PSD's prolonged absence from national power over the past ten years has impacted on the party's finances. Not only has it meant an automatic reduction in state subventions, but PSD sources also admitted donations are more forthcoming when the party is in power. However, there appears to be increased political activity for the PSD, as shown in Figure 1, which presents the general expenditure, income and annual subventions received by the PSD over the past decade.

The decline in subventions in the period 1996–2001 is consistent with the decline in the party's vote, with the general annual subvention over the 1995–2004 period being equal to 1/225 of the monthly minimum wage multiplied by the party's vote in the last legislative elections. Over half of the PSD's general income over this period was from state subventions, confirming Katz and Mair's (1995) prediction of a considerable reliance on the state by political parties as the grassroots organizations wither. Moreover, this pattern is likely to be strengthened in the coming years. The reform of party financing law of 2003 has led to a 66 per cent increase in the annual subvention per vote as of 1 January 2005. This will no doubt further consolidate the centrality of state subventions in the PSD's financial fortunes.

Playing a Waiting Game: The PSD's Competitive Strategy

Two central elements can be discerned in the PSD's competitive strategy over the last ten years. The first is in terms of its key objective of regaining national office, and

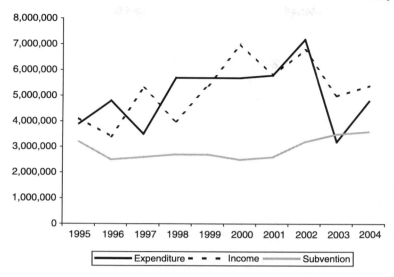

Figure 1 General Expenditure, Income and Subvention Income for the PSD, 1995–2004 (euros). *Sources*: Expenditure and income, 1995–2002: Martins (2005, p. 32); 2003–4: 2004 PSD annual report, submitted to the Constitutional Court. Subvention income: own calculations.

consequently its competition with the Socialist Party; the second is its equivocal stance vis-à-vis the CDS–PP throughout the last decade.

Received wisdom in Portuguese politics has it that elections are incumbents' to lose rather than challengers' to win, and no party has clung on to this notion more tenaciously than the PSD. This was certainly evident during the PSD's period in power, when it was not averse to a degree of demand management in order to bolster economic conditions, as was the case in the run-up to the 1980, 1987 and 1991 elections. This belief is perhaps not entirely misplaced—Portuguese national election studies confirm the importance of short-term political factors—notably, the evaluation of economic conditions and government record—for voter choice in Portugal (Jalali 2004). As Gunther and Montero (2001, p. 142) point out, the Portuguese case is a somewhat 'anomalous' one in terms of electoral behaviour, an anomaly that emerges from the inconsistency between the weakness of traditional cleavages such as class and religion in predicting voter choice, and a context where socioeconomic cleavages and religious practice appear to be relatively strong. This anomaly can be explained by the emergence of another dimension of conflict, centring on regime choice, which dominated the revolutionary context of 1974–75 and divided the parties—and their military allies—favouring liberal democracy (PS, PSD and CDS) from those that sought alternatives elsewhere (notably, the Communists and the extreme-left).

Crucially, this decisive dimension of conflict was to emerge at the crucial moment of mass political mobilization in Portuguese society, after almost 50 years of authoritarian rule. Partisan support was thus encapsulated over this conflict, which was to impinge on class and religion (Jalali 2004). At the same time, with both the PS and PSD on the same side of the regime-choice cleavage, this decisive conflict was to produce a relatively flimsy differentiation between the two dominant parties, accentuated by the weak politicization of the traditional cleavages. This helps explain the substantial apolitical electorate in post-1974 Portugal, whose vote is swayed by short-term political factors (notably, economic performance, political scandals and leader perceptions) rather than determined by established cleavage structures. By all accounts, this electorate has become crucial for electoral success and winning government, particularly since the mid-1980s, providing the swing in the electoral wicket for the PS and PSD (Jalali 2002; 2004).

This pattern of electoral behaviour has inevitably impacted on the PSD's competitive strategy over the past decade, with ideology and clear programmatic options eschewed in favour of an emphasis on the party leader and the incumbent government's record. In particular, it has meant that the party's strategy towards the PS while in opposition over the last decade has been largely limited to a waiting game. PSD leaders in opposition have thus concentrated on riding out the successive waves of internal factionalism until a change in the economic climate or scandals might undo the incumbent PS government.

However, the PSD was unable to settle on a strategy to deal with the junior party of the Portuguese right, the CDS–PP, while in opposition. The growth of the CDS–PP in the 1995 elections, which more than doubled its vote from 4.4 per cent to 9.1 per cent, as well as its increasing combativeness towards the PSD, has made it a thorn in the PSD's side since the early 1990s. In particular, a dilemma arose between choosing to compete or ally with the CDS. Indeed, much of the PSD's internal factionalism since 1995 stems from opposing visions of how to deal with its rival on the right. On the one hand, some within the PSD saw the proximity between the two parties as pointing to the necessity of an alliance on the right to defeat the socialists. In turn, others argued that an alliance would move the party away from the centrist vote it had to wrest from the socialists to win government. The matter became all the more entangled by the ill-disguised loathing of CDS–PP leader Paulo Portas by much of the PSD apparatus. This equivocal stance was intensified as relations with the CDS became fodder for PSD internal conflict. At the same time, the party's stance towards the CDS reflects the extent to which the party's key parameter for action is the exercise of power. As such, the party's strategy can be quickly reversed if need be. The relative ease with which Barroso was able to form and work in a coalition government with the CDS and Portas in 2002—despite the fact that he had been the foremost critic of the 1999 alliance with the very same party—is a clear reflection of the extent to which power can be an effective balm for Portugal's Social Democrats.

Leaving it to the Professionals: PSD Electoral Campaigning

Campaigning in Portugal is now largely professionalized and market-based, and the PSD has been very much at the forefront of this development. While the logistical aspects of the campaign are organized in-house, the party has been turning to professional marketing consultants for its campaign conception over the past ten years, beginning with the campaign for the 1995 legislative elections under Fernando Nogueira. In addition, there has been a marked personalization of the PSD's electoral campaigns, confirming notions of a 'presidentialization of politics' in Portugal.

By all accounts, campaigns tend to be prepared on a very ad hoc basis. Thus, the PSD does not have a permanent in-house election team comprising media and electoral marketing specialists. Rather, campaign coordination is left to small ad hoc teams, selected by the party leader and composed of people loyal to him. These teams are appointed a few months (sometimes as little as three months) before elections, and normally deal only with the logistical aspects of the campaign. Inevitably, this pattern has been accentuated by the internal convulsions in the party over the past decade, with leaders sometimes installed shortly before elections.

The conception of the actual campaign content—in terms of slogans or outdoor advertising—is contracted to outside consultants. Interestingly, these marketing consultants tend also to be chosen on an ad hoc basis, often being a personal choice of the party leader. Thus, the PSD hired for the 2005 legislative elections a Brazilian publicist, Einhart Jacome da Paz, who had previously been responsible for Santana Lopes's (successful) bid for the Lisbon city hall in 2001. Indeed, the PSD campaign for the 2005 elections—largely focusing as it did on the personality of the party leader, Santana Lopes—was the brainchild of Mr da Paz. The emphasis on the marketing and communications side of the campaign is reflected in the campaign budgets, with the bulk of the budgets devoted to party propaganda (accounting for 87.5 per cent of the PSD's expenditure in the 1995 elections, for instance).

At the same time, the centrality of party leaders within the electoral campaign should not be underestimated. Not only can they rely on a loyal campaign team, but they also retain a veto on the campaign's marketing, and it is not unheard of for leaders to reject ideas put forward by the outside consultants. Equally, there are no in-house polling experts, and the intense polling analysis seen in American politics—where pollsters are increasingly an integral part of the campaign team—appears to be virtually non-existent.

The main mode of political communication for the PSD's campaigns is television. This is relatively unsurprising, since, as the Portuguese national election survey of 2002 highlighted (Barreto et al. 2002), the Portuguese rely overwhelmingly on television as their main source of political information: some 73 per cent of those questioned said they watched news or programmes about politics on TV at least once a week, a figure more than twice as large as those who use the radio or newspapers.

While the PSD has adapted to the technological advances of the past years—notably, running an effective website and creating a blog for the party leader during the 2005 legislative campaign (<http://pedrosantanalopes.blogs.sapo.pt/ >)—the predominance of television as a source of information for the Portuguese means that the PSD campaigns remain in the 'TV Age', to use Farrell and Webb's typology (2000). This is particularly noticeable in terms of campaign resources and themes, where the PSD neatly fits the second stage of development posited by Farrell and Webb (2000, pp. 102-3), notably in terms of a 'growing prominence of "specialist" consultants [but with] politicians still in charge', a focus on television debates and 'pseudo-events' as key campaign events, and a catch-all targeting of voters.

Concurrently with these processes, the role of the rank-and-file party militant has virtually vanished. The PSD—like most other parties—now pays private firms for the placement of its posters, mainly because it lacks the manpower to do this. The majority of party militants appear in the campaign only for the party rallies (largely bussed in by the various neighbouring local party organizations), with handfuls of party youth members accompanying the candidates in the handing out of party literature and publicity materials, with the latter—which include plastic bags, T-shirts, postcards and even playing cards and dominoes—by far the more popular. Even this youthful enthusiasm is not entirely cost free for the PSD, since the accompanying party youth members often are paid a stipend for their efforts on the campaign. Meanwhile, rallies are carefully orchestrated for their televisual impact. The PSD—like the other main parties—now deliberately chooses relatively small and confined venues to give the televisual image of a full house. This is in stark contrast with the early period of the Second Republic, when large party rallies were held, often in football stadiums, and poster display was done by party militants.

Conclusion

The past ten years provide a useful period for analysing change within the PSD, particularly since it was during this period that the party was out of power for the first time since democratic consolidation. Certainly the examination of this period cautions against conclusions of 'party decline' in the case of the PSD. Indeed, the PSD remains a central element of the Portuguese party system. To use Mair's (1997) framework, it remains within the main dimension of competition of the party system. Indeed, if anything, its position has been reinforced by the more centripetal direction of competition and the relative closure of the structures of competition in the party system since the mid-1980s, which has led to a greater domination of the party system by the two centrist parties, the PS and PSD. Moreover, while the party is characterized by weak social rooting and a thin organizational structure, the fact is that these characteristics are by no means new, given the genetic imprint of the revolutionary period. As such, rumours of the decline of the PSD appear to be exaggerated.

Equally, there has been little change to the PSD's policy preferences and programme. The party remains within poorly defined ideological boundaries and retains a catch-all electoral appeal. Despite its relatively prolonged absence from power, there are few incentives for the PSD to change. As shown above, 'old' cleavages (class, religion) only weakly differentiate it from its main competitor, the Socialist Party. At the same time, survey data suggest that the PSD has little to gain by drifting towards 'new' cleavages. Indeed, post-materialist orientations in the Portuguese electorate are very weak, with only four per cent of those questioned in 2002 indicating a post-materialist orientation, and respondents with a materialist orientation outnumbering those with a mixed orientation (Jalali 2004); and only one per cent of those asked in 2004 listed immigration as one of the two priority issues for Portugal (Jalali et al. 2005).

At the same time, the variance in the party's access to national power over the past ten years has thrown into relief a number of internal party patterns obscured by the previous decade's dominance. Most notably, it calls into question two hitherto received pieces of wisdom regarding the PSD. The first concerns local–national party relations. Previous analyses pointing to a hierarchical relationship appear to be misguided, the pattern emerging over the past ten years being rather of a more stratarchical nature, with power as the oil that greases the points of contact between the different party levels. Secondly, the PSD's characterization as a party dependent on leader charisma is also questioned. Rather, the party is dependent on access to power, and the perceived 'charisma' of a leader is in fact a direct correlate of the power (or, at the very least, the promise of power) he embodies.

Notes

[1] The Social Democratic Party was initially called PPD (Popular Democratic Party). The appearance of a radical right-wing Partido Social Democrata Cristão (Christian Social Democratic Party) forced a last minute alteration of name to PPD in 1974, in order to avoid any possible confusion. It adopted its 'real' name of PSD in October 1976, though PPD was to remain as a prefix (Manalvo, 2001:35–6, 64–5). To avoid confusion, we solely use the acronym PSD here.

[2] With two brief exceptions: the grand coalition of 1983–85 and the short-lived attempts by President Eanes at presidential government in 1978–79.

[3] The PSD and CDS had previously formed an electoral alliance in the 1979 legislative elections, subsequently maintained in the 1980 legislative elections, called the Democratic Alliance, whose acronym was AD. The original AD won a parliamentary majority in both these elections, before the ensuing government coalition collapsed in 1982. While the proposed alliance in the 1990s had a slightly different name, it maintained the AD acronym of its earlier incarnation.

[4] For accounts of the convoluted revolutionary period of 1974–75, and the risks of civil war it carried, see Robinson (1979) or Maxwell (1995).

[5] For full party statutes, see 'Estatutos do Partido Social Democrata Aprovados no XXVIII Congresso—Março de 2006', available from the PSD website: < http://www.psd.pt/partido/ download/estatutos_2006.pdf > .

[6] This was incorporated into the statute of deputies as Law No. 3/2001 of February 2001.

[7] 'Militantes do PSD têm pela primeira vez oportunidade de eleger directamente o líder', *Público online*, 5 May 2006.

References

Barreto, A., Freire, A., Lobo, M. C. & Magalhães, P. (eds) (2002) *Comportamento Eleitoral e Atitudes Políticas dos Portugueses—Base de Dados 1*, Instituto de Ciências Sociais, Lisboa.

Bruneau, T. C. & MacLeod, A. (1986) *Politics in Contemporary Portugal: Politics and the Consolidation of Democracy*, Lynne Rienner, Boulder, CO.

Burton, M., Gunther, R. & Higley, J. (1992) 'Introduction: elite transformations and democratic regimes', in *Elites and Democratic Consolidation in Latin America and Southern Europe*, eds J. Higley & R. Gunther, Cambridge University Press, Cambridge, England, pp. 1–37.

Carty, R. K. (2004) 'Parties as franchise systems: the stratarchical organizational imperative', *Party Politics*, vol. 10, no. 1, pp. 5–24.

Dalton, R. J. & Wattenberg, M. P. (2000) 'Unthinkable democracy: political change in advanced industrial democracies', in *Parties without Partisans: Political Change in Advanced Industrial Democracies*, eds R. Dalton & M. Wattenberg, Oxford University Press, Oxford, pp. 3–16.

Farrell, D. M. & Webb, P. (2000) 'Political parties as campaign organizations', in *Parties without Partisans: Political Change in Advanced Industrial Democracies*, eds R. Dalton & M. Wattenberg, Oxford University Press, Oxford, pp. 102–126.

Frain, M. (1997) 'The right in Portugal: the PSD and CDS/PP', in *Political Parties and Democracy in Portugal*, ed. T. C. Bruneau, Westview Press, Boulder, CO, pp. 77–111.

Gillespie, R. & Gallagher, T. (1989) 'Democracy and authority in the socialist parties of Southern Europe', in *Southern European Socialism: Parties, Elections and the Challenge of Government*, eds T. Gallagher & A. Williams, Manchester University Press, Manchester, pp. 163–187.

Gunther, R. & Montero, J. R. (2001) 'The anchors of partisanship: a comparative analysis of voting behaviour in four Southern European countries', in *Parties, Politics and Democracy in the New Southern Europe*, eds P. N. Diamandouros & R. Gunther, Johns Hopkins University Press, Baltimore, pp. 83–152.

Gunther, R. & Diamond, L. (2003) 'Species of political parties: a new typology', *Party Politics*, vol. 9, no. 2, pp. 167–199.

Jalali, C. (2002) 'The Evolution of the Portuguese Party System in Comparative European Perspective Since 1974', DPhil. thesis, University of Oxford, Oxford.

Jalali, C. (2004) 'As mesmas clivagens de sempre? Velhas clivagens e novos valores no comportamento eleitoral português', in *Portugal a Votos: As Eleições Legislativas de 2002*, eds A. Freire, M. Costa Lobo & P. Magalhães, Imprensa de Ciências Sociais, Lisboa, pp. 87–124.

Jalali, C., Nunes, F. & Santo, A. E. (2005) *Eurobarómetro 62: A Opinião Pública na União Europeia, Outono de 2004*, European Commission, Brussels.

Katz, R. S. & Mair, P. (1995) 'Changing models of party organization: the emergence of the cartel party', *Party Politics*, vol. 1, no. 1, pp. 5–28.

Kirchheimer, O. (1966) 'The transformation of the Western European party systems', in *Political Parties and Political Development*, eds J. LaPalombara & M. Weiner, Princeton University Press, Princeton, NJ, pp. 177–200.

Koole, R. (1994) 'The vulnerability of the modern cadre party in The Netherlands', in *How Parties Organize: Change and Adaptation in Party Organizations in Western Democracies*, eds R. S. Katz & P. Mair, Sage, London, pp. 278–303.

Koole, R. (1996) 'Cadre, catch-all or cartel? A comment on the notion of the cartel party', *Party Politics*, vol. 2, no. 2, pp. 507–523.

Le Galés, P. (2002) 'The changing European state: pressures from within', in *Governing Europe*, eds J. Hayward & A. Menon, Oxford University Press, Oxford, pp. 380–394.

Lopes, P. S. (1989) 'P.P.D./P.S.D.: a dependência do carisma', in *Portugal: o Sistema Político e Constitucional, 1974–1987*, ed. M. Baptista Coelho, Instituto de Ciências Sociais, Lisboa, pp. 181–192.

Mair, P. (1997) *Party System Change: Approaches and Interpretations*, Clarendon Press, Oxford.

Manalvo, N. (2001) *PSD: A Marca dos Líderes*, Editorial Notícias, Lisboa.

Martins, M. M. (2004) *Participação Política e Democracia, o Caso Português (1976–2000)*, Instituto Superior de Ciências Sociais e Políticas, Lisboa.

Martins, M. M. (2005) 'Os "custos da democracia" em Portugal', *Revista de Assuntos Eleitorais*, no. 9, pp. 29–39.

Maxwell, K. (1995) *The Making of Portuguese Democracy*, Cambridge University Press, Cambridge, England.

Montero, J. R. & Gunther, R. (2002) 'Introduction: reviewing and reassessing parties', in *Political Parties: Old Concepts and New Challenges*, eds R. Gunther, J. R. Montero & J. Linz, Oxford University Press, Oxford, pp. 1–35.

Morlino, L. (1995) 'Political parties and democratic consolidation in Southern Europe', in *The Politics of Democratic Consolidation: Southern Europe in Comparative Perspective*, eds R. Gunther, H. J. Puhle & P. N. Diamandouros, Johns Hopkins University Press, Baltimore, pp. 315–388.

Morlino, L. (1998) *Democracy between Consolidation and Crisis: Parties, Groups and Citizens in Southern Europe*, Oxford University Press, Oxford.

Pereira, P. (2001) 'Grau Zero', *Público online*, 6 September.

Panebianco, A. (1988) *Political Parties: Organization and Power*, Cambridge University Press, Cambridge, England.

Robinson, R. (1979) *Contemporary Portugal: A History*, George Allen & Unwin, London.

Sousa, M. R. de (2000a) *A Revolução e o Nascimento do PPD, 1 Volume*, Bertrand Editora, Venda Nova, Portugal.

Sousa, M. R. de (2000b) *A Revolução e o Nascimento do PPD, 2 Volume*, Bertrand Editora, Venda Nova, Portugal.

Ware, A. (1996) *Political Parties and Party Systems*, Oxford University Press, Oxford.

The Importance of Winning Office: The PS and the Struggle for Power*

Marco Lisi

Introduction

The Partido Socialista Português (Portuguese Socialist Party, PS) played an important role in the transition and consolidation of Portuguese democracy. After the 1974 military coup, the PS emerged as the leading party in the 1975 elections for the constituent assembly and in the first legislative elections held in 1976. From the earliest days of the new democratic regime the PS participated in minority or coalitional governments, giving priority to the building of the new democratic institutions rather than to the implementation of socialist policies. In the 1980s, the PS spent a very short period in office (1983–85) taking part in the Bloco Central (Central Bloc), a coalition between the PS and the centre-right Partido Social Democrata (Social Democratic Party, PSD). The rise of the Partido Renovador Democrático (Party of Democratic Renewal, PRD) in 1985—supported by President Ramalho Eanes—led to a huge electoral defeat for the PS, opening an entire decade in opposition which was marked by two absolute majorities of the PSD (1987–95). Yet, since the period of 'military tutelage', the socialists have been able to secure the presidential office first with Mário Soares (1986–96) and then with Jorge Sampaio, who was elected for the first time in 1996 and then re-elected with a strong majority in 2001. Since 1995, the PS has begun a new cycle of relative or absolute parliamentary majorities, broken only by a two-year

*The author would like to thank Marina Costa Lobo for her valuable comments and for providing the data of the 2005 post-electoral survey of the Institute of Social Science.

period of centre-right coalitional government. After the two minority governments led by António Guterres (1995–2002), in February 2005 the PS gained its first absolute majority since Portuguese democratization under the leadership of José Sócrates.

These institutional and governmental experiences reflect an underlying feature of the socialist and social democratic parties of Southern Europe: since their formation they may be characterized as catch-all parties, giving priority to governmental power and the winning of office. This is a key point for understanding the evolution of the PS over the last three decades. Thus, it will be argued that the main challenges the party had to face in the recent period are related to the struggle for power. In particular, the relative stability of the main features of the political and electoral environment since the mid-1980s has led to a substantial continuity in different party dimensions. However, party changes took place when party leaders had to face challenges—within or outside the party—and needed to improve the electoral performance or to acquire more resources in order to achieve (or maintain) power.

This work will focus on the main dimensions of change and adaptation in the PS from 1995 to 2005. First the PS electoral performance and its political challenges between 1976 and 2005 will be examined. Then, the analysis will focus on the evolution of the PS programmatic orientations and ideological stances, while the third part will deal with changes in party membership and organization, stressing the relationship between the different faces of the party. The following sections will examine the competitive strategy and the organization of electoral campaigns. Finally, causes of party change will be pointed out in the conclusions, considering the whole trajectory of change undergone by the PS.

From Minority to Majority: The PS Electoral Performance

During the first decade of democratization, the PS held between 22 and 40 per cent of the parliamentary seats and it consolidated its position as one of the two largest Portuguese parties (Table 1). However, after the first socialist minority government led by Soares in 1976, the fragmentation of the party system made it necessary for the PS to join two coalition governments with the right-wing parties (in 1978 and again in 1983), since the orthodox Marxism–Leninism of the Communist Party (PCP) made a left-wing cabinet impossible.

This period was also characterized by a high degree of factionalism which finds its primary cause in the ideological heterogeneity of the groups that joined the PS during the early years of democratization.[1] Until the late 1970s the party's internal life was marked by several splits, while at the same time new groups entered the PS (Sablosky 1997). Consequently, Soares had some difficulties maintaining the party's unity and cohesion, as shown by his demise as secretary-general when the party decided to support Eanes's re-election as president of the Republic in 1981. However, after the internal adjustments and the fading of ideological divisions within the PS, Soares was able to re-establish his control over the party's organization and strategy.

Table 1 PS Votes, Seats, Secretary-Generals and Participation in Government (1976–2005)

Election YEAR	PS votes* %	PS seats N	%	PS secretary-general	Governments		
					Prime minister	Inauguration date	Type of cabinet
1976	34.8	107	40.6	Mário Soares	Mário Soares (PS)	July 1976	Minority
					Mário Soares (PS–CDS)	Jan. 1978	Majority
					Nobre da Costa (Nonpartisan)	Aug. 1978	Presidential
					Mota Pinto (Nonpartisan)	November 1978	Presidential
1979	27.3	74	29.6	Mário Soares	Pintassilgo (Nonpartisan)	July 1979	Presidential
1980	26.6	71	28.4	Mário Soares	Sá Carneiro (PSD–CDS–PPM)	January 1980	Majority
					Pinto Balsemão (PSD–CDS–PPM)	January 1981	Majority
					Pinto Balsemão (PSD–CDS–PPM)	September 1982	Majority
					Pinto Balsemão (PSD–CDS–PPM)	December 1982	Majority
1983	36.1	101	40.4	Mário Soares	Mário Soares (PS–PSD)	June 1983	Majority
1985	20.7	57	22.8	A. Almeida Santos	Cavaco Silva (PSD)	November 1985	Minority
1987	22.2	60	24.0	Vítor Constâncio	Cavaco Silva (PSD)	September 1987	Majority
1991	29.1	72	31.3	Jorge Sampaio	Cavaco Silva (PSD)	October 1991	Majority
1995	43.7	111	48.7	António Guterres	António Guterres (PS)	October1995	Minority
1999	44.0	115	50.0	António Guterres	António Guterres (PS)	October 1999	Minority
2002	37.7	96	41.7	E. Ferro Rodrigues	Durão Barroso (PSD–CDS)	March 2002	Majority
					Santana Lopes (PSD–CDS)	July 2004	Majority
2005	45.0	121	52.6	José Sócrates	José Sócrates (PS)	February 2005	Majority

Source: Secretariado Técnico dos Assuntos para o Processo Eleitoral (STAPE). *Percentage of valid votes.

After reaching its lowest share of votes in 1985 (20.7 per cent) due to the rise of the PRD, the PS was able gradually to increase its support. The first success was the victory in local elections in 1989, which led Sampaio to be elected mayor of Lisbon; then signs of electoral recovery emerged in 1991, when the socialists reached 29.1 per cent of the vote at the expense of the Communists. However, the election of Soares as president in 1986 led to a leadership crisis inside the party and opened a period of internal struggles. After the attempt to elect Soares's right-hand man, António Almeida Santos, as party leader (1985), Vítor Constâncio was chosen as secretary-general in June 1986. The lack of control over the party's organization and the electoral defeats led to his replacement by Sampaio in 1989. The difficulties of being in opposition, after the second absolute majority obtained by Cavaco Silva, were to undermine Sampaio's leadership and party unity. Thus, in 1992 a new secretary-general was elected, António Guterres, who started a process of organizational and programmatic renewal. With the rise of Guterres a new generation of top leaders replaced the old cadres, as shown by the high turnover of the main party bodies—more than 80 per cent in the executive organ and 70 per cent in the deliberative one. Moreover, in 1993 Guterres started a process called *Estados Gerais* (General States), aimed at discussing the main programmatic orientations through the participation of independents and civil society in order to present a more attractive electoral manifesto.

In the 1995 elections the PS fell short by four seats of obtaining an absolute majority in the Portuguese parliament and formed a minority cabinet. This success was the consequence of the gradual move towards the centre of the political spectrum undertaken by Guterres. In addition to the new socialist leadership and programme, two factors—the crisis of the PSD government and its intra-party conflicts—contributed to the success of the PS strategy in the second half of the 1990s. However, the lack of a parliamentary majority led the PS to negotiate with the opposition, adopting a pragmatic orientation through ad hoc alliances with different parties. This contributed to the demobilization of the socialist sympathizers and to the rise of abstention in the 1999 elections, when the PS gained a higher percentage in terms of votes and seats, but did not manage to win an absolute majority.

The second Guterres government was marked by growing public dissatisfaction and the lack of coherent political action (Lobo & Magalhães 2002). Several cabinet reshuffles took place in 2001, showing the increasing difficulty of the Prime Minister to control both the executive and the relationship between the party and the government. In this sense, although Guterres officially resigned in December 2001 as a result of the defeat at the local elections, the crisis of the socialist government was due to the malaise emerging within both the PS and public opinion. The demise of Guterres as secretary-general led to the election of a new party leader, Eduardo Ferro Rodrigues, who had to face the negative conditions predicted for the socialists in the 2002 elections: the decrease in the government's popularity and the worsening of the economic situation. As foreseen, the socialist vote decreased by 6.3 per cent and the party went back to opposition (Table 1); yet, this was only the beginning of a new phase in the PS's history, characterized by a deep crisis at both the leadership and the civil society levels.

On the one hand, the loss of governmental resources made it difficult for the socialist leader to manage the centrifugal forces in the party elite and to stabilize the dominant coalition. On the other hand, the situation complicated further in 2003 with the involvement of some socialist leaders, close to the secretary-general, in a scandal involving child abuse. As a consequence, the support for the PS in the electorate dwindled and Ferro Rodrigues had to endure increasing criticism not only from voters but also within the party, as shown by the request of several socialist leaders that the secretary-general be removed, while others suggested convening a new congress and electing new party organs.

The 2005 early elections led to the return of the PS to government, this time with a comfortable absolute majority (45 per cent of the vote), the party's best result since 1976. The path to electoral success started with the election of José Sócrates as secretary-general in September 2004, after Ferro Rodrigues had resigned due to the political crisis that had led to the replacement of Durão Barroso—leader of the centre-right coalition and prime minister—by Pedro Santana Lopes (see Jalali, this volume). However, the recovery of the PS was due not only to the new leader—and the way he conducted the electoral campaign—but also to the programmatic incoherence of the new centre-right government and the inability of Santana Lopes to coordinate the executive. This seems to confirm what, according to Aguiar (2000, p. 73), is becoming a rule of the Portuguese party system: the electoral outcomes of the two main parties are linked, so that a party must benefit from the other party's failure in order to win a parliamentary majority. The high level of inter-bloc volatility (more than 98 per cent of total volatility) demonstrates that the PS was able to appeal to voters dissatisfied with the centre-right government (Magalhães 2005, p. 180).

Towards the Centre: The Ideological and Programmatic Evolution of the PS

The move of the PS towards the centre of the political spectrum has been gradual and constant over the last three decades. Notwithstanding the Marxist ideological legacy inherited from the revolutionary period, the need to differentiate from the PCP and competition with the PSD forced the PS to adopt a moderate orientation. As various authors have stressed (Sabloski 1997; Canas 2005), the governmental responsibility of the PS during the first decade of the democratic regime represented a challenge for the ideological and programmatic evolution of the party. In a period characterized by a deep economic and financial crisis and international constraints—related to access to the European Community—the socialists had to adopt and implement pragmatic and realistic policies that ran counter to their ideological orientation.

The process of adaptation began in 1979 through the adoption of a new plan ('Dez anos para mudar Portugal' [Ten Years to Change Portugal]) developed under the coordination of Guterres, at the time only 30 years old. This was to constitute the guidelines for the PS's action throughout the 1980s, embracing democratic socialism and a mixed economy (Puhle 2001, p. 283). The effort of the party to modify its identity culminated at the 1986 congress in the discarding of any references to Marxism from the party statutes. Besides the support of the PS for the European integration process—which has been the major dimension of continuity in the socialist programme since democratization—the new ideological orientations were based on political and economic pluralism, on the one hand, and on a commitment to improve the social and cultural conditions of citizens, on the other. After 1992, when Guterres became secretary-general, the move towards the centre was steered by the need to improve the country's social and economic modernization, but also by the greater proximity between the new party leader—with strong links to the Church—and Catholic voters. The party also adopted a new symbol—a rose instead of the traditional closed fist—as a sign of the renewal and moderation chosen by the party leadership. Finally, Guterres set out a more appealing political programme that was centred on social policies rather than on ideological issues.

Accordingly, in the 1995 electoral programme, the PS adopted a 'third way' orientation that combined pragmatic liberalism, the implementation of new social policies and financial orthodoxy (Lobo & Magalhães 2004). The constraints imposed by the EU were the most important factor in determining the economic and financial plans of the socialist governments. The European requirements not only made the PS collude with the opposition (especially the PSD) to adopt a number of economic policies,[2] but they also served as legitimizing principles of governmental choices. Notwithstanding parliamentary collaboration, the PS differed from the PSD in emphasizing the importance of education, through the implementation of the information society, and solidarity, through the reform of the welfare state in terms of health care regulation and the social security system.

These programmatic orientations have shown great continuity, even since the PS's return to power with José Sócrates. In the 2005 general elections the programme set out by the PS focused on a set of modernization policies (a package known as the 'technological shock'), such as the deepening of the information society both in public administration and in the education system, and the implementation of social policies. Thus, neither did the new socialist leaders decide to include new issues in their programme, nor have there been substantial changes in PS stances since the mid-1990s.

The evolution of the PS's ideology and programme over the past decades is confirmed by opinion surveys. In 1978 the electorate's average placement of the PS was 4.6 on a ten-point scale (from left to right), while in 1985 the score was five. Since then, the PS has swung from 4.6 to 5.2 but without a linear trend (4.8 in 1989; 4.6 in 1993; 4.7 in 1999; 5.2 in 2002 and 4.7 in 2005).[3] Yet these data underline an important pattern in the voters' perception of the PS, that is, when the party is in office voters tend to attribute a more moderate position to the socialists (the move to the centre in 1985, 1999 and 2002), whereas when the party is in opposition it is perceived to be more to the left. This seems to suggest that the electorate is more sensitive to the policies implemented by the socialist governments than to changes in ideological principles.

In conclusion, two factors have contributed to the socialists' maintenance of the same programmatic stances: the first is the centripetal competition with the PSD, while the second is the continuity in the PCP's ideological orthodoxy and its exclusion from the national government (Jalali 2002; Lobo & Magalhães 2004). Interestingly, up to now the Bloco de Esquerda (Left Bloc, BE)[4] has monopolized the post-materialist themes. Even if the importance of these issues for the Portuguese electorate seems to be increased in the last decade, the socialist leaders have preferred to compete basically on the socio-economic and religious dimensions, instead of introducing a new dimension of competition (Freire 2005, pp. 346–347). This has enhanced the centripetal strategy of the PS and it has limited the ideological distance between the two main parties.

The Organizational Change: Towards What Type of Party?

Organizational Structure and Party Membership

The PS built its organization according to the socialist mass party model, privileging a vertical structure, although it has never developed the participation of members inside the party—except in electoral periods—and it has endowed the membership with more rights than obligations, so that members only play a secondary role in party activities (Van Biezen 1998).

The main deliberative party bodies are the congress, the national commission and the political commission, while the executive bodies of the PS are the secretary-general (the party leader) and the executive committee (the secretariat). In addition to the main party bodies, the permanent commission has developed the important function of managing the relationship between the party in public office and the extra-parliamentary party. This body acts under the control of the party leader and includes members from the secretariat. In practice, the permanent commission has emerged as the inner circle of the party leadership under Guterres. In 2003 the commission disappeared from the party statutes but was restored in 2005, with the Sócrates government, first under the leadership of Jorge Coelho and then, after January 2006, under the direct control of the prime minister. The evolution of this party body shows the weak institutionalization of the PS.

The organizational model changed in 1992 after the rise of Guterres as secretary-general, as the PS structure was completely rebuilt—at least formally—with the introduction of a convention and the abolition of the congress. The national commission was now elected directly by party members and it replaced the congress as the main party body by electing all the remaining national organs (the political commission, the secretariat and the secretary-general). However, as observed by Van Biezen (2003), the convention model was bound to be just an intermezzo. In 1998 the PS leadership decided to return to the traditional model, reintroducing the congress as the main party body. One of the reasons adduced for the change was the lack of enthusiasm of party members and the failure to achieve a deeper mobilization during inter-elections periods. Therefore, the transformation undertaken in 1998 can be seen as a device to re-establish the influence of the 'barons' within the party organization by controlling the election of delegates through the party federations (Van Biezen 2003, p. 72).

Turning now to the PS membership, a brief glance at its size shows the limited capacity of the party to establish strong links with the citizens. The low level of socialist members as a percentage of voters and of the electorate make clear how far the PS is from the classic mass party model, especially when compared with the PCP (Table 2). This is a relevant feature of the two main Portuguese parties—the PS and the PSD— which have shown more interest in attracting voters than members.

However, the most striking feature of the evolution of party membership concerns the deep qualitative changes undertaken in 2003. If we look at the channels for members' access and participation, the statutes approved in 2003 established new forms for the

Table 2 PS and PCP Membership, 1974–2005

Year	PS members	PS membership (% of voters)	PS membership (% of electorate)	PCP membership (% of voters)	PCP membership (% of electorate)
1974	35,971	—	—	—	—
1975	81,654	3.77	1.31	10.6	1.60
1976	91,562	4.85	1.39	14.6	1.75
1978	96,563	—	—	—	—
1979	107,732	6.63	1.48	14.6	2.27
1980	115,762	7.21	1.61	18.6	2.60
1981	121,460	—	—	—	—
1982	125,648	—	—	—	—
1983	130,279	6.36	1.77	19.5	2.73
1984	—	—	—	—	—
1985	—	3.90	0.59	22.3	2.56
1986	46,655	—	—	—	—
1987	—	3.71	0.58	28.9	2.51
1989	62,117	—	—	—	—
1990	55,558	—	—	—	—
1991	59,869	3.58	0.70	32.4	1.93
1992	65,447	—	—	—	—
1993	68,498	—	—	—	—
1994	74,127	—	—	—	—
1995	81,358	3.7	1.01	27.8	1.60
1996	90,062	—	—	—	—
1997	96,107	—	—	—	—
1998	103,872	—	—	—	—
1999	114,974	4.2	1.06	27.1	1.51
2000	124,611 (100,000)[*]	—	—	—	—
2001	122.548 (80,000)[†]	—	—	—	—
2002	66,917	3.6	0.84	34.6	1.47
2003	74,949	—	—	—	—
2005	—	2.9	0.85	18.5	0.91

Sources: Martins (2004) and Silva (2005) for PS membership; Jalali (2002) for PCP membership as a percentage of voters. [*]Van Biezen (2003, p. 60). [†]*Público*, 24 April 2001.

integration of members, based not only on geographical criteria but also on thematic interests. Moreover, the possibility has been introduced of setting up cyber sections and to form 'politics clubs', which are informal structures promoted by members and open to citizens not necessarily linked to the party. Therefore, the status of 'sympathizer' was formally recognized, a sympathizer being 'any person who identifies with the programme and the Declaration of Principles' (PS 2003). Despite the lack of specific criteria to distinguish the different types of members, the statutes establish that sympathizers have the right to take part in several activities inside the party but without the right to vote, and they also have the chance to be registered in a specific file controlled by the secretariat. Overall, these changes show the loosening of the boundaries between members and voters, as well as the attempt to enhance the links between the party and civil society.

Another important change regards the recruiting system of the party, since according to the 2003 statutes the national organization—through the secretariat— controls the recruitment of party members, instead of local sections as happened in the past. However, there have been difficulties with the institutionalization of this change because of the conflicts between the central and local bodies of the party: at the end of 2003 the national commission re-established the payment of dues at the section level. This was interpreted as the result of the pressures from some powerful federations that wanted to counteract the increasing concentration of powers in the national party bodies (Lopes 2005, pp. 367–368).

Despite the tensions within the party regarding the delegates' election to the party congress and the recruiting system, the territorial cleavage—centre versus periphery— seems not to be a relevant feature of the PS organization. Since the early 1980s there has been a process of centralization and concentration of powers in the national party organs. This concerns the candidates' selection, party financing, the composition of national party bodies, and the strategy and organization of the electoral campaign (see below). Nevertheless, the organizational balance of power should be distinguished from the governmental dynamics; in this sense, holding a local office constitutes a key resource in order to gain an important position at the national level, namely, in the party national leadership or in the main political institutions (that is, government and parliament). Thus, local office holders are able to use their power to achieve more autonomy—often through clientelistic practices—and to influence party life in their own district or municipality for their own interests or careers, to the detriment of national party objectives and policies (Jalali 2002; Lopes 2005).

Party Leadership and the Internal Balance of Power

As regards the national party bodies, we must consider two different aspects: the first concerns the evolution of the size of deliberative and executive organs, whereas the second relates to the powers attributed to these organs. Observing the changes in the size of the national party bodies, it is possible to distinguish two different periods: the first, with Guterres as secretary-general, is characterized by the increase in the number of members of the secretariat and the permanent commission, while the second, starting with Ferro Rodrigues, is marked by a huge rationalization of national organs. Until 2001 the expansion of the executive bodies was a device used by the secretary-general to reward the more careerist leaders through appointments *ex officio*. However, under Ferro Rodrigues the size of the party executive was reduced in order to revitalize the party leadership, as also shown by the frequency of meetings of the political commission, which changed from intervals of two months to intervals of three weeks.

A closer look at the powers of the national party bodies shows that the underlying feature of the PS between 1995 and 2005 is the increasing concentration of powers in the executive organs and, in particular, in the hands of the secretary-general. This is due not only to the control of important organizational resources such as the management of party funding and the selection of candidates,[5] but also to the institutional role played by the PS, mainly through the governmentalization of party organs (Lobo 2003). This means that when the party achieves governmental power there is a strong overlap between the party leadership and the members of the cabinet, but gradually the party in government, and especially the party leader, acquires more autonomy, leading to control over the rest of the party. Although formally the secretary-general has maintained almost the same prerogatives vis-à-vis the national party bodies, in practice between 1995 and 2005 there has been a deeper concentration of powers in the party leader's hands. This evolution is reflected in the introduction of the direct election of the party leader.

The mechanism for the selection of the PS secretary-general has changed several times since 1976. While originally the socialist leader was elected by the party congress, after the introduction of the 1992 statutes the power to select the secretary-general was attributed to the national commission. Finally, in 1998 direct election of the party leader by party members was introduced. This is probably the most important organizational change in the last decade; after the failure of the convention model, this change was considered by the socialist leadership a mechanism to expand internal participation and legitimacy. The secretary-general is elected by the majority of votes polled by the party members.[6] At the same time, the secretariat is elected through a closed list presented by the secretary-general, who also chooses the members of the permanent commission. This allows the party leader to have strong support within the executive organs. Similar to what has been observed for other European parties, the direct election of the secretary-general does not entail greater intra-party democratization; instead, it seems that this organizational change prompts an increasing concentration of powers because of the 'atomization' effect on the membership and the neutralization of the middle-level elite (Mair 1994; Lobo 2003).

Centripetal Dynamics and Bilateral Oppositions: The PS's Competitive Strategy

The policy of alliances followed by the PS reflects both the characteristics of the democratic transition—through the formation of the party identity in opposition to the radical socialism advanced by the PCP and extreme-left groups—and the evolution of the Portuguese party system towards a bipolar system. These two elements are the main causes of the continuity of the socialist strategy of alliances since the mid-1980s. The underlying features of the competitive strategy adopted by the PS are the strengthening of the competition towards the centre of the political spectrum and the refusal to form any kind of alliance with the left-wing parties (PCP, BE) at the national level.

Since 1987 the Portuguese party system has become less fragmented, as shown by the decrease in the effective number of parliamentary parties (ENP). In the first decade of the democratic regime the average ENP was 3.3, which diminished to 2.5 in the 1987–2005 period (Martins & Mendes 2005, p. 104). This was the consequence of the increase in the share of votes for the centre parties (PS and PSD), which contrasted with the progressive weakening of the extreme parties (CDS and PCP). The sudden rise and fall of the PRD and the resulting high level of vote shifts have also benefited the PS and the PSD in the long term (Magalhães 2005). Between 1975 and 1985 the average share of the vote for the two main centre parties was 63 per cent, substantially below the 75.8 per cent of the following period (1987–2005). This suggests a progressive strengthening of the centre and a shift to a more centripetal competition, although this trend was partially reversed in the 2005 elections. The semi-presidential system has also contributed to reinforcing the bipolarization of the system—left versus right—as it forces the small parties in each bloc to support the PS and the PSD candidates for the presidency in the runoff election at the cost of eroding their partisan loyalties.

The second characteristic of the socialists' competitive strategy is the refusal to form alliances with the left-wing parties. Despite the Communists' attempts to enter an alliance with the PS, the socialist leadership—namely Soares—has always avoided any cooperation with the PCP at the national level. Initially, this strategy stemmed from the ideological differences emerging between the two parties in the revolutionary period. Things seemed to change in 1989, when the socialist leader Jorge Sampaio ran for the presidency of the Lisbon municipal chamber in alliance with the PCP, becoming mayor of the capital city. The rise of Guterres to the party leadership and the Communists' electoral decline since 1991, at both national and local level, were to interrupt any further rapprochement between the two left-wing parties. Yet, the 2002 and 2005 elections have shown that this issue still represents an important puzzle for the socialist leadership. While an absolute parliamentary majority allows parties of government—mainly the PS and the PSD—to overlook the smaller parties of their own bloc, a relative majority endangers governmental stability (Jalali 2002). In the 2002 electoral campaign, for instance, the socialist leader Ferro Rodrigues suggested that if the PS had obtained a relative majority it would have probably entered into an alliance with one of the smaller left-wing parties (PCP or BE). Likewise, the 2004 election of the secretary-general showed that the strategy of alliances was one of the main issues that divided the three candidates. While João Soares (Mário Soares's son) did not assume a clear position on this issue, Sócrates maintained the competitive position adopted by Guterres, as opposed to Manuel Alegre—supported by the party left wing—who suggested the possibility of negotiating an alliance with the left parties, especially if the PS were not able to achieve a strong parliamentary majority.

In the evolution of the competitive strategy undertaken by the PS, the main change took place in the mid-1980s through the progressive adaptation of the socialists' policy of alliances to the party system dynamics. During the Soares leadership the PS tried to play a pivotal role in forming the governmental majorities. Thus, the party's basic aim was to maximize its governmental potential through the establishment of alliances with the centre-right parties, while denying any kind of compromise with the PCP. After 1985, with the beginning of the rotation in government between the PS and the PSD, the Socialist Party (under Constâncio and Sampaio) tried to win the parliamentary majority by running alone and presenting itself as the only viable alternative to the centre-right parties. According to this strategy the PS was to become the 'common house' of centre-left voters. Since then, and despite the hesitations of some leaders, the competitive strategy has shown great continuity. However, as observed by Nunes (2005, p. 193), the bipolarization prompted by the PS after the mid-1980s took a different form with Guterres. Under the leadership of Constâncio and Sampaio the PS attempted to maintain a leftist identity in order to represent the left pole of the party system, whereas Guterres aimed to compete directly with the PSD in order to maximize the share of votes and to win a parliamentary majority.

Guterres's strategy was based on the appeal to the centre electorate and the direct competition for the PSD's social basis of support. Since democratization PS electoral campaigns have targeted voters with a centrist position and weak party attachment, without particular reference to any specific social class. Yet this strategy became clearer under Guterres, not only through the formulation of a more moderate and liberal programme, but also through the appeal to the Catholic vote. In addition, he attempted to mobilize potential abstainers, who constitute an important factor in determining which party will win the majority of parliamentary seats (Aguiar 2000; Freire 2001). This was indeed a priority of the message launched in 1999 for the winning of an absolute majority and also the basis of the 2005 electoral success.[7] In this sense, the competitive strategy adopted by Guterres has shown remarkable continuity and still characterizes the relationship between the PS and the other parties.

More Responsive or More Efficient? PS Electoral Campaigns

The organization of the electoral campaigns for the Portuguese parties has developed in the context of mass politics and the widespread use of mass media. As a consequence the PS has always attributed great importance to television through media-based events (conventions, rallies) and the face-to-face debates between the main party leaders which take place on the eve of elections. Moreover, the increasing importance of the means of communication and the dynamics of the presidential elections have enhanced the personalization of the electoral competition and the role played by party leaders (Lobo 2005). However, when compared with previous socialist campaigns, the 1995 campaign strengthened the technocratic and professionalized approach to the electoral competition; this was the result of the constitution of a specific electoral body—the electoral technical committee—on the one hand, and of the use of external consultants regarding marketing activities, on the other.[8] With the exception of the 2002 elections, these two elements have represented a constant feature of the socialist campaigns since the mid-1990s.

As regards campaign organization, the PS relies on ad hoc electoral committees rather than on a permanent department. While in 2002 and 2005 the committees were created as soon as the date of the early elections was known, in 1995 and 1999 Guterres was able to prepare the electoral campaign at least one year before the date of the elections. The party leader usually forms an electoral team with some of his closest collaborators—normally members of the executive committee—in order to decide the electoral strategy and to supervise and coordinate the campaign. From this point of view, the PS campaign is highly centralized as regards the conceptualization of the main strategy, and the secretariat and the permanent commission take care of all aspects of the leader's campaign. Party federations and local branches, however, usually have more freedom in making plans and supporting the candidates in their own districts. The prevalence of the central executive over the party local organizations also emerged during the 2005 elections, when a committee under the coordination of the PS organizational secretary, Jorge Coelho, and including some of the main party leaders (for example, António Galamba and António Vitorino), was established to supervise and plan the electoral campaign. More than for their expertise, the members of the committee were chosen according to the personal trust and confidence of the party leader, who maintained tight control over the whole process.

The most important change in the organization of electoral campaigns since the mid-1990s regards electoral marketing. While the national party bodies—usually the executive committee—took charge of marketing activities until the late 1980s, since the election of Guterres as secretary-general there has been an increasing use of external consultants; in particular, advertising agencies were asked to prepare posters, hoardings, slogans and other outdoor publicity. Experts on marketing and communication usually follow the guidelines of the electoral committee, though they are responsible for the conception of the material and the communication strategy. The use of opinion polls varies according to the institutional position of the party: when the PS is in government there is a widespread use of opinion polls, so that the party undergoes a sort of 'permanent campaign'. On the other hand, when the party is in opposition, it usually relies on opinion polls and other kinds of data produced by newspapers or magazines, although in specific situations the party leaders can decide to ask private agencies to monitor public opinion in order to have some kind of feedback. This activity usually takes place four or five times a year, but intensifies on the eve of elections.

The shift towards—and strengthening of—'new campaign politics' is shown also by the evolution of party funding. Between 1995 and 2005 two trends have emerged: the first is the huge increase in the expenditure on national legislative elections, while the second is the rise of state subventions (Martins 2004). Since 1995 there has been a

Table 3 PS Revenue and Expenditure for Electoral Campaigns, 1995–2005 (thousands of euros and percentages)

	1995	%	1999	%	2002	%	2005	%
State subventions	284.8	11.6	346.6	13.9	1,310.2	49.4	3,453.7	74.3
Donations from companies	296.7	12.1	—	—	—	—	—	—
Donations from individuals	1,866.5	76.2	—	—	154.7	5.9	—	—
Fundraising campaigns	—	—	—	—	41.8	1.6	448.9	9.6
Contributions from the party	—	—	1,657	66.6	1,134.5	43.1	744.4	16.0
Other	—	—	481.4	19.0				
Total revenue	2,448.5	99.9	2,485	99.5	2,632.2	100	4,647.2	99.9
Total expenditure	2,470.0	—	2,490	—	2,631.6	—	4,647.2	—

Sources: Van Biezen (2003, p. 195) for 1995 and 2002; Comissão Nacional de Eleições for 1999; PS for 2005 (provisional data).

linear increase in the PS's expenditures. As Table 3 shows, in 2005 the cost of the electoral campaign almost doubled compared with 2002.[9] On the other hand, the funding for the electoral competition is based mainly on public subventions. In the 2005 elections state contributions accounted for more than 70 per cent of the electoral budget of the PS, while only 25 per cent was financed by party canvassing and party contribution. The weight of public subventions allows the Portuguese parties to give less importance to canvassing activities and to the contributions of their members, while electoral success has emerged as the guarantee for survival without other kinds of income.

Conclusions

This work aimed to examine the evolution of the main dimensions of change and continuity in the Portuguese Socialist Party. It has been argued that since the mid-1980s the PS has undergone important changes in terms of its ideological and programmatic orientations, as well as its competitive strategy. These changes, which went hand in hand with the shift from a multipolar to a bipolar political system, culminated in the leadership of Guterres.

More complex is to evaluate the organizational changes, since the analysis of the party statutes must be complemented with the evolution of the internal balance of power. Even if the powers of the national party bodies did not formally change during the decade 1995–2005, the relevance of the executive and deliberative organs varied according to the institutional role played by the party—whether in opposition or in government. Thus, incumbency is a major factor that influenced the PS's changes from the mid-1990s onwards. As the evolution of the size of the main party bodies and the increasing concentration of powers in the party leader have shown, during the two

Guterres mandates the secretariat and the political commission played a secondary role; on the other hand, when the party was in opposition the executive committee emerged as the most powerful body. Overall, the variation of the internal distribution of power has shown an increasing autonomy and concentration of powers in the executive committee and in the party leader in particular (Canas 2005).

These organizational changes entail some considerations on the causes of party change. To explain the PS's changes, the most significant variable seems to be electoral performance: in effect, the changes undertaken under Guterres have uncovered a growing electoralist vocation and an increasing dependence on governmental power. The second variable that must be considered is the party leadership: intra-party consensus building has become a necessity of contemporary parties in order to present themselves as united and cohesive. The first challenge for the leadership of electoralist parties is thus to gain strong support within the party before appealing to voters. Meanwhile, the importance of party leadership depends on institutional resources: while it is easy for party leaders to ensure control over internal party life when they hold governmental power, this seems to be much more difficult in opposition. In this sense, the winning of elections is an important instrument for gaining more resources (and power) to spend both within and outside the party. The increasing concentration of power in the party leader can represent, however, an element of vulnerability by weakening the party organization and increasing its dependency on government resources at both the national and local level.

Notes

[1] Besides the ideological factionalism, different tendencies emerged in the mid-1980s around different leaders (or 'barons'). This 'personalized' factionalism (Lopes 2005, p. 363) was the consequence of the pattern of democratic transition, the process of party building and the disappearance of the ideological conflicts after the mid-1980s.

[2] The pragmatic and moderate stance undertaken by the first Guterres government is reflected in the percentage of laws passed in parliament with the support of the centre-right parties, as opposed to that of the Communists (almost 20 per cent against eight per cent; see Filipe 2002, pp. 251–252).

[3] See Freire (2004) for 1978, 1985, 1989, 1999 and 2002; Gunther & Montero (2001) for 1993; and Barreto et al. (2005) for 2005.

[4] The Left Bloc is a coalition of three extreme-left parties (Socialist Revolutionary Party, PSR and People's Democratic Union, UDP) and a political movement (Politics XXI) which ran for the first time in the 1999 legislative elections.

[5] Besides the control of the extra-parliamentary party over the parliamentary group through the party discipline, according to the 2003 statutes the party leader has the right to appoint 30 per cent of the candidates for the legislative elections, while the political commission has a veto power on the remaining candidates—who are chosen formally by the party federations.

[6] In order to be a candidate for the party leadership it was necessary to be a member of the party for at least one year and to present the signatures of 1,000 party members. With the statutes approved in 2003, the limit of the signatures decreased to 100 in order to encourage intra-party competition. Only in 2004, however, has there been a real competition between different

candidates; before Sócrates' election, the selection of the party leader was a top-down process, since the secretary-general was de facto chosen by the main party leaders.

[7] The correlation coefficients between abstention and the socialist support at aggregated level are statistically significant both for the 1995 and 1999 elections; while in the first case the PS increased its votes where the amount of abstentions decreased ($r = -0.30$), in the second case the socialist losses corresponded to an increase in abstentions ($r = -0.13$; see Freire & Magalhães 2002, pp. 105–106).

[8] Most of the information about the PS political campaign is based on data collected through newspapers and magazines, as well as interviews with Socialist leaders.

[9] By and large, data on the financing of political parties in Portugal lack reliability and must be considered with care due to the limits of internal and external control.

References

Aguiar, J. (2000) 'Eleições, configurações e clivagens: os resultados eleitorais de 1995', *Análise Social*, nos 154–155, pp. 55–84.

Barreto, A., Freire, A., Lobo, M. Costa, Magalhães, P. & Espírito Santo, A. (2005) *Base de Dados: Inquérito Pós-eleitoral*, Instituto de Ciências Sociais, Lisboa.

Canas, V. (2005) 'O PS: que partido é?', in *O Partido Socialista e a Democracia*, ed. V. Canas, Celta Editora, Oeiras, pp. 3–28.

Filipe, A. (2002) *As Oposições Parlamentares em Portugal*, Vega, Lisboa.

Freire, A. (2001) *Mudança Eleitoral em Portugal*, Celta Editora, Oeiras, Portugal.

Freire, A. (2004) 'O Significado da Divisão entre Esquerda e Direita: Portugal, Espanha e Grécia em Perspectiva Comparada', DPhil thesis, Instituto de Ciências Sociais, Lisboa.

Freire, A. (2005) 'Geografia e sociologia do voto no Partido Socialista', in *O Partido Socialista e a Democracia*, ed. V. Canas, Celta Editora, Oeiras, pp. 327–351.

Freire, A. & Magalhães, P. (2002) *A Abstenção Eleitoral em Portugal*, Instituto de Ciências Sociais, Lisboa.

Gunther, R. & Montero, J. R. (2001) 'The anchors of partisanship: a comparative analysis of voting behaviour in four Southern European countries', in *Parties, Politics and Democracy in the New Southern Europe*, eds P. N. Diamandouros & R. Gunther, Johns Hopkins University Press, Baltimore, pp. 83–152.

Jalali, C. (2002) 'The Evolution of the Portuguese Party System in Comparative European Perspective since 1974', DPhil thesis, University of Oxford.

Lobo, M. C. (2003) 'A elite partidária em Portugal, 1976–2002', in *Elites, Sociedade e Mudança Política*, eds A. Costa Pinto & A. Freire, Celta Editora, Oeiras, Portugal, pp. 249–275.

Lobo, M. C. (2005) 'The presidentialization of Portuguese democracy?', in *The Presidentialization of Politics*, eds T. Poguntke & P. Webb, Oxford University Press, Oxford, pp. 269–288.

Lobo, M. C. & Magalhães, P. (2002) 'The return of the Portuguese right: the 2001 local government elections and the 2002 legislative elections', *South European Society & Politics*, vol. 7, no. 1, pp. 72–89.

Lobo, M. C. & Magalhães, P. (2004) 'The Portuguese socialists and the third way', in *Social Democratic Party Politics in Contemporary Europe*, eds G. Bonoli & M. Powell, Routledge, London, pp. 83–101.

Lopes, F. F. (2005) 'Perfil organizativo do Partido Socialista', in *O Partido Socialista e a Democracia*, ed. V. Canas, Celta Editora, Oeiras, pp. 353–370.

Magalhães, P. (2005) 'Eleições, partidos e instituições políticas no Portugal democrático', in *Portugal Contemporâneo*, ed. A. Costa Pinto, Publicações Dom Quixote, Lisboa, pp. 173–192.

Mair, P. (1994) 'Party organization: from civil society to the state', in *How Parties Organize*, eds R. S. Katz & P. Mair, Sage, London, pp. 1–21.

Martins, M. M. (2004) *Participação Política e Democracia—O Caso Português (1975–2000)*, Instituto Superior de Ciências Sociais e Políticas, Lisboa.

Martins, M. M. & Mendes, M. de F. A. (2005) *30 Anos de Democracia: Retrospectiva das Eleições para a Assembleia da República (1975–2005)*, Comissão Nacional de Eleições, Lisboa.

Nunes, F. (2005) 'A nossa via. A política e as políticas nos programas eleitorais do Partido Socialista (1980, 1987 e 1995)', in *O Partido Socialista e a Democracia*, ed. V. Canas, Celta Editora, Oeiras, pp. 181–203.

PS (2003) *Estatutos*, Partido Socialista, Lisboa.

Puhle, H. -J. (2001) 'Mobilizers and late modernizers: Socialist parties in the new Southern Europe', in *Parties, Politics and Democracy in the New Southern Europe*, eds P. N. Diamandouros & R. Gunther, Johns Hopkins University Press, Baltimore, pp. 268–328.

Sablosky, J. A. (1997) 'The Portuguese Socialist Party', in *Political Parties and Democracy in Portugal: Organizations, Elections and Public Opinion*, ed. T. C. Bruneau, Westview Press, Boulder, CO, pp. 55–76.

Silva, A. S. (2005) 'Os socialistas portugueses à entrada do século XXI: os militantes e a estrutura do PS', in *O Partido Socialista e a Democracia*, ed. V. Canas, Celta Editora, Oeiras, pp. 295–326.

Van Biezen, I. (1998) 'Building party organizations and the relevance of past models: the Communist and Socialist Parties in Spain and Portugal', *West European Politics*, vol. 21, no. 2, pp. 32–62.

Van Biezen, I. (2003) *Political Parties in New Democracies*, Palgrave Macmillan, New York.

If It Isn't Broken, Don't Fix It: The Spanish Popular Party in Power

Javier Astudillo & Elena García-Guereta

Introduction

The 30-year-old history of the Spanish Partido Popular (PP) can be divided into two distinct periods. In the first, between 1976 and 1996, the party suffered deep and frequent changes, affecting its organization, leadership, ideology and programmes. In the second, between 1996 and 2005, changes have almost been absent. The PP was born as Alianza Popular (Popular Alliance, AP) in October 1976, when Spain was starting its transition to democracy. It entered the new Spanish party system as a very rightist and minor party, which managed to become the main opposition party by 1982, and to reach national government between 1996 and 2004, when unexpectedly it lost general elections and returned to opposition.

Parties are especially conservative organizations,[1] and few if any changes are expected when a party succeeds; so between 1995 and 2005 the PP behaved basically as party change theories would have predicted. However, the PP's lack of recent changes makes it an interesting exception among political parties in Europe in general, and Southern Europe in particular, that have experienced different processes of organizational or programmatic changes. The PP also constitutes an interesting exception in another sense: it has been in office precisely at the time when leftist parties or coalitions of the centre-left terminated long periods of conservative rule in most Western European countries (Chandler 2002, p. 7).

In this work we analyse how these particular features are inextricably linked. The PP's previous changes paved the way for its coming to power and its electoral and policy success made substantial party changes unlikely. We will start by reviewing the history of the PP, and how party changes took place before the party's coming to power. In the following three sections we analyse its competitive strategies, campaign politics and organizational format, and in the final section we look at how its programmatic changes were implemented after coming to power through its public policies.

AP-PP 1976–2006: From Opposition to Government and Back to Opposition[2]

The PP, which by the late 1990s seemed to be a model for fellow right-wingers across the continent (*The Economist*, 21 January 1999), was founded at the beginning of the Spanish democratic transition as a coalition of seven 'liberal' politicians from the Franco regime (Montero 1987, p. 10). Under the leadership of Manuel Fraga, the party—named Alianza Popular between 1976 and 1989—intended to become the main Spanish conservative party. However, the first democratic elections, in 1977, were won by the Union of the Democratic Centre (UCD), a wide coalition of small centrist parties presided over by Adolfo Suárez, who after being appointed prime minister in July 1976, successfully ended the Franco era and started the Spanish transition to democracy.

The AP's poor performance in the 1977 elections (8.6 per cent of the vote and 16 seats out of 350) led to the most drastic changes that this party ever experienced. Only two years later, Fraga was the only party founder who remained as a party leader, and the AP entered a coalition (Democratic Coalition) that attempted to compete with the governing UCD for the centrist voters in the 1979 general elections (Montero 1987, p. 13). This drastic party change worsened the AP's electoral fortunes to such an extent that the party's very existence was at risk: it obtained only six per cent of the vote and its leader resigned. But the party survived, Fraga returned to preside over it, and its previous strong transformation allowed it to become the main opposition party when the collapse of the UCD forced early general elections. In 1982 the AP, in coalition with the Popular Democratic Party (PDP) that had split with the UCD, and with some minor regional parties, obtained 106 seats and 26.4 per cent of the vote. In spite of this success, however, the AP continued to be perceived as a clearly rightist party by most Spanish voters (Montero 1987), and in the general elections of 1986 it got 105 seats with 26 per cent of the vote, while the centrist Social Democratic Centre (CDS), the party founded by Adolfo Suárez when the UCD split into several parties, grew from two to 19 seats.

The AP's electoral stagnation added to the failure of the coalitional strategy followed by Fraga to generate both internal dissent and criticisms, as well as external distrust in his capability to lead the AP to national government. By the end of 1987, Fraga resigned as party leader, and Hernández Mancha, a young politician from Andalucía, was elected the AP's president. However, the national party apparatus had supported an alternative candidate for the presidency, and Mancha never counted on its support. By 1988 the intra-party conflicts had become an open and public battle, which led the AP into a profound crisis and worsened its electoral prospects. To remedy the situation Fraga returned to the party presidency, temporarily, to pacify the party, and to integrate smaller centre-right parties into a 'refounded' party.

In January 1989 the ninth party congress approved Fraga's agreement with the elites of the Christian democrat PDP and a minor liberal party, former AP coalition partners during the 1980s, which dissolved their parties and entered the renamed Popular Party. Hence, 12 years after its foundation, the AP, reborn as the PP, was finally able to encapsulate all the national centre-right and right political families.

A few months later, Fraga proposed to appoint José María Aznar as the party candidate for prime minister for the 1989 general elections, and that was approved. Aznar was both a relevant member of the party's dominant coalition and the young president of the Castilla-León autonomous government. The PP obtained in the 1989 elections a similar result to that in 1986, but it was considered a success, given that after less than two months as party leader Aznar had recovered the electoral support that the PP had lost between elections. From his arrival as leader, Aznar presented himself as a member of a new political generation, and tried to move the party to the centre of the political spectrum, changing both the party's image and some of its traditional programmatic stances. At the same time, Aznar considered that the prerequisite to transform the PP into a governing party was to build a cohesive organization.

Meanwhile, in the first half of the 1990s the PP's main national rivals, the governing Socialist Party (PSOE) and the centrist CDS, started to experience serious internal problems. The PSOE suffered from a series of corruption scandals and internal feuding while the country entered a deep economic crisis. In 1991 the CDS had to face the resignation of its charismatic leader, Adolfo Suárez. By 1993 Aznar had achieved its two initial goals: to build a cohesive and efficient organization, and to occupy the central space of the political spectrum. However, the PP had been unable to achieve office. When the PP faced the next general contest, in 1996, it presented a moderate electoral manifesto, and tried to fight the electoral battle on competence, rather than ideology.

Finally, after 20 years in opposition, and 14 years of the PSOE's rule, the PP won the 1996 general elections. It obtained 38.8 per cent of the vote, compared with 37.6 per cent for the PSOE. The narrow margin of its victory, however, forced Aznar to seek the parliamentary support of the Catalan, Canary Islands, and Basque regional nationalist parties. In May 1996 Aznar formed his single-party minority government, which was by all standards a 'party government', including members from each of the PP's ideological families and historical stages.

During his first term in office, Aznar worked hard to build a consensus for most of its reforms. His main socio-economic policies were oriented primarily towards helping economic growth and Spain's joining the monetary union. At the same time, and in part as the price for the support of the regional nationalist parties, the devolution of authority from the centre to the regional governments increased.

A cease-fire declared by the Basque terrorist group opened the possibility of putting an end to the violence in the Basque Country. However, in spite of the political stability, economic prosperity and social peace that characterized the first years of the Aznar government, opinion polls never indicated that it would reach an absolute majority in the following elections.

At last, and unexpectedly, the PP won an outright majority in the March 2000 general elections: 183 seats and 44.5 per cent of the vote. The electoral victory granted Aznar much more power to implement his programme, although he made public his intention to continue seeking agreements for his reform policies with the regional nationalist parties and even with the PSOE.[3]

In January 2002 the PP achieved its sweetest moment, coinciding with its 14th national congress. Aznar was re-elected as party president for the last time—he reaffirmed that he would not stand again as leader, or as party candidate. So Aznar presented his 'legacy': a political programme for the following decade whose chief goal was to transform Spain into one of the main democracies in the world. However, his 'legacy' also showed a shift in his political priorities, since terrorism and nationalism had become his principal worries.

A few months later, things became more complicated for the PP. In spring 2002 Spanish trade unions organized a general strike against the government reform of unemployment benefits. This, in combination with Aznar's highly unpopular pro-American stand in the war on Iraq, weakened PP electoral prospects and gave the socialist opposition party a lead in the polls by some six percentage points. The local and regional elections of May 2003 were won by the PSOE, which achieved their first victory in a nationwide contest after ten years of defeats, although the Socialists won by a smaller margin than expected. Given the circumstances, the PP did unexpectedly well, coming first in 35 out of 52 cities, and nine out of 13 regions.

At the beginning of September 2003 Aznar's nominee to succeed him, Mariano Rajoy, was elected as the new electoral candidate by the party governing organs. Rajoy was an expected successor, and started his electoral campaign promising a continuation of Aznar's agenda. While the PP's lead had been narrowing, opinion polls predicted a win for the PP. However, the general elections of 2004, held only three days after the March 11 terrorist attacks,[4] was won by the Socialist Party. Its leader, Rodríguez Zapatero, obtained 42.6 per cent of the vote, whereas the PP got only 37 per cent. This unexpected electoral result has not brought any relevant party changes so far. Rajoy has not been held responsible for the electoral defeat, generally attributed to the exceptional circumstances preceding the election day. Hence, in October 2004 the PP called its 14th congress, and elected Rajoy as the new party president.

Moving to the Centre: Electoral and Competitive Strategies

Since the beginning of the transition, Spanish conservatism was divided among different organizations, both nationally and regionally. After 1982–83, this division became much more pronounced. At the national level, the collapse of the governing

UCD left the national centre-right and right forces more divided than before, and in a very weak competitive position. At the regional level, the decentralization process started by the Spanish constitution gave way to the emergence of regional governments, parliaments and specific party systems. By 1983 the new institutional structure was completed. As a result, regional right-wing forces emerged in many more regions than Catalonia and the Basque Country, where nationalist right-wing parties had successfully established their presence in the first democratic elections.

In other terms, the success of the AP in the 1982 general elections, when it became the main opposition party, was also the worst performance for the Spanish right-wing parties so far (Montero 1986), since the three national right-wing parties competing in those elections (AP, UCD and CDS) obtained together 36 per cent of the vote, a share that the UCD had almost gained alone in the previous elections. Throughout the 1980s, AP electoral strength stagnated at 26 per cent of the vote, although the progressive decline of the Socialists (from 48 per cent in 1982 to 40 per cent in 1989) decreased the electoral distance between the governing PSOE and the main opposition party.

When in 1989 Aznar was elected PP candidate for the post of prime minister, the party's competitive position had improved greatly. The *refundación* (refoundation) of the AP as the PP had integrated all the national centre-right and right political forces into the PP, though the central space of the political spectrum remained occupied by the CDS. From the very moment Aznar was elected party president (at the tenth party conference, in March 1990), it became clear that its main competitive strategy would be to occupy the central space of the political spectrum, while the fight for the electorate of regional right-wing forces would be a complementary but secondary strategy.

The 1991 local and regional elections were the first test of Aznar's strategy. They showed not only that the PP was growing spectacularly among the urban and well-informed electorate (López-Nieto 1998), but, more importantly, that the PP was succeeding in its attempt to attract the centrist voters. The CDS dropped from 9.8 to four per cent of the vote, leading to the resignation of its charismatic leader, Adolfo Suárez. Immediately after those elections, Aznar declared that the Socialist and Popular electorates had become adjacent, showing clearly that his future competitive strategy would also be directed to attract those moderate voters who so far had been voting for the PSOE. The 1993 general elections showed, this time more clearly, that Aznar's competitive strategy was paying off: although the PP lost again, its share grew from 26 to 35 per cent of the vote, while the centrist CDS became an extra-parliamentary party, and the governing PSOE lost its absolute majority. Thus, in 1993 the PP had finally become the only national party representing in parliament the centre-right and right of the political spectrum.

Hence, the PP did not change its competitive strategy, but reinforced it. By 1994 the success of that strategy seemed astounding: for the first time in history the PP surpassed the PSOE in a European, but nationwide, election and it did so with a margin of almost ten percentage points. The PP repeated its triumph in the 1995 regional and local elections: it received the highest number of votes in 11 out of 13 autonomous communities and also won, for the first time, the municipal elections.

This strategy remained unchanged until the 1996 general elections, which the PP faced as the obvious favourite. However, against expectations, the PP won with a very narrow majority: less than 300,000 votes separated the two main parties. This result left the PP in a difficult position, since to form a government it had to reach an agreement with the Catalan Nationalist Party (CiU), which between 1993 and 1996 had supported the Socialist government, and with other regional parties (Gunther et al. 2004).

Again, the narrow electoral victory did not lead to any fundamental change in the party's competitive strategy (Martínez & Méndez 2004, p. 89). However, on coming to power the PP changed the way in which its strategies were carried out. The electoral victory enhanced the PP's chance of making its strategies successful, in two regards. Firstly, to gain more votes the PP no longer had to rest on pure rhetorical arguments. From the very moment at which Aznar was elected prime minister, he developed his 'drizzling rain theory': governmental policy outputs and the piecemeal fulfilment of electoral promises would slowly convince citizens that the PP was a moderate party, capable of governing efficiently, and therefore would slowly improve the PP's electoral fortunes. Secondly, the agreement reached between the PP and the main regional centre-right parties offered the conservatives the opportunity to get closer to their nationalist Basque and Catalan counterparts, something that could have helped to improve the PP's electoral fortunes in those regions. But, as we explain later, the different views of the PP and these nationalist parties (CiU and the Basque Nationalist Party, PNV) about what should be the final territorial distribution of powers in Spain kept them as far apart from each other as they were before 1996.

Until December 1998 Aznar's 'drizzling rain theory' did not seem to be working. Opinion polls showed that the PP held a very narrow lead over the PSOE. So Aznar used the 13th party congress, held in 1999, to reinforce the party's middle-of-the-road message, and to some extent to renovate the party leadership, replacing Álvarez Cascos, the party's secretary-general since 1989, with Javier Arenas, who was generally considered a more moderate politician.

The general elections held in March 2000 gave the PP a very clear victory. The electoral alliance of the Socialists with the former Communists had helped the PP to present themselves as the only party representing the centrist and moderate electorate. Post-electoral studies (Varela 2004) have shown that between 1996 and 2000 the profile of PP voters changed significantly and became more evenly distributed across social classes than in the past. In addition, the PP overtook the PSOE as the largest party among voters aged 60 and over, an electoral niche of utmost importance, since they represented 27 per cent of the total electorate. However, the large and unexpected conservative majority did not mean that the Spanish electorate had massively shifted to support the conservatives. In fact, the PP received 600,000 more votes in 2000 than in 1996, while the Socialists lost 1.5 million and the Communists 1.4 million. In other words, the electoral outcome was due rather to the abstention of former leftist voters (the abstention rate rose from 22 to 31 per cent) than to the PP's success in attracting new voters (Barreiro 2001; González 2002).

The 2000 electoral victory allowed the PP to govern by itself. Needless to say, the success did not provoke any relevant change in the party's competitive strategy. Although the party electoral candidate changed in September 2003, when Aznar was replaced as leader by Rajoy, this did not affect its competitive strategy, something completely logical, since Rajoy had been one of the main PP electoral strategists for the previous 14 years.

Campaign Design and Organization

Under Fraga's leadership, the party electoral machinery used to be activated only a few months before elections. But under Aznar the PP became more electorally oriented, to the extent that at first he planned to have the electoral machinery in almost permanent readiness. In March 1990, right before his election as party president, Aznar announced his intention to professionalize the electoral and organizational party areas. At the same time, he declared that he had already established an electoral team devoted full-time to prepare for the local and regional elections due 18 months later.[5]

However, the professionalization announced by Aznar was not really such. What Aznar did was, on the one hand, to devote the work of some members of its central apparatus permanently to various electoral activities, and on the other, to hire an external sociologist specializing in analysing surveys and electoral behaviour, Pedro Arriola, who became one of Aznar's closest advisors, and was therefore hired by the party on a permanent basis.

In general, the PP has not relied on external professionals to design and organize its campaigns. Instead, its campaigns have usually been designed and organized by the top party leadership, normally by those who meet weekly with the president at the *reuniones de maitines* (matins meetings), the real daily decision-making party body.[6] External consultants and marketing professionals have been contracted to select the campaign slogan and to translate its main ideas to the public through advertising. But usually the party leadership has also played a central role in adopting the final decisions on their electoral advertising campaigns.

Typically, a few months before elections a campaign director or coordinator is appointed. Under Aznar's leadership, the campaign director has always been one of the party highest leaders, who has headed a campaign committee comprising members of the party electoral and organizational areas. This committee takes care of the logistical aspects of each campaign, such as organizing the party rallies and producing the 'candidate handbook'.[7] The campaign director usually oversees the preparation of an electoral study based on the previous elections, in order to identify which provinces should be given priority in each electoral campaign. This territorial strategic map is used to design the campaign of the party president, and of the other relevant party leaders.

The general election campaigns in Spain have always been characterized by a marked personalization, and the PP strategies have, at least since 1993, consciously tried to polarize the campaign on the two main parties, and more specifically, on their leaders.[8] This was also reflected in the PP's internet campaign in 2000, when the electoral webpage was not the party page, but the candidate's page. The PP started to use the internet for both political and electoral purposes around 1996, but, as internet users are still a minority in Spain,[9] television is the main mode of political communication for parties during a campaign.[10]

Between 1995 and 2005 the content of the PP campaigns markedly changed, as a result of its coming to power. The PP started its campaigns publicizing the government's policies and their results (Martínez & Méndez 2004, p. 87). This constituted a first phase of the PP electoral campaigns, which was followed by the traditional party campaigning, based on explaining the party policy proposals. The policy evaluation documents 'Balance of Government'—produced previously by the ministerial departments—were of the utmost importance for this new phase of the PP electoral campaigns, since they eased its preparation by the party electoral teams, as well as the preparation of the party manifesto.

Finally, the 2004 campaign was slightly different from those before. The new party candidate, Mariano Rajoy, had been the director of most of the PP electoral campaigns since the beginning of the 1990s, so in principle there was no reason to expect changes. However, Rajoy was to benefit from Aznar's legacy. Hence, Aznar was given a prominent role in the campaign, although Rajoy was the running candidate, and the campaign had a kind of dual leadership. The other change affected the campaign director, for Rajoy appointed a second-level politician, thus breaking with the tradition of appointing one of the top party leaders.

PP Organization: Cohesiveness as a Goal

Research has typically found that the centre-right is weakest where it is divided either into separate parties or into factions within more inclusive centre-right parties (Girvin 1988; Cordell 2005). In Spain, however, the centre-right ideological family seemed to have reduced this problem, since it is characterized by organizational unity, internal cohesiveness and centralization of decision making. These organizational features were achieved well before the PP came to power in 1996. Its leadership considered these features to be the key to its success,[11] and obviated any experimental processes of party revitalization by empowering its rank and file, like other Western European parties on the left and right of the ideological spectrum.

Party Membership

We begin our analysis of the PP's structure by studying its membership growth and role. Although parties in new democracies tend to have very low levels of membership (Van Biezen 2003), the PP's membership has grown steadily since the early 1980s, in both absolute and relative terms (Table 1). This membership growth is the result of an

Table 1 PP Membership, Yearly Increase and Ratio of Party Membership to Party Voters and Total Electorate, 1977–2005

	PP membership	Yearly increase in membership (%)	PP members as percentage of voters	PP members as percentage of electorate
1977	27,225	—	1.9	0.1
1982	85,412	—	1.5	0.3
1983	144,960	69.7		
1984	163,062	12.5		
1985	202,777	24.4		
1986	236,068	16.4	4.5	0.8
1987	240,235	1.8		
1988	246,678	2.7		
1989	262,755	6.5	5.0	0.9
1990	284,323	8.2		
1991	300,988	5.9		
1992	326,960	8.6		
1993	375,232	14.8	4.6	1.2
1994	429,293	14.4		
1995	490,223	14.2		
1996	540,218	10.2	5.6	1.7
1997	570,879	5.7		
1998	584,341	2.4		
1999	586,000	0.3		
2000	601,731	2.7	5.8	1.8
2001	631,882	4.8		
2002	640,000	1.3		
2003	—	—		
2004	667,073	—	6.8	1.9
2005	707,000	6		

Sources: 1977 (Van Biezen 2003, p. 94); 1982–92 (Gangas 1995); 1992–99 (García-Guereta 2001); 2000–5 (PP 1999b; <www.pp.es>).

organizational strategy implemented since the beginning of the 1980s as a way of reinforcing the party organization, and also as a vehicle for electoral growth. But in the PP there has been no process of empowering, at least formally, the rank and file, either by increasing individual members' involvement in candidate selection for public offices, in the elaboration of electoral platforms or in the selection of party leaders.

The low profile of the PP's membership is reflected in the way delegates to the party congress are allocated. Thus, instead of establishing the number of congress delegates in relation to the size of the membership organization as in the classic mass party, since the 1980s the PP has used a combination of membership size and level of electoral support, in a ratio of about 60 to 40 (Van Biezen 2003, p. 96). In addition, the national congress, formally its highest decision-making authority, is composed not only of members elected by the PP provincial and local assemblies, but also of *ex officio* members. The latter include holders of national committee offices, national members of parliament and representatives of the party's youth organization. The number of elected members has to be at least four/five times higher than the number of *ex officio* delegates (García-Guereta 2001).

A 'Presidentialist' Cohesive Party

At the beginning the AP was a rather odd creature. From 1978 until the late 1980s, it had a dual structure, being simultaneously a unified party and a federation of parties. As pointed out earlier, in 1989 the AP invited its previous coalition partners to join a new 'refounded' organization, the PP. The AP-PP's internal structure has always been similar to that of other classic mass parties. Formally, and in addition to its national congress, its main governing bodies—which have existed throughout the history of the AP-PP—have been the national directive committee (*junta directiva nacional*), the main organ between congresses (which has increased the number of its members from around 270 in the mid 1980s to around 600 at present), and the national executive committee (*comité ejecutivo nacional*; see Table 2). Both organs are composed of *ex officio* members, and members elected by the national congress. Finally, day-to-day party activities have been carried out by informal weekly meetings of the national party leader with his personal appointees (around ten members), the *reuniones de maitines*.

Since 1979 the AP-PP has also been a 'presidentialist' organization. The power of the national president—institutionalized as a 'unipersonal' party organ—has been reinforced by the way of electing the party president and the members of the national executive committee, except for a brief interlude between 1986 and 1989. The elected members of the executive committee are voted for according to a majority system through a closed and blocked list along with the presidential candidate at the PP congress.[12] The PP president also has the prerogative of 'proposing' to the executive committee which of them are going to occupy top offices such as the secretary-general (the second most important political office within the party after the president), the

Table 2 Size and Renewal of the PP's National Executive Committee (NEC)

| PP congress | Size | Re-elected members[*] | | | New members | |
		N	As % of the old NEC	As % of the new NEC	N	As % of the new NEC
9th (1989)	46					
10th (1990)	38	29	63.0	76.3	9	23.7
11th (1993)	50	27	71.1	54.0	23	46.0
12th (1996)	60	40	80.0	66.7	20	33.3
13th (1999)	79	48	80.0	60.8	31	39.2
14th (2002)	89	62	78.5	69.7	27	30.3
15th (2004)	81	55	61.8	67.9	26	32.1

[*]Members of the national executive that sat in the previous executive.
Source: Updated from García-Guereta (2001) with PP congress documents.

deputy secretaries, the area coordinators and executive secretaries. The president's power was reinforced at the beginning of the 1990s. The tenth congress, in 1990, which elected Aznar as president, eliminated the deputy presidencies, which in the past had been used to erode the party leader's authority (García-Guereta 2001). In 1993 the party president acquired the *ex officio* leadership of the parliamentary groups in the lower and upper chambers, thus reinforcing party control over them.

But the power of the PP president cannot simply be attributed to the prerogatives conferred by the party statutes. We cannot forget that 'presidentialism' was already a formal characteristic of both the UCD and the AP, and in both cases national party leaders were forced to resign on several occasions (Hopkin 2000; García-Guereta 2001). That Aznar managed to obtain so much power within the party must be attributed mainly to his renewal of the internal party leadership, and above all to the expectations that this renewal—in addition to programmatic and strategic change—could eventually lead to electoral success. Accordingly, the electoral gains this party made from 1989 onwards, and in particular its 1996 and 2000 electoral victories, reinforced his power.

However, elite renewal has been attained more by addition than by replacement, and this explains, at least partly, why leadership renewal has been accompanied by internal peace and cohesion. As Table 2 shows, even when Aznar was elected party president (1990), 63 per cent of the old members of the party executive were re-elected, and when in 1993 Aznar's team took over the party executive (46 per cent of its members were new), 71 per cent of the old executive members were retained. Rajoy's election as party president in October 2004 did not change this pattern, since almost 62 per cent of the old executive members were re-elected.

Since 1983 the PP's organization has also adapted to the Spanish decentralization process. Accordingly, in addition to the national structure the party also has local, provincial and regional structures, each having its own organs of self-government. Formally these sub-national organs are in charge of party activities at their respective level of government, although their level of autonomy is highly restricted in practical terms. As Astudillo and García-Guereta (2005) have shown, the PP has been de facto a highly centralized party. Thus, its statutes have provided the national leadership with the prerogative of vetoing the sub-national organs' decisions on the most salient activities, such as candidate selection for local office and regional parliaments, or forming alliances with other parties.

The party structure and internal functioning have varied little since the PP came to power in 1996, but some changes have been introduced to adapt the party to its new governing status. Firstly, the PP national leadership has striven to maintain the coordination between the national and regional levels of government, as well as among the party apparatus, the parliamentary delegation and the national government. The PP's cohesiveness was reflected in the small number of internal disputes, and in the reliable behaviour of its parliamentary delegation. Thus, during its first term in office the PP government was able to enact 89 per cent of its proposed legislation, in spite of its minority status. As Gunther, Montero and Botella (2004, p. 388) have pointed out, since the re-establishment of democracy only the legislative success rate of the Socialist government of 1982–86 (which enjoyed an absolute majority in parliament) exceeds this figure. In its second term in office, the Aznar government did not suffer defections from its parliamentary group when supporting the unpopular American and British invasion of Iraq in 2003. This coordination was secured in the PP to a large extent through the overlapping of party and governmental offices. Thus, in addition to Aznar being prime minister and party president, the four party heavyweights occupied the most salient ministries, and two of them were also appointed as deputy prime ministers. Thus the party secretary-general, Francisco Álvarez Cascos, was appointed first deputy prime minister and minister of the presidency. One of the three deputy secretaries, Rodrigo Rato, was appointed second deputy prime minister and minister of finance, while the other two, Jaime Mayor Oreja and Mariano Rajoy, became minister of the interior and minister of public administration, respectively.

In addition, the traditional matins meetings also acquired a new role in party–government coordination, but this meant a new body was needed in charge of the daily organizational management of the party. Consequently, after coming to power a new party position was created, the 'party coordinator' (appointed by the executive committee), and the 1999 PP congress established a new formal permanent executive organ: the *comité de dirección* (management committee). This comprises the top party leadership: the secretary-general, the executive secretaries and the spokespersons of the PP parliamentary groups, closely resembling the reduced composition of the original (1979) executive committee (PP 1999a, pp. 31–32; AP 1979, art. 13).

Finally, in summer 2003 Aznar honoured his promise of staying in power just for two terms, renouncing the PP candidature for prime minister in the 2004 elections and also stepping down from the post of party leader. After informally consulting the party elites, he proposed Mariano Rajoy as his successor. Rajoy received the explicit support of every prominent party leader,[13] including those who had been considered co-candidates to succeed Aznar, and was formally elected by the *junta directiva nacional* as the new secretary-general and the next party candidate for prime minister.[14] Finally in October 2004 the 15th national congress elected him as party president. That congress also introduced some changes in the party's power structure. The party's deputy secretaries-general, which since 1993 had been the highest-power positions after the national president and the secretary-general, were eliminated (PP 2004). This kind of organizational change closely resembles what Aznar did with the deputy presidents when he was elected party president. But the party's dominant coalition in the PP has not fundamentally changed.

PP Goals and Policies: A Neo-liberal Party?

As regards party goals and policies, the PP has responded to some of the new challenges the European centre-right is facing. As is well known, since the late 1970s and early 1980s the diverse traditions of the centre-right have converged around the neo-liberal agenda, especially after the demise of Keynesian macroeconomic management (Ware 1996). Its earlier and easier conversion to a new 'neo-liberal' consensus than the centre-left seemed to be politically advantageous (Girvin 1988). But, recently, it has been suggested that the adoption of a policy mix of market and welfare state by social democrats has deprived the centre-right of its electoral advantage over the left (Wilson 1998; Sturm 2002). If the welfare state is economically viable if some structural reforms are implemented, voters may be coming to accept the need to sacrifice some social benefits and state protections, but they might want these changes made by parties that seem able to do so without the doctrinal convictions and enthusiasm of the right.

As a consequence, European centre-right parties seem to face today the dilemma of either intensifying their commitment to the neo-liberal agenda, or offering another version of the social-democratic policy mix and a sort of 'compassionate conservatism'. If the first option moves the centre-right parties away from the median voter, the second one dilutes their alternative to the policies of the social-democratic third-way parties (Wilson 1998; Sturm 2002). How did the Spanish PP react to these policy challenges? Did it intensify its commitment to the neo-liberal agenda? Or did it try to find another policy area where it could offer a distinctive policy? In addition, scholars such as Ware (1996) and Wilson (1998) argue that subtle differences in party values are less evident in party electoral manifestos than they are in actual implementation, since party manifestos may reflect more what parties expect voters want to hear, according to their professional advisers, pollsters and market researchers. Accordingly, we have to study the PP's governmental policies as well as its party manifestos.

As is well documented by studies of the ideological position of the PP, and as reflected in its electoral manifestos, the party gradually moved towards the centre by moderating its ideology and policy proposals (Ramiro-Fernández 2005). Thus, in the late 1970s the PP focused on traditional conservative issues such as strong state, unity of Spain, public morality, law and order, and defence of the family. From the early 1980s the PP moved gradually towards a kind of neo-liberal stance on economic and social issues, while keeping its conservative position on those moral and law-and-order issues (García-Guereta 2001). But as the social policies of the PSOE were those most preferred by the Spanish electorate (Maravall 1995), the adoption of a clear-cut neo-liberal position by the PP was detrimental to its electoral returns. To make matters worse, its defence of traditional moral and law-and-order issues made large sections of the electorate identify the conservative party with the Spanish authoritarian past (Montero 1988, p. 157), an identification harmful for the Spanish centre-right party's advancement, as also happened in Portugal and Greece (Pappas 2001). Thus, under the new Aznar leadership the PP not only eliminated those old-fashioned issues from its electoral programmes, but also progressively proposed a policy mix of liberal economic policies and sustainable welfare social policies. This policy mix was defended through the PP's eight years of government.[15] Was that just a way of disguising its true neo-liberal convictions?

In the PP's first term in office, paramount in Aznar's programme of government was meeting the macroeconomic convergence criteria imposed by the European Union as a prerequisite for joining the initial group of countries adopting the euro as their new currency (Powell 2001a). Therefore, the PP government carried out a policy of fiscal consolidation and market liberalization. All this was complemented by the privatization of large parastatal firms that was one of the most ambitious in the Organization for Economic Cooperation and Development (OECD 2000) and, almost at the end of its first term in office, a cut in income tax rates. These policies were maintained during the PP's second term in office. As a result, the budget deficit was reduced to 3.1 per cent of GDP in 1997 from almost seven per cent in 1995. By 2002 public finances were in balance. Public debt was reduced to 52 per cent of GDP in 2003, 16 points less than in 1996 (OECD 2005).

A doctrinal commitment to the neo-liberal agenda is, however, more difficult to find in other policy areas. According to the conventional parties-do-matter hypothesis, whereas leftist governments opt for, and achieve, full employment, centre-right governments emphasize the control of inflationary pressure (Schmidt 2002). But the PP did not reduce inflation at the expense of employment. Annual inflation was cut from 4.7 per cent in 1995 to 1.8 per cent in 1998, and unemployment also went down from 18.1 per cent[16] at the end of 1995 to 15 per cent at the end of 1998. Later, inflation went up again to a maximum of 3.6 per cent in 2001, but unemployment continued to go down to 10.5 per cent in that year, staying around that level until 2004. In addition, employment creation was not achieved at the expense of its quality. True, when the PP left office, the temporary job rate was one of the highest in the OECD, but it had actually fallen from 33.8 per cent in 1996 to 30.6 per cent in 2004.

Furthermore, this record was achieved without imposing unilateral reforms or weakening the Spanish trade unions, even though at the end of 1995, a few months before the PP came to power, the Spanish unemployment rate had been 18.1 per cent, and the OECD had recommended reforms to the pension system, health care and labour market (OECD 1998). On the contrary, 1997 marked the beginning of an unprecedented period of social peace. Consequently, tripartite agreements were reached on the promotion of open-ended contracts and regulation of temporary jobs, occupational training, resolution of labour disputes, pensions, collective bargaining in public administration, and risk prevention.[17] It is also remarkable that, in spite of obtaining an absolute parliamentary majority in 2000, the PP failed to implement the structural reforms in the pension system, the labour market and the collective bargaining system according to the OECD guidelines (OECD 2000; 2003). Its most controversial legislative development during its second term in office—a royal decree law reforming unemployment benefits issued by the government in May 2002—was withdrawn after the first, and only, general strike organized by the Spanish trade unions on 20 June.

As regards social policies, there was no major welfare retrenchment either, although certainly the previous process of converging on social spending in other advanced Western European countries had ended (Gunther et al. 2004). There were some timid movements towards a kind of 'liberal' welfare state regime, but no major cuts were introduced in pensions and health care. Given the economic growth, total social protection expenditure as a percentage of the Spanish GDP did fall to 20.2 per cent in 2002, as compared with 22.1 per cent in 1995. But if we look at social protection expenditure per capita, there was only a reduction in 1997, and by 1999 it had recovered to the 1996 level (Eurostat 2005). Does this mean, then, that by implementing this policy mix the PP lacks a distinct policy profile vis-à-vis a 'third way' *avant-la-lettre* PSOE?

The first thing to say is that the PP expected to make its profile on economic issues distinctive by superior performance rather than by offering markedly different or specific policies. Thus the Aznar government hoped that by participating in the euro area from the outset, his government would gain among the Spanish electorate a reputation for economic and political competence. It may be true that European parties are offering today a similar policy mix in their electoral manifestos, but they may still differ in their ability to implement them once in government. As a result, voters may think which party wins the elections continues to make a difference.

In the second place, Aznar developed a new 'nationalistic' policy profile, especially during his second term in office. As several authors have underlined, nationalism has traditionally been used by conservatives for political mobilization (Girvin 1988; Marks & Wilson 2000). In the Spanish context, with the existence of a profound centre–periphery cleavage, nationalism does not only mean 'promoting' the standing of Spain in international scenarios and enhancing the national esteem and confidence of Spaniards (Aznar 2005). It also means that national and peripheral centre-right parties hold strongly different conceptions of what should be the distribution of powers between the central state and the regions, since the PP opposes semi-sovereignty claims by Basque and Catalan nationalists for their regions (Aznar 2005).

In the PP's first term in office, since it needed the support of the regional nationalist parties, this new nationalistic concern could only be reflected in foreign affairs. Thus, in spite of the political and economic progress made under the PSOE administration, Spain was still regarded in Northern European countries as another member of the idle 'Club Med' with Portugal, Greece and Italy (Powell 2001a; Aznar 2005). Therefore, joining the EMU from the start was intended to enhance the international credit of Spain.

But it was after ending its parliamentary dependence on the regional nationalist parties in the 2000 elections that Aznar was able to intensify his nationalistic profile (Gunther et al. 2004). From an external point of view, the election of the republican candidate, George W. Bush, as US president in 2000 represented a window of opportunity for Aznar's policy of international 'prestige promotion'. If González's social democratic governments had contributed to the process of European integration, Aznar could contribute instead to the rebuilding of the transatlantic alliance under US leadership (Calduch 2004; Aznar 2005). Thus, the Aznar government made a U-turn in Spain's traditional foreign policy by enthusiastically supporting the American and British invasion of Iraq in 2003 and their fight against international terrorism. His support of the Iraq invasion, however, met overwhelming opposition from the general public, as shown in opinion polls and public demonstrations, helping the PSOE to become the party with the most votes in the local elections of May 2003.

The nationalistic character of the PP government was also reflected internally in its effort to re-emphasize the importance and value of Spanish history and culture, and its rejection of the deepening of the decentralization process (Aznar 2005).[18] Between 1996 and 2000, the PP government increased the powers transferred to the Spanish regions, as the price for the support of the regional nationalist parties. At the same time, the government completed the devolution of powers to those autonomous communities that had acquired autonomy more slowly, transferring to them decision making on education and health issues, thus fulfilling the 'Autonomic Pact' agreed with the PSOE in 1992.

The PP argued that once all these transfers were completed, the cession of powers from the state to the regions would stop, and maintained that Spain should reach a stable territorial distribution of powers. On the other hand, the Catalan and Basque nationalists demanded both more powers and the status of nation for their regions. As a consequence, the PP's political cooperation with the regional nationalist parties worsened. In the case of the Basque PNV the relationship, already strained because of the PNV's connections with separatist groups, ended in open confrontation. In Catalonia the left separatist party, ERC (Republican Left of Catalonia), surged from 8.6 per cent of the vote in the 1999 regional elections to 16.4 per cent in 2003. At the national level, the Spanish electorate perceived that the PP moved towards the right in its second term in office.[19] A policy of restoring Spain's prestige and pride, in other words 'nationalism' and not neo-liberalism, would be the policy field that gave the PP its clearest profile vis-à-vis centre-left governments during its second term in office.

Conclusion

Since the mid 1990s, unlike other Western European political parties and its own previous history, the PP has experienced only minor organizational and programmatic changes. At the same time, again unlike other Western European centre-right parties, the PP was in office until March 2004. From 1995 until 2004 it achieved its best electoral results ever, and fulfilled its primary goal for the first time in its history. These two significant features are inextricably linked. The PP's previous organizational, programmatic and leadership changes paved the way for its coming to power in 1996 and its renewal in 2000. At the same time, its electoral and policy success made substantial party changes unlikely. In addition, since the unexpected electoral defeat in March 2004, the party has experienced only minor organizational and leadership adjustments.

As the party literature has shown (Janda et al. 1995), defeat is the mother of party change. Thus, when political parties find an organizational format, a leadership and a programme that prove to offer electoral returns and lead to government, that is, to fulfill their main goals, it is very unlikely that either vote-seeking, office-seeking or policy-seeking parties would change substantially. The PP's recent change of leadership, from José María Aznar to Mariano Rajoy, is surely important, but its full programmatic and organizational consequences are still to be seen.

The PP is today the single national centre-right party in Spain, and up to now there are few signs of an extreme right party's emergence. The PP is therefore considerably luckier than other centre-right parties in Europe that have to face bilateral competition. The PP, however, is not the only Spanish centre-right organization, since regional nationalist parties also exist, and they seem to be increasingly distant from the party headed by Mariano Rajoy.

Notes

[1] Janda et al. (1995) summarize parties' conservative nature, stating that their guiding principle is 'If it isn't broken, don't fix it'.

[2] This section summarizes 30 years of party history. For a more detailed account, see Powell (2001b), García-Guereta (2001, pp. 71–200) and Baón (2001).

[3] Aznar ruled out reaching agreements with the moderate Basque Nationalist Party (PNV), because of their accord with the political wing of the Basque terrorist organization Basque Homeland and Liberty (ETA).

[4] The electoral consequences of the worst terrorist attacks in Spanish history are still the subject of academic debate.

[5] Most of the information included in this section comes from anonymous interviews carried out by García-Guereta with the party elites between 1995 and 1996 (García-Guereta 2001), and from analysing electoral campaigns in the Spanish press.

[6] Martínez and Méndez (2004, p. 109) have argued that the 2000 electoral campaign was really designed by Aznar's cabinet. However, at the same time they recognize that important strategic decisions were made by the campaign director, Mariano Rajoy, and the team he led.

[7] This document has some content common to every election (about how to behave in front of the media and how to give a speech at the party rallies), and some election-specific content, such as about campaign style and principal messages.

[8] At least since 1993 the PP's campaigns have been candidate centred (*El País*, 19 April 1993).

[9] In fact, by September 2004, only 25 per cent of Spanish households had internet access, when the European average was 45 per cent (*El País*, 15 September 2004).

[10] In 2000, television was the daily source of campaign information for 44.9 per cent of the voters. See the CIS Estudio no. 2.384, available at < www.cis.es>. On the 2000 campaign, see Martínez and Méndez (2004, pp. 119–124).

[11] Aznar, guest speaker at the founding congress of the French UMP (Union pour un mouvement populaire) (November 2002), declared, 'The model that you have chosen today works ... [on three conditions]... One party, not two or three, a single set of policies, and one team, one only, not several teams' (quoted by Cordell 2005, p. 198).

[12] The only significant experience of increasing the internal democracy ended in party feuding. At its seventh national congress, held in 1986, an open list system was introduced. This democratization weakened the already narrow party cohesion. At the following congress one year later, called after Fraga's resignation, for the first and only time in the party's history two candidates stood for the party presidency. The result was a resurgence of factionalism within the party and a further deterioration of its electoral prospects.

[13] Minutes of the national executive committee held on 1 September 2003.

[14] In addition Aznar delegated to him as secretary-general all his powers as party president, a possibility formally permitted in the PP's statutes.

[15] Motions approved at the 13th (1999) and 14th national party congresses (2002). See Aznar's 'State of the Nation' addresses (1997–2003) in the Spanish parliament (<www.congreso.es>).

[16] According to the recalculation made in 2001 after a new method to measure unemployment was adopted by the Spanish Active Labour Force Survey.

[17] See the reports 'Annual Review for Spain' (1997, 1998, 1999, 2000) of the European Industrial Relations Observatory (<www.eiro.eurofound.eu.int/2005/country/spain.html>).

[18] Thus, the government implemented an education reform that increased the mandatory teaching load of Spanish history and language all over Spain (Llamazares 2005).

[19] The Spanish electorate still placed the PP in a clearly right-wing position in 1996 (7.9 on a ten-point left–right scale). In 2000 the PP was placed in a slightly more centrist position (7.4), but moved to the right in 2004 (7.8). This evolution of the ideological position of the PP was to some extent also perceived by its voters, although they always perceived it less to the right (7.3 in 1996, 7 in 2000, and 7.1 in 2004). Data from the post-electoral surveys of the Centro de Investigaciones Sociológicas.

References

AP (1979) *Estatutos, III Congreso Nacional*, Madrid.

Astudillo, J. & García-Guereta, E. (2005) 'La distribución territorial del poder en los partidos políticos: el caso del Partido Popular español', paper presented at the VII Congreso Español de Ciencia Política y de la Administración, Madrid, 21–23 September.

Aznar, J. M. (2005) *Ocho Años de Gobierno: Una Visión Personal de España*, Editorial Planeta, Barcelona.

Baón, R. (2001) *Historia del Partido Popular: del Franquismo a la Refundación*, Ibersaf Editores, Madrid.

Barreiro, B. (2001) *Los determinantes de la participación en las elecciones de 2000. El problema de la abstención en la izquierda*, Working Paper no. 171, Instituto Juan March, Madrid.

Calduch, R. (2004) 'Política exterior y de seguridad de España en 2003', *Anuario Internacional CIDOB 2003*, Fundació CIDOB, Barcelona, pp. 25–36.

Chandler, W. (2002) 'Conservatism in crisis?', in *Christian-Democratic and Center-Right Parties in Europe and North America: Selected Perspectives*, eds C. Clemens & G. Hirscher, Academy for Politics and Current Affairs, Munich, pp. 7–24.

Cordell, J. (2005) 'Unity and plurality in the French right', *South European Society & Politics*, vol. 10, no. 2, pp. 191–206.

Eurostat (2005) *European Social Statistics: Social Protection, Expenditure and Receipts*, European Commission, Luxembourg.

Gangas, P. (1995) 'El Desarrollo Organizativo de los Partidos Políticos Españoles de Implantación Nacional', DPhil. thesis, Centro de Estudios Avanzados en Ciencias Sociales, Madrid.

García-Guereta, E. (2001) 'Factores Externos e Internos en la Transformación de los Partidos Políticos: el Caso de AP-PP', DPhil. thesis, Centro de Estudios Avanzados en Ciencias Sociales, Madrid.

Girvin, B. (1988) 'Introduction: varieties of conservatism', in *The Transformation of Contemporary Conservatism*, ed. B. Girvin, Sage, London, pp. 1–12.

González, J. J. (2002) 'Las elecciones generales de 2000: voto ideológico/voto racional', *Revista Internacional de Sociología*, no. 32, pp. 7–33.

Gunther, R., Montero, J. R. & Botella, J. (2004) *Democracy in Modern Spain*, Yale University Press, New Haven.

Hopkin, J. (2000) *El Partido de la Transición: Ascenso y Caída de la UCD*, Acento Editorial, Madrid.

Janda, K., Harmel, R., Edens, C. & Goff, P. (1995) 'Changes in party identity: evidence from party manifestos', *Party Politics*, vol. 1, no. 2, pp. 171–196.

Llamazares, I. (2005) 'The Popular Party and European integration: re-elaborating the European programme of Spanish conservatism', *South European Society & Politics*, vol. 10, no. 2, pp. 315–332.

López-Nieto, L. (1998) 'The organizational dynamics of AP/PP', in *The Organization of Political Parties in Southern Europe*, eds P. Ignazi & C. Ysmal, Praeger, London, pp. 254–269.

Maravall, J. M. (1995) *Los Resultados de la Democracia: Un Estudio del Sur y el Este de Europa*, Alianza Editorial, Madrid.

Marks, G. & Wilson, C. (2000) 'The past in the present: a cleavage theory of party response to European integration', *British Journal of Political Science*, vol. 30, pp. 433–459.

Martínez, A. & Méndez, M. (2004) 'Las campañas de los partidos', in *Las Campañas Electorales y sus Efectos en la Decisión del Voto*, vol. 2, *La Campaña Electoral de 2000: Partidos, Medios de Comunicación y Electores*, ed. I. Crespo, Tirant lo Blanch, Valencia, pp. 67–132.

Montero, J. R. (1986) 'El sub-triunfo de la derecha: los apoyos electorales de AP-PDP', in *Crisis y Cambio: Electores y Partidos en la España de los Años Ochenta*, eds J. J. Linz & J. R. Montero, Centro de Estudios Constitucionales, Madrid, pp. 345–432.

Montero, J. R. (1987) 'Los fracasos políticos y electorales de la derecha española: Alianza Popular, 1976–1986', *Revista Española de Investigaciones Sociológicas*, no. 39, pp. 7–43.

Montero, J. R. (1988) 'More than conservative, less than neoconservative: Alianza Popular in Spain', in *The Transformation of Contemporary Conservatism*, ed. B. Girvin, Sage, London, pp. 145–163.

OECD (1998, 2000, 2003, 2005) *Economic Surveys: Spain*, Paris.

Pappas, T. S. (2001) 'In search of the center: conservative parties, electoral competition, and political legitimacy in Southern Europe's new democracies', in *Parties, Politics, and Democracy in the New Southern Europe*, eds P. N. Diamandouros & R. Gunther, Johns Hopkins University Press, Baltimore and London, pp. 224–267.

Powell, C. (2001a) *Fifteen Years on: Spanish Membership in the European Union Revisited*, Working Paper no. 89, Center for European Studies, Harvard University, Cambridge, MA.

Powell, C. (2001b) *España en Democracia: 1975–2000*, Plaza y Janés, Barcelona.

PP (1999a) *Estatutos, XIII Congreso Nacional*, Madrid.

PP (1999b) *Acta del XIII Congreso Nacional*, Madrid.

PP (2004) *Acta del XV Congreso Nacional*, Madrid.

Ramiro-Fernández, L. (2005) 'Programmatic adaptation and organizational centralization in the AP-PP', *South European Society & Politics*, vol. 10, no. 2, pp. 207–223.

Schmidt, M. (2002) 'The impact of political parties, constitutional structures and veto players on public policy', in *Comparative Democratic Politics*, ed. H. Kamen, Sage, London, pp. 166–184.

Sturm, R. (2002) 'A different ball-game? Conservative parties react to third way policies', in *Christian-Democratic and Center-Right Parties in Europe and North America: Selected Perspectives*, eds C. Clemens & G. Hirscher, Academy for Politics and Current Affairs, Munich, pp. 47–52.

Varela, I. (2004) 'La campaña del PSOE', *in Las Campañas Electorales y sus Efectos en la Decisión del Voto*, vol. 2, *La Campaña Electoral de 2000: Partidos, Medios de Comunicación y Electores*, ed. I. Crespo, Tirant lo Blanch, Valencia, pp. 180–194.

Van Biezen, I. (2003) *Political Parties in New Democracies: Party Organization in Southern and East-central Europe*, Palgrave Macmillan, Basingstoke, England.

Ware, A. (1996) *Political Parties and Party Systems*, Oxford University Press, Oxford.

Wilson, F. (1998) 'The center-right at the end of the century', in *The European Center-Right at the End of the Twentieth Century*, ed. F. Wilson, St Martin's Press, New York, pp. 247–270.

Turning the Page: Crisis and Transformation of the Spanish Socialist Party*

Mónica Méndez Lago

Introduction

During the past decade the Partido Socialista Obrero Español (PSOE) has gone from government to opposition and, more recently, back into office after the 2004 general elections. When the PSOE lost the general elections in 1996, after having been in government since 1982, it faced the major challenges of relaunching the party organization and undertaking a process of leadership and programme renewal in order to regain political credibility, and eventually to return to power.

This work looks at the way the PSOE has responded to these challenges. It identifies two distinct phases: one from 1996 to 2000, characterized by the difficulties experienced by the PSOE in adjusting to its new position as the main party in opposition and in finding ways to renew its organization and strategy; and a second phase, starting in 2000, when José Luis Rodríguez Zapatero, the current party leader

*I would like to express my gratitude to the PSOE for providing me with documents and interviews that were very useful in writing this work. Many thanks also go to the participants at the workshop 'Party Change in Southern Europe' (Florence, September 2005). All outstanding errors are mine.

and prime minister, was elected as secretary-general. While the period between 1996 and 2000 was mostly lived 'inwards', that is, the party's efforts were directed at confronting the internal challenges it had to solve, such as the election of a new leader, in the second phase it concentrated on the overhaul of its organization while at the same time attempting to renew its policies and regain the support of large sectors of society. This phase ended with the unexpected victory of the PSOE at the 2004 general elections which brought the party back into office.

A Decade of Challenges: The PSOE between 1996 and 2004

In the mid-1990s the PSOE was going through a deep crisis on several fronts. After more than ten years in office, it was suffering from general government wear and tear. Just as the initial hopes raised by the coming of the socialist government had been very high, so was some of the disillusionment ten years later. Intra-party disputes, the fatigue of Felipe González, secretary-general since 1974 and prime minister since 1982, and his doubts about whether to stand as candidate in the following general elections in 1996, the economic crisis, the opposition of the labour movement and the aggressiveness of part of the media were the main defining characteristics of the political atmosphere. While the 'party on the ground' was disillusioned and demobilized, the 'party in public office' was starting to lose support and credibility and, after internal tensions emerged, it became increasingly distant from the 'party in central office', especially from 1991 onwards when Alfonso Guerra, the main protagonist with Felipe González of the PSOE's reconstruction at the end of the 1970s, was no longer deputy prime minister and concentrated exclusively on his position as PSOE's deputy secretary-general.

All these reasons contributed to the erosion of the image and popularity of the PSOE in public office (government) and of the PSOE as a party organization. However, the erosion of the socialist government's image among the general public in the early 1990s was mainly due to the emergence of several corruption cases, which were denounced by the press and followed by judicial investigations (Maravall 1991). Internal struggles within the party between *guerristas* (named after followers of Alfonso Guerra) and *renovadores* (renewers) were also damaging the party's image. The *renovadores* were a heterogeneous group favouring a change in the party discourse, style and internal organization, which they considered excessively rigid and monolithic. Allegiance to each of the groups was very much a matter of personal loyalties and political careers and there were many cases of switches from one camp to the other, especially from the *guerristas* to the *renovadores*, particularly after it became more evident that Felipe González was leaning towards the *renovadores*.

The translation of all of these problems into the electoral arena became clear in 1993 when the socialists lost their absolute majority of seats in the Congress of Deputies (38.8 per cent of the vote), and even more so in June 1994, when the Popular Party (Partido Popular, PP) obtained its first victory over the socialists at the European elections. The following year the PP also won the local and regional elections, and in

1996 it won the general elections (38.8 per cent), although by a smaller margin over the PSOE (37.6 per cent) than was expected from the various surveys published throughout the 1993–96 term.

Although there was an increasing awareness of the need to turn the page, the party experienced great difficulties in starting a new phase out of office. In fact, it had to be Felipe González himself who triggered the process of change when, without notice, he announced his decision not to stand again for the post of secretary-general in his opening speech to the 34th party congress in June 1997. The void was quickly filled by Joaquín Almunia, an ex-minister and close collaborator of Felipe González, who was elected secretary-general at the same party congress. Critics of the way the leadership question was resolved thought that Almunia had been elected because he had been presented as Felipe González's choice. There was therefore widespread criticism of the lack of debate about the leadership succession (Méndez Lago 2005).

Shortly after having been elected as secretary-general, in April 1998 Joaquín Almunia decided to call internal primary elections for the post of candidate to become prime minister in the next general elections, which were due in 2000. It is likely that he made this move thinking that winning these internal elections would provide him with the legitimacy he lacked because of the circumstances in which he had become secretary-general. However, the unexpected outcome of these primary elections was the victory by a clear margin (55 to 44 per cent) of Josep Borrell, a left-winger who had also served as a minister with Felipe González.

About a year after having won the primaries, Josep Borrell resigned. Although he formally resigned as a result of the revelation of corrupt behaviour by several functionaries whom he had appointed while he served as a minister, the lack of clear support by the party elite was also an important factor in this decision. His resignation ended a difficult period of cohabitation with Almunia, who was still secretary-general. After initial confrontation, they had managed to reach an agreement to share power, urged to do so by regional 'barons', who had acquired power and visibility in the context of a weak central leadership.

The resignation of Borrell meant that the party was left with no candidate for the 2000 general elections less than a year before they were due. In the absence of other options, Joaquín Almunia became the party's candidate to become prime minister. If the March 1996 general election results were characterized as a 'sweet defeat', those of March 2000 were very bitter. The PP obtained an absolute majority of seats in the lower chamber while the PSOE suffered its worst result since 1979 (34.2 per cent of the vote). These disastrous results finally acted as a catalyst for the transformation of the PSOE. Joaquín Almunia resigned from the leadership on election night. The election of the new party leader would take place in July 2000 at the 35th congress and there were four contenders for the post. The one with more explicit support of most of the party establishment was José Bono, who had been president of the autonomous community of Castilla-La Mancha. Although he had never participated in any of González's governments, Bono belonged to the same political generation and in the eyes of public opinion he was clearly not a new face. The other candidates were Rosa

Díez, a popular politician who had been a candidate in one of the first primaries in the PSOE's Basque federation, and Matilde Fernández, who had served as a minister with Felipe González, but belonged to the *guerrista* group. The fourth contender was José Luis Rodríguez Zapatero, who had been an MP since 1986. He had been a backbencher, unknown to the public and even to the party, so he was a 'new' face, but he had many years of experience in parliamentary and intra-party life.

When the 35th party congress started it became clear that the central issue in the election of the new leader was not ideology, but the question of whether it was time that the generation that had carried out the transition to democracy and had held governmental positions during the 1980s and 1990s should give way to a new generation. In the speech in which he presented his candidacy Rodríguez Zapatero concentrated on this idea, but neither renounced nor explicitly criticized the party's past. Another theme in the candidates' speeches to the party delegates, especially in Rodríguez Zapatero's, was the need to renew the party organization, style and strategy of opposition so as to start a new phase (López-Alba 2003). In the end Bono was narrowly defeated by Rodríguez Zapatero (who obtained 41.7 per cent of the vote to Bono's 40.8 per cent). Thus, in spite of the support that most party elites at the central and regional levels had expressed for Bono, a majority of delegates supported the candidate who represented a clearer wish for change. The victory of Rodríguez Zapatero was facilitated by the renewed composition of the delegations and by the change of rules in the way delegates vote in party conferences which was adopted in the mid-1990s, by virtue of which the block vote by regional delegations was replaced by secret individual ballot, which lessened the control of regional delegations by the party leaders.

The main challenge for Rodríguez Zapatero was to consolidate his leadership. He gradually managed to do so, helped by the good ratings obtained in public opinion polls, but also by other factors. First, he became leader of the PSOE after the disastrous 2000 general elections, and thus represented the 'last hope' for the party. Second, he had a long experience in internal party life. Rodríguez Zapatero was not very well known inside the party, but both he and his collaborators in the federal executive commission had held positions in party bodies and had a good understanding of the intricacies of intra-party life. Finally, the electoral results of the PSOE started improving during the second term of the PP. This is not to say that the electoral improvement can automatically be attributed to the new leader, but it certainly helped him to secure his position.

Rodríguez Zapatero launched a new strategy of opposition to the PP government that was referred to as 'quiet opposition'. As a result of this style of non-confrontation, the PSOE reached pacts with the PP in several policy domains such as the reform of the judiciary and the fight against terrorism. The opposition style became more aggressive when the PP approved a large-scale reform in the educational system and particularly when it backed the war against Iraq.

The context in which the 2004 general elections were held, just three days after the al-Qaeda terrorist attack in Madrid, makes it difficult to analyse the results and evaluate the extent to which the victory of the PSOE can be explained by its policy offers and the opposition style it had developed previously. There is serious controversy among academics in assessing the effects of the attack on the vote (Lago & Montero 2005; Michavilla 2005; Torcal & Rico 2004; Santamaría 2004; Barreiro 2004). All voting intention polls published before the elections forecast a victory for the PP, although the margin varied considerably according to each particular survey. A few surveys showed a very close race in which the margin of the estimated victory for the PP was smaller than the margin of error, and there was therefore a chance that the socialists could win. It seems clear, though, that the margin of victory of the PSOE was larger than expected (42.6 per cent of the vote, against 37.7 per cent for the PP). Irrespective of the context, the PSOE had managed to recover enough credibility to win the elections and had managed to put behind it a decade of crisis and transformation. The next section moves on to analyse the way the PSOE confronted the challenges of renewing its organizational structure and functioning, its campaign design, its ideology and discourse and its competitive strategy.

Revitalizing a Languishing Party Organization

When the PSOE left office in 1996 there was a clear perception of a sclerotic, languishing party organization, even if the debate on the need to renew the party had been there since the early 1990s. One sign of paralysis was the very low rate of turnover in membership of the federal executive commission, the most important governing body of the party, in the 1980s and early 1990s. After the end of the 1970s, most of the members of the executive commission were re-elected at each party congress, and usually renewal came through an increase in the size of this body rather than through actual change of its members (see Table 1).

This stagnation can be attributed partly to the organizational strategy followed by the party in the late 1970s and 1980s, which was based on three pillars: the leadership of Felipe González, the intense concentration of power in the hands of the party leaders, González himself and Alfonso Guerra, and the maintenance of a high degree of internal cohesion. The strategy also involved intense coordination between the party in government, the parliamentary group and the party organization, facilitated by the presence of the leading figures in all three arenas.

In addition to the intense concentration of power, the PSOE suffered a void in the 1980s when many cadres and leaders took up governmental positions after the party came to power. All the energies were put into governing, rather than into developing the party as an organization. By contrast, from the 1990s the party organization became the centre of attention, but this was due to increasing internal divisions. Instead of helping revitalize the party organization or increase its visibility, these divisions portrayed an image of inwardly oriented party elites, concentrating mainly on power struggles.

The debate over opening up the processes of candidate selection through primary elections started in the late 1990s, when the diagnosis of increasing centralization and

Table 1 Degree of Renewal in the PSOE's Federal Executive Commission (FEC)

PSOE congress	Size	Re-elected members[*] N	Re-elected members[*] as % of the old FEC	Re-elected members[*] as % of the new FEC
27th (December 1976)	19			
Extraordinary (September 1979)	24	9	47	37
29th (October 1981)	25	17	71	68
30th (December 1984)	17	17	68	100
31st (January 1988)	23	13	76	56
32nd (November 1990)	31	20	87	64
33rd (March 1994)	36	17	55	47
34th (June 1997)	33	11	30	33
35th (July 2000)	25	4	12	16
36th (July 2004)	31	10	40	32

[*] 'Re-elected members' represent the number of members of the executive commission who were already members in the previous term.
Source: Adapted from Méndez Lago (2000).

paralysis had started to be a major worry. The primary elections were first adopted in 1997 as a mechanism that would allow members to participate in the selection of party candidates for the post of mayor and could help to break that image of a top-down centralized organization. The surprise came when Almunia adopted this mechanism in 1998 to choose the candidate for prime minister at the 2000 general elections. Although it was perceived as a way to consolidate his leadership because of the way his election had been decided upon at the 1997 congress, it also meant giving an impulse to primary elections as an internal mechanism for selecting candidates.

The specific problems resulting from the 1998 primary elections due to the difficult coexistence between the winner, Josep Borrell, and the secretary-general, Joaquín Almunia, provoked a questioning of primaries. Those who were critical of this system argued that primary elections introduced confrontation within the party, and were particularly detrimental to the electoral prospects of incumbents, who had to fight against fellow party members and sometimes see their image weakened in the eyes of voters. Another argument referred to the potential conflict between direct and indirect democracy, that is, between the legitimacy that resulted from the one-member-one-vote system and the one that emerged from a delegate system, in which members elect local committees and delegates to higher-level assemblies who take decisions on their behalf.

Some changes were introduced into the regulation of primary elections at the 2001 political conference, so as to limit their use and their potentially damaging effects for the party. These regulations limited the possibility that this mechanism would be used in municipalities with a population below 50,000 inhabitants, as well as in places where the PSOE was in office. These limitations could be overruled by a majority of the members of the federal, regional and provincial committee (depending on the electoral level concerned), or by 40 per cent of the local branch members in the case of local elections (PSOE 2001, pp. 52–53). However, the debate about the advantages and disadvantages of primary elections continues.

At the leadership level primaries created a 'double-headed' party. If Almunia had won the primary elections, there could have been a possibility that this mechanism would have been adopted for subsequent elections of the party leader. Since this did not occur, when Almunia resigned from his post after the 2000 electoral defeat, the new secretary-general was elected, as usual, by party delegates at the party congress, but with a new one-round secret ballot system. The election of Rodríguez Zapatero was accompanied by a substantial renewal of the composition of the federal executive commission, elected at the same congress: only four members of the previous executive remained (see Table 1). The political conference held in 2001 established further mechanisms to enhance internal renewal such as term limits for internal party positions.

During the period 1996–2004 there was also a 'qualitative' renewal of the party leadership, illustrated by the increasing presence of women in executive bodies and in public office (Threlfall 2005). The take-off point was the approval of a 25 per cent quota of representation of women at the 31st congress (1988), but the most recent development in this direction was the principle of parity approved at the 34th congress (1997). The presence and say of representatives from the youth section of the party, Juventudes Socialistas de España (Socialist Youth of Spain), has also increased since the 34th congress. The next section turns to an analysis of change in an area that has experienced a deep transformation during the last two decades: the territorial structure of the party and the power of regional leaders within the party.

Territorial Party Structure and Power Relations

There have not been major changes in the formal structure of the party since its reconstruction at the time of the transition to democracy. The PSOE rebuilt its organization on a territorial basis. According to the statutes approved at the 27th party congress held in December 1976, the PSOE has a federal structure composed of four territorial layers, the *agrupación local* (local branch) and the provincial, regional[1] and national levels. The main governing body is the federal congress, the highest decision-making body of the party, which meets every three to four years, sets the main policy lines and elects both the secretary-general and the federal executive commission (*comisión ejecutiva federal*), which is the most important day-to-day decision-making party body. Finally, the federal committee (*comité federal*) is elected partly at the federal congress and partly by regional federations, and its main tasks include controlling the executive commission and deliberating on the main political decisions of the party.

The reconstruction of the party organization at the time of transition to democracy was closely controlled by the central leadership and, especially, by Alfonso Guerra. The control of the process of territorial expansion by the federal authorities of the party facilitated the subsequent centralization of resources and of decision-making capacity. Juliá (1997) claims that it is extremely important to take into account that the reconstruction of the party and the command of the dominant coalition took place *before* regional or local elites had time to develop. Provisions were made so that the federal bodies had the power to decide on political alliances, and to veto candidates on the lists for public office.

During the late 1970s and early 1980s the federalization of the party was considered one of the main priorities to be undertaken by the organizational secretariat. The term 'federalization' referred to the creation of regional federations while keeping their provincial equivalents. The process started around 1979 as an attempt to adjust the party structures to the organization of the state approved in the 1978 constitution.[2] Even at that time there was some internal debate over the difference between a federation of parties and a federal party. The leaders of the PSOE insisted that the party was federal in its structure and functioning, but not a federation or confederation of parties, expressing their fear that federalization would entail a lack of a unified message across the Spanish territory.

The 1980s witnessed the expansion of the regional federations and the increase in power of their leaders, the regional barons. Since the mid-1980s, regional barons, helped by the process of political decentralization that led to the development of the autonomous communities, began exploiting their own command of votes and patronage, and sometimes of large party congress delegations, in order to assert some autonomy from the federal party authorities (Gillespie 1992, p. 8). As Table 2 shows, in the 1980s the federal executive commission started to include regional party leaders among its members. Not all regional leaders gained the same amount of influence, but particularly those who had great experience within the party and who had won office repeatedly in their own regions, such as José Bono (Castilla-La Mancha), Rodríguez Ibarra (Extremadura) and Manuel Chaves (Andalucía).

Table 2 Composition of the PSOE Federal Executive Commission

	Government members[*] N	Women (%)	Heads of regional federation	Heads of regional government
1976	—	5	0	0
1979	—	8	0	0
1981	0 (+5)	12	2	0
1984	2 (+3)	23	0	0
1988	3	22	3	1
1990	2 (+1)	21	4	2
1994	4	31	9	4
1997	—	42	3	1
2000	—	35	7	3
2004	3	37	3	2

Source: Adapted from Méndez Lago (2000).
[*] The figures refer to the point at which the commission was formed, whereas the figures in brackets reflect changes occurring between party congresses.

Thus, the conditions that facilitated the control of the central party authorities changed over the 1980s, but the real effects of these changes only became evident in the 1990s. As Table 2 shows, the presence of regional leaders in the federal executive commission increased particularly in 1994, at a time when internal struggles for party control between *guerristas* and *renovadores* were most intense. Later on, regional barons would take a very active part in all important party decisions, such as the replacement of Felipe González as leader of the party, and the division of tasks and areas of influence between Almunia and Borrell. The presence of regional leaders was also high in the executive commission that came out of the congress at which Rodríguez Zapatero was elected secretary-general, but diminished at the following congress (2004), when his leadership had been consolidated. In short, the new balance of power between the centre and the periphery inside the party asserted itself when the leadership was vulnerable—in the early 1990s in a context of internal divisions, and later on at the end of the decade when there was no central leadership at all—and diminished when the central leadership strengthened again (Méndez Lago 2004, pp. 44–48).

Although there are differences among regional federations, the increasing federalization of the party has meant reaching a sort of *stratarchy*, in which regional federations have gained autonomy when developing their strategies and drafting their manifestos for elections, as well as in dealing with intra-party affairs, even though central supervision has always remained a competence of the federal party bodies.

The most noticeable transformation in the party's structure related to the increasing presence of regional leaders in the decision-making process is the creation of the territorial council (*consejo territorial*). It was created at the 34th party congress (1997) as a means to have a formal reflection in the party's organization chart of the increasing power of regional leaders. Its current composition includes the PSOE's secretary-general, its regional general secretaries, the presidents of the autonomous communities governed by the PSOE, the speaker of the socialist parliamentary group at the Congress of Deputies and the Senate, the president of the Spanish federation of municipalities (if he/she belongs to the PSOE, or the highest-ranking socialist in that organization), the secretary-general of the Juventudes Socialistas, the federal organizational secretary and the member of the federal executive commission who deals with political matters regarding autonomous communities.[3] In 2005 there was an attempt to enhance the powers of this body, in order to avoid endless negotiations among party leaders to have a representative from their federation in the executive commission. However, party federations still try to have a presence in the executive, since it is the most important party body. The activity and meetings of the territorial council have been limited so far, although there are increasing attempts to make this body visible to the general public as the forum that sets out the 'official' position of the party in relation to the State of Autonomies (even though this position is usually achieved in other negotiations *before* the meeting takes place). This was easier to achieve when the PSOE was in opposition. While in government the visibility of the council (and of the party as a whole) has diminished and its meetings have become more irregular, but there has been an effort to convey the idea that the council had some relevance in forming the socialist position regarding the current reforms of the State of Autonomies.

Party Membership

Spanish parties are well known to have very little organizational presence in civil society. Levels of party membership and party identification are comparatively low (Mair & Van Biezen 2001). This has been attributed, among other reasons, to the context in which parties were created anew or reconstructed. That context was characterized by widespread mass media that gave parties very few incentives to develop mass parties. In addition, the availability of public finance for political parties helps to explain why Spanish parties had few incentives to build large membership organizations. Voters could be mobilized by other means than building a large organization, which would entail a large investment in both material and human resources. This is not to say that a party that developed in this new environment did not need members, but the type of organization of the PSOE, a social-democratic party, was likely to be different from its counterparts in other Western democracies (Van Biezen 2003).

During the first stage of reconstruction of the PSOE, from the beginning of the transition to the 1982 elections, its organizational strategy was governed by the need to grow numerically and to improve its territorial spread. Thus membership growth was an important concern both to provide candidates for office at the local, regional and national levels, and to have the minimal capacity to organize election campaigns. Since the departure point was a political group with virtually no members, the goal of organizational growth was a fairly obvious one that all intra-party actors shared. Party strategists and organizers also believed it was important to convey an image of a strong organization, given that the other party on the left, the communists, had a strong membership base at that time. Seeking members was an important aim of the party, but was conditioned to the main organizational concern: maintaining discipline and internal cohesion.

Once it won the 1982 general elections, the PSOE enjoyed a huge number of resources with which to influence society. Having access to government meant having to fill many positions and having access to patronage. In short, it opened a pool of resources that went far beyond the existing and the potential party's organizational resources, and diminished the necessity and the 'profitability' of investing in the party organization. In addition to that, as has been mentioned already, the institutional, political and social context in which the PSOE operated did not provide incentives to build a mass membership party.

Thus, except for the initial attempts during its early years in office to find candidates for local elections or the membership drives designed to convert electoral support into organizational resources, there was a decreasing emphasis on recruiting and maintaining members. As Table 3 shows, this does not mean that the PSOE's

Table 3 PSOE Membership and Ratio of Party Membership to Party Voters and total electorate, 1976–2004

	PSOE membership	Yearly increase in membership (%)	PSOE members as percentage of voters	PSOE members as percentage of electorate
1976	9,141			
1977	48,635	432.1	0.9	0.2
1978	65,296	34.3		
1979	80,389	23.1	1.5	0.3
1980	88,446	10.0		
1981	96,418	9.0		
1982	115,945	20.3	1.1	0.4
1983	136,561	17.8		
1984	148,957	9.1		
1985	158,257	6.2		
1986	185,429	17.2	2.1	0.6
1987	217,478	17.3		
1988	235,099	8.1		
1989	249,970	6.3	3.1	0.8
1990	280,052	12.0		
1991	316,676	13.1		
1992	329,308	4.0		
1993	351,463	6.7	3.8	1.1
1994	364,477	3.7		
1995	364,457	0.0		
1996	371,599	2.0	3.9	1.1
1998	400,000	7.6		
2000	407,821	2.0	5.2	1.2
2004	460,000[*]	12.8	4.2	1.3

[*] Data for 2004 include members and sympathizers.
Source: Calculated from data provided in PSOE's documents and by the PSOE organizational secretariat.

membership stopped growing, but the party organization made fewer efforts to recruit members and the pace of growth declined (Méndez Lago 2000, Chapter 5).

The revitalization and modernization of the party organization were among the main goals of the new leadership elected at the 35th party congress. Within this programme a special committee was elected to revise the membership census. The federal office of membership register (*oficina federal del censo de afiliados*) carried out this task in the period 2000 to 2004, when it contacted all party members to ask whether they wanted to maintain their membership. In that case, they would have to provide a bank account number so that membership dues would automatically be paid, instead of paying them at their local branch.[4] With the current system, the census is kept by the federal organizational secretariat and automatically updated every time it is needed, by simply looking at the number of members paying their dues through their bank account. Those who were consulted and did not proceed to authorize bank payment were made 'sympathizers'. Current membership figures therefore include both 'militants' (those who pay dues) and sympathizers. Party members who stop paying their dues for more than six months become sympathizers until they pay their debt.[5] The last figure in the first column of Table 3 thus represents the total number of members, which includes both full members and sympathizers. The figure shows that the new party leadership and the victory at the 2004 election had the effect of increasing the number of socialist militants and sympathizers.

During the last decade there have been changes in the inclusiveness that has characterized the membership strategy of the party, that is, in the 'height of barriers separating members from other supporters' (Scarrow 1996, p. 30). Becoming a party member has become easier. Now it is possible to enrol through the internet, rather than going to the local branch, and the need for two people to 'introduce' new members has been removed. Regarding another important aspect of 'inclusiveness', the definition of the rights and duties of members, there have also been some changes during the last decade, particularly the extent to which members can participate in the process of candidate selection through primary elections. However, these changes are limited by the fact that primary elections are only used to select the head of the party list and that, in any case, their use has been limited.

As for sympathizers, they receive information about the party and training, especially when they carry out tasks as representatives of the party at polling stations on the election day. They may also participate in the thematic branches (*organizaciones sectoriales*) and therefore, indirectly, be represented at party bodies through these organizations.[6] However, in the party there is resistance to involving sympathizers in the election of intra-party bodies and the PSOE statutes are vague in defining how they can participate in the selection of candidates for public office. For all these reasons there is currently an open debate in the party on the possibility of extending sympathizers' rights to participate in party life.

Campaign Design and Organization

During the last decade the PSOE has made little change to the way it designs and organizes campaigns. This obviously refers to the organizational aspects of campaigns, not to their content. In spite of the lack of formal regulation, the general procedure of organization has been roughly similar in all the election campaigns since 1977. After an election is called, the federal executive appoints a campaign coordinator who is in charge of the planning and coordination of the various tasks involved in the campaign. For all the general elections held between 1977 and 1993 the general coordinator was Alfonso Guerra. Later on this responsibility was taken over by the organizational secretary; thus in 1996 and 2000, the coordinator was Cipriá Ciscar, and in the 2004 general elections it was José Blanco (organizational secretary since the 35th party congress). The renewal of the party leadership that took place at that congress facilitated a change in the composition of the team in charge of designing and organizing election campaigns, although the structures and procedures hardly changed from the previous phase.

The responsibilities of the campaign coordinator include the organization of all activities related to campaigning: orientation, organization, and strategic and operational management.[7] He or she appoints the other members of the federal election committee, the team that is in charge of the organization of election campaigns. The work of the election committee is based on a 'horizontal' and 'vertical' division of labour. The horizontal division of labour is achieved though the internal division of tasks among the members of the team. The vertical division consists in the creation of election committees at different territorial levels, among which the most important are the provinces (the electoral districts). It is important to note that candidate selection and the development of the party electoral programme are carried out not by the election committee, but by the federal committee and the federal executive commission, respectively.

In addition to its internal team, the PSOE makes intensive use of external personnel in election campaigns, especially for the design and production of leaflets, placards and videos, on one hand, and to commission surveys and electoral behaviour studies on the other. In the most recent general elections the party hired a different publicity firm from previous occasions (Campmany 2005), but the cooperation between external and internal teams of experts was similar to that in previous election campaigns.

One important novelty in the field of political communication is the internet. The party has made use of the internet since the 1996 general elections, although its importance increased in the 2000 and 2004 electoral campaigns. New technologies are also used for internal communication purposes between central and provincial electoral boards and with party members.

Another concern of the party regarding electoral campaigns and political communication in general involves the development of these tasks in non-electoral periods. In 1994, at the 33rd party congress, an electoral and communication department was created, but then disappeared a few years later without being replaced by a similar body. The department was part of the organizational secretariat and was run by a person appointed by the federal executive. It had three main tasks: the analysis of the political situation, the formulation of communication and political strategies, and the training of a national network capable of mobilizing the party at any moment. Since 2000 there has been increasing concern over the lack of a stable specialized body in the area of election analysis and political communication, but no steps have yet been taken to create one formally.[8] There is a sort of 'informal' body, comprising the party leaders and organizers who take part in the electoral boards; they remain in charge of these tasks between elections, but their work is carried out on a fairly informal basis.

Recovering Credibility: Party Values and Ideology

When the PSOE went into opposition in 1996, the main challenge had less to do with ideological and programmatic renewal than with the need to recover credibility and trust among citizens. Unlike other social-democratic parties, the PSOE had moderated its ideological stances as early as 1979, when it explicitly renounced Marxism. During its time in office it adopted orthodox market-oriented policies, which were combined with a commitment to welfare policies.

The main steps towards regaining credibility and developing a range of new policies were taken once Rodríguez Zapatero was elected as party leader in 2000. The political conference held in July 2001 provided the guidelines as to how the new Socialist leadership defined its ideological stances. It made reference to the main values of socialism: equality, freedom, pluralism, social justice and solidarity, giving special emphasis to freedom, claiming that 'socialism is freedom' (*Socialismo es libertad*), the slogan of the first party congress held in Spain in 1976, after many years of exile.

The strategy of opposition to the PP which Rodríguez Zapatero adopted from his election made it clear to the electorate that there were fields in which the PSOE had similar views to the PP, or found it necessary to reach consensus with the party in government, but also helped to point up the areas in which there was no consensus, such as foreign policy and the war in Iraq, some aspects of labour market policy, or the way the PP handled the crisis caused by the sinking of the *Prestige*.[9] His position on the war on Iraq was so salient among the PSOE's electoral commitments that the withdrawal of the troops became the first decision the new socialist government made once in office.

The PSOE did not question the main elements of the economic policy carried out by the PP government, although it placed greater emphasis on classic social-democratic policies such as education and housing. Rodríguez Zapatero also insisted on dialogue and consensus building, thereby accusing the PP, and especially José María Aznar, of having an authoritarian way of governing. Changing the government style would later become a primary concern of the PSOE when it came to power in 2004. Since his election as prime minister, Rodríguez Zapatero has insisted on holding regular meetings with the leader of the main opposition party (which had not been the case during the last term of the PP in office), and with all the autonomous communities by establishing the 'regional prime ministers' conference' (*conferencia de presidentes*).

After Rodríguez Zapatero became secretary-general, the PSOE placed greater emphasis on non-economic policies, such as institutional reform and civil rights. The reform of the Senate and the revision of the current State of Autonomies were included in the election programme and became part of the government's agenda (PSOE 2004). Issues related to women have also received great attention from the new government: one of its first decisions was to launch an ambitious law to fight domestic violence against women. Appointing a gender parity cabinet of eight women and eight men was also a way to show the relevance of this issue on Rodríguez Zapatero's agenda. Finally, the new government has focused on the development and extension of civil and political rights. The first concrete development was the passing of the law allowing homosexuals to get married and adopt children (June 2005).

Reconquering Lost Ground: The Competitive and Electoral Strategy 1996–2004

The competitive environment in which the PSOE has developed its electoral strategies during the last decade is very different from the one it faced in the 1980s, when it dominated the electoral scene at national, regional and local levels. Since the overwhelming victory of the socialists in 1982, the electoral support for the party steadily declined (from 37.7 per cent of the electorate in 1982 to 30.6 per cent in 1986 and 27.4 per cent in 1989), but the PSOE's predominant position in the party system did not suffer greatly from this decline because the main party in the opposition (Alianza Popular, known as Partido Popular since 1989) did not manage to increase its share of the vote during this time.

In the 1990s, after the PP went through a process of leadership renewal and ideological moderation, the electoral scene became more competitive. Although the PSOE won the 1993 elections, for the first time since the socialist accession to power there was a widespread feeling that the PP could win. The PP finally won the 1996 elections by a narrower margin than expected, although in the 2000 general elections it managed to increase substantially its advantage over the socialists. Post-electoral analysis indicated that roughly one million left-wing voters abstained in the 2000 elections, while another million switched their vote to the PP (González 2002). As Table 4 shows, the PSOE had faced the problem of demobilization of voters on the left of the political spectrum during the 1980s and 1990s. In the 2000 elections the demobilization of left-wing voters was the highest since 1986.

At the time the PSOE lost office, its electoral base had changed a great deal compared with what it was in the early 1980s. While in 1982 PSOE voters were mostly urban, educated and middle class, some ten years later they came mostly from rural areas, the working class and the economically inactive groups (pensioners, the unemployed and housewives), and had a lower educational attainment (González 2001; 2002).

The main aim of the renewed PSOE in the 2004 elections was to return to office. In order to do that, its electoral strategy was first to regain the support of those voters

Table 4 Percentage of Abstainers by Position on the Left–Right Scale

	1986	1989	1993	1996	2000	2004
Extreme left (1–2)	7.6	7.1	5.6	7.2	13.3	8.7
Left (3–4)	4.2	6.0	5.6	7.3	11.1	7.2
Centre-left (5)	6.2	9.6	8.5	7.4	8.2	11.3
Centre-right (6)	5.8	4.2	5.4	2.2	4.6	6.1
Right (7–8)	3.6	4.8	3.1	2.3	3.0	9.1
Extreme-right (9–10)	3.5	1.3	1.4	2.7	3.1	11.3
No declared ideology[*]	20.1	22.5	20.9	15.2	20.1	25.3

Source: Barreiro (2002, p. 186), updated with data from the Centro de Investigaciones Sociológicas for 2004 (Study no. 2559).
[*] Includes respondents who did not declare their ideological position (Don't know/No answer).

who had abstained in 2000 and previously (particularly those who had voted for the PSOE at any previous election), to recover the support of those ex-voters who had voted for the PP in 2000, to obtain the maximum support among young people and first-time voters and finally to attract as many left-wing voters as possible (Campmany 2005, p. 215).

Analyses of vote transfers carried out after the 2004 elections (Michavila 2005) suggest that the three million additional votes for the PSOE came mostly from previous non-voters (one-and-a-half million), transfers from other parties, in particular from the PP (around 700,000 votes) and the communist United Left (300,000 votes) and from new voters (around 500,000). These analyses also show that the PSOE was successful in reversing the tendency of support to be concentrated in the least active strata of society: it managed to increase its votes among the young, the middle classes, the employed and those with university degrees (Sanz & Sánchez-Sierra 2005). As Table 4 shows, the tendency to abstain among voters on the left of the political spectrum also diminished at the last general elections, compared with the 2000 elections, while the demobilization among right-wing voters was the highest since the mid-1980s. It remains to be seen whether the PSOE can retain the support of its newly gained electorate.

Concluding Remarks

When the PSOE lost the 1996 general elections it confronted huge challenges, such as adapting to its new role as the main party in the opposition, revitalizing the party organization, promoting a programme renewal and, finally, the most difficult one, replacing Felipe González as the main leader of the party. Although he was still considered a very charismatic leader by the end of his last term as prime minister, it was difficult to believe that the party could successfully deal with the challenges it faced and return to power unless it carried out a deep transformation, which would most likely include its leadership.

The difficulties experienced by the PSOE in accomplishing these goals, especially at the end of the 1990s, can be partly explained in terms of the party's recent history, that is, by looking at the way the party rebuilt its organization at the time of the transition to democracy and its early years in government during the 1980s. The strategy followed by the PSOE at that time was based on the intense concentration of power in the hands of the party leaders and placed great emphasis in internal cohesion and discipline. These organizational traits proved to be an advantage at the end of the 1970s and beginning of the 1980s, in a context of uncertainty regarding the stability of democracy and of intense competition from other political parties. The lack of competitiveness in the party system for most of the 1980s, on the other hand, contributed to the stabilization of these characteristics: there were few external challenges to act as catalysts for change and there were also few intra-party incentives to initiate reforms.

In the late 1990s, however, the strategy based on internal cohesion and leadership control was clearly unsuitable for dealing with a political environment that had become increasingly competitive. In addition, these organizational features became a burden to the party when it tried to change them at the time of leaving office. Thus, the choices taken at the time the party was reconstructed during the 1970s acted as a sort of 'genetic imprint' that conditioned the subsequent development of the party, slowing its pace and intensity.

This was evident in the way the party confronted the challenge of renewing its leadership, which was a very important step in helping the organizational and ideological transformation to take off. Replacing Felipe González consumed most of the time and energy of the PSOE during the first five years after leaving office. It took a parliamentary term and a severe electoral defeat in the 2000 general elections for the party to react to the external stimulus and choose a younger leader with no connection with the past, and thus in a good position to make the PSOE recover its credibility among voters. In addition, the difficulties in choosing a new leader which the party had experienced during the 1996–2000 period acted as a learning process and made it easier for Rodríguez Zapatero to gain enough margin of manoeuvre to concentrate on carrying out the party's task as the main opposition to the governing PP. One noticeable transformation during these years, the increasing power of regional party leaders, became very visible during the times when central leadership was weaker.

The renewed party's executive commission, led by Rodríguez Zapatero, managed to leave the internal party struggles behind and to concentrate on modernizing the party organization and on programme renewal. In terms of party organization, the new leadership revised the party's membership register and relaunched the debate on the need to blur further the line between members and non-members by increasing the role of sympathizers in party life. The new leadership also found a more suitable environment to put forward new policy proposals: although there was no great change in the party's orientation towards economic policies, more emphasis was placed on non-economic issues such as institutional reform, the promotion of gender parity and the extension of civil rights.

The extent of transformation in these two areas, organization and ideology, should not be overstated. However, it is not so much the extent of the change that counts as the ability of the new leadership to divert the attention of public opinion from intra-party affairs and struggles to the policies offered by the PSOE. These processes helped the party to regain credibility among Spaniards, to gradually recover its electoral support, and, eventually, to win the 2004 general elections, even if the special circumstances in which these elections were held, just three days after the al-Qaeda attacks in Madrid, forces us to be extremely cautious about interpreting the link between the election results and the strategies developed by the PSOE. Leaving this question aside, what seems clear is that the PSOE's new leadership managed to turn the page and start a new phase in the party's development.

Notes

[1] The exception is the Catalan case (Partit dels Socialistes Catalans), which is in fact a different party organization, which has established a stable coalition with the PSOE since 1978.

[2] Author's interview with Joaquín Almunia (June 1996).

[3] Party statutes approved at the 36th congress (2004), art. 48.

[4] Because the weight of local branches at provincial congresses depended upon membership, it was widely known that some branches 'paid' dues for more members than they actually had enrolled. Author's interview with Oscar López, member of the federal organizational secretariat (September 2005).

[5] Party statutes approved at the 36th congress (2004), art. 8.

[6] There are now six thematic organizations devoted to education, environment, citizen participation, health, new technologies, and entrepreneurs and the self-employed.

[7] Author's interview with Ignacio Varela (November 1996). Varela has participated in the design of PSOE's election campaigns since 1977. As a result of this participation over the years, he has developed a professional career in this field.

[8] Author's interviews with Ignacio Varela and Oscar López.

[9] The *Prestige* was an oil tanker whose sinking in 2002 off the Spanish coast caused a huge oil spill. The decisions taken by the authorities before and after the sinking were the subject of deep political controversy.

References

Barreiro, B. (2002) 'La progresiva desmovilización de la izquierda en España: un análisis de la abstención en las elecciones generales de 1986 a 2000', *Revista Española de Ciencia Política*, no. 6, pp. 183–205.

Barreiro, B. (2004) '14-M: elecciones a la sombra del terrorismo', *Claves de Razón Práctica*, no. 141, pp. 14–22.

Campmany, J. (2005) *El Efecto ZP. 1000 Días de Campaña para llegar a la Moncloa*, Planeta, Barcelona.

Gillespie, R. (1992) *Factionalism in the Spanish Socialist Party*, Working Paper no. 59, Institut de Ciències Polítiques i Socials, Barcelona.

González, J. J. (2001) 'Clases, cohortes, partidos y elecciones: un análisis de la experiencia española (1986–1996)', *Revista Internacional de Sociología*, no. 29, pp. 91–113.

González, J. J. (2002) 'Las elecciones generales de 2000: voto ideológico/voto racional', *Revista Internacional de Sociología*, no. 32, pp. 7–33.

Juliá, S. (1997) *Los Socialistas en la Política Española 1879–1982*, Taurus, Madrid.

Lago, I. & Montero, J. R. (2005) 'Los mecanismos del cambio electoral. Del 11-M al 14-M', *Claves de Razón Práctica*, no. 149, pp. 36–44.

López-Alba, G. (2003) *El Relevo. Crónica Viva del Camino hacia el II Suresnes del PSOE*, Taurus, Madrid.

Mair, P. & Van Biezen, I. (2001) 'Party membership in twenty European democracies 1980-2000', *Party Politics*, vol. 7, no. 1, pp. 5–21.

Maravall, J. M. (1991) 'From opposition to government. Politics and policies of the Psoe', in *Socialist Parties in Europe*, eds. J. M. Maravall et al. Institut de Ciències Polítiques i Socials, Barcelona, pp. 5–34.

Méndez Lago, M. (2000) *La Estrategia Organizativa del Partido Socialista Obrero Español (1975–1996)*, Centro de Investigaciones Sociológicas, Madrid.

Méndez Lago, M. (2004) *Federalismo y partidos políticos: los casos de Canadá y España*, Working Paper no. 232, Institut de Ciències Polítiques i Socials, Barcelona.

Méndez Lago, M. (2005) 'The Socialist Party in government and in opposition', in *The Politics of Contemporary Spain*, ed. S. Balfour, Routledge, London, pp. 169–197.

Michavila, N. (2005) *Guerra, terrorismo y elecciones: incidencia electoral de los atentados islamistas en Madrid*, Working Paper no. 13, Real Instituto Elcano, Madrid.

PSOE. (2001) *Resoluciones. Conferencia Política*, Madrid.

PSOE. (2004) *Merecemos una España mejor. Programa electoral, elecciones 2004*, Madrid.

Santamaría, J. (2004) 'El azar y el contexto. Las elecciones generales de 2004', *Claves de Razón Práctica*, no. 146, pp. 28–40.

Sanz, A. & Sánchez-Sierra, A. (2005) *Las elecciones generales de 2004 en España: Política exterior, estilo de gobierno y movilización*, Working Paper Online Series no. 45, Universidad Autónoma de Madrid, <http://www.uam.es/centros/derecho/cpolitica/investigacion/papers/48_2005>.

Scarrow, S. (1996) *Parties and Their Members. Organizing for Victory in Britain and Germany*, Oxford University Press, Oxford.

Threlfall, M. (2005) 'Towards parity representation in party politics', in *Gendering Spanish Democracy*, eds M. Threlfall, C. Cousins & C. Valiente, Routledge, London, pp. 125–161.

Torcal, M. & Rico, G. (2004) 'The 2004 Spanish general election: in the shadow of al-Qaeda?', *South European Society & Politics*, vol. 9, no. 3, pp. 107–121.

Van Biezen, I. (2003) *Political Parties in New Democracies. Party Organization in Southern and East-Central Europe*, Palgrave Macmillan, Basingstoke, England.

Forza Italia: A Leader with a Party

Francesco Raniolo

Introduction

Forza Italia (FI, Go Italy!) is a young party, only 11 years old. It is also a totally new party. Berlusconi himself (2001, pp. 76–77) defined it as 'a completely new type of free organization of men and women electors'. The manner and the timing of its entry into the political arena were also new and for this reason FI has been called an 'instant' or 'plastic' party. New, too, were its particular organizational and strategic characteristics and its political culture. In addition, it is a new party because it represents a non-political answer or, perhaps better, an anti-political answer to the crisis and subsequent collapse of the Italian political system and an entire political class (1992–94). Thus it is an 'anti-party party' and, as such, a 'subversive party'. There are elements of truth in these labels. FI is all these things together but also more.

Several aspects are relevant here. First, to be successful a new party has to overcome institutional and competitive barriers; as will be seen, this is no problem for FI because of the collapse, by means of the judiciary, of the Italian party system. Second, it has to solve the problem of making its policy proposals distinctive. It must build up and assert its own identity. Third, it has to deal with the problem of organization and mobilization of resources and, lastly, with strategic innovation (coalition building and political marketing). All these aspects will be dealt with in the next four sections.

The Short History of a New Party

In the early 1990s the long-term conditions that had characterized the Italian Republic (Morlino & Tarchi 1996) no longer existed. Instead there were real incentives for political change. These factors provided all the essential elements for the emergence of a new political subject. All that was needed was to link them in a suitable way. For this a 'political entrepreneur' was needed: Silvio Berlusconi. We will now discuss the most meaningful moments in FI's (short) life.

The Foundational Phase (1994–96)

On 26 January 1994 Silvio Berlusconi announced his entry into politics to the nation, presenting his creation: 'the political movement Forza Italia'. In the March elections, after an electoral campaign that had no precedent in the history of Italian politics in terms of the enormous sums of money involved and the role played by television and electoral marketing, FI won 21 per cent of the proportional representation votes and 15.7 per cent of the seats in the Chamber of Deputies. Over 8 million electors gave their vote to FI.

This surprising result was the fruit of three effective operations. First of all, in only a few months and starting from scratch, thanks to the support of the business and finance group of which he is head (the Fininvest), Berlusconi was able to set up a formidable machine to win over the consensus of electors. Secondly, he succeeded in building up an exceptional and asymmetrical coalition: in the north with a regional party, the Northern League, within the Polo delle libertà (Pole of Freedoms) and in the centre-south with the National Alliance (AN)—the heir of the neofascist Italian Social Movement (MSI)—within the Polo del buon governo (Pole of Good Government). With the exclusion of the Christian Democratic Centre (CCD), the political group coming from the old Christian Democracy, the centre-right coalition had an anti-political common denominator. Its main themes, embodied in FI, the AN and the League were a mixture of reaction to statism and party politics and a dislike for the political regime itself (the First Republic and the 1948 constitution). Thirdly, Berlusconi succeeded in defining and imposing the main points on the agenda for the electoral campaign and the political contest (the welfare crisis, the privatizations, the modernization of the state, etc.).

These three aspects, that is, mobilization of private resources, coalition management and political marketing, were Berlusconi's strong points, but also his weak ones. In fact, as will be seen, in one way or another all three aspects made the consolidation of FI a difficult accomplishment. To begin with, the first Berlusconi cabinet confirmed that electioneering was one matter and that governing was another and very different one. The heterogeneous nature of the governmental coalition, the absence of 'high-profile figures with political and professional experience, and the inclusion in the government of collaborators or employees... financially linked to the premier' (Ignazi & Katz 1995, p. 39) were all factors of weakness in that first cabinet. Thus, after only seven months the first Berlusconi cabinet was obliged to resign (December 1994).

There followed a period of institutional tensions, characterized by a conflict with the head of state, and political uncertainty. The competitive advantages gained in 1994 were lost after only a year. It was necessary to start again from the beginning.

Crossing the Desert (1996–2000)

In the 1996 elections FI won 20.6 per cent of the vote (7,715,342 votes) and obtained 123 seats in the Chamber of Deputies (47 in the Senate). The elections were won by the centre-left coalition led by the economist Romano Prodi. The coalition was formed by L'Ulivo (The Olive Tree) backed by the Party of Communist Refoundation (PRC). How did this result come about? Three basic reasons can be suggested and they mirror what had happened in 1994. Firstly, Berlusconi made a number of serious mistakes when building up the electoral coalition. The League stood as an independent party list and the leaders of the Pole also underestimated the need for agreements with the smaller lists. Secondly, even Berlusconi's image seemed less attractive and less able to sway the moderate electorate and, in addition, his electoral campaign was constrained by the approval of the regulations regarding *par condicio*.[1]

Thus, began FI's 'crossing of the desert'. These were the years of strengthening the party organization and of establishing it throughout the country. The European and regional elections that followed also provided the opportunity for a new alliance with the League. The results of these elections indicated that the balance of power had now again tipped in favour of the centre-right. Lastly, FI and its leader became better known on the European scene with the party's disputed entry into the parliamentary group of the European Popular Party (EPP) in December 1999.

Back in Office (2001–6)

The elections of 13 May 2001 were 'the first legitimate, peaceful changeover in the Italian political system, decided by the electorate and accepted by the losers' (Pasquino 2002, p. 19). But the elections were especially important for the 29.4 per cent won by FI, that is, 10,923,146 votes. More than 50 per cent of the votes went to the Casa delle libertà (House of Freedoms), the new name for the centre-right coalition. In contrast to 1994, there was also a considerable gap between FI and the second national party, the Democrats of the Left (DS), which only got 16.6 per cent of the vote. In parliament FI won 187 seats in the lower chamber and 83 in the Senate. It thus became the first party in Italy for its nationwide size, 'capable of establishing itself anywhere and everywhere' (Diamanti 2003, p. 90). In the 2001 elections FI spread and geographically extended the consensus, since it was the first party in 81 provinces and came second in 20. There were two electoral strongholds: Lombardia, with the area of the former industrial triangle, and Sicilia. FI was no longer the party movement of 1994. Now it seemed a strong organization, well rooted throughout the country.

The second Berlusconi cabinet will be remembered as the longest in republican Italy. However, a number of internal conflicts took place between the leader and his partners in the cabinet, and between the different components of the cabinet, that is, between 'technical' ministers and 'political' ministers and, among the latter, between representatives of the League and those of the other incumbent parties. Comments have been made on Berlusconi's style in the management of internal conflicts, which was 'reactive rather than preventive' (Cotta 2002, p. 179). Signs of crisis became more evident after the results of the European (2004) and regional and local (2005) elections. The outcome of this negative trend was the resignation of the Berlusconi cabinet and the formation of a new one: the so-called Berlusconi *ter* (23 April 2005).

Party Identity between Hybridization and Personalization

Berlusconi's party was born with a negative identity, characterized by its anti-party statements and the image built by its competitors: the 'primary, fundamental, original and irreplaceable factor' in FI is its anti-communist attitude (Are 1997, p. 186). However, is there a positive identity of FI? First of all, it is a problematic identity, based on the attempt to bring together different values that come from 'strongly rooted Italian political traditions' (Berlusconi 2003, p. 13). The result is a cultural and ideological hybridization that FI shares with other moderate and conservative parties in Europe (Raniolo 2000).

However, the basis for the mobilization and identification of electors and supporters can be found in a specific set of cleavages. They reflect FI's reference values, that is, its 'ethos', as well as its programme or 'doctrine'. The position of the party on the first two cleavages, that is, the state vs. market and individualism vs. authoritarianism, places it within the ideological family of neo-conservative parties, in the wake of Reagan and Thatcher, who complemented economic free enterprise, the breaking-up of the state, and market centrality with an authoritarian vision of society. This means the deregulation of economic behaviour and at the same time the regulation of social behaviour. The third cleavage, that is, the pro/anti-regime cleavage, is typical of a new party with an anti-political culture: 'FI is, first of all, in favour of a new constitution' (Baget Bozzo 1997, p. 28). Actually, Berlusconi's position regarding constitutional and electoral reforms has been anything but stable and coherent (Sartori 2004). Lastly, with regard to international politics, a pro-American feeling and a Eurosceptic attitude have characterized FI since the beginning.

These positions on cleavage configuration make up the core of FI's set of values. They have not undergone much change since 1994, except in terms of selective emphasis or the radicalization of specific issues. The assessment of the incoherence between official values and congress delegates' attitudes is a meaningful way of going more deeply into such an analysis.[2] In the first place, 66.5 per cent of those interviewed held a realistic view of peace, which was not considered an absolute, unconditioned value, but could be achieved by other means (including war). In addition, in the trade-off between freedom and security, 63 per cent chose freedom. At the same time, 81 per cent chose freedom in the trade-off between freedom and equality. In both choices freedom prevails, but this conceals a contradictory aspect. On the one hand, the realistic position of the delegates regarding peace is mitigated by a post-materialist refusal of security as a principal value. On the other hand, the free-enterprise position on economic policy is attenuated by the fact that 70 per cent of the delegates affirmed that the state (rather than the market) should guarantee essential public services.

But what was the delegates' perception of the level of importance of the issues in the FI programme? First of all (see Table 1), several issues stand out because they are highly symbolic or because they concern crucial interests (the highest-frequency figures are shown in the first two columns). These are value issues that can be taken for granted and show a high level of coherence between the party's official goals and how delegates viewed them. They include, in order of importance, justice, crime, health, education, unemployment, inefficiency in public administration, and taxes (with a lower value than expected). Then, there are the issues seen as less important (frequency figures are highly dispersed across the four columns). They include inflation, political corruption, pollution, tax evasion and immigration. Finally, for a limited number of issues, the opinions are more diversified: on Italy's integration in Europe (only 31 per cent of those interviewed thought it was a very important problem), on pluralism in information (36 per cent) and on federalism (almost 17 per cent). These are probably areas of major political conflict (information) or on which the party's position is low-profile or ambiguous (Europe, federalism).

Contrary to the official picture of a centre party, 62.3 per cent of the delegates considered FI a centre-right party and 2.9 per cent even considered it right-wing. These data are fully consistent with those regarding self-placement: 61.3 per cent of the delegates placed themselves on the centre-right, while nine per cent considered themselves on the right. Furthermore only 31 per cent described FI as a centre party. This profile is coherent with the results of the surveys of voters (Schadee & Segatti 2002, p. 359), which place FI on the left–right continuum (1 to 10 scale) at 7.99, before the AN (8.60), but after the League (7.77) and the CCD (6.31).

Some incongruities emerge from these data between the orientation of delegates and the official party position. As has been noted, the delegates have a less liberal and more statist vision of economic and social policies. Moreover, some specific issues, such as taxation and federalism, both central to FI's rhetoric, arouse less interest among delegates. This inconsistency in FI's system of values, as well as in the issues included in the programme, is explained by the delegates' previous political affiliation—52 per cent had had experience of other parties, chiefly Christian Democracy and the Socialist Party—and by the ideological eclecticism of FI (catch-all politics). From this initial evaluation there emerges an ideological profile of the FI cadres as liberal-conservatives, if not really neo-conservatives.

A Model of Loose Party Institutionalization

How is a new party organized, a party created by an outsider? Berlusconi stated, 'We had no intention of turning Forza Italia into a real party, we thought it was right to go on being an electoral committee to gather voters at election time . . . We wanted to be

Table 1 Relevance of Political, Social and Economic Issues (raw and per cent* values) According to the Delegates of the Second Forza Italia Congress (2004)

	It is a very important problem	It is a quite important problem	It is a secondary problem	It is not really important
1. Unemployment	215 (59.2)	123 (33.9)	23 (6.3)	2 (0.6)
2. Health	225 (61.6)	126 (34.5)	8 (2.2)	6 (1.6)
3. Crime	233 (64.4)	116 (32.0)	12 (3.3)	1 (0.3)
4. Justice	260 (71.2)	96 (26.3)	6 (1.6)	3 (0.8)
5. Taxes	178 (48.8)	159 (43.6)	23 (6.3)	5 (1.4)
6. Tax evasion	122 (34.8)	158 (45.0)	66 (18.8)	5 (1.4)
7. Education	212 (60.2)	116 (33.0)	20 (5.7)	4 (1.1)
8. Immigration	162 (45.8)	130 (36.7)	52 (14.7)	10 (2.8)
9. Federal reform	59 (16.9)	131 (37.5)	108 (30.9)	51 (14.6)
10. PA inefficiency†	191 (52.5)	138 (37.9)	31 (8.5)	4 (1.1)
11. Pollution	113 (31.3)	169 (46.8)	67 (18.6)	12 (3.3)
12. Under-development of southern Italy	147 (40.7)	135 (37.4)	65 (18.0)	14 (3.9)
13. European integration	111 (30.8)	133 (36.9)	71 (19.7)	45 (12.5)
14. Inflation	86 (24.0)	163 (45.4)	86 (24.0)	24 (6.7)
15. Political corruption	103 (28.4)	124 (34.2)	106 (29.2)	30 (8.3)
16. Pluralism in information	130 (35.6)	118 (32.2)	64 (17.5)	53 (14.5)

Source: Osservatorio sulle trasformazioni dei partiti politici, unpublished data.

*Percentages do not add up to 100, since 'Don't know' and 'No response' are not included.

†PA = public administration.

free of any form of organization' (Berlusconi 2000, p. 39). The desire to make FI a sort of 'formless' party arose from a clear ideological and anti-party political choice: the refusal of the organizational shape of the mass ideological parties that had characterized the past history of Italy. It also arose from a need: creating a mass party well rooted throughout the country in a few months would have been impossible. The alternative was to form something Berlusconi knew well: a post-industrial organization such as the Fininvest group. FI came into being to wage and win a 'lightning war': the immediate conquest of power. Once the party came to power, the task of the 'machine' was over but, at the same time, the weaknesses in the organization became visible. Would a political *ad-hocracy* be able to last, or was its destiny that of an instant party? What level of congruence could it ensure between the three components in any political party: the party on the ground, the party in central office and the party in public office? These three different faces of the party are now examined.

The Party in Central Office

From the beginning FI appeared a 'light' party. This is certainly true with regard to the central organs, which are somewhat limited if compared with those of parties run by professional politicians. Some 40–50 full-time staff are involved in the day-to-day running of the party and 20–25 in the regional and provincial offices (Poli 2001). This tendency has more or less continued in the different organizational models adopted. It became established with the Previti[3] model (1994), that is an 'American party' without party members and run by the elected representatives (see below). Previti believed that the main framework of the party should be made up of the coordinators of the 475 electoral districts (the elected MPs) and of 20 regional coordinators to be appointed from the top. In addition, democratic participation was ensured though a nationwide network of FI clubs, which were organized on a national level in the national association of FI clubs (Anfi).

The second model adopted (1995) was that of the *filiere* (organizational lines) proposed by Giuliano Urbani.[4] When the inadequacies of the light party became evident with the crisis of the first Berlusconi cabinet, FI was obliged to revise its party model. Consequently, party organization was planned along six lines—local institutions, clubs, departments, fundraising, *promotori azzurri* (blue promoters, actually FI's militants) and the internet. In addition, according to Urbani's proposal, the structure included 20 regional coordinators, 103 provincial coordinators and 475 constituency coordinators as well as other activists in each town. This organizational solution, however, did not last long. Claudio Scajola, a minister in the second Berlusconi government and FI coordinator (1996–2001), led the way to the refounding of the party and to a new statute (18 January 1997). His aim was to establish the party throughout the country following the example of the old Christian Democratic Party. In this respect, the new statute had two innovations: a geographical articulation that reflected the traditional administrative divisions and therefore eliminated the constituency level; and the establishment of party assemblies at various levels (town assembly, provincial congress, national congress) with the main task of electing the different executive bodies. The only level not affected by this reform was the regional one, whose coordinators were directly appointed by Berlusconi.

The reorganization carried out by Scajola is considered one of the reasons for the victory in the 2001 elections. FI is no longer the 'party that is not', nor is it a 'flash party'. However, despite the electoral achievement this model did not consolidate. This is probably due to a consequence of the original model of FI: a light party created as an electoral machine for the success of a leader who addresses the electors directly through the mass media. As Randall and Svåsand (2002, p. 19) state, 'personalistic leadership [can] contribute at the initial stage to party cohesion and survival but in the long run... it [can] inhibit institutional development'. Later on, organizational discontinuity was brought about by the appointment of Sandro Bondi as party coordinator in September 2003. Unlike Scajola, Bondi appeared to pursue again the centrality of the 'party of the elected'. There was a return to the party-institution model with minimal organization, based on the elected representatives, and the national leader as the only source of identity. The negative electoral cycle of 2003–5, however, reopened the debate between a 'light' party and a 'heavy' party in terms of organization. Consequently, during the 2005 regional elections FI hired and paid at least 1,000 militants to try to slow down the electoral crisis. This solution was inspired by Publitalia, the market research company of Fininvest, rather than by a conscious decision to implement a party model more integrated in the country.

Thus, on the whole, FI is a 'minimal' party. By contrast, the central level is 'maximum', because of the absolute concentration of power resources in the hands of the leader. The hypothesis that I submit here is that the different organizational solutions were only variations within the initial 'plan' of the personal party (Gunther & Diamond 2003; Calise 2000). If so, there are a number of important consequences. First, FI was born as an 'indirect structure' (Duverger 1954), that is, a structure based on already existing organizations. Its formation called for 'considerable use of human and logistic resources which, almost without exception, came from companies in the group of which Berlusconi was the founder and president' (Poli 2001, p. 30). From this point of view FI is an 'individual business party' (Diamanti 1995), a 'business firm party' (Hopkin & Paolucci 1999) or, to recall Weber (1986), a 'patrimonial-type apparatus' or 'neo-patrimonial' party (Maraffi 1995; Ginsborg 2003), where the dividing line between public and private, as well as between business and party, is blurred.

Secondly, with regard to the legitimization of the new political party, 'FI's identity originates in, and is nourished by Silvio Berlusconi's personality and biography' (Frattini 2003, p. 76). There is no shortage of charisma in this identity, even if it is largely an impure charisma. There are Messiah-like components: 'Mr. Berlusconi presented himself as endowed with a saviour's mission: to rescue the country from the danger of a still Communist Left, and to lead it out of general crises toward a brilliant future' (Cavalli 1994, p. 11). Moreover, the existence of a serious social and political crisis, quite typical in the case of 'situational charisma' (Panebianco 1988), complemented by a careful process of image-building of the leader, which involves also his physical aspect, leads one to consider it a 'mediatic charisma' or, better, a 'manufactured charisma' (Ginsborg 2003).

Thirdly, the very nature of the organizational framework is conditioned by leadership. In the first place, all the power in FI is in the hands of the president, who is formally elected by the national congress—the main assembly within FI—for three years and can be re-elected. Actually, up to now there has been a mechanism based on the acclamation of one single leader. There is also a system of relationships based upon loyalty and closeness to the leader. This sort of 'clan' dimension is particularly evident among the leader's closest collaborators, who came entirely from companies of the Fininvest group in the foundation phase (1994–95). Later on such symbiosis with the leader became very relevant for the composition and functioning of all the party's main bodies. This is particularly true for the national council and the presidential committee, that is, the two main top executive bodies in FI.

On the characteristics of the leadership, the answers given by the party delegates are of great interest: 61 per cent of those interviewed believe that FI still depends on Berlusconi and 15 per cent even consider this dependence on the figure and actions of the leader to have increased. Moreover, 57.5 per cent consider Berlusconi the European leader who is most worthy of admiration (only 15 per cent indicate Blair and 14 per cent Aznar). Berlusconi is still the 'symbolic centre' of FI and there is no other personality who could obscure him. This is evident in the answers to three crucial questions on the matter. Who, inside FI, could replace Berlusconi as the head of the government? Who, after Berlusconi, best interprets the spirit of FI? Who, in this moment, wields the greatest influence in FI? Various names come up, but, excepting Berlusconi, all of them achieve low percentages. In answering the first question, those obtaining more votes are Frattini, a former minister and currently a European commissioner (21 per cent), and Formigoni, the president of the Lombardia region (20 per cent). Cicchitto, deputy party coordinator, comes first in reply to the second question (23.5 per cent), while in reply to the third question Bondi, the present party coordinator, obtains 40 per cent of the preferences.

The Party on the Ground

Since the beginning FI has had an ambivalent relationship with its members. In Previti's proposal for party organization, at the end of 1994, there was no provision for members and no membership campaign. Even the formal requests to join—more than 5,000 in 1994—were suspended. Behind this solution there is FI's refusal to become a mass party and the preference for an 'American party' model, where the central organization, according to a metaphor used by FI leaders, is like a thin 'breadstick' (*grissino*). Requests to join the party were again accepted from 1996 onwards, but it was in the 1997 statute that the system of membership was finally formalized. Three types of members were envisaged: ordinary members, supporters and *benemeriti* (meritorious members)[5]. This change was probably the answer to the need for democratic legitimization. However, it also reflected more practical demands, such as the need for voluntary work and for the mobilization of other resources in addition to the public ones.

Table 2 shows data on FI membership. From 1997 to 2000 there was a significant increase in membership (170 per cent), which has been seen as a valid indicator of the level of organizational consolidation achieved. Yet the rank and file remained smaller than that of other parties, such as the DS (see Giannetti & Mulé, this volume).

FI attracts support at election time, but does not 'integrate' its electors. In 2001, for example, FI lost more than 40,000 affiliates, while in 2004 a drop of about 68,000 members indicated a real collapse of the associative base. In the same vein, the party's membership levels were weakest in the regions where the party won a higher number of votes, such as Lombardia and Sicilia (Diamanti 2003). One gets the same impression examining the history of the other original component of the party on the ground: the clubs.[6] Despite plans that placed them at the centre of party life, their role has always been limited. No primaries have been held, although they were a central point in Previti's plan. Nor have members been involved in other ways. However, 77 per cent of the delegates interviewed at the 2004 congress stated that the selection of candidates should take place at a local level; in addition, more than 50 per cent of those interviewed complained that in the pre-congress debates in which they had participated, opinions had varied very little or not at all, and 31 per cent affirmed that in the pre-congress debates there had been a lack of discussion.

Such a lack of interest in internal forms of participation and democracy brought about a party with 'shadow members', that is, people with no rights. This is obviously neither a specific problem of FI, nor an Italian one. But in FI it is aggravated by the charismatic-populist aspect of the party, which seems to tolerate only the ritual of democracy by acclamation.

Table 2 Forza Italia Membership and Ratio of Party Members to Party Voters and Total Electorate, 1994–2004

	Forza Italia members	Forza Italia voters	Total electorate	FI members as % of FI voters	FI members as % of electorate
1994	5,200	8,119,287	48,135,041	0.06	0.01
1995	—				
1996	116,000	7,715,342	48,744,846	1.50	0.24
1997	139,546				
1998	161,319				
1999	190,399				
2000	312,863				
2001	271,751	10,923,431	49,256,295	2.48	0.55
2002	222,631				
2003	239,252				
2004	171,273				

Source: National Membership Office of Forza Italia.

The Party in Public Office

After the 1994 elections the 'party of the elected' was the only structured organizational sub-system with its own autonomous (parliamentary) resources. However, there is no doubt that the MPs carried out important party functions as constituency delegates and coordinators at different levels in the country (the Previti model). The organizational developments that followed (the Bondi model) have not changed the role played by the MPs; they did, however, offer more opportunities for the integration of the MPs into the party in central office. Thus, at the end of the 1996–2001 legislature, 66 per cent of the positions available on a national level were occupied by senators and deputies (Poli 2001, p. 222). The 1997 statute had formalized this organizational integration by affirming the right of those elected to participate in the various councils (national council, national congress and local assemblies). However, these observations should not mislead us.

FI could be labelled a 'party of the elected', but not in the sense that it is led by the elected. It is not a modern cadre party which concentrates power resources in the 'parliamentary party complex' (Koole 1994, p. 291). The low level of professionalization of the MPs needs to be stressed. In 1994 more than 91 per cent of FI deputies and senators were elected for the first time. This figure went down to 49 per cent in 1996, but went up again to 50 per cent in 2001 (Verzichelli 1997; 2002; Lanza & Piazza 2002). Among the Italian parties FI has the youngest parliamentary class with regard to parliamentary experience. In addition, a fairly high turnover is a recurring feature. Consequently, FI MPs have no autonomy in candidate selection, electoral campaigns or parliamentary activities. In short, the parliamentary groups are strictly controlled by Berlusconi. Besides, with the 1997 statute this sort of centralization was formalized: article 23 states that the presidential committee should coordinate the parliamentary groups' activities.

The party in public office is especially important in centre–periphery relationships. If we consider the party of the elected as a sort of iceberg, the parliamentary groups represent the part above water, with the government as the tip, while the part under the water is made up of FI representatives at the regional, provincial and municipal levels. From this perspective the institutionalization of FI can be seen as the result of the direct networking carried out by local representatives, rather than in the traditional terms of the mass-party framework. But this is not an easy road to party institutionalization.

FI is characterized by a potentially problematic division of labour between the centre and the periphery. On the one hand, the electoral success at the national level depends on the role played by Berlusconi; on the other hand, maintaining support at the local level depends on FI local representatives. The latter, however, come from the group of 'former Christian-democrat and socialist leaders, who have chosen Forza Italia as a way to promote their careers' and are strictly linked to local interest groups and economic organizations (Diamanti 2003, p. 131). Therefore, thanks to their own support networks, FI local representatives preserve a high degree of autonomy from the centre. Consequently, the party's institutionalization remains loose (Fava 2005; Paolucci 1999). The result of all this is a configuration of the 'organized anarchy' type, where relations between the three faces of party organization are not tied up and vertical integration between the centre and the periphery remains intermittent.

Competitive Innovation, Political Marketing, and Populism

FI is a light party created for electoral purposes. The organizational structure is seen as a cost in terms of efficiency and as an obstacle in terms of ideology. Its action is bound by a strategic imperative: winning as many votes as possible to come to power. This calls for an adequate competitive strategy and effective election campaigning. Ever since Berlusconi entered the field, both these needs have been abundantly clear, tightly linked and tackled using market-oriented methods. It was a question of (1) 'product' innovation—the leader with his personal party; (2) competitive innovation—alliance politics; and (3) innovation in the electoral campaign (political marketing). Having analysed the product innovation, we now turn to the last two areas of novelty.

The theme of alliance politics is a key element in FI's success. The double coalition of 1994, with the League in the north and the AN in the south, was a winning move on Berlusconi's part. Accordingly, the lesson the centre-right learnt from this experience was 'united we win' (Di Virgilio 2001). This inclusive strategy gave a more decisive push in the direction of a bipolar party system. Moreover, building a coalition with Berlusconi as guarantor made it possible to anchor political forces that were partially anti-system or were perceived as such, that is, the Northern League and the MSI/AN. At the same time, FI performed a key role as a glue holding together pieces that would otherwise conflict: 'moderates and extremists, partisans of the North or South of Italy, secessionists and nationalists, believers in the free enterprise and welfare state supporters' (Diamanti 2005, p. 20). In this situation, Berlusconi appeared the only leader able to hold the coalition together, to choose and impose the issues for political contest and to keep FI alive.

Consequently, Berlusconi's leadership was very important. But in the case of recurrent electoral failures, an unmovable leadership can turn a strength into a weakness. In addition, FI's electoral crisis in 2003–5 was a destabilizing factor within the Casa delle Libertà coalition. On the one hand, the other partners took advantage of the FI crisis: in 1994–96 the League absorbed the FI's votes and in 2004–5 the centre-right successors to Christian Democracy did the same. But here there is more: by winning those votes the allies were able to increase their internal veto power in policymaking, but they were not able to guarantee the holding together of the alliance.

From an organizational point of view it can be said that political marketing has determined FI's structure since the beginning. One aspect of this influence relates to the systematic hiring of outside specialists: public relations experts, pollsters, advertisement experts, political consultants and similar professionals. This tendency is implicit in the very creation of FI and in its symbiotic relationship with Fininvest. It is reflected, too, in the creation of marketing-oriented structures outside the party. This is the case with Diakron (1993), a public opinion research institute founded by Gianni Pilo, the manager of the Fininvest marketing office who prepared and directed FI's debut (Poli 2001). In 1999 Diakron was replaced by a market research company outside FI, Luigi Crespi's Datamedia, which participated in all Berlusconi's strategic choices up to 2001. Another sector in which party professionalization has reached levels that were unattainable by the other Italian parties is that of candidate selection, which is the task of specialized business consultants, although from a different perspective. In this case it was another external market research company, Sinergetica, which organized the selection of candidates in the 2000 regional elections and the 2001 general election (Poli 2001; Cattaneo & Zannetto 2003).

Marketing strategies also strengthened the centralization of power in the hands of Berlusconi and his staff. The communication sector in the central party 'establishes and communicates to the outside world the framework, also in a symbolical sense, within which candidates are to act' (Mancini 2001, p. 41). Another significant innovation is the Tavolo per l'Italia (the Round Table for Italy), a kind of Blair 'war cabinet', with weekly meetings—held in Berlusconi's villa at Arcore—involving internal communication experts, external professional figures and Berlusconi himself: 'the job of the *tavolo*, in accordance with Fininvest experience, is to establish the guidelines for FI communication, adapting it to the different circumstances' (ibid.).

Thus, the revolution in political communication carried out by FI has mainly brought about two important and lasting organizational effects: professionalization and centralization. Other relevant aspects concern campaign modernization. As is well known, besides the organizational aspect at least three other elements characterize a political campaign: technical, thematic and resource developments (Norris 2002; Farrell 2002). Technical elements will be discussed first.

Despite a strategy diversification, FI basically developed a campaign organization within the context of TV campaigns, which are modern rather than post-modern (Norris 2002; Farrell & Webb 2000). However, for large numbers of Italian voters 'politics' means above all 'politics on television' (Legnante 2002, p. 245). Moreover, for many voters the television is the main source of political identification. Casa delle Libertà voters prefer the Mediaset network, the group of television channels belonging to the Berlusconi family; while those who vote for L'Ulivo prefer the Rai network, that is, the public television company (Sani 2001; Sani & Legnante 2002). The Rai–Mediaset opposition has become the basis for a new cleavage. Empirical support for this can be found in the interviews with the delegates at the 2004 FI congress: 73 per cent of those interviewed had little or no trust in the Rai channels, while they had some or a lot in the Mediaset ones; moreover, 78 per cent had little or no trust in the press. This lack of trust, however, is reduced to 50 per cent of those interviewed in the case of the radio and 35 per cent in the case of the internet.

As regards campaign issues, discussion here will be limited to the problem of personalization, which has been a relevant aspect of the Italian political scene for quite a time. The terms 'telecracy' and 'telepopulism' were used for the first time during the 1994 electoral campaign (Bentivegna 1995). Data processed by the Osservatorio di Pavia (Sani & Legnante 2001) confirm this 'hard' regularity in FI's campaigns. In the years 1997–99, although he was in opposition, Berlusconi was the politician who was most seen on Italian television: 13,497 minutes, closely followed by D'Alema, leader of the DS, with 13,435 minutes. Other politicians followed at a considerable distance. However, if a distinction is made between 'presence', that is, a direct appearance on TV and 'attention', that is, indirect news about the candidates given by the TV, Berlusconi comes out clearly above D'Alema as regards direct presence—6,645 minutes, as opposed to 4,307—and it is no surprise to discover that Berlusconi is more present on the Mediaset channels (4,569 minutes) than on the public ones. A more surprising fact is that the Mediaset channels pay more attention to Berlusconi and FI to the detriment of the other centre-right leaders and parties. This situation did not change during the 2001 electoral campaign.

Media and personalization reinforce each other and contribute to give meaning and coherence to an otherwise weakly linked party organization. FI is, therefore, a media-mediated personality party (Seisselberg 1996). The political–media circuit acts also as connective tissue in its relationship with the electors: FI 'was born from a direct connection between Berlusconi and the electors when no party existed' (Baget Bozzo 2003, p. 91). Berlusconi and the 'people', the leader and the movement, are the two poles, ever in a state of tension, of FI's identity; a state of affairs that brings to mind the idea of populism (Tarchi 2003).

Lastly, marketing orientation means mobilizing huge financial resources. In political finances, some of the problems related to the nature and role of FI come to light: the unclear intertwining of politics and Berlusconi's private assets. From the beginning the party's two main objectives regarding finance were: self-financing and expenditure reduction (Poli 2001). These were, in reality, two objectives that remained out of reach. FI spends a large sum, not on organization, which remains 'light', but on strategies (professionalization, mediatization and permanent campaign), which are financially 'heavy'. The most critical point in FI's political finances was the 2001 permanent campaign, which cost more than €18 million. This is a considerable amount of money compared with that spent by the other parties. Between 1994 and 1998 FI spent, on average, a total of €17.5 million and this figure leapt up to €37 million and €52.5 million in 1999 and 2000, respectively, which were the years of the greatest 'commercial' drive to help the party to return to power (Bechis 2001, p. 3; Poli 2001, p. 275). Expenditure on surveys and external consultancy has progressively increased since the 2001 elections.

Compared with these financial demands, it is not surprising that the money coming in always appears to be limited. Even if insufficient, electoral reimbursement is the main source of income. Moreover, self-financing is subject to the uncertainties of a fluid organization. In 2000, with 260,000 members, FI raised about €10 million. In 2002 it raised €9 million, and in 2003 over €10 million. This was a substantial sum when compared with state contributions in non-electoral periods and in 2004/5, with the membership collapse, it could constitute a serious economic problem.

Conclusions

FI is a new party, which defines itself as a 'post-ideological container' (Frattini 2003, p. 78). It came into being as a consequence of the serious crisis the Italian party system went through in the 1990s. Ever since its appearance it has carried out a double function of systemic integration. On the one hand, it has filled the gap left by the disappearance of governing parties; on the other hand, it has made a decisive contribution to bipolar dynamics in a party system that is still fragmentary and in which there are heterogeneous coalitions. For FI the main sources of change and development have been both internal and external. As has been observed, changes of internal origin have been connected with the resilience of the original model of a personal party and with the prevalence in the dominating coalition of people identified with this model. External sources of change, instead, are concerned with the transformations that affect the institutional and competitive context (system of government, electoral law, party financing, number of parties, ideological distance between them, etc.) in which the party exists. These changes have been connected with the need to maintain competitive advantages in an unstable political scenario.

In all this there can be found two constraints on FI's actions and also a paradox. The first constraint is organizational: the weaker the institutionalization of FI, the greater the instability of the party system. The second constraint is an institutional one. Italian bipolarism continues to limp, because the institutional guarantees for its consolidation, in particular adequate electoral reform, are missing. But after the disastrous results in the 2005 regional and local elections, Berlusconi's strategy has gone in the opposite direction. Goals based on surviving as a government and maintaining the leadership have forced him to agree to the requests of some of his partners to go back to a more proportional system. Such an electoral reform might strike a deadly blow at bipolarism. And herein lies the paradox. Berlusconi came to power because of the emergence of bipolarism in the party system and later he has decided to put an end to it.

Notes

[1] This expression is used to describe the decrees issued in March 1995 aimed at limiting electoral expenditure, abolishing television electioneering during the electoral campaign and favouring equal access to the state television for all political parties.

[2] Data drawn from a questionnaire distributed to the party delegates (468 interviewed) at the second FI congress (Milan, 27–29 May 2004); the survey was organized by the Osservatorio italiano sulle trasformazioni dei partiti politici (Italian observatory on political party change) of the Universities of Florence, Bologna, Catania and Trieste.

[3] Cesare Previti was a minister in the first Berlusconi government and also the FI coordinator (1995–96).

[4] Giuliano Urbani was one of the founders of FI as well as a minister in two of the Berlusconi governments.

[5] This distinction is based on the different party dues paid (€50 for ordinary members, €100 for supporters and €250 for *benemeriti*) but this does not imply any difference in the rights and duties of members.

[6] In 1998 there were 2,200 clubs affiliated to FI, with about 91,000 members. In 2004 there were about 2,700 clubs with about 104,000 members (Possa 1998).

References

Are, G. (1997) 'I riferimenti culturali', in *Forza Italia. Radiografia di un evento*, ed. D. Mennitti, Ideazione Editrice, Roma, pp. 183–195.

Baget Bozzo, G. (1997) *La cultura politica di Forza Italia*, Forza Italia, Roma.

Baget Bozzo, G. (2003) 'La Berlusconi generation', *Liberal*, no. 15, pp. 89–91.

Bechis, F. (2001) 'Forza Italia, il buco è già a 84 mld', *Milano Finanza*, 3 July, p. 3

Bentivegna, S. (1995) 'Attori e strategie comunicative della campagna elettorale', in *L'alternanza inattesa. Le elezioni del 27 marzo 1994 e le loro conseguenze*, ed. G. Pasquino, Rubbettino, Soveria Mannelli, pp. 99–130.

Berlusconi, S. (2000) *L'Italia che ho in mente*, Mondadori, Milano.

Berlusconi, S. (2001) *Una storia italiana*, Mondadori, Milano.

Berlusconi, S. (2003) *La nuova strada*, Fondazione Liberal, Roma.

Calise, M. (2000) *Il partito personale*, Laterza, Roma and Bari.

Cattaneo, A. & Zannetto, P. (2003) *(E)lezioni di successo*, Etas, Milano.

Cavalli, L. (1994) *The Personalization of Leadership in Italy*, Working Paper no. 2, Centro Interuniversitario di Sociologia Politica, Firenze.

Cotta, M. (2002) 'Berlusconi alla seconda prova di governo', in *Politica in Italia. I fatti dell'anno e le interpretazioni*, eds P. Bellucci & M. Bull, Il Mulino, Bologna, pp. 163–184.

Diamanti, I. (1995) 'Partiti, modelli', *Politica ed Economia*, special issue, pp. 71–80.

Diamanti, I. (2003) *Bianco, rosso, verde . . . e azzurro. Mappe e colori dell'Italia politica*, Il Mulino, Bologna.

Diamanti, I. (2005) 'Il Cavaliere senza partito', *La Repubblica*, 17 April, p. 20.

Di Virgilio, A. (2001) 'Uniti si vince? Voto e politica delle alleanze', *Il Mulino*, no. 4, pp. 635–644.

Duverger, M. (1954) *Political Parties*, Methuen, London.

Farrell, D. M. (2002) 'Campaign modernization and the West European party', in *Political parties in the New Europe. Political and Analytical Challenges*, eds K. R. Luther & F. Müller-Rommel, Oxford University Press, Oxford, pp. 63–83.

Farrell, D. M. & Webb, P. (2000) 'Political parties as campaign organizations', in *Parties without Partisans. Political Change in Advanced Industrial Democracies*, eds R. J. Dalton & M. P. Wattenberg, Oxford University Press, Oxford, pp. 102–128.

Fava, T. (2005) 'Forza Italia. I limiti di un'organizzazione leggera', *Il Mulino*, no. 5, pp. 883–893.

Frattini, F. (2003) 'Una grande svolta', *Liberal*, no. 15, pp. 76–78.

Ginsborg, P. (2003) *Berlusconi. Ambizioni patrimoniali in una democrazia mediatica*, Einaudi, Turin.

Gunther, R. & Diamond, L. (2003) 'Species of political parties. A new typology', *Party Politics*, vol. 9, no. 2, pp. 167–199.

Hopkin, J. & Paolucci, C. (1999) 'The business firm model of party organisation: cases from Spain and Italy', *European Journal of Political Research*, vol. 35, no. 3, pp. 307–339.

Ignazi, P. & Katz, R. (1995) 'Introduzione. Ascesa e caduta del governo Berlusconi', in *Politica in Italia. I fatti dell'anno e le interpretazioni*, eds P. Ignazi & R. Katz, Il Mulino, Bologna, pp. 27–48.

Koole, R. (1994) 'The vulnerability of the modern cadre party in The Netherlands', in *How Parties Organize*, eds R. Katz & P. Mair, Sage, London, pp. 278–303.

Lanza, O. & Piazza, G. (2002) 'Il ricambio dei parlamentari', in *Dall'Ulivo al governo Berlusconi. Le elezioni del 13 maggio 2001 e il sistema politico italiano*, ed. G. Pasquino, Il Mulino, Bologna, pp. 239–273.

Legnante, G. (2002) 'Tra influenza e incapsulamento. Cittadini, comunicazione e campagna elettorale', in *Le ragioni dell'elettore. Perché ha vinto il centro-destra nelle elezioni italiane del 2001*, eds M. Caciagli & P. Corbetta, Il Mulino, Bologna, pp. 233–273.

Mancini, P. (2001) 'Il professionismo della *war room*: come cambiano i partiti politici', *Comunicazione Politica*, vol. 2, no. 1, pp. 29–45.

Maraffi, M. (1995) 'Forza Italia', in *La politica italiana. Dizionario critico (1945–95)*, ed. G. Pasquino, Laterza, Roma and Bari, pp. 247–259.

Morlino, L. & Tarchi, M. (1996) 'The dissatisfied society, protest and support in Italy', *European Journal of Political Research*, vol. 30, no. 1, pp. 41–63.

Norris, P. (2002) 'Campaign Comunications', in *Comparing Democracies 2*, eds L. LeDuc, R. G. Niemi & P. Norris, Sage, London, pp. 127–147.

Panebianco, A. (1988) *Political Parties. Organization and Power*, Cambridge University Press, Cambridge, England.

Paolucci, C. (1999) 'Forza Italia a livello locale: un marchio in franchising?', *Rivista Italiana di Scienza Politica*, vol. 29, no. 3, pp. 481–516.

Pasquino, G. (2002) 'Un'elezione non come le altre', in *Dall'Ulivo al governo Berlusconi. Le elezioni del 13 maggio 2001 e il sistema politico italiano*, ed. G. Pasquino, Il Mulino, Bologna, pp. 11–22.

Poli, E. (2001) *Forza Italia. Struttura, leadership e radicamento territoriale*, Il Mulino, Bologna.

Possa, G. (1998) 'Il processo di strutturazione organizzativa di Forza Italia e il futuro dei club,' party document presented at the first FI Congress, Milano, 16–18 April.

Randall, V. & Svåsand, L. (2002) 'Party institutionalization in new democracies', *Party Politics*, vol. 8, no. 1, pp. 5–29.

Raniolo, F. (2000) *I partiti conservatori in Europa occidentale*, Il Mulino, Bologna.

Sani, G. (ed.) (2001) *Mass media ed elezioni*, Il Mulino, Bologna.

Sani, G. & Legnante, G. (2001) 'La comunicazione politica in televisione (1997–1999)', in *Mass media ed elezioni*, ed. G. Sani, Il Mulino, Bologna, pp. 127–157.

Sani, G. & Legnante, G. (2002) 'Quanto conta la comunicazione politica?', in *Dall'Ulivo al governo Berlusconi. Le elezioni del 13 maggio 2001 e il sistema politico italiano*, ed. G. Pasquino, Il Mulino, Bologna, pp. 117–137.

Sartori, G. (2004) *Mala tempora*, Laterza, Roma and Bari.

Schadee, M. A. & Segatti, P. (2002) 'Informazione politica, spazio elettorale ed elettori in movimento', in *Le ragioni dell'elettore. Perché ha vinto il centro-destra nelle elezioni italiane del 2001*, eds M. Caciagli & P. Corbetta, Il Mulino, Bologna, pp. 339–369.

Seisselberg, J. (1996) 'Conditions of success and political problems of a media-mediated personality party', *West European Politics*, vol. 19, no. 4, pp. 715–743.

Tarchi, M. (2003) *L'Italia populista. Dal qualunquismo ai girotondi*, Il Mulino, Bologna.

Verzichelli, L. (1997) 'La classe parlamentare', in *Forza Italia. Radiografia di un evento*, ed. D. Mennitti, Ideazione Editrice, Roma, pp. 49–77.

Verzichelli, L. (2002) 'Da un ceto parlamentare all'altro. Il mutamento del personale legislativo italiano', in *Maggioritario finalmente?La transizione elettorale 1994–2001*, eds R. D'Alimonte & S. Bartolini, Il Mulino, Bologna, pp. 319–361.

Weber, M. (1986) *Economia e società*, Comunità, Milano, vol. 2.

The Democratici di Sinistra: In Search of a New Identity*

Daniela Giannetti & Rosa Mulé

Introduction

The Italian Democrats of the Left (Democratici di Sinistra, DS) is the largest Italian left-wing political party, heir of the former Communist Party (Partito Comunista Italiano, PCI). In recent years, the party has undergone fundamental changes, which involved reforming its ideological identity and its organizational structure. These changes are best understood in the context of the transformation of the Italian political system in the early 1990s. Two related factors help to explain that sweeping transformation: the downfall of communism in 1989 and the effects of judicial investigations that revealed the widespread corruption network linking political leaders, public administrators and businesspeople. As a result, the Italian party system and political institutions were overhauled. The success of the 1991 and 1993 referenda prompted a change in electoral rules at both national and local level. After about 40 years of almost pure proportional representation (PR), in 1993 Italy adopted a mixed

*We would like to thank Luca Billi (DS Bologna Federation), Emiliano Citarella (DS Central Office) and Elisabetta De Giorgi for their help. We are solely responsible for any errors or omissions.

electoral system where 75 per cent of the seats were allocated by plurality and the remaining 25 per cent were allocated by PR.[1] Three elections have been held under the mixed electoral law: in 1994, 1996 and 2001. Two important points are worth noting. The first relates to the dynamics of electoral competition, whereby the new electoral system created incentives for the formation of pre-electoral coalitions in the plurality tier, with a tendency for these electoral cartels to present themselves to the voters as potential governments. At the same time, however, parties retained separate identities within these cartels, and remain sovereign actors in the post-electoral legislative politics of government formation.

This work analyses the complex interplay between the restructuring of the DS party and the transformation of the Italian political system. We find that the main changes concern the structure of the party organization, marked by a process of growing factionalization and a policy shift towards the centre of the ideological space. Thus, the next section sketches recent party history and describes the DS's electoral trends. The second examines changes in policy positions at three levels of party politics: leaders, members and voters. The third section deals with the organizational restructuring of the party. The fourth analyses the DS's competitive strategy, while the fifth looks at campaign politics. Some concluding remarks are presented in the final section.

Recent Party History: In Search of a New Identity

The recent history of the DS can be summarized in terms of three main aspects: changes in party identity as reflected in modifications of party name/label, changes in electoral trends, and changes in its role from opposition to government party. Research on party politics has convincingly argued that changes of party name signal major shifts in policy stance (Panebianco 1988; Harmel & Janda 1994). This assertion sits squarely with the experience of the PCI-PDS-DS, where party re-labelling reflects the main splits and fusions of the past 15 years.

The starting point for analysing the party's recent history is 1991, when the PCI held its 20th congress in Rimini. In response to an initiative launched by the party leader, Achille Occhetto, to disengage the Italian left from the collapse of communism in Eastern Europe, the PCI changed its name to Partito Democratico della Sinistra (Democratic Party of the Left, PDS), starting a process of transformation aimed at placing the party within the European socialist tradition. A group of dissenters split forming an extreme left party, the Partito della Rifondazione Comunista (Communist Refoundation Party, PRC). In February 1998 the PDS held a national convention at which the party opened its doors to several outside groups with left-wing leanings: Laburisti (a splinter of the former Italian Socialist Party, born in 1994), Cristiano Sociali (splinter of the former Christian Democracy movement, formed in 1993), Comunisti Unitari (splinter of the PRC, formed in 1995) and Sinistra Repubblicana (splinter of the former Italian Republican Party). As a result, the party changed its name to Sinistra Democratica (Democratic Left, DS). Finally, at the last party congress held in February 2005 a large majority of the party delegates approved another change to the party label, which explicitly confirms the DS affiliation to the European Socialist Party.

A second major change regards the electoral and legislative strength of the party. Electoral results for the Chamber of Deputies from 1987 to 2001 are given in Table 1. The percentages after 1992 refer to the PDS-DS vote share in the PR tier, which gives a very clear indication of the relative strength of individual parties. Table 1 also shows the electoral results for PCI-PDS-DS in the European elections from 1984 to 1999. These results give some measure of the party's electoral strength, despite the fact that turnout in European elections is usually lower than in national elections. Party vote share for 2004 is not available, because the DS contested the European elections by joining a list called Uniti nell'Ulivo (United in the Olive Tree), which included other centre and socialist parties. The list gained 31.1 per cent of the vote. Currently in the European Parliament the DS has 12 MEPs, who belong to the Party of European Socialists group.

The national elections of April 1992 are widely regarded as a turning point in Italian politics. All the traditional parties suffered a vote loss, with the Christian Democracy (DC) falling below the 30 per cent threshold for the first time in its history. As Table 1 shows, the PCI-PDS vote share dropped from 26.6 per cent in 1987 to 16.1 per cent in 1992. This loss was only partially due to the 1991 split, given that the PRC gained 5.6 per cent of the vote.

In March 1994, the first elections under the new electoral law were held. The centre-left coalition was defeated, though the PDS increased its vote share (20.3 per cent). However, new elections were held just two years later. On 21 April 1996, the centre-left coalition, named L'Ulivo (The Olive Tree), won the election. The PDS vote share remained stable at 21.1 per cent. In the national elections of 13 May 2001, the Ulivo

Table 1 PCI-PDS-DS Electoral Results, 1987–2005

	Vote and seats in the Chamber of Deputies*			Vote share in the European elections		Vote share in the regional elections		
Year	Votes	PR vote share (%)	Total seats	Year	Vote share (%)	Year	Vote share	Vote share (%)
1987	10,254,591	26.6	177	1984	33.0			
1992	6,317,962	16.1	107	1989	27.6			
1994	7,855,610	20.3	115	1994	19.1	1995	6,470,445	24.6
1996	7,897,044	21.1	172	1999	17.4	2000	4,150,950	17.7
2001	6,145,569	16.6	136	2004	—	2005	1,511,405†	17.0

Source: Minister of Interior and the political parties' websites.
*Vote share percentages in 1994, 1996 and 2001 refer to the PR tier. Seats refer to the total number of seats (plurality and PR). DS electoral results for 2004 European Elections are not available because the party joined the list Uniti nell'Ulivo.
†DS electoral results for 2005 regional elections are available only for five regions. In the remaining nine the party joined the left-wing coalition Uniti nell'Ulivo. The Ulivo alliance gained 34.2 per cent of the vote share (in the nine regions).

coalition was defeated, and the PDS-DS dropped to a modest 16.6 per cent of vote share (about the same vote share the party had in 1992). Within the Ulivo, voters' preferences shifted in favour of the centre-left group, La Margherita (The Daisy), which gained 14.5 per cent of the total vote share, while PRC barely passed the five per cent threshold in the PR tier. Electoral results at the regional level show a similar pattern.

Despite this declining electoral trend, in the past decade the PDS-DS has succeeded in shifting from opposition to government for the first time in the history of the Italian Republic. After victory in the 1996 elections, the centre-left coalition led by Romano Prodi, former leader of the DC, formed a government that included nine PDS ministers controlling important portfolios such as the interior, finance and education ministries. The PDS strongly supported the Prime Minister's economic policy aimed at ensuring that Italy would enter the first round of European monetary union. However, the Prodi government was intrinsically weak because it depended upon the external support of the PRC.[2] Eventually, in October 1998, the government collapsed after the PRC leader refused to support its annual budget bill.

A new government led by the DS secretary general, Massimo D'Alema, replaced the Prodi cabinet. The government coalition was supported by the former partners of the Prodi government and by two parliamentary factions that formed during the inter-electoral stage: the Partito dei Comunisti Italiani (Party of Italian Communists, PdCI), a PRC splinter whose members stayed loyal to the Prodi government, and a small but crucial group of deputies previously elected as members of the right-wing coalition, the Unione Democratici Europei (Union of European Democrats, UDEUR).

The first D'Alema government was short-lived. It fell in December 1999, following a change in the parliamentary party system.[3] The birth of a new legislative centrist faction called I Democratici (The Democrats), which had successfully contested the 1999 European election, determined a change in the composition of the cabinet.[4] The second D'Alema government lasted only four months. This time the main reason for government termination was the defeat of left-wing parties in the regional elections held in April 2000. D'Alema resigned and was replaced as prime minister by the former socialist leader Giuliano Amato. The left-wing coalition remained in power until the national elections of 2001.

While in government, and even more so in opposition, the DS party was plagued by internal divisions. A significant proportion of DS deputies regularly voted in different ways on key rollcall votes on foreign policy (Giannetti & Laver 2004). In 1999, the decision of the centre-left government to send Italian troops to support NATO military intervention in Kosovo provoked a major split among DS members in the legislature. Similarly, after 2001, when the right-wing government supported the Enduring Freedom military operation, a significant proportion of DS deputies dissented from the party line, voting against Italian military involvement. These party splits clearly indicated dwindling party discipline and suggested that a process of power dispersion within the party elite was gradually developing.

Party Values and Programmes: Towards the Centre

Such transformations at the elite level affected the DS political identity as well. Scholars agree that from 1991 onwards the PDS-DS gradually committed itself to a more moderate leftist posture. First of all, the party detached itself from the old Marxist tradition and moved toward full acceptance of liberal democracy (Occhetto 1991). Consequently, the two major policy areas in which PDS-DS party values and programmes underwent significant changes are economic and foreign policy (Baccetti 1997; Bellucci et al. 2000). As far as economic policy is concerned, the main debate revolved around appreciation of the economic institutions of capitalism, market-oriented economic ideas and rethinking the role of the state in the economy. In foreign policy matters, which had shaped the traditional identity of Italian communism, the central issue concerned the position of Italy in the international system and its affiliation to military alliances. After the fall of the Soviet Union, the official position of the PDS was explicit support for a common foreign and security policy in the European Union and participation in NATO.

Moreover, the literature has pointed out changes not only in party policy positions, but also in the salience of particular issues, such as women's rights, civil rights and environmental policy (Bellucci et al. 2000). To these we can surely add the increased salience of the institutional reform issue that has dominated the Italian political scene since the early 1990s (Giannetti & Sened 2004).

In what follows we present some quantitative estimates of party policy positions along the most significant dimensions. The most widely used source of data for estimating party positions is the content analysis of party manifestos undertaken by the Manifesto Research Group (MRG). The MRG dataset covers almost all the post-war period for a wide range of countries (Budge et al. 2001). Expert survey data are usually assembled for a specific time point. However, comparable datasets of party policy positions in several European democracies, including Italy, are available for the years 1992 and 2004 (Laver & Hunt 1992; Laver & Benoit 2006).

MRG-based estimates of economic left–right positions for PCI-PDS-DS show a trend toward a more centrist position along the economic left–right dimension from -0.80 in 1992 to -0.47 in 2004.[5] This means that while the importance of spending versus taxes remains relevant, the emphasis on the former is less marked. Expert survey-based estimates suggest a clear difference between the two time points, with the PDS-DS mean position rising from 3.0 in 1992 to 6.7 in 2004 on a 20-point scale (from left to right).

As far as foreign policy is concerned, we cannot compare 1992 and 2004 expert survey-based estimates because the questions asked to country experts changed considerably. For instance, data published in 1992 provide estimates about relations with the former Soviet Union, which obviously disappeared in the dataset collected in 2004. As a proxy, we might use a pro/anti-Europe stance, comparing for example the DS position with the PRC position. This comparison helps to gauge the DS movement towards the centre with the PRC inheriting the more radical traits of the former PCI.

Seen in this light, it is worth noting that the DS had a mean score of 6 and the PRC a mean score of 12, on a 20-point scale where 1 means being in favour of European involvement in domestic affairs and peacekeeping operations. All of these estimates refer to the 'official' position of the party, which is considered to be a unitary actor. As research on party politics suggests, the unitary assumption should be relaxed because it takes as parametric what is instead strategic (Panebianco 1988; Mulé 2001). Strategic dynamics are ubiquitous in party organizations, where the equilibrium of power can only be understood as the result of factional strife.

Strategic dynamics have marked the evolution of the DS party in the last decade, with the emergence of distinct factions. To our knowledge, the only documents that have been systematically analysed in order to derive policy positions of the DS party factions are the motions that were debated at the recent party congresses held in Turin (2000) and Pesaro (2001) (Giannetti & Laver 2004). This analysis shows very significant differences between the mean position of the leadership faction members (-0.15) and the mean position of members of the radical left faction (-1.08), giving some indication of significant policy differences inside the party.[6] In short, looking at the party elite level, from 1991 onwards there have been substantial changes in PDS-DS policy positions, with the party moving progressively toward the centre of the political spectrum. At the same time, the left-wing hardliners have maintained significant policy differences. For instance, on matters of foreign policy, they have been closer to the pro-peace and anti-NATO position of the splinter PRC.

An interesting question is whether similar trends are detectable for congress delegates, rank-and-file members and voters. Bellucci et al. (2000) provide survey estimates on the self-placement of congress delegates. Delegates were asked to place themselves and the party on a ten-point left–right scale. In 1990, about 70 per cent of the party delegates placed themselves on the left, while in 2000 this was true for only 20 per cent of those interviewed. More than two-thirds labelled themselves centre-left. A similar pattern characterizes the placement of the party by delegates on the same scale. These results suggest that there was little difference between the way party delegates perceived themselves vis-à-vis the party. By contrast, more recent survey results show that about 70 per cent of the rank and file still place themselves on the left, while only about 53 per cent place the party on the left (Mulé, forthcoming). What this means is that a sizeable proportion of party members believe they are ideologically more committed than party leaders. Such a finding adds weight to the so-called 'law' of curvilinear disparity (May 1973), which states that rank and file are more radical than party elites.

Finally, to examine DS voters' positions, we draw on Eurobarometer data, which provide estimates of the self-placement of voters on a ten-point left–right scale. Data about the median left–right positions of DS voters show convergence toward the centre. Voters for the PCI-PDS-DS have been slowly drifting rightwards over the last three decades, with the median position rising from 1.38 in 1973 to 3.05 in 2002, while the median position within the entire electorate remained more or less constant over time (from 4.76 to 5.18). [7]

Party Organization: Looser Internal and External Ties

The most important organizational changes involve the 'party on the ground' and the 'party in central office'. This section shows that while the number of members enrolled in the DS has dropped dramatically since the early 1980s, the intensity of involvement seems to be growing. Moreover, in the decade under examination, the party organization saw modifications in the cohesion and stability of its dominant coalition. A party's dominant coalition is composed of those organizational actors who control the most vital resources necessary for the functioning of the party. Of the usual terms used to indicate a party's elite, such as the 'inner circle', we prefer the term 'dominant coalition' because organizational power is not necessarily concentrated in the internal or parliamentary positions of that party (Panebianco 1988, pp. 37–40).

Changes in the DS dominant coalition meant stronger decentralization, the consolidation of organized factions and, more generally, greater dispersion of power among party groupings. The new distribution of power brought about several important organizational changes: (a) the creation of a diarchy following the formation of a new organizational position in 2000 (the party president); (b) changes in the formal mechanisms of party leadership selection; (c) the end of the unanimity rule, which had characterized the approval of political documents at party congresses; (d) the capacity of DS factions to run official candidates for party leadership. In what follows we look at these modifications in more detail.

Membership: Dropping Quantity, Increasing Quality?

Parties with large, formally enrolled memberships have been one of the most distinctive, and most successful, forms of political organization in the twentieth century (Scarrow 1996). International comparisons show that Italy enjoys one of the highest number of party members in Europe, reaching about 1,974,040 members in 1998 (Mair & Van Biezen 2001, p. 9). We know however that membership enrolment is dropping fast, reflecting a general crisis in political participation in the Western democracies (Dalton & Wattenberg 2000).

How much, then, is the PDS-DS party still a membership-based organization? Table 2 shows that between 1985 and 2005 the number of party members dropped to about one-third of the members of the old PCI. The most significant change happened in 1991, when the number of party members decreased by about 330,000. This sharp decline is not surprising, since 1991 was the year of major transformation of the party's identity and symbols. However, from 2002 onwards, the data indicate a reverse trend, with a modest increase in party members.

Table 2 also sets out the ratio between membership figures and party vote share, and between membership and the total electorate in 1994, 1996 and 2001. The figures for 1994 and 1996 are relatively stable. The increase in 2001 in party membership/party vote share stems from a drop in the party's vote share, while the decrease in party

Table 2 PCI-PDS-DS Membership, 1985–2005

Year	Party members (absolute number)	Party members as percentage of voters	Party members as percentage of electorate
1985	1,595,281		
1986	1,551,576		
1987	1,508,140		
1988	1,462,281		
1989	1,417,182		
1990	1,319,305		
1991	989,708		
1992	769,944		
1993	690,414		
1994	698,287	8.9	1.8
1995	682,290		
1996	686,713	8.7	1.8
1997	640,838		
1998	613,412		
1999	656,146		
2000	555,171		
2001	598,082	9.7	1.2
2002	534,358		
2003	549,372		
2004	560,141		
2005	561,193		

Source: Data from 1985 to 1994: Ignazi & Katz 1995; from 1995 to 2005: provided by DS central and local offices.
Note: Party vote refers to PR absolute number of valid votes.

membership/total vote ratio derives from an increase in the total vote from 48,744,846 in 1996 to 49,256,295 in 2001.

As far as the recruiting system is concerned, there have been no changes between 1994 and 2005. Local party offices control the individuals enrolling as party members. However, one notable innovation was introduced at the Pesaro congress in 2001, when the party agreed to begin collecting socio-demographic data on the membership (*anagrafe*). This means that membership data are now based on a coherent framework and are organized at the national level. Previously, such information was assembled by local federations, which applied their own method of data collection, thus rendering comparisons between federations more problematic.

One of the most interesting questions about party members is their degree of involvement. Survey data about DS party members show various degrees of involvement (Mulé, forthcoming).[8] In order to probe the levels of activism within the party, members were asked, 'How active do you consider yourself to be in the DS?' Table 3 sets out the responses of DS members, with a breakdown of recruitment years before and after 1991. The data show significant differences between 'old' and 'new' party members in terms of degree of activism. Three aspects are considered: contacts between party members, participation in party meetings and the number of hours

Table 3 Activism among DS Members (percentage)

	'Old' members*	'New' members[†]
How frequently have you had contacts with other members in the past year?		
Never	10.6	7.5
Rarely (1 or 2 times)	23.1	17.9
Sometimes (3 to 5 times)	25.7	21.9
Often (6 to 12 times)	20.1	20.1
Very often (more than 13 times)	20.4	32.6
Total	100.0	100.0
(*N*)	(1,402)	(402)
How frequently have you attended party meetings in the past year?		
Never	31.6	26.6
Rarely (1 or 2 times)	28.1	18.9
Sometimes (3 to 5 times)	17.7	14.2
Often (6 to 12 times)	12.7	17.9
Very often (more than 13 times)	9.9	22.4
Total	100.0	100.0
(*N*)	(1,401)	(402)
How much time, on average, do you devote in a month to the party?		
None	51.8	41.7
Up to 5 hours	25.7	21.9
From 5 to 10 hours	10.0	12.6
From 11 to 15 hours	4.8	9.5
From 16 to 20 hours	2.4	3.3
More than 20 hours	5.4	11.1
Total	100.0	100.0
(*N*)	(1,339)	(398)

Source: Mulé (forthcoming).
* 'Old' members joined the DS before 1991.
[†] 'New' members joined after 1991.

devoted to party activities. Regarding the first aspect, 'new' party members have more frequent contacts (32.6 per cent) than 'old' party members (20.4 per cent). Another way of looking at party members' involvement is given in the second section of Table 3. The data show that 22.6 per cent of 'old' members participate 'often' or 'very often' in party meetings, while this percentage doubles for 'new' members (40.3 per cent). The number of hours party members devote to party activities offers a more precise measure of activism. The figures show a high degree of apathy among 'old' party members, with more than 50 per cent saying that they were never involved. These results support our previous findings that 'new' members exhibit a higher degree of activism. About 11 per cent devote more than 20 hours per month to the party, as opposed to 5.4 per cent of 'old' members.

In order to stimulate membership participation, party leaders have tried hard to strengthen the distribution of incentives. One important project, named 'Cantiere dell'innovazione del partito' (Mapping out the Party Renewal), is set out in the 2003

Party Report (DS 2004). The aim of the project is threefold. First, to increase participation by collecting detailed socio-economic data on party members; second, to improve 'knowledge and skills' by organizing seminars, debates and meetings on specific issues; third to intensify 'communication' between party leaders and followers by using new technologies (that is, the internet, text messages, satellite).

According to the 2005 statute (art. 29), party leaders take account of members' opinions through internal referenda. In practice, however, this instrument of direct democracy is never used. This should not be taken as a sign of neglect on the part of the leadership. For example, there are surveys administered by the national organization that are specifically designed to get the members' feedback. On a more regular basis, the preferred way for internal communication is holding local meetings.

As one might expect, advances in internal communication between leaders and followers have been helped by the spread of the internet. In 2000, the DS created their own website where interested citizens can gather information on the day-to-day life of the organization and learn about its internal structure and functioning. We should, however, note that progress in the use of the internet has been rather slow. While a number of parties now have websites that members can access with suitable credentials, this is not yet possible for DS members. Therefore, the party website is more a means of publicity, visibility and communication with the electorate, and less a means of consultation between leaders and members.

The Organization: The Emergence of a Factional Structure

One way of examining the organizational structure of the DS party is to look at its dominant coalition (Panebianco 1988). We analyse changes in both the cohesion and stability of the dominant coalition and changes in relations between the party and its flanking organizations. Stability of the dominant coalition reflects the leaders' capacity to reach long-term agreements, while cohesion points to the level of power concentration, indicated by the presence or absence of organized factions.

Usually, organizational instability and divisiveness are positively correlated, and the DS party is no exception to this rule. We have explored in detail above the emergence of factions and the corresponding difficulty of party leaders in reaching stable agreements on platforms and competitive strategies. As we shall see below, the party statute has recently formalized the process of factionalization, thus sanctioning the transformation of the DS from a strongly to a weakly institutionalized party. The central difference between these two types of party organization is the presence or absence of organized factions, that is, internal groups with strong and stable ties (Panebianco 1988).

Before proceeding, it should be noted that a party's statute is generally little more than a point of departure for the organizational analysis of a political party. However, we are not looking at the DS statutes to understand its internal power structure. Rather, we are examining how the emerging factional structure has been incorporated into the party's internal rules. As the theory of party organization indicates, formal rules are a vital resource of organizational power. Consequently, the control of formal rules allows certain actors to swing power games to their advantage. For this reason we believe that the importance of changes in party statutes should not be underestimated.

The main amendments to the DS party's statutes in the decade under scrutiny were introduced in 2000 and in 2005. At the congress held in Turin in 2000, a new statute was approved, introducing several important changes in the internal structure of the party. First, the party organization became more decentralized. The idea was to create a 'federal' party, with regional units (*unioni regionali*) as the basic organizational level. It should be noted that the organizational structure of the DS was already based on regional federations with their own statute. However, the federations had little or no political autonomy. The novelty introduced in 2000 lies in the fact that the regional units acquired decision-making independence from the centre. Second, this new statute gave party groupings the right to set their own rules and regulations. It recognized the formation of the *associazioni di tendenza* (factions of principle), which are organized factions open to members and non-members. These are national political associations with their own offices and networks. Hence, for the first time in the party's organizational history, the statute acknowledged the programmatic and organizational autonomy of party groupings. In this way the party seems to be ending the transition from the monolithic power structure of the PCI to a more pluralistic structure where the equilibrium of power is the outcome of a compromise between different factions.

Further modifications were introduced in 2005 with the creation of a new decision-making body, the national council. The national council (also called the national assembly) sets party policies based on the general programme established by the national congress. It elects the national executive, which makes the most important and strategic decisions. The chief reason for setting up the national council was to establish a deliberative body to act as a permanent link between the national executive and the national congress (which meets every three years). Prior to 2005, the national executive was a larger body, partly because it was the only committee connecting the leader with the party congress. The national congress defines the main programme of the party and ratifies the election of the party secretary (see next section).

The creation of new decision-making bodies and the setting up of political clubs give evidence of loosening internal ties. A parallel process of power dispersion developed between the party and its traditional flanking organizations. The most important flanking organizations of the old PCI were the trade union CGIL (Italian General Confederation of Labour), the cooperative movement (Lega delle Cooperative), the recreation and cultural association (ARCI), the Youth Federation now replaced by the Youth Left, and the women's organization. It has been well documented that after the birth of the PDS in 1991 relations between the party and its environment became looser, with a notable weakening of the traditional linkages (Pamini 1998).

Leadership Selection: The Changing Competitive Climate

The most important DS leader is the party secretary. The secretary defines the party programme; she/he is responsible for the party symbol, calls the national executive and approves the setting up of the 'factions of principle'. From 2000 onwards, the secretary is directly elected by party members, on the basis of the votes obtained in the local party congresses. As a matter of fact, party members cast a vote for a motion, which is signed by a prospective candidate. Delegates at the national congress, who are elected proportionally to the support gained by the motions, simply ratify party members' choices. In the past, it was the delegates who elected the party leader.

In 2000 the DS created the office of the party president, occupied by D'Alema as the then head of the Italian government. The reason for this position was related to internal party politics. D'Alema was a prominent DS leader who wished to retain influence in the party. Since 2001, the president has been elected by the delegates at the national congress, who cast a secret ballot. The president calls and chairs the national council. Hence, the formal mechanisms of leadership selection have changed significantly in the past decade. Even though the party secretary retains the main role, a dual leadership has been formalized. This has potentially important consequences for the cohesion of the dominant coalition. Table 4 summarizes the major changes in the party statutes and in the party leadership in the 1994–2005 period.

Another important point is that the process of factionalization has deeply affected the dynamics for the election of the party secretary, in terms of number of motions and candidates. From the mid-1990s leadership selection became increasingly more competitive. For example, in 1994 the contest for the leadership explicitly involved two candidates, Massimo D'Alema and Walter Veltroni. D'Alema was committed to a more traditional social democratic culture, while Veltroni advocated the opening of the party to outside groups. D'Alema defeated Veltroni with about 60 per cent of the vote. In 1997, despite the fact that only one motion was debated at the PDS congress, internal dissent was evident as reflected in several amendments proposed by the radical left faction and by the Veltroni faction. Eventually, D'Alema was re-elected

Table 4 PDS-DS: Changes In Name, Leadership and Party Statutes, 1994–2005

Year	Party leader	Change in statute			
1994	Massimo D'Alema				
1998		PDS changes name to DS			
2000	Walter Veltroni	Leader directly elected by party members	Party president	Regional units acquire more decision-making independence from the centre	Formation of political clubs (*associazioni di tendenza*)
2001	Piero Fassino				
2005		National Council			

secretary with 88 per cent of the delegates' vote. Moreover, at the Turin congress in 2000 two alternative motions were debated—the first endorsed by Veltroni, the second by the DS leftist faction. Veltroni was elected as party leader with 79.9 per cent of the delegates' vote.

The Pesaro congress, which was held because of the 2001 electoral defeat, provides further evidence of the changing competitive climate for leadership selection. For the first time in the party's history there were three official candidates for the leadership, each one endorsing a motion: Piero Fassino (majority component), Enrico Morando (liberal component) and Giovanni Berlinguer (radical left faction). Fassino was elected leader with 61.7 per cent of the vote ahead of Berlinguer and Morando (34.1 and 4.2 per cent, respectively). Finally, at the 2005 congress four motions were debated. Fassino was re-elected leader with 79.1 per cent of the members' vote. No other candidate was present, but left-wing candidates ran for congressional delegates.

To recapitulate, between 1994 and 2005, key elements of party organization have been modified. The trend in membership enrolment has been dramatically declining, although this might be offset by the intensity of participation of the new members. Moreover, the dominant coalition has become less cohesive and more divided, as manifested in the consolidation of organized factions. This new distribution of power brought about important changes in the party statutes, such as the creation of a diarchy at the top, and the loosening ties with traditional flanking organizations.

Political Competition: The Dilemma between Merging Strategy and Party Identity

In the post-1993 Italian political system, competitive strategies of political parties are strictly connected to coalition building. This is because the plurality component of the mixed electoral system lead to a coalition formation phase *before*, rather than *after*, the election. In essence, the pre-electoral stage and the coalition formation stage were inextricably intertwined. However, parties were competing on separate identities in the PR tier. Keeping in mind this duality, we now look at the main changes in the PDS-DS competitive strategy.

Starting with the pre-electoral coalition politics, the PDS contested the 1994 election as a member of the left-wing coalition named Progressisti (Alliance for Progress). This coalition included the PRC, the Greens, the anti-Mafia party called The Network, remnants of old centre parties and a new movement of moderate leftist forces, Alleanza Democratica (Democratic Alliance, AD). Given the disarray of the Christian Democrats and other traditional centre parties, the predominant mood was that of an unavoidable triumph of the left. The entry of Forza Italia (FI), a party formed just a few months before the elections, and its charismatic leader Silvio Berlusconi, changed the picture entirely. The elections resulted in a major transformation of the political scene, with FI becoming the first national party (see Raniolo, this volume).

After the fall of the centre-right government led by Berlusconi, in 1996 new elections were held. The 1996 elections saw significant changes in the PDS competitive strategy.

First of all, the party formed the Ulivo centre-left coalition. The coalition included the Partito Popolare Italiano (Italian Popular Party, PPI), which comprised the former Christian Democrats, the Greens and several other minor groups and local parties. Secondly, and most importantly, the PRC was no longer a member of the left-wing alliance as it had been in 1994.[9] What is more, coalition members agreed to a binding electoral platform and supported Romano Prodi as prospective prime minister. The new competitive strategy paid dividends in that the PDS finally became a governing party after the Ulivo won the election.

In the 2001 elections the DS competitive strategy aimed at consolidating the centre-left alliance. The Ulivo was now composed of the DS, the new centre-left group La Margherita, an aggregation of Greens and socialists labelled Il Girasole (The Sunflower), and the PdCI. In contrast to the 1996 national elections, the PRC did not strike any formal electoral deal with the Ulivo. In this way, the DS strategy signalled a further detachment from extreme left positions.

As far as the identity of the party *within* the coalition is concerned, two different views emerged. One view, strongly advocated by the former secretary D'Alema, saw the Ulivo as a mere electoral coalition between the PDS-DS and other centre forces. Such a view was in sharp contrast with the expectations of Prodi and Veltroni (deputy prime minister in the Prodi government), who conceived of the Ulivo as a first step in the process of merging the PDS-DS into a wider alliance, a unified Democratic Party. This dispute about strategic positioning remains unresolved. After the electoral debacle in 2001, D'Alema's strategy of shaping a party with a distinct left-wing identity waned and the current party leader Fassino tried to strike what seems to be a difficult compromise between supporters and opponents of what we can call 'the merging strategy'.

At present, it is hard to predict how the DS competitive strategy is likely to evolve. On October 16 2005 for the first time open primaries were held in order to choose the leader of the centre-left alliance in preparation for the 2006 national elections. Even more significant is the approval of new electoral rules on December 2005 by the current right-wing government introducing stronger elements of proportionality. These two developments will probably affect the evolution of the merging strategy between the DS and other centre-left forces.

Campaign Politics: Slowly Shedding Tradition

Between 1994 and 2005, political communication rapidly modernized in all Western democracies, involving a widespread use of mass media and information technology. For instance, survey research conducted by the Italian National Election Study on the impact of different media on voting behaviour suggests that TV programmes have increasingly become the chief source of political information. While in 1990 62.1 per cent of the respondents declared that TV was their main source of information, in 2001 this was true for about 77 per cent of Italian voters. The percentage of respondents declaring that their main sources of political information were traditional media, such as newspapers, dropped from 19.7 per cent in 1990 to 6.4 per cent in 2001. The internet is still the least popular way of accessing information: in 2001 only 0.1 per cent of respondents relied on it as their main source of information (Legnante 2002).

The evolution in political communication strategies gathered speed after the change in the electoral system and especially after the entry of the media tycoon Berlusconi into the domain of political competition in the mid-1990s. Berlusconi initiated innovations in election campaigning, stressing electoral marketing techniques and systematic recourse to outside specialists. Consequently, research on political communication and campaign politics in Italy has focused mostly on FI and its leader. Berlusconi's unexpected success in the 1994 elections deeply affected the subsequent campaign strategies of his competitors, including the DS.

In order to understand the impact of the new electoral communication techniques on the PDS-DS campaign, we should keep in mind that the organizational structure of the party has been based on the mass party model. This means that for decades the party successfully relied on rallies, door-to-door canvassing, party press (*L'Unità*) and local mobilization of the membership. Up to the early 1990s these traditional means of communication seemed adequately to address the PCI-PDS core constituency. However, they proved less powerful to compete for support in the new electoral and political scenario.

To analyse the most significant changes in campaign politics, we look at the following aspects: the organizational and technical features and the thematic development of the campaign (Farrell 2002). As far as organizational aspects are concerned, the authors of the electoral campaign are not just the party bureaucracies and activists as in the past. Nowadays there is a sort of 'permanent campaign' based on party departments devoted to preparing and designing the campaign. The party has in-house media and electoral marketing specialists who are responsible for the electoral campaign. In addition to this, the party sometimes employs campaign consultants and advertising agencies external to the party. Surveys are widely used to obtain feedback about the campaign. There are targeted campaign messages directed at specific categories of voters.[10]

From informal talks with DS party members and official documents (DS 2004) we gather that party leaders are planning to invest increasing resources in communication strategies. The aim is to improve the use of the party's website, the online newsletter and mobile phone messages as direct chains of communication. The party report provides evidence for the increasing intensity of the electoral campaign, pointing to the steady growth of the Feste de l'Unità, a kind of political festival organized once a year throughout the country. The number of such festivals rose from 2,200 in 2001 to about 3,000 in 2003, thus increasing by approximately 30 per cent in less than three years (DS 2004, p. 18). To give but one example of this trend at the local level, in 1999 the DS Bologna Federation organized 62 Feste de l'Unità over a total of about 700 days, while in 2005 there were 84 Feste over a total of 816 days.[11]

As far as the general electorate is concerned, the aim is to rely more on electoral marketing specialists. One reason is that the party wishes to 'adopt a type of communication characterized by a stronger emotional impact' (DS 2004, p. 19), primarily to try to counterbalance the fierce competition from the right-wing alliance in terms of financial resources.

More generally, it has been pointed out that Italian elections have become increasingly candidate-centred, with the leader being a major theme of the campaign and an important part of the party's political assets. This process is in line with international trends towards the presidentialization of the electoral campaign (Campus 2002). In Italy, however, in the light of the peculiarities of party competition mentioned above, the process of presidentialization has had greater impact on the image and role of coalition leaders than of party leaders.

Conclusions

Over the past decade, the DS has undergone a process of momentous change. This change was the outcome of a complex interplay between party evolution, on one hand, and the radical transformation of the party system and political institutions, on the other. Such a sweeping transformation brought about a dramatic decline in the party's vote share as well as changes in the party's values, organization and competitive strategy.

To understand the reasons for party change, our paper has focused on party politics and organizational development. As far as the first point is concerned, we argue that the dual structure of party competition affected party positioning and competitive strategies. Our results show a steady shift toward more moderate policy positions on the left–right dimension. Competitive and coalition-building strategies also reveal a move toward the centre of the political spectrum. In the last decade, the pattern of political alliances has created a dilemma between merging strategy and party identity. While at the level of competition within the party system the DS seems to be motivated by convergence towards the centre, embracing more moderate policies and joining a wider alliance, within the coalition the party seeks to retain its own image and programme.

In the process of transformation the DS has slowly moved away from the old class cleavage to new cleavages such as environmental issues and women's rights. What is more, in international policy the DS has progressively detached itself from the old ideological divide between Eastern and Western Europe, firmly accepting a pro-European point of view.

Between 1994 and 2005 there was also a turning point in the Italian political history when the major left-wing party abandoned its long-standing role of opposition party to become a government party in 1996. The sudden switch from opposition to government probably accelerated the DS's ideological shift towards the centre, pushing party leaders to change the party name for the second time in less than ten years.

Changes in the party identity and name were associated with a process of party factionalization. The main reason for greater dispersion of power within the party lies in the fact that the decision to radically reshape the party's identity in 1991 deeply divided the dominant coalition, offering new opportunities to minority groups. We have documented the emergence of the factional structure and its implications for leadership selection as well as for the cohesion and the stability of the dominant coalition.

Another important finding of our work is that 'new' party members, that is, those joining after the PRC split, are more active than 'old' party members. This may mean that while the number of party members is declining, the intensity of participation is increasing. The reason for this apparent change is worthy of further research.

All these ideological and organizational changes unfolded while the political system was adjusting from a multipolar to a bipolar structure, following modifications in the electoral rules and the entry of Forza Italia as a strong, innovative and successful political competitor. These events helped the DS leadership to craft a more ideologically flexible party.

Notes

[1] The effects of the new electoral law are extensively analysed in Bartolini and D'Alimonte (1995) and D'Alimonte and Bartolini (1997; 2002). Party responses to these political upheavals have been analysed in Bardi (2004) and Morlino (2001).

[2] The Ulivo coalition controlled 279 seats and needed the support of the 34 deputies of the PRC to reach a majority (315).

[3] A striking feature of Italian party politics since 1996 has been the fluidity of the legislative party system. See Verzichelli (1996), Giannetti and Laver (2001) and Heller and Mershon (2005) for an analysis of party switching at parliamentary level.

[4] I Democratici negotiated their participation in the second D'Alema government, obtaining four important portfolios.

[5] Party positions based on MRG data range from -2 (left) to $+2$ (right); see Laver (2001) for details.

[6] Motions and speeches were analysed using a computer-based content analysis technique developed by Laver, Benoit and Garry (2003). Scores range from -2 (left) to $+2$ (right). Reported estimates refer to speeches made at the Turin congress, but similar results hold for the Pesaro congress.

[7] The data derive from the Mannheim cumulative Eurobarometer trend file (1970–2002). Median estimates are used here, since they have the advantage of being less sensitive than the mean to the presence of extreme values.

[8] The data are based on a questionnaire mailed in May 2003 to 5,000 party members of the DS (about one per cent of the target population), with a response rate of 36 per cent. The survey used proportional stratification of a random sample of party members, based on the membership figures of provincial federations.

[9] Notwithstanding this separation, the Ulivo and the PRC reached an electoral agreement (called *desistenza*) to avoid contesting the same plurality seats. The PRC supported the Ulivo candidates except in two districts; the Ulivo supported PRC candidates in 27 single member districts for the election of the lower chamber and 17 for the election of the Senate.

[10] What follows is mainly based on personal communication with Luca Billi from the DS Bologna Federation.

[11] Data from the DS Bologna Federation.

References

Baccetti, C (1997) *Il Pds. Verso un nuovo modello di partito?*, Il Mulino, Bologna.

Bardi, L. (2004) 'Party responses to electoral dealignment in Italy', in *Political Parties and Electoral Change. Party Responses to Electoral Markets*, eds P. Mair, W. C. Müller & F. Plasser, Sage, London, pp. 111–144.

Bartolini, S. & D'Alimonte, R. (eds) (1995) *Maggioritario ma non troppo: le elezioni politiche del 1994*, Il Mulino, Bologna.

Bellucci, P., Maraffi, M. & Segatti, P. (2000) *PCI, PDS, DS. Le trasformazioni dell'identità politica della sinistra di governo*, Donzelli, Roma.

Budge, I., Klingemann, H., Volkens, A., Bara, J. & Tanenbaum, E. (2001) *Mapping Policy Preferences. Estimates for Parties, Electors and Governments 1945–1998*, Oxford University Press, Oxford.

Campus, D. (2002) 'Leaders, dreams and journeys: Italy's new political communication', *Journal of Modern Italian Studies*, vol. 7, no. 2, pp. 171–191.

D'Alimonte, R. & Bartolini, S. (eds) (1997) *Maggioritario per caso: le elezioni politiche del 1996*, Il Mulino, Bologna.

D'Alimonte, R. & Bartolini, S. (eds) (2002) *Maggioritario finalmente? La transizione elettorale 1994– 2001*, Il Mulino, Bologna.

Dalton, R. J. & Wattenberg, M. P. (eds) (2000) *Parties without Partisans: Political Change in Advanced Industrial Democracies*, Oxford University Press, Oxford.

DS (2004) 'Per un partito riformista: quattro progetti per il 2004. Comunicazione, anagrafe/tesseramento, formazione politica, risorse finanziarie', Area Comunicazione e Formazione Politica, < www.dsonline.it > .

Farrell, D. M. (2002) 'Campaign modernization and the West European party', in *Political Parties in the New Europe. Political and Analytical Challenges*, eds K. R. Luther & F. Müller-Rommel, Oxford University Press, Oxford, pp. 63–83.

Giannetti, D. & Laver, M. (2001) 'Party systems dynamics and the making and breaking of Italian governments', *Electoral Studies*, vol. 20, no. 4, pp. 529–553.

Giannetti, D. & Laver, M. (2004) 'Party factions and split roll call voting in the Italian DS', paper delivered at the Annual Meeting of the American Political Science Association, Chicago, 2–5 September.

Giannetti, D. & Sened, I. (2004) 'Party competition and coalition formation: Italy 1994–1996', *Journal of Theoretical Politics*, vol. 16, no. 4, pp. 483–515.

Harmel, R. & Janda, K. (1994) 'An integrated theory of party goals and party change', *Journal of Theoretical Politics*, vol. 6, no. 3, pp. 259–287.

Heller, W. B. & Mershon, C. (2005) 'Party switching in the Italian Chamber of Deputies, 1996–2001', *Journal of Politics*, vol. 67, no. 2, pp. 536–559.

Ignazi, P. & Katz, R. S. (eds) (1995) *Politica in Italia. I fatti dell'anno e le interpretazioni*, Il Mulino, Bologna.

Laver, M. (ed.) (2001) *Estimating the Policy Positions of Political Actors*, Routledge, London.

Laver, M. & Benoit, K. (2006) *Party Policy in Modern Democracies*, Routledge, London.

Laver, M. & Hunt, W. B. (1992) *Policy and Party Competition*, Routledge, New York.

Laver, M., Benoit, K. & Garry, J. (2003) 'Estimating the policy positions of political actors using words as data', *American Political Science Review*, vol. 97, no. 2, pp. 311–331.

Legnante, G. (2002) 'Tra influenza e incapsulamento. Cittadini, comunicazione e campagna elettorale', in *Le ragioni dell'elettore. Perché ha vinto il centro-destra nelle elezioni italiane del 2001*, eds M. Caciagli & P. Corbetta, Il Mulino, Bologna, pp. 233–273.

Mair, P. & Van Biezen, I. (2001) 'Party membership in twenty European democracies 1980–2000', *Party Politics*, vol. 7, no. 1, pp. 5–21.

May, J. (1973) 'Opinion structure of political parties: the special law of curvilinear disparity', *Political Studies*, vol. 21, no. 2, pp. 135–151.

Morlino, L. (2001) 'The three phases of Italian parties', in *Political Parties and Democracy*, eds L. Diamond & R. Gunther, Johns Hopkins University Press, Baltimore and London, pp. 109–142.

Mulé, R. (2001) *Political Parties, Games and Redistribution*, Cambridge University Press, Cambridge, England.

Mulé, R. (forthcoming) *Chi sono e cosa pensano gli iscritti ai DS*, Il Mulino, Bologna.

Occhetto, A. (1991) 'Per il partito democratico della sinistra', motion presented at the 20th PCI Congress, Rimini, 31 January–3 February.

Pamini, M. (1998) 'From militants to voters: from the PCI to the PDS', in *The Organization of Political Parties in Southern Europe*, eds P. Ignazi & C. Ysmal, Praeger, Westport, CT, pp. 134–156.

Panebianco, A. (1988) *Political Parties. Organization and Power*, Cambridge University Press, Cambridge, England.

Scarrow, S. (1996) *Parties and Their Members. Organizing for Victory in Britain and Germany*, Oxford University Press, Oxford.

Verzichelli, L. (1996) 'I gruppi parlamentari dopo il 1994. Fluidità e riaggregazioni', *Rivista Italiana di Scienza Politica*, vol. 22, no. 2, pp. 391–413.

From Opposition to Power: Greek Conservatism Reinvented

Takis S. Pappas & Elias Dinas

You will be safer in the middle. (Ovid, *Metamorphoses*, Book II, no. 137)

Introduction

Nea Democratia (New Democracy, ND) was founded by Konstantinos Karamanlis shortly after the transition of Greece to democracy in July 1974, and became the standard bearer of Greek liberal conservatism. Although the party drew on an old party lineage originating from the interwar years, Karamanlis tried to give it a modern image—and one untainted by past political struggles—so as to render it fitter for the new political conditions. In the first democratic elections in November 1974, with the majority of the population still excited by the unexpected change of regime, but also confident about the way Karamanlis was almost single-handedly managing the transition, ND received an impressive 54.3 per cent of the national vote. The party would remain in power for the next seven years, during which it completed the consolidation of democracy and the accession of the country into the European Community (January 1981). Meanwhile, in May 1980, Karamanlis was elected head of state, and his positions of prime minister and ND party leader were filled by Georgios

Rallis, a moderate liberal politician. Under Rallis, the electoral decline of ND, which had become evident in the 1977 elections, continued to the advantage of the rapidly ascending socialist PASOK (Panhellenic Socialist Movement), which eventually triumphed in the elections of 1981, thus relegating ND to the opposition.

From 1981 to 2004, apart from a brief, and rather dismal, spell of power in 1990–93, ND remained the chief opposition party in the newly established two-party system (on the consolidation of two-partyism in Greece since 1981, see Pappas 2003). With respect to ND's efforts to regain power, this long period can be effectively divided into two distinct phases: one from the electoral defeat of 1981 to that of 1996, during which the party was plagued by serious deficiencies (to be analysed in the following section), while PASOK enjoyed full political dominance; the second phase from 1996 to 2004, marked by the gradual recovery of ND and its eventual return to power. In effect, ND's story since the mid-1990s is that of a large and established party, long deemed in opposition, preparing for a comeback to power. To the comparison-minded reader, ND's successful return to power may recall the British Labour Party's success after the election of Tony Blair as its leader (Hindmoor 2004). On the other hand, and limiting our view to South European party politics, ND seems to present the opposite picture to Portugal's PSD, which, after losing office in 1995, remains unable to recover and show a credible promise of returning to power any time soon (see Jalali, this volume).

This work examines the major changes in the development of ND during the last ten years and asks what it took to regain power. In the course of the process, ND elected a new leader, developed an encapsulating competitive strategy, enhanced its organizational structure, and introduced novel campaign tactics. These changes are analysed in the following sections. Before that, however, we need to understand the reasons that had kept ND away from power for such a long time.

The Background: Three Obstacles on ND's Road to Power, 1981–96

After its grave electoral defeat in 1981, ND was to remain in opposition for the best part of two decades, apart from the interlude of 1989–93. During that period, and while PASOK was enjoying an exceptionally long term of office, ND suffered from three chronic deficiencies, which moreover seemed to be interconnected: a leadership deficit, its ideological drift away from the centre, and persisting organizational maladies.

From the time the charismatic Constantine Karamanlis departed from the party leadership until the mid-1990s, when his nephew, Kostas Karamanlis, rose to occupy this same post, the party had a succession of four leaders. Of these, none managed to keep the party together, to provide it with an unambiguous and appealing ideological profile, or, of course, to surpass in popularity PASOK's leader Andreas Papandreou. During this long period, ND was harmed by frequent internal dissension and splits, suffered ideological confusion, and lost many elections to a party that lacked a clear ideology or coherent programme but was led by a strong leader. Rallis's leadership was relatively brief and ended with the 1981 electoral defeat. Immediately after that, ND's parliamentary group elected Evangelos Averoff, an old party strongman and staunch right-winger, as the new party leader. He reinforced the party's organizational base but, in sharp contrast to his predecessors, also led ND to ultra-conservative positions. Embracing the far right and employing scaremongering as his key tactics in the political confrontation with PASOK, Averoff led the party into an ideological blind alley. ND lost the 1984 European Parliament elections, after which Averoff resigned from the party leadership and was promptly replaced by Constantine Mitsotakis, an arch-enemy of Papandreou from the pre-dictatorship years. Following PASOK's June 1989 election defeat, ND participated in the coalition governments of 1989–90. Then in 1990, Mitsotakis was finally able to lead ND to power with a very narrow parliamentary majority. Once in office, ND applied a programme of neo-liberal policies, which, however, failed in the face of widespread popular reaction and for lack of intra-party accord. In the 1993 elections, ND lost to the re-emergent PASOK and, once more, its leader was forced to resign. But the new leader, Miltiades Evert, also failed to rejuvenate the demoralized party by giving it a new programme and clear ideology. No wonder, then, that, although PASOK now had a new leader, following Andreas Papandreou's death, ND was not able to avoid another electoral defeat in 1996.

The second chronic deficiency of ND throughout the 1980s and early 1990s was its ideological drifting and, consequently, its inability to rid itself of the taint of being an ultra-conservative and non-progressive (even reactionary) party. When Karamanlis created ND, he tried to bring it closer to the political centre and dissociate it from its rightist pre-dictatorial past. Initially, his centrist strategy was successful. Just before the 1977 elections, utterly dissatisfied with ND's moderation and reformist policies, the nostalgic fringe of the extreme right split and formed its own party, Ethniki Parataxis (National Front, EP). In the elections, EP received 6.8 per cent of the total vote, most of it at the expense of ND. And yet, Karamanlis, far from trying to recapture the votes that had been lost to the far right, continued his centrist strategy even more determinedly. That strategy was frustrated by his successors (Pappas 2001, pp. 240–248). Shortly before the critical 1981 elections and faced with the prospect of defeat, Georgios Rallis, however reluctantly, decided to reabsorb the EP breakaways into ND. That move did not bring his party electoral victory. Still worse, it destroyed the centre-right image that Karamanlis had tried so hard to create and effectively alienated many liberal voters. Subsequently, the victorious PASOK came to dominate the centre (without toning down its fierce anti-right rhetoric), while ND drifted away from it. Besides, to the extent that the far right remained sheltered within ND and able to blackmail its leadership, PASOK found it easy to move into the centre where most of the electorate was to be found. Once again, for the average voter, ND was an unattractive right-wing party.

The third persistent deficiency of ND was related to its organizational form and functions. Founded by a charismatic leader and confronted by the increasingly massified socialist party, ND was faced from the beginning with two formidable tasks: to build an organization in which charisma would be 'routinized' and to allow it to function effectively in facing PASOK, its main political opponent. The first task was carried out in the 1970s by Karamanlis himself, who well understood that institutionalizing the party organization served both of his chief political aims—the consolidation of Greek democracy and the survival of the party he had founded (Pappas 1999). During that period, ND created a nationwide organization with regional and local branches, and party membership jumped from 20,000 in 1976 to 150,000 in 1979 (Loulis 1981, p. 72; New Democracy 1979). By the time Karamanlis departed from its leadership, ND had been transformed into a highly institutionalized and modern party. However, as form failed to match substance, ND's organization remained ineffective vis-à-vis PASOK. In the period that followed its 1981 electoral defeat, as if to verify Duverger's 'contagion from the left' hypothesis, ND built a formidable mass organization, which was preserved well into the 1990s. By 1994, membership had risen to 420,000 members (New Democracy 1994), which made ND the largest party among its European conservative counterparts (Kalyvas 1998, p. 99). Nonetheless, during the entire period ND remained torn by internal factionalism, which led twice to the creation of splinter parties, and lacked professionalization. The problem of intra-party factionalism figures conspicuously in many an academic account, personal memoir, and journalistic report from that period (for instance, Alexakis 1993; Loulis 1995; Seitanidis 1997; Bratakos 2002; Voultepsis 2005). Internal strife took place across ideological lines (moderates versus ultras), as well as among the main party subunits (that is, the party leader, the parliamentary group, and the rank and file) over the distribution of intra-party power (Pappas 1998). As a result, besides being unable to improve upon its effectiveness, by the mid-1990s ND had suffered two major splits that led to the creation of splinter parties.[1]

After suffering yet another electoral defeat in 1996, ND reinvented itself. Initially hesitantly, but progressively more resolutely, and always painstakingly, the party succeeded in the end in removing all three obstacles that, for two decades, had blocked its way to government. In early 2004, ND won the national elections and came to power. Meanwhile it had undergone a change of leadership, developed a new, winning strategy, redesigned its organizational structure, and applied novel electoral tactics. These changes are analysed in the sections that follow.

New Leadership

After its electoral defeat in 1996, ND was a party 'on the verge of decomposition' (Loulis 2001, p. 207). Just one day after the election, former party leader Georgios Rallis publicly admitted that the unity of ND had long been 'artificial', and expressed fears about its future (cited in Bratakos 2002, p. 686). For months thereafter, the party presented a deplorable picture. As a prominent cadre described the situation, 'Today, the various factions and groups within ND, encouraged by personal ambitions. . . the incompetence of most party cadres, the selfish pursuits of part of the leader's entourage, and the lack of steady ideological direction, are not far from a real break into at least two camps: one liberal, and the other conservative (traditional right)' (Christidis 1997, p. 51). Such fears of an eventual break-up were widespread in ND; some even counted on its occurrence (Macridis 1996).

The 1996 electoral defeat, and its aftermath, was the cumulative outcome of three causes, two internal to the party, and one external to it. First of all, party leader Miltiades Evert had been unable to contain intra-party factionalism, which, during his leadership, was both extensive and intense (for detailed documentation of internal party rifts during this period, see especially Bratakos 2002, pp. 605–683). In such a climate of endemic internal disputes, it is not surprising that Evert was not able to pursue significant organizational reforms. A new party charter, adopted at the third party congress in 1994, included only minor innovations, the most notable of which was the expansion of the participation of the party's grassroots in decision-making procedures (New Democracy 1994). The second reason for electoral defeat was that ND failed to reverse the negative public image it had acquired during its last government during 1990–93. Its abortive attempt to apply an enormously unpopular neo-liberal agenda had long-lasting effects that were to haunt ND for many years to come. Thirdly, ND's major opponent, PASOK, had displayed remarkable durability, as well as adaptability in the changing conditions. When Andreas Papandreou resigned due to ill health in 1996, he was succeeded as party leader by Kostas Simitis, an uncharismatic personality but well known for both his reformist agenda and technocratic style of management. Taking full advantage of ND's chronic deficiencies, he promptly broke away from PASOK's most populist aspects, and steered it decisively towards the moderate centre. At the same time, ND found it harder than ever to rid itself of its unappealing right-wing image.

Such were the circumstances when ND, at its fourth party congress in early 1997, elected a new leader, Kostas Karamanlis. At election time, Karamanlis was young (in his forties) and inexperienced (never having held any ministerial post); on the other hand, he was not personally burdened by the negative aspects of his party's past. The new leader, to be sure, did not metamorphose ND right away. As a political analyst (and Karamanlis's chief consultant) would bluntly put it as late as 1999, the ND party was still 'a faded product. . . that had been tested during the past 20 years and was basically rejected in most cases' (Loulis 2001, pp. 341, 370). As it would turn out, however, despite several partial failures, turnarounds, and delays, the new leader would succeed where his four predecessors had failed, that is, in unifying the party and giving it a new image, applying a winning strategy, and, eventually, leading it to power.

Once in the party leadership, Karamanlis was faced with two pressing tasks: invigorating the party mechanism and unifying the internal party factions. Towards the first aim, he established a 'shadow government' consisting of ND parliamentary cadres, each charged with the monitoring of a particular area of current governmental activity. In the long run, this initiative helped create a number of experienced party cadres who, moreover, by continuous media exposure of PASOK's faults and shortcomings in the areas of their particular responsibility, both communicated the ND's positions to the mass public and helped improve its image. The task of enforcing party discipline was more difficult. Yet, unlike his predecessors, Karamanlis, early in his leadership, did not hesitate to expel from the party several prominent cadres— among them Stefanos Manos, an outspoken advocate of neo-liberalism, and Georgios Souflias, the defeated contender in the recent party leadership contest. From then on, Karamanlis would remain virtually unchallenged in the party leadership, and factionalism would subside considerably.[2]

The next step for Karamanlis was to apply strong opposition to the government, as well as to overcome the negative image of his party as being right-wing and socially insensitive. To this end, contrary to his predecessors, who had either turned the party to the right or, perhaps more harmfully, led it to ideological confusion, he chose to apply a centrist strategy (of which more in the next section), thus confronting Simitis's PASOK on ground where the latter appeared stronger. Karamanlis's new strategy soon produced results. After a very good performance in the local government elections of 1998, ND also won the 1999 European Parliament elections. The latter was the party's first electoral victory in the entire decade. Next came the national elections of 2000. In a bitterly fought contest, ND lost to PASOK for a third consecutive time by a margin of only 70,000 votes. Despite the defeat, however, the election was a personal vindication for Karamanlis and his centrist strategy—which he would carry on basically unaltered until the next electoral contest.

Shortly after the 2000 elections, Karamanlis called an extraordinary party congress with the purpose of absorbing tensions and preventing disputes within ND, as well as to confirm the continuation of his electoral strategy. Only one year later, with PASOK already losing much of its popularity, ND convened its fifth regular congress. This would have remained a rather unexciting event had it not been marked by Karamanlis's public invitation to G. Souflias to return to the party. The latter's acceptance was well received by the party base and, moreover, added valuable experience to the ND power team and reinforced the party's centrist image. As the elections of 2004 approached, Karamanlis's popularity had risen higher than that of the PASOK's leader. Interestingly enough, Karamanlis now gave the impression of being a more sensitive and human leader than socialist Simitis. As indicated by repeated public opinion surveys, when questioned about their degree of trust in the leaders' ability to tackle social problems, the electorate preferred Karamanlis to Simitis by a large margin (*MRB Trends*, various years).

In early January 2004, less than three months prior to the scheduled election, Simitis decided to resign as party leader in favour of Georgios Papandreou, son of Andreas. By that time, however, it was already too late for the new leader to turn around the result of the contest. Papandreou sent ambiguous ideological messages, ran a badly organized campaign, and seemed unable to control PASOK's strongmen. Perhaps worse, Papandreou, a poor orator, also performed rather badly in the pre-election televised debate (Dinas 2005).

New Centripetal Strategy, New Political Programme

In the mid-1990s, Greek politics appeared to enter a new era. In contrast to the high politicization and deep polarization that had marked the previous decades, society now seemed to take a step away from active politics, and to clamour for stability and governmental efficiency. More specifically, one could identify five major changes in Greek public opinion around that time (Loulis 2001, pp. 57–59): (a) a marked decline of statism, most notably in the belief that economic growth should not be left entirely to the state; (b) the ascendancy of political pragmatism over the radicalism and ideologization that had prevailed in the past; (c) the growth of the centre vote and the dramatic reduction in voters placing themselves on the left; (d) widespread disillusionment with politics, which resulted in the tendency of the electorate to vote, not for the 'best' party, but for the 'least bad'; and (e) high vote volatility, which severed past electoral alliances and caused significant shifts in political allegiances from one election to the next.

The foregoing changes caused the transformation of both the electorate's make-up and the dynamics of party competition. Unlike previous decades, when the electorate appeared to be almost uniformly dispersed along the left–right ideological continuum, and strongly anchored in their respective positions, by the mid-1990s a new picture had emerged. The voters placing themselves on the centre (and the right) increased precipitously, while at the same time those on the left decreased. The percentage of the voters who, either out of indifference or political agnosticism, declined self-placement also grew (see Figure 1). Remarkable as these changes may be, there is a further facet to them: in contrast to the centre voters of previous decades, who were ideology sensitive, highly politicized, and mostly in favour of the state, the new ones (like the non-committed floating voters) were pragmatists with no

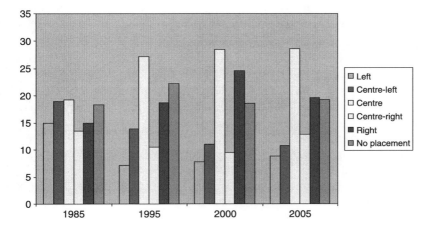

Figure 1 Voters' Political Self-Placement *Source:* MRB, *Trends*, various years.

ideological baggage and very little trust in the state. No wonder, then, that most of them accepted as true the statement that 'the notions of right, left, and centre are by now meaningless' (Loulis 2001, p. 86).

Soon after his rise to the party leadership, in line with the suggestions of his close team of advisors, Karamanlis decided to follow a consistent centripetal strategy for capturing the middle ground. Far from committing the party to a particular set of ideological principles, this strategy emphasized political moderation, pragmatism, and social sensitivity. According to Karamanlis himself, choosing his words carefully, the new strategy was meant to

> express ND's opening to the entire society [and] underline our wish to fight for enhancing the quality of democracy... *[The strategy] anything but introduces some new kind of political geography, or signifies specific ideological direction.* It rejects [political] entrenchments, divisions, and discriminations. It wards off fanaticism, dogmatism, and yesterday's rigidities. It expresses our vision for a society of solidarity and compassion, [ready to] apply policies for all the citizens. The standards of political behaviour it sets are moderation, prudence, seriousness, [political] morality, respect for all the citizens, as well as our political opponents. Our basic principles are cooperation, the blending of opinions and ideas, the advancement of national unity and cohesion. (Karamanlis 2000, emphasis added)

The new centripetal strategy was not lost in easy verbiage; moreover it included specific changes in ND's political programme. Up to the mid-1990s, the party programme had remained essentially unaltered, revolving around three broad themes: political sovereignty, national traditions, and social cohesion (Konstantinidis 2004). Since then, and especially under the leadership of Karamanlis, ND has been able to renew its programmatic appeal so as to attract the voters in the middle. The new political programme focused on a number of important non-ideological issues (such as education, health, social order and state efficiency, culture, and the environment), as well as on problems related to the management of the state and the economy (bad administration and state inefficiency, tax evasion, corruption, etc.). In parallel, ND adopted ideas and policies traditionally identified with the social-democratic left, such as the improvement of social security schemes.

The new strategy was not accepted without internal party protests (Makris 2001, p. 97). To some in the party's youth organization, for instance, it appeared 'an unjustified acceptance of the most commonplace and easy to digest ideas in society... [that] dispenses with the essence of politics and weakens the internal party tissue'; others feared that the middle-ground strategy 'causes confusion in relation to the ideological profile of the party' (Bratakos 2002, pp. 880–881). By that time, however, Karamanlis and his team of advisors had charted a clear course to lead the party to the middle. The return of the moderate Souflias to ND in early 2001 almost coincided with Karamanlis's personal decision to expel from the party a high-profile deputy who had often advocated extreme-right ideas. The latter promptly created a new ultra-conservative party, the so-called Laikos Orthodoxos Synagermos (Popular Orthodox Rally, LAOS), thus effectively clearing ND of any formal associations with the far right.

Not much later, ND also became dissociated from neo-liberalism when the latter's two most vocal advocates, S. Manos and A. Andrianopoulos, decided to abandon the party. Shortly before the 2004 elections, and to the general electorate's surprise, both politicians were recruited by Georgios Papandreou and given prominent positions in his party's electoral lists. Meanwhile, ND, now rid of both its extreme right and neo-liberal elements, could credibly claim to represent the 'middle ground'.

Changes in Party Organization

To repeat a truism, political parties, far from being unitary actors, consist of subunits constantly struggling between them for power (Sartori 1976; Katz & Mair 1992). In a previous study of ND's first two decades of organizational development, one of the present authors (Pappas 1998) identified three such subunits (the party leader, the parliamentary party, and the party's rank and file), and attempted to explain their intra-party dynamics through consecutive phases of party development. In this work, we propose to follow up that earlier study with a particular eye to innovations, discontinuities, and organizational reversals. Most notably, besides the three traditional party subunits, we have now added a fourth—professional party cadres.

Table 1 ND Party Subunits and the Distribution of Intra-party Power

	1993–97	1997–2000	2000–05
a. Party leader			
Mass popularity	1	2	3
Domination over parliamentary group	1	2	3
Control of formal party organization	1	2	3
General assessment	**3**	**6**	**9**
b. Parliamentary group			
Free scope for nomination in party ticket	1	1	1
Influence in leader's election	3	2	1
Potential for factional autonomy	3	2	1
General assessment	**7**	**5**	**3**
c. Mass organization			
Numerical strength	3	2	2
Influence in party decision-making	1	2	2
Importance in party competition	3	2	1
General assessment	**7**	**6**	**5**
d. Professional cadres			
Involvement in party's strategy	1	2	3
Active role of experts' thinktanks	1	2	3
Participation in party organs	1	2	3
General assessment	**3**	**6**	**9**

Note: All numbers have cardinal meaning and show the relative performance of the party subunits in the periods indicated. 1: no/to no extent; 2: yes/to some extent; 3: yes/to a great extent.

Furthermore, to assess relative intra-party strength, or feebleness, we identify for each of the four party subunits a set of criteria, or indicators, both quantitative and qualitative. Those appear in condensed form in Table 1 and in the text are analysed in more detail.

Party leadership, first, is evaluated on the basis of the following criteria: the leader's mass popularity, his degree of domination over the party's sitting deputies, and control over the party organs. Despite a rather auspicious beginning, Evert's popularity never reached high levels. While the media relentlessly presented him as 'an ignorant and inadequate contender for power' (quoted in Bratakos 2002, p. 681), the electorate found his leadership style uninspiring and rather dull. Even supposing that such an unfavourable perception was due to the fact that, in the earlier part of his leadership, Evert had to confront the charismatic Andreas Papandreou, things hardly improved after the latter's death. Evert's popularity remained markedly below that of PASOK's new leader, and worsened further after their televised debate just before the 1996 elections. More than his personal image, however, low popularity and bad press publicity damaged Evert's status within his party. As has been abundantly documented, during his leadership internal disputes and factionalism became endemic in ND. And, unsurprisingly, his inability, or reluctance, to face these problems led to several cases of indiscipline and frequent challenges to his rule. This picture changed dramatically under the leadership of Kostas Karamanlis. The latter not only maintained respectable levels of personal popularity among the electorate, but also shortly after the elections of 2000 surpassed PASOK's leader in popularity, and stayed ahead until Simitis's resignation from the leadership. In addition, unlike his predecessor, Karamanlis remained largely unmolested by his potential intra-party opponents thanks to a mixture of penalties (the expulsions early in his leadership) and new regulations. Most notable were the decision of the 1997 congress to increase the proportion of deputies required to challenge the party leader from one-third to 50 per cent of their total number, and the suspension of the past ND leaders' prerogative to participate ex officio in the highest party organs. Finally, Karamanlis also succeeded in gradually controlling the vast majority of the party grassroots and, therefore, the party congress decisions. At the sixth ND congress that was convened right after the elections of 2004, it was estimated that Karamanlis influenced no less than 85 per cent of the members of the party's central committee (Zoulas 2004).[3] This organ then promptly elected as party secretary-general the person suggested by the party leader, who, not unpredictably, was the only candidate.

To assess the relative intra-party position of ND's parliamentary group, we employ the following variables: independence from the leader for nomination in the party ticket, degree of influence in the election of the leader, and potential for factual autonomy. Of these variables, the first has remained constant throughout the period under examination, since the party leader is fully responsible for candidate nominations. The other two variables have changed considerably, to the detriment of the parliamentary party. This is evident in the diminishing influence of ND's sitting deputies in electing the party leader. In 1993, Evert was elected by a closed electoral body totalling just 183 members, in which the parliamentary majority outnumbered the representatives of the party base by a 2:1 ratio. By contrast, in 1997, Karamanlis was elected by a broadened party congress, in which the party deputies were but a minority. As in 2004 the congress membership increased even further, the capability of the party deputies to control future leader-election procedures seemed to be further undermined. Finally, in terms of internal factionalism, the contrast between the mid-1990s, when Evert was at the party helm, and the post-1997 period could not be sharper. During Evert's leadership, one could identify within ND two broad factions, or camps, with personal, ideological, and strategic differences: one revolving around Evert himself (and projecting an old-fashioned conservative ideology with heavy reliance on the state), the other around Mitsotakis (advocating a mostly neo-liberal agenda). When Karamanlis came to party power, and after the initial wave of expulsions, factionalism subsided significantly and party unity was established.[4] Besides that, as shown in Table 2, in both elections ND fought under the leadership of Karamanlis, the party ballot lists were filled with a new generation of parliamentarians who were younger and, often, recruited from non-political areas (such as the private sector, academia, etc.); the proportion of women was also increased.

The evaluation of the internal dynamics of ND's mass organization is made on the basis of three criteria: numerical strength, degree of influence in party decision-making processes, and the significance of the mass organization in party competition. Of these, numerical strength is the hardest to assess. From the scarce and, perhaps, not wholly reliable data available, we learn that in 1996 ND had 383,428 members distributed across 3,500 local branches (*To Vema*, 24 March), while in 2005 the party membership stood at 350,000 (authors' interviews with party officials). Although there is no information about fluctuations during that decade, it seems that until 2004 membership declined slightly. After that, however, and rather paradoxically for a party in office, it levelled off again and, today, even seems to be on the rise. What has undoubtedly been enhanced since the 1997 change of leadership is the influence of the mass organization in party decision-making processes. First of all, the convention of party congresses at regular intervals became institutionalized—and congresses did really take place.[5] During the same period, the number of participants at consecutive party congresses rocketed from 1,286 at the third ND congress (1994) to 3,604 at the

Table 2 Key Characteristics of ND's Parliamentary Party since 1996 (percentages)

	1996	2000	2004
< 40[*]	11.8	16.0	16.8
41–55[†]	56.9	51.3	52.7
56 >[†]	31.3	32.7	30.5
Political newcomers	19.0	31.0	37.0
Women deputies	5.6	8.0	11.5

Sources: [*]*Eleftheros Typos*, special edition, 1996; [†]*Eleftherotypia*, special editions, 2000, 2004.

fourth and fifth congresses (1997 and 2001) to no less than 4,500 at the last party congress (2004). At an equally substantial level, in 1997 the party congress was granted the right (up till then an exclusive prerogative of the parliamentary party) to challenge the party leader once an issue had been raised by one-third of its participants. Furthermore, and despite the persistence of strong centralism in ND organization, local party branches have been given a clear voice in the party decision-making processes.[6] And yet, despite its impressive numerical potency and upgraded role in vital functions of the party life, ND's mass organization played an increasingly diminished role in party competition. As a consequence of fast-growing professionalization (of which more below), mass organization seemed a rather redundant and inflexible means for winning electoral battles. To that end, party modernization was much preferred to mass mobilization.

Here enters the fourth party subunit, the professional cadres, by which we simply mean party officials of a new type, most often appointed directly by the leader, who participate in the party's higher ranks by virtue of their specific professional qualities rather than their ideology, party membership, or other political affiliation. Of course, such professionals (campaign consultants, spin-doctors, opinion pollsters, communication experts, etc.) have never been absent from ND, especially during election periods. In fact, the third party congress institutionalized a large number of new bodies ranging from the Constantine Karamanlis Institute of Democracy, to an office for 'party documentation', to a department responsible for providing research assistance to party deputies preparing for parliamentary debate. Even when those organs and offices did not remain empty shells, as was usually the case, they became staffed by traditional, and often retired, party cadres looking for a role in a decaying party. As is shown in the following section, a growing body of professional cadres acquired a key role in internal party life after the 1997 change in the party leadership. Since then, either individually or through the various thinktanks they created, but always in cooperation with the new party leader, they became fully responsible in charting the party strategy, in the process colonizing several party organs.

To sum up and conclude this section, a number of observations can be made with relation to the intense intra-party developments that took place in the course of the last decade. First, the leader amassed significant power to control the party and, essentially unchallenged, to steer it in his preferred direction. A similar trend is evident in relation to the professional party cadres who, progressively, turned into a really powerful unit. As they provide the leader with expertise and advice in turn for tenure in ND's higher ranks, there seems to have developed within the party a stable alliance between the two most powerful party subunits. In contrast, the relative power of the parliamentary party, once a real powerhouse within ND, has been significantly reduced, and today appears to be the weakest of the party components. Mass organization, on the other hand, however weakened overall, still retains a good deal of its formal authority—which, to a large extent, also lends credibility to the party's claim to internal democracy. This said, to the extent that organizational fine-tuning was considered to be a key factor for electoral success, emphasis was put more on matters of efficiency than on improving intra-party democracy. In a changing political environment, where traditional grassroots mobilization was replaced by centrally organized and media-centred campaigns, ND had to become a professional party.

Upgrading the Party's Public Image

In Greece, as in many other countries, electoral campaigning has traditionally taken three main forms: charismatic appeal, when some charismatic leader exists; barnstorming, complete with its customary clientelist trappings; and mass mobilization, via organized rallies, media propaganda, or local canvassing. Although all three forms are still present, none can adequately capture the workings of ND's contemporary campaigning. The current party leader may be strong and popular, but certainly is not charismatic; barnstorming by promise-delivering deputies ceases to be effective when promises are repeatedly not kept; at the same time, in a society of growing depoliticization and apathy, mass mobilization is becoming costly, and even counterproductive. Faced with new challenges in a changing political environment, ND was forced to change its campaign politics. As this section will attempt to show, that change included nothing less than a thorough modernization of the party and, especially, the professionalization of the party cadres. More particularly, in what follows we ask: Who are responsible for planning ND's campaigns? How are electoral campaigns waged? How is the issue agenda set and why?

Political consultants, communication specialists, and electoral strategists have played important roles in the ND campaigns at least since the mid-1980s. In all six elections conducted between 1985 and 1996, ND electoral campaigns were coordinated mostly by foreign advertising companies (among them Soyer and Communication Company), electoral strategists (such as Clinton's former consultant John Carbel), and survey analysts (Kennan Research). Typically, these were recruited ad hoc shortly before election time and, during the campaign, collaborated directly with the party leader, bypassing the permanent party organization. Things changed under Karamanlis's leadership. Not long after he came to the helm, he created a small, in-house team of communication experts and political analysts to whom he entrusted the planning of ND's future strategy. It was this team that, besides elaborating ND's centripetal strategy, also became responsible for running the party's electoral campaigns in both 2000 and 2004. Throughout, this team collaborated with other liberal thinktanks, publicized its opinions in the daily press, conducted its own surveys, and produced a plethora of party propaganda material. Of key importance for working out, and applying, the new strategy was the Constantine Karamanlis Institute of Democracy, a thinktank established by ND in 1998 and thereafter serving as generator of policy ideas and strategic plans, as well as a multitude of publications mostly related to current political developments. ND was, in fact, the first Greek party to include such a thinktank among its organs in response to the changing needs of party modernization and general political competition.

The contrast with the past could not be sharper. Whereas electoral campaigns were previously seen as last-ditch efforts to enhance an already tarnished party image, now they simply became the peak points of a continuous strategy designed both carefully and a long time ago. Today, with ND in government, the core of the same team is still in place, and coordinates the party strategy with a view to the next elections, and beyond. As emerges from the newest output of party materials (Loulis 2004, p. 329; Karachalios 2004; Dimitrakos 2005), the target for the near future is already set and includes ND's credible transformation into a centre party and its consolidation on the ideological centre-right. This already foretells the chief themes of ND's next electoral campaign.

With regard to the means of political communication, ND's most recent campaigns have changed significantly from the past. The erstwhile low-technology, ideology-sensitive, mass-oriented campaigns have been substituted by technology-intensive, issue-focused, and specific-audience-targeted ones. As expected, television plays an ever greater role (Chondroleou 2004). In contrast to campaigning based on public mass rallies, where success depends on crowd size and enthusiasm, TV-centred campaigning serves those parties trying to project their leader's personality, complex political issues, and specific policy preferences (Yannas 2002). Under Karamanlis's leadership, ND, already a more confident party with a clear strategy, able leader, and specific programme, looked for novel means of political communication. In 2000, instead of the traditional party rally in Athens, ND organized a concert in the Olympic stadium. In the elections of 2004, the party reverted to the logic of (relatively fewer) mass rallies, but also launched a series of speeches by the party leader to specifically targeted electoral groups (women, young people, farmers, middle-class businessmen), in which emphasis was given to political dialogue and interpersonal communication. In addition, abundant use was made of electronic and visual media in campaigning. Already in the 1999 European Parliament elections, ND had introduced a three-digit telephone number providing information about the elections. It had also launched a series of television spots (featuring mostly negative political advertising—a tactic abandoned in subsequent elections). Moreover, as televised debates between party leaders had become a key component of electoral campaigning since 1996 (Papathanassopoulos 2000, p. 54), ND campaign strategists paid great attention to them. Finally, ND began utilizing the internet around the 2000 elections. On the official party webpage one can find speeches by the party leader and other top party officials, the party programme and its organizational structure, and numerous policy reports. Somewhat more unusually, there are also to be found several self-congratulatory analyses about PASOK's recent electoral defeats, complete with suggestions for that party's modernization in the future.

Turning now to the issue of agenda setting for electoral campaigning during the last decade, several changes are visible. The centripetal movement that was decided early in Karamanlis's leadership put an end to both the party's rightward drifting and strategic prevarications (such as Evert's unfortunate decision on the eve of the 1996 election to cancel the mass rally in Athens so as to avoid the stain of populism). When Karamanlis entered the electoral arena as ND's leader in 1999, two things became clear: firstly, that his party was set to follow a firm strategy consistent with its new ideological orientation and, secondly, that this strategy was targeting real people (burdened by real problems, fears, and expectations) rather than ideology-minded voters (supposedly divided between left and right). To this end, the ND campaign concentrated heavily on issues related to people's everyday lives, such as education, health, unemployment, and criminality. It is worth emphasizing that the choice and prioritization of issues were not accidental; each and every one of them was picked after careful examination of public opinion surveys—a practice ND still employs to this day. Encouraged by its success in the 1999 European Parliament elections, ND went to the 2000 general elections with a similar issue agenda. This time, of course, ND made an extra effort to present itself as a middle party. To succeed, it needed to appear politically moderate (in the face of PASOK's polarizing tactics) and a socially sensitive force (hitherto a monopoly of the parties on the left). Its marginal electoral defeat notwithstanding, ND succeeded on both fronts thanks to its leader, who, following his team's advice, waged a successful 'middle-of-the-road' campaign to the effect that, in the end, he imposed himself on the party rather than the party imposing itself on the leader (Loulis 2004, p. 322).

In the aftermath of the 2000 elections, it was evident that PASOK was losing steam fast, while ND was in the ascendancy. Only a few months into the new government's life, opinion polls showed ND to have overtaken PASOK; since then, it never lost its electoral advantage. Within the confines of an almost perfect two-party system, ND, having established a clear hegemony in the centre-right political space, was now in a position to plunder PASOK's vote. As the elections of 2004 approached, and the distance between the two parties constantly increased, PASOK seemed doomed to electoral defeat.

As in previous elections, ND focused its 2004 campaign on burning social issues and stressed the social fatigue from PASOK's long rule. This time, however, ND carefully avoided any negative advertisement about its opponent and focused on criticizing the government on very specific issues. Karamanlis not only refrained from engaging in personal disputes, but also did not hesitate to praise the personal qualities of his opponent (Georgios Papandreou, newly elevated to the PASOK leadership). With the fortunes of the two party opponents so dramatically reversed, ND won an impressive victory of almost seven per cent over PASOK, and returned to power after 11 long years.

In Conclusion: ND in Government and Beyond

Three months after its victory in the 2004 national contest, ND went on to win the European Parliament elections by a landslide. Only one month later, in July, the party convened its sixth party congress. The difference between this congress and the one that had followed ND's electoral defeat in 1996 could not be greater. Whereas the former had been seen as 'the congress of a fearful and insecure party' (Loulis 2001, p. 207) that was simply trying to muddle through without serious losses, the more recent congress was a rather self-flattering event, full of enthusiasm and optimism.

It also confirmed Karamanlis's unchallenged leadership of the party. ND had not only won two consecutive elections by large margins; even more substantially, in a relatively short time, this party had also overcome the chronic deficiencies that had plagued it for almost two decades—the leadership deficit, an unappealing right-wing image, and ineffective organization. Already in government, ND seemed to be an ideologically re-branded party, led by a strong leader, and professionally organized. At present, all signs point to the party's determination to take advantage of its newly acquired characteristics.

ND's persistent centripetalism, primarily, as well as its insistence on depolarizing the political struggle, has helped it break away from the negative connotations of the traditional right, and reposition itself in the political centre. Considering its success, ND's centripetal strategy is certain to remain unaltered in the near future. To this end, ND is bound to continue its 'middle-of-the-road' electoral tactics, and also to exploit the creation of the ultra-conservative LAOS at the far end of the political spectrum. An early indication of centripetalism was given shortly after ND's ascent to power, when Karamanlis nominated Carolos Papoulias, a founding member and prominent minister in successive PASOK governments, for the position of president of the Greek Republic. As the ideological and programmatic differences between the two major parties become increasingly blurred (Featherstone 2005, p. 223; Lyrintzis 2005, p. 254), ND is at present better suited to capture the middle vote than the twice defeated, organizationally weakened, and ideologically bemused PASOK.

Strong leadership is the second feature of contemporary ND. The clear winner of two electoral contests, Karamanlis is today the undisputed leader of the party. Once in office, he made a determined effort to keep the party's old 'barons' out of ministerial positions, most of which he assigned to a relatively new and younger generation of cadres. What kind of leadership is Karamanlis most likely to exercise? Greek politics, to be sure, has in the past been a favourable terrain for the emergence of both charismatic leaders (Pappas 2002) and parties depending on a single personality (Clogg 1987). Neither of these fits current realities, however, as Karamanlis cannot be said to be charismatic, nor is ND bound to decay after its leader is past and gone. Of course, as in many other places (Kaase 1994; Wilke & Reinemann 2001; King 2002; Street 2003), there is in ND a certain degree of personalism, which becomes particularly evident in the presidentialization of the electoral campaigns (Mughan 2000). It seems to us, however, that contemporary ND fits the type of 'non-charismatic personalist party' in which, according to Ansell and Fish (1999, p. 284) the leader 'represents the party itself. At the same time, however, as in the case of charismatic leadership but in contrast with rational–legal authority, the basis for the leader's legitimacy is personal.'

The creation of a permanent professional organization that both is controlled by and aims to aid the leader is the third ubiquitous feature of today's ND. Unlike in the past, the party organization has not atrophied since ND came to office. Instead, in addition to some increase in membership, it also shows signs of both independence from the government and growing professionalization. Indeed, ND is said to be a professional party in Panebianco's (1988, p. 264) sense. Besides being highly personalized, it attributes a central role to career-oriented professional cadres, and emphasizes vertical rather than horizontal ties. In addition, both during and between elections, ND adheres to the image of a pragmatic party focusing on very specific (non-ideological) issues. A crucial issue will be whether ND will eventually give in to the accumulated clientelist demands of its organized base. Clientelism, of course, is an entrenched characteristic of Greek society (Sotiropoulos 1993), but, given the tightness of budgets and the controls imposed by the European Union, any government now employs such traditional practices at its own peril.

Notes

[1] The first split occurred in 1985, when Kostis Stefanopoulos, a prominent conservative figure and recent contender for the ND leadership, left ND to create a new reformist party called Dimokratiki Ananeossi (Democratic Renewal). The second split happened in 1993 and was the responsibility of the then foreign affairs minister Antonis Samaras. After leaving ND, he created a new party, the so-called Politiki Anoixi (Political Spring). Neither of the foregoing parties was able to survive in the long run, yet they both caused ND considerable electoral damage and, in the case of Political Spring, the downfall of the ND government in 1993 after it lost its slim majority in parliament.

[2] A split from ND occurred in 2001, when prominent cadre and successful mayor of Athens Dimitris Avramopoulos decided to create his own party. Soon realizing, however, that in the changing conditions of that time his chances for success were minimal, he decided to suspend the new party's operation by early 2002 without ever competing in national elections. Thereafter, he accepted an unconditional return to the mother ND party.

[3] Evidently, by controlling the central committee, the party leader is also in control of the party's executive committee (renamed after 2001 the 'political council'). This organ consists of the party leader, the party secretary-general, the parliamentary party leader, the party youth organization leader, and another 14 members, of which seven come from the parliamentary party and the other seven from the local party organizations.

[4] It is characteristic, in this respect, that, for the first time since 1985, no splinter parties appeared in the elections of 2000 (and, then, again in 2004) to contest ND's supremacy in the centre-right.

[5] Of the six regular congresses ND has convened since its foundation in 1974, three (together with two extraordinary ones) took place *after* 1997.

[6] Witness, for instance, the decisions of recent party congresses to introduce the direct participation of party members in the election of local administrative bodies (1997), the provision for local referenda, the novelty of establishing regional councils with the purpose of facilitating two-way communication between the central party and its grassroots (2001), as well as more recent attempts to fine-tune local party committees by both specifying and invigorating their functions (New Democracy 2004).

References

Alexakis, E. G. (1993) 'The Greek Right: Structure and Ideology of The New Democracy Party', PhD dissertation, London School of Economics.

Ansell, Ch. K. & Fish, S. M. (1999) 'The art of being indispensable: noncharismatic personalism in contemporary political parties', *Comparative Political Studies*, vol. 32, no. 3, pp. 283–312.

Bratakos, A. (2002) *Η ιστορία της Νέας Δημοκρατίας* [The History of New Democracy], Livanis, Athens.

Chondroleou, G. (2004) 'Public images and private lives: the Greek experience', *Parliamentary Affairs*, vol. 57, no. 1, pp. 53–66.

Christidis, C. (1997) 'Κεντροδεξιά: ορολογία, ιδεολογικό υπόβαθρο, προτάσεις για εκσυγχρονισμό' [The centre-right: terminology, ideological foundations, proposals for modernization], *Epikentra*, vol. 21, no. 2, pp. 50–53.

Clogg, R. (1987) *Parties and Elections in Greece: The Search for Legitimacy*, C. Hurst, London.

Dimitrakos, D. (2005) 'Κοινωνικό κέντρο και σύγχρονος φιλελευθερισμός' ['Social centre' and modern liberalism] *E-logos*, <http://www.e-logos.gr/articles.asp?subject_id=41&subject2_id=&article=324&lang=GR > .

Dinas, E. (2005) *Was it Karamanlis who won it or Papandreou who last it? The impact of leaders' image in the 2004 election*, paper presented at the 2nd Hellenic Observatory Symposium, London School of Economics, London.

Featherstone, K. (2005) 'Introduction: "modernisation" and the structural constraints of Greek politics', *West European Politics*, vol. 28, no. 2, pp. 223–241.

Hindmoor, A. (2004) *New Labour at the Centre: Constructing Political Space*, Oxford University Press, Oxford.

Kaase, M. (1994) 'Is there personalization in politics? Candidates and voting behavior in Germany', *International Political Science Review*, vol. 15, no. 3, pp. 211–230.

Kalyvas, S. N. (1998) 'The Greek right: between transition and reform', in *The European Center-Right at the Turn of the Century*, ed. F. L. Wilson, St Martin's Press, New York, pp. 87–115.

Karachalios, N. (2004) Recorded interview on the Greek radio station SKY, 21 June.

Karamanlis, C. (2000) 'Speech to ND's Executive Committee', Athens.

Katz, R. S. & Mair, P. (eds) (1992) *Party Organizations: A Data Handbook on Party Organizations in Western Democracies 1960–90*, Sage, London.

King, A. (2002) *Leaders, Personalities and the Outcomes of Democratic Elections*, Oxford University Press, New York.

Konstantinidis, I. (2004) 'Μεταβολές στο περιεχόμενο των πολιτικών προγραμμάτων των ελληνικών κομμάτων: η αξία τησ προσαρμοστικότητασ' [Policy changes as pictured in the electoral manifestos issued by the Greek parties: the value of adaptability], *Greek Political Science Review*, no. 24, pp. 105–139.

Loulis, J. C. (1981) 'New Democracy: the new face of conservatism', in *Greece at the Polls; The National Elections of 1974 and 1977*, ed. H. R. Penniman, American Enterprise Institute for Public Policy Research, Washington and London, pp. 49–83.

Loulis, J. (1995) *Η κρίση της πολιτικής στην Ελλάδα. Εκλογές, κοινή γνώμη, πολιτικές εξελίξεις 1980–1995*, [The Crisis of Politics in Greece. Elections, Public Opinion, Political Developments 1980–1995] I. Sideris, Athens.

Loulis, J. (2001) *Τα είκοσι χρόνια που άλλαξαν την Ελλάδα: Κερδισμένοι και χαμένοι* [The Twenty Years that Transformed Greece: Winners and Losers], Livanis, Athens.

Loulis, J. (2004) *Το τέλος μιας κυριαρχίας. Πως και γιατί το Πα.Σο.Κ. έχασε τις εκλογές* [The End of a Dominion. How and Why PASOK Lost the Elections], Livanis, Athens.

Lyrintzis, C. (2005) 'The changing party system: stable democracy, contested "modernisation"', *West European Politics*, vol. 28, no. 2, pp. 223–241.

Macridis, N. (1996) 'Μήπως η διάσπαση είναι αναγκαία ή και χρήσιμη; Η κρίση στους κόλπους της Νέας Δημοκρατίας' [Would a party break-up be necessary or even useful? The crisis within ND], *Epikentra*, vol. 20, no. 1, pp. 57–59.

Makris, S. (2001) 'Η ιδεολογία της Νέας Δημοκρατίας στο κατώφλι του 21^{ου} αιώνα' [ND's ideology at the threshold of the 21st century], *Emfasi*, vol. 6, pp. 89–100.

Mughan, A. (2000) *Media and Presidentialization of Parliamentary Elections*, St Martin's Press, New York.

New Democracy (1979) Α΄ συνέδριο. Πρακτικά [First Congress. Minutes], Athens.

New Democracy (1994) Γ΄ συνέδριω. Πρακτικά [Third Congress. Minutes], Athens.

New Democracy (2004) Καταστατικό [Statutes], Athens.

Panebianco, A. (1988) *Political Parties: Organization and Power*, Cambridge University Press, Cambridge, England.

Papathanassopoulos, S. (2000) 'Election campaigning in the television age: the case of contemporary Greece', *Political Communication*, vol. 17, pp. 47–60.

Pappas, T. S. (1998) 'Nea Democratia: party development and organizational logics', in *The Organization of Political Parties in Southern Europe*, eds P. Ignazi & C. Ysmal, Praeger, Westport, CT and London, pp. 221–237.

Pappas, T. S. (1999) *Making Party Democracy in Greece*, Macmillan/Palgrave, Basingstoke, England.

Pappas, T. S. (2001) 'In search of the center: conservative parties, electoral competition, and political legitimacy in Southern Europe's new democracies', in *Parties, Politics, and Democracy in the New Southern Europe*, eds P. N. Diamandouros & R. Gunther, Johns Hopkins University Press, Baltimore and London, pp. 224–267.

Pappas, T. S. (2002) 'Το τέλος του χαρισματικού; Πολιτική κρίση, χαρισματική ηγεσία και δημοκρατία στην Ελλάδα του 20ού αιώνα' [The end of charisma? Political crisis, charismatic leadership, and democracy in twentieth-century Greece], *Greek Political Science Review*, no. 19, pp. 22–58.

Pappas, T. S. (2003) 'The transformation of the Greek party system since 1951', *West European Politics*, vol. 26, no. 2, pp. 90–114.

Sartori, G. (1976) *Parties and Party Systems. A Framework for Analysis*, Cambridge University Press, Cambridge, England.

Seitanidis, D. A. (1997) Τα αίτια της χρόνιας κρίσης στην ελληνική κεντροδεξιά [The Causes of Chronic Crisis in the Greek Centre-Right], Papazisis, Athens.

Sotiropoulos, D. (1993) 'A colossus with feet of clay: the state in post-authoritarian Greece', in *Greece, the New Europe and the Changing International Order*, eds J. Psomiades & S. B. Thomadakis, Pella, New York, pp. 43–56.

Street, J. (2003) 'The celebrity politician: political style and political culture', in *Media and the Restyling of Politics*, eds J. Corner & D. Pels, Sage, London, pp. 85–98.

Voultepsis, J. Th. (2005) Δέκα σκληρά χρόνια στη Νέα Δημοκρατία, 1984–1993 [Ten Hard Years in New Democracy, 1984–1993], Proskenio, Athens.

Wilke, J. & Reinemann, C. (2001) 'Do candidates matter? Long-term trends of campaign coverage. A study of the German press since 1949', *European Journal of Communication*, vol. 16, no. 3, pp. 291–314.

Yannas, P. (2002) 'The role of image-makers in the Greek political scene', *Journal of Political Marketing*, vol. 1, no. 1, pp. 67–89.

Zoulas, S. (2004) 'Η ΝΔ τοποθετείται στο κέντρο' [ND is being placed at the centre], *I Kathimerini* 27 June.

Party Change in Greece and the Vanguard Role of PASOK

Michalis Spourdalakis & Chrisanthos Tassis

Following the end of a full-scale civil war in the 1940s, the Greek polity operated in such a way that it could only formally be called democratic, since parallel undemocratic structures cancelled out the very essence of parliamentary democracy—such as that of party change in government. The effect of this 'guided democracy' was that party competition was to a great extent founded on past cleavages and much less on current issues. It is ironic that the epitome of this 'cackectic democracy' (Nicolacopoulos 2001), the seven-year dictatorship (1967–74), put an end to the poorly functioning democratic regime and opened a new era for political parties.

Thus, with the fall of the colonels' regime and the *Metapolitefsi* (the Political Change of 1974), we witnessed a gradual but steady move away from the old structures and habits, leading to a completely new party system and a democratic regime with, by Greek standards, unprecedented qualities. The settling of the monarchy issue, the legalization of parties with communist ideological orientation (53 party formations identified themselves as communist in 1974), the clearly European orientation of the country, the recognition of the anti-fascist movement, along with the recognition of the institutions of organized interests as legitimate expressions of society and contributing actors to the policy-making process are some of the key developments of this new era. Political parties were not only conditioned by these developments but were instrumental in them.

No political party of the pre-1967 period appeared in the new *Metapolitefsi* era with a lasting presence. All political parties that came to play an important role in the now 30-year-old Third Greek Republic were new and made an effort to distance themselves from the pre-dictatorship party system. Even in the first years of the *Metapolitefsi*, when political leaders of the past remained protagonists in the political arena, no party, with the obvious exception of the Communist Party of Greece (KKE), accepted any association with the pre-junta party formations. Furthermore, political personnel from all parts of the political spectrum made a point of distancing themselves from the political practices of the past. However, old habits die hard, and, despite the sincere intentions of the individuals involved, it would have been wrong to expect that a modern party system would evolve automatically. If the Greek party system is today on a par with its European counterparts, that is to a great extent due to the role played by the Panhellenic Socialist Movement (Πανελλήνιο Σοσιαλιστικό Κίνημα, PASOK) both in opposition and in government. To put it differently, PASOK has been a pivotal factor in modernizing the Greek party system. For this reason an examination of this party's development and changes is key to an understanding of the developing trends and dynamics of almost all political parties in the country. In the following pages, after a brief reference to the party's historical development and its modernizing impact upon the Greek party system, we will focus on the changes that led it to become the dominant party of the country. Thus, we will analyse the changes PASOK underwent in values and programme, in its organization and in its competitive strategy and campaign politics. Finally, we will see how these changes have become its main challenge, especially since 2004, when it found itself in opposition.

Party History: A Remarkable Story (1974–94)

PASOK is a relatively new political grouping. Andreas Papandreou and a number of activists from both liberal and left-wing backgrounds founded the party in the aftermath of the fall of the junta. In its founding document, the legendary *Declaration of September 3rd* (1974), PASOK entered the political scene of the infant Greek democracy with a clearly radical discourse. The party's political and ideological coordinates and particularly its organizational premises were at a distinct distance from those of other parties. The nationalization of key industries and sectors of the Greek economy, its anti-NATO, anti-European and even wholesale anti-Western rhetoric and the promise of a mass membership based party organization were some of the key traits that set it apart, even from the left end of the political spectrum.

Table 1 PASOK Votes and Seats (1974–2004)

	Votes (%)	Seats (%)
17 November 1974	13.6	5.0
20 November 1977	25.3	31.0
18 October 1981	48.1	57.3
2 June 1985	45.8	53.7
18 June 1989	39.1	41.7
5 November 1989	40.7	42.7
8 April 1990	39.3*	41.7†
10 October 1993	46.8	56.7
22 September 1996	41.5	54.0
9 April 2000	43.8	52.7
7 March 2004	40.5	39.0

*Percentages include the vote from the five single-seat constituencies where PASOK and Synaspismos run common candidates.
†The number of seats includes the four elected MP's who have been supported jointly by Synaspismos and PASOK in single-member constituencies.
Source: Ministry of Interior, Public Administration and Decentralization

After the first elections, marked by the party's relatively modest performance (Table 1), along with those who were anxious to capture power, the PASOK leader, Andreas Papandreou, started systematically to change the party's political rhetoric and orientation. Wisely interpreting the changing political environment, which was steadily moving away from the *Metapolitefsi*'s radicalism, the leadership of the party did away with its internal opposition, and crafted the strategy that could safely, but most importantly quickly, lead the party to power. 'PASOK's short march' to power came to an end in October 1981, just seven years after its first appearance on the Greek political scene (Spourdalakis 1988).

Although in government PASOK marked a clear contrast to its initial political profile, there is no doubt that for its first two terms, that is until 1989, the party maintained some of its radical rhetoric, although this now contained tones of nationalism and a rather simplistic view of 'changing society' (*allage*) which led many to consider it a merely populist party. The truth of the matter was that, when in government, Papandreou's party was confronted with the structural restraints and needs of state power, on the one hand, and the often high expectations and demands of society, on the other. As a consequence, the party had to conform to these and drastically compromise its original political plans.

One must recognize that PASOK was faced with challenges that no other party before or since had confronted. It was the first non-right-wing party—in fact a party with left-socialist aspirations and programme—to take power in half a century, in a country that had experienced a bloody civil war and a dictatorship. This occurred during a negative international political conjuncture—the second Cold War instigated by Ronald Reagan in the early 1980s and the economic recession were far from conducive to the implementation of PASOK's programme. At the same time, one has also to recognize that the challenges PASOK faced from society were to a great extent a backlash against its own political opportunism, which had led it to numerous promises that it could not fulfil.

This is not to say that PASOK did not introduce some important reforms in various fields, such as in state administration, family law, education and health, but rather that it took a number of initiatives and created conditions that were in clear contrast to its original ideological coordinates. The legislation that made the right to strike almost impossible to exercise, the crude colonization of the state apparatus, the party's scandalous relations with business interests, which resulted in unprecedented instances of corruption, and, finally, its fickle and erratic foreign and especially European policy are some of the most striking examples of its programmatic and value changes (Spourdalakis 1998; Givalos 2005; Voulgaris 2001).

PASOK's reign lasted eight years. 1989 was not just the annus mirabilis of world history, as for many it ended the 'short twentieth century', but also for Greece. Under the weight of the exposure of a huge corruption network involving top government cabinet ministers, bankers and large media networks and the impasse of the government's financial and social policy, PASOK was defeated at the June elections. However, due to the electoral law, New Democracy (ND) could not form a majority government. This led to two, by Greek standards, unprecedented coalition cabinets: first between the ND and the Synaspismos of Left and Progress, in which the Communist Party was the main component, and later a short-lived all-party cabinet (1989–90).

Greece is a country with a traumatic experience of a civil war, policies that discriminated against the left wing and even liberal citizens, a political culture characterized by a zero-sum mentality, and political antagonisms over-determined by past cleavages. Thus, the developments around the 1989–90 elections were of historical importance. As the events of corruption and/or slander which accompanied them were engraved in the DNA of Greek politics, a widespread cynicism arose and past cleavages were demystified, which in turn contributed to a further de-ideologization of political discourse and to a political competition based on managerial proposals of state requirements merely to secure the reproduction of the social balance of power.

In fact, clear tendencies of managerial orientation had appeared by the end of the previous period of PASOK's development. The party's 1989 electoral programme ('The Programme for the Third Term') was already far removed from the visionary rhetoric of the past and it was made clear that the prime goal was now the achievement of high rates of growth, which would guarantee the country's participation in European integration (PASOK 1989). In the same vein, PASOK's opposition to the ND majority government formed on 9 April 1990 was rather technocratic, realistic and strongly influenced by the hegemony of neo-liberal ideas. In his effort to have a triumphant and somewhat vindictive comeback, given the animosity with Konstantinos Mitsotakis (from the ND), Papandreou declared that PASOK would exercise 'responsible opposition' (Papandreou 1990). Setting aside the demarcation of governmental strategy as 'extremely neo-liberal' and the polemical rhetoric that it would lead 'the country to an economic and social impasse' (ibid.), PASOK called for a new 'National Strategy' based on three axes—'stability, development, social protection'. The government's role was to be limited and the state would be reduced to a planning headquarters that would control only the activities of 'economic importance', while the rest would be given to the private sector (PASOK 1989).

The conflicts within the Mitsotakis government, along with its thin majority in parliament and the crisis over the 'Macedonian issue', in combination with extensive social discontent caused by high rates of inflation (almost 20 per cent), frozen wages and rising unemployment, prematurely ended the ND term. The 1993 election brought PASOK triumphantly back to power (Table 1). However, it was clear that this was already a different PASOK. Even the title of its electoral programme ('For the Present and the Future of Greece. Renaissance Everywhere') was indicative of the new trend. The aftertaste of the party's old radicalism was now wrapped in nationalist overtones, for the new call was a rally to 'rejuvenate Greece and the entire Greek nation'. However, neither this nor the presence of the strong, though ageing, leader could hide the fact that the demand for 'modernization' put forward by a number of organized interests under the auspices and with the support of the media had found its way into PASOK. In fact it was around the issue of modernization that the internal party conflicts were structured, since the debates over its content were to determine the competition for the imminent leadership replacement and the future direction of the party itself.

From Dominant Party to Oppositional Impasse (1995–2005)

A number of prominent members of the party (members of the executive bureau and former cabinet ministers), who objected to the style of Papandreou's leadership, rallied around the demand to renew the party's agenda and supported the overall demand for modernization. For the first time Papandreou appeared incapable of renewing the party's strategy and in addition he seemed to be trapped in a maze of personal and extra-institutional procedures and relationships. For a period the party was stagnant, searching for a new strategic orientation. Its internal critics were of two minds and, roughly speaking, divided into two groups. The first, apace with the European project, demanded a more rational, realistic direction, seeking through modernization to place the country at the forefront of European integration. The second appeared rather romantic, since its proposals derived from the party's origins, and was fanatically opposed to the modernizing tendency. As Papandreou's leadership became weaker, the friction between the two party tendencies became more intense. Finally, the pro-modernization group won the ideological battle, thanks to systematic media promotion and the mobilization of a good part of the intelligentsia. A significant split took place when Tsovolas, former minister of finance, left the party and founded the Democratic Social Movement (DIKKI) in October 1995, a move that strengthened the modernizers.

Thus, it did not come as a surprise, when following Papandreou's resignation due to illness (15 January 1996), the party's parliamentary group replaced him with Kostas Simitis, a former cabinet minister and prominent advocate of modernization. Only those who had not realized that PASOK had already entered a new phase and that its further development and strength were tied to the logic of the state and the management of governmental affairs failed to understand how the modernizers, a rather weak tendency within the party at the time, became hegemonic and dominant. The reasons for Simitis's rise to power and his strength should not be sought within the party. For the first time PASOK's internal balance of power and developments were legitimized primarily, if not exclusively, outside the party and as a result of the need to secure its capacity to govern. In fact this was put forward as the key factor in mobilizing and even expanding its popular support (Spourdalakis 1998, p. 71).

Policies that could be classified as moves towards modernization had already appeared following PASOK's return to power in 1993. However, with the rise of Simitis to the party leadership—at the fourth congress (June 1996), when he was elected party president with a commanding 54 per cent of the vote, soundly defeating his opponent Akis Tsochatzopoulos—modernization became the prime mobilizing factor and the legitimizing basis for PASOK's political initiatives and strategy.

Under the leadership of the modernizers, PASOK came closer to the economic orientation and strategy that are hegemonic worldwide and are presented as if 'there is no alternative'. Its coordination with the political hegemony of the time was enriched and further supported by the country's candidacy to participate in the Euro-zone (Greece applied officially in March 2000 and was accepted in January 2001). This, in combination with the inability of the opposition to put together a convincing alternative governmental programme, led to Simitis's impressive electoral victory in 1996.

Turning the country's membership of the Euro-zone into the sole national dogma for the country, Simitis's government created a significant social deficit. The popular discontent generated was not enough to challenge PASOK's modernizing discourse. The party insisted that the privatization programme would be realized; promising that completing all the infrastructure projects would make the country competitive in the international division of labour, which in turn would lead to economic development (Simitis 2000). Of course, to be fair it was this stubbornness that led to Greece's participation in the Euro-zone and secured the third slim victory of PASOK (Mavrogordatos 2000).

After 2002, with the country's membership in the Euro-zone, PASOK's popularity fell drastically as the social deficit created strong currents of social and political discontent. The rhetoric and practices of the government created a huge space for the representation of popular demands, which could not but be expressed in a populist fashion. ND and its new leader, Karamanlis, by promising everything to everyone, managed to fill this gap and climb to power. In the March 2004 elections PASOK was defeated, despite the mobilization around its new leader Giorgos Papandreou, who had gained a strong mandate in an open referendum-like election, in which over one million people participated.

For PASOK the defeat was a shocking experience and, so far, the party has not displayed signs of recovery. This would require a redefinition of the party's values and programme, which have been drastically transformed, particularly in the preceding decade or so. We now turn to the presentation and analysis of this programme.

Party Values and Programme

Even if one takes into account the fact that PASOK entered the 1990s having completely altered its initial radical identity and orientation, the changes that have taken place since are arguably of such magnitude that the party today no longer resembles the political Socialist Movement that entered Greek politics in 1974. Indeed, shifts in the party's values from the call for immediate transition to socialism in 1974 to its programme in the 1993 election, which aimed at 'Development and Stability', were strikingly clear. During its first 20 years PASOK had gradually moved to an orientation that was more realistic and certainly closer to state policy as it was determined both by the fading of the post-junta radicalism and the country's commitment to the EEC/EU. The latter, in combination with the tremendous side effects of the fall of the East European regimes, which in Greece, due to the strong communist left, played an important role in defining political identities, shifted the centre of the political spectrum. More concretely, these changes meant that the party had moved away from: (a) the unquestionable primacy of the state; (b) explicit reservations concerning the market; and (c) a visionary political discourse.

However, values and programmatic traits since 1996 have surpassed the shifts and changes of the first 20 years of the party's life. The new leader Kostas Simitis marked his era with a new set of values and programmatic goals which, under the banner of modernization, signified the fact that PASOK's values had changed radically. Although these changes, as we have seen, did not come out of the blue, even a brief analysis of the main coordinates of this modernization will verify that the PASOK of the Simitis era was a new one.

Under Simitis's leadership, PASOK's modernization started off with an intense critique of the 1981–85 and 1987–89 governmental economic and social policies and claimed that the entire orientation of the party's government programme should change. This revision was not far from the proposals of the Bank of Greece, the Association of Greek Industries and the International Monetary Fund (Papademitriou 1995; Paraskevopoulos 1995). This does not mean that the party's modernization did not include moral and ethical goals or certain sociological perceptions that strengthened the modernizers' project.

A clear example is the idea they promoted of society. To the modernizers of the new PASOK it was not collective social subjects that actually 'give the tone to politics' but rather 'every [individual] citizen (who composes) ... the very civil society' (Simitis 2000). This perception of society and politics led to a kind of elitism that collided with populism, its opposite current. In fact the modernizers' elitism managed to label as populist every popular demand and need of the lower social strata, which led to a political impasse, as it further separated society from government and state management. It was not only un-socialist but also proven to be politically distorting and electorally disastrous.

A systematic evaluation of the Simitis era for both Greek politics and PASOK remains to be done.[1] However, without great risk we can argue that its key policies and even discourse were not far from the coordinates that dominated the labour, socialist and social democratic European parties (such as New Labour in Great Britain, the SPD in Germany, the PVDA in The Netherlands, and the SAP in Sweden). The new strategic goal of the party was the creation of a 'powerful Greece'. The latter was identified with 'a powerful economy', based upon the strengthening of the economic accumulation structures and processes, the drastic control of inflation and deficits, extensive privatization programmes and a strong currency (Simitis 1998). This economic plan was seen to be of prime importance. As a result, popular, working class and general social demands were at times condemned by the government as 'sectarian interests', 'populist' or 'regressive' and at all times were conditional upon the success of its monetarist policies.

After its unquestionable success in the 2000 elections, PASOK failed to put forward a new general, 'national' goal capable once again of mobilizing the population. It was probably the poor performance at the Gallup polls that led Simitis, who was always seen as a better person for the top job than the ND leader, to put forward the 'Convergence Charter' (10 September 2003). This was a plan that touched upon some social issues as the key axes towards convergence with the country's partners in the EU (Simitis 2003a).

However, under the circumstances, when fiscal policies were given priority and competition and entrepreneurship were elevated to 'holy' principles, very few things could be done by the Greek socialists to close the gap between Greece and the EU countries on key social issues (Simitis 2003b). The modernizers' reference to social 'sensitivities' sounded more and more opportunistic, as, quite often, their initiatives in government and their discourse made it clear where their priorities lay. Three months after the Charter, Simitis, speaking on the strategic goals of the European left, made clear that he intended to 'promote the demands of the dynamic strata of society. We recognize the value of the market economy, of private initiative and creativity. We are working for development, an increase of productivity and the competitiveness of the Greek economy' (Simitis 2003c). In addition to these, the reason PASOK did not manage to change its political and ideological image and orientation is the fact that its organizational structure, as its leadership abandoned it, was in a shambles and in a state of disintegration. It is to this issue that we now turn.

Party Organization

The organizational structure of PASOK, its flexibility and adaptation to the challenges of the 1995–2005 decade and its modernizing effects on the Greek party system led some early observers to characterize it as exceptional and even sui generis. More recent analyses that discuss and distinguish between party formation and party adaptation, especially with regard to new democracies (Van Biezen 2005), sound convincing with regard to other cases, especially Eastern Europe. However, they do not apply to PASOK, whose adaptation followed the patterns of its counterparts in older democracies. This is because during its 30 years of existence, PASOK managed to experience practically all the historical phases of party organizational development: from cadre (1974–75) to mass party (1975–77), catchall (1977–85) and cartel or rather state-confined party (1986–2005). After the short cadre phase that marked its founding stages of development, PASOK evolved into a fully developed mass party and in record time became not only a key positive factor in the delicate process of transition to democracy but also a model for the entire party system.

In fact, it is in this sense that PASOK, under the leadership of its founder Andreas Papandreou, played a crucial role in the modernization of the Greek party system, which until then had been *terra incognita* for modern, democratic and participatory party structures. PASOK's organization legitimized mass party structures of the traditional left and, most importantly, became the model for the right-wing ND, which after its loss of power (1981) started to modernize its organization to become a modern mass party, in striking contrast to its past practices. Needless to say, PASOK's organizational development and modernizing effect were far from ideal, since collective democratic practices did not necessarily prevail over personalized and parochial structures and procedures. However, within the context of Greek political development, PASOK's rupture with the past party system was very clear, even if one takes into consideration the dominance of Andreas Papandreou over the party and some striking irregularities, such as the fact that the party only managed to organize its first congress ten years after its entrance into politics.

The evolution of PASOK's organization can be traced by looking at its relationship to the parliamentary group. The party's entrance into the Greek political arena was followed by the perception that its MPs and parliamentary activities should be subordinated to the party's political strategy and to the will of the party apparatus. Soon after the 1974 election, however, Papandreou's party gradually but steadily crafted an electoralist strategy, complemented by clear catchall organizational characteristics. In the course of this development—the epitome of which was PASOK's triumphant entrance to power in 1981—the parliamentary group gained significant power and became, if not dominant, at least as important as the party's collective bodies, the central committee and the executive bureau. During the 1985 elections the political conjuncture imposed strict discipline on the parliamentary party, capable of guaranteeing the election of the new president of the republic, and thus one witnessed a temporary overturning of this trend as the closed candidate lists were put together by the party's central committee. By the end of the 1980s, however, the powers of the parliamentary group no longer remained on a par with the party's collective bodies. As PASOK became increasingly stuck in the mire of government, parliamentarians started to interfere with and even control almost all party local and regional organizations, whose main activity was now to mobilize support for the government and to function as a campaign organization for certain ambitious individuals. The empowerment of the MPs reached its peak in 1995, when the party's central committee decided that in the event of the prime minister having to be changed while the party was in power, the parliamentary group should elect him/her.

Indeed it was during this period that PASOK displayed characteristics that systematically undermined previous party organization and internal functions through the adoption of mass and even catchall parties. The trends that developed, especially in the 2000–5 period, support our argument that PASOK has been transformed in such a way that, from the point of view of its organization, we will soon have a *non-party party*. An examination of a few aspects leads to this conclusion.

To begin with, the definition of membership has changed. The basic trait of mass political parties—in addition to mass membership—was that the party members were organized into local or professional sections that were not open to followers or party sympathizers. Since PASOK's first congress in 1984, when the definition of membership was rather strict, we have witnessed a *de facto* withering away of such strictness. This fuzziness of the border line between member and non-member, which became a mainstream trait of the party's organization under the leadership of K. Simitis (1996–2004), was retained and found its way into the party's 2005 Statutes. Sympathizers can now participate with voting rights in all party processes and they are enrolled in a separate registry (PASOK 2005, art. 20). Thus, essentially there is no longer a distinction between genuine members and other citizens involved in party life. Consequently, there is a free-floating membership in the party. PASOK's membership in December 2003 was 200,000. In January 2004 over one million people voted for the election of Giorgos Papandreou to the leadership. In February 2005, 400,000 people participated in the debates in preparation for the seventh congress and in June 2005, 250,000 people voted for the local/municipal and regional party bodies. In addition, there has been an effort to institute a 'cyber membership', where relationship of the members to the party is open-ended and contact is made primarily through the internet (e-referendums, chat rooms, etc.). However, given the low percentage of internet connections in the country, this will merely have a symbolic effect indicating only the new leadership's orientation towards looser and more flexible membership. Although the party has rarely given out its actual membership numbers, reliable estimates demonstrate their fluidity (Table 2).

Probably, the most significant development in the party's latest restructuring efforts is the abolition of the professional branches and the unification of all local units into only one per municipality. The latter is a rather modernizing move, since it makes the manipulation of the local base by candidates and prominent party members more difficult. The abolition of the professional units demonstrates the tendency to move away from direct links with specific social groups. This tendency also led to the exclusion of references to social classes in the party programme and the adoption of a rhetoric which gave emphasis on the vague notion of civil society. In fact, the party Statutes (PASOK 2005) have introduced a new working committee called the

Table 2 PASOK Membership and Ratio of Party Members to Party Voters and Total Electorate, 1974–2004

Election year	PASOK membership	PASOK members as percentage of PASOK voters	PASOK members as percentage of electorate†
1974	8,000	1.2	0.1
1977	27,000	2.1	0.4
1981	110,000	4.0	1.6
1985	220,000	7.5	2.5
1989 June	90,000	3.5	1.1
1989 November	90,000	3.3	1.0
1990	82,489	3.2	1.0
1993	112,088	3.5	1.2
1996	155,642	5.5	1.7
2000	125,000	4.2	1.3
2004*	250,000	8.3	2.5

*Includes both members and sympathizers.
†It should be mentioned that the register of those enabled to vote in Greece is not renewed very often and therefore the number of registered voters is underestimated.
Source: Own calculations and official party data (Spourdalakis 1998).

'Everyday Citizen' (art. 48), which aims directly at mobilizing civil society and whose purpose is to 'broaden dialogue with active citizens, social initiatives and voluntarism as it promotes cooperation with Civil Society'. A further striking example of this trend is the abolition of the long-standing action committees, which coordinated PASOK's presence in trade unions, in the cooperative and agriculture movement and in mass and women's movements.

A simple comparison of the new names of the collective bodies of the party and their electoral base and functions is sufficient to illustrate the difference in the spirit according to which the party operates. More concretely one should note the striking change in the election of the party's president. The party's founder, Andreas Papandreou, was never elected. Kostas Simitis was first elected by the parliamentary group as prime minister, and then as the party's president during PASOK's fourth congress (1996). Finally, in 2004 Giorgos Papandreou rose to the leadership after a vote open to the electorate, where he was the only candidate. Furthermore, according to the 2005 statutes, the party's central committee (composed of 176 members elected by the party congress) changed its name—to 'national council'—and composition (287 members composed of elected members, the parliamentary group and other appointed party dignitaries), while its executive bureau became the political council. The party organization is not only radically different from the mass party we observed in the historical development of the party system in Western Europe but even from its own past. The parliamentarians of the party have been promoted even further in the party hierarchies, as in their *ex officio* participation in the national council.

Thus, the emphasis of the leadership on participation and 'participatory democracy' has had no practical effects so far. In fact we could argue, along with similar studies (Seyd 1999), that the effort to increase party membership, in combination with the promotion of participatory democracy and a plebiscite type of membership mobilization, works to strengthen the leadership itself. In other words, this organizational trend contributes to the further concentration of power in the person of the leader, who now enjoys more autonomy than ever before. The consequence of this development is that very little room is left to the periphery for recruitment initiatives. These initiatives are left to the leader, who appeals to the membership and the citizenry directly, a pattern that actually nullifies the mediating function of numerous party bodies.

This recent organizational development and dynamic of PASOK are vividly displayed by the structure of its financing. According to the published budget of the party, in 2004, membership dues represented only five per cent of revenues, down from 14 per cent just ten years before. The rest of the party's financial needs are covered by legislated state remittances, which are based on the popular vote gained by the party. The actual procedures of the party's seventh congress (2005) are also characteristic of these trends. The delegates discussed the statutes and the political principles of the party separately. With the exception of the speeches of K. Simitis and G. Papandreou, there were no common sessions and there was no opportunity for true participation and debate or collective party-wide decision making at any point. The fragmentation of the delegates into four or five parallel sessions did not allow much room for proposals that would represent the real pulse of the party, nor could these important collective processes perform the function of leadership recruitment.

To be fair, one should add that these organizational trends of the Greek socialists developed and were strengthened by the drastic changes in the political mobilization patterns of the country. Indeed since the early 1990s the lopsided power enjoyed by the mass media, especially television, has influenced party mobilization. Party membership is at best on the sidelines of this process while the media play a decisive role in all party functions, including political recruitment, political mobilization and even policy formation. Given the party's dependency on the media, PASOK in turn increasingly depends on external expert consultants, as well as on the symbolic and material resources of politicians who are recruited regardless of their political background or ideological orientation. The inclusion of two prominent neo-liberal leaders on the party's ticket (S. Manos and A. Andrianopoulos) and the overall management of the electoral campaign are the most typical examples of these trends.

Competitive Strategy and Campaign Politics

Despite the organizational changes the competitive strategy of PASOK has remained essentially the same. With minor variations the party's strategy revolves around two key points. The first is that, despite its anti-right-wing political rhetoric, the Greek socialists have not attempted any kind of real cooperation with the parties of the traditional left. This discreet but clear distance from the left is not only articulated on the central political scene but, with marginal and insignificant exceptions, also with regard to all aspects of public life, for example, local and regional government, and institutions of organized interests. While this has been a key trait of PASOK since 1974, one could point to the striking exception to this pattern, the party's participation in the 'all party government' (1989–90) that followed the crisis and the brief electoral stalemate of 1989. However, this short-lived experience did not seem to have altered either PASOK's strategy or the overall political attitudes on party and political competition. The second key characteristic of its strategy vis-à-vis its prime political rival (the ND) was to preserve this (anti-right) rivalry on the basis of the cleavages of the past. The weight of these cleavages is purely historical and their current importance is the result of political inertia.

In other words, PASOK's strategy in this field is characterized by the maintenance, on the one hand, of a solid anti-right-wing rhetoric and, on the other, by the exercise of a softer criticism of the left and, occasionally, the promoting of rhetoric for cooperation. To the extent that the old civil war cleavages work, they are updated, interpreted and enriched with new political values and a programmatic orientation. Of course, the latter would have been very difficult given the programmatic convergence of the party with the ND. However, its often tactical use of these dated cleavages, even by the newly elected liberal leader Giorgos Papandreou, constitutes a clear trend. The party's relationship with the left, however, reveals a rather opportunistic strategy. It is the incapacitating sectarianism of the left (Synaspismos and KKE) that has made this strategy rather beneficial for the party's influence.

If the competitive strategy of PASOK displays clear signs of inertia and continuity, its campaign politics have changed drastically. By today's standards the campaign politics of the party until the end of the 1980s were rather primitive. After the first election (1974), when the campaign was spontaneous and decentralized, the party's overall strategy was redrafted and the electoral campaigns became more centralized as they were left in the hands and to the charisma of A. Papandreou. Although on the surface the methods used were not much different from those that characterized party politics in the 1960s, we should note that PASOK introduced some important innovations in its first 20 years of political presence. These included the replacement of informal and personalized networks with a well-organized party capable of carrying out the decisions made by the party hierarchy. Local and regional electoral committees, which were appointed just before every election, were under the control of the party's central committee and especially the executive bureau.

By the beginning of the 1990s, in the context of a political and electoral stalemate and with the framework of a rapidly and radically changing world of media and mass communications in the country, technocrats and electoral marketing experts were hired to assist the party's leadership in the details of its strategy. The presence of advertising experts and the adoption of internationally applied campaign techniques would become the main trait of the organization of electoral campaigns in the next phase of the party's development (Papathanassopoulos 2000).

Indeed PASOK's recent development is vividly displayed in its campaigning politics. During the period under examination (1995–2005) the preparation of the electoral campaigns changed radically. Contrary to the first two decades of the party's life, when planning was the responsibility of the party's leadership (especially the president and the executive bureau), campaigns have gradually passed into the hands of marketing experts. Following the general trend, PASOK relies almost exclusively on a whole series of experts and technocrats in the field of marketing and communication.

The key features of PASOK's electoral campaigns include the hiring of communication consultants, often working exclusively for the party leader, the use of opinion polls, reliance on new media and emphasis on the candidates' and especially the leader's image.

This is not of course something that is exclusive to the Greek socialists. In fact, since all major Greek political parties (including those on the left) employ to a great extent the same methods and display the same characteristics in their campaign politics and since these patterns are associated with American politics, it would not be an exaggeration to claim that PASOK participates, if not pivotally, in what has been convincingly called the 'americanization of Greek politics' (Kotzaivazoglou & Ikonomou 2005). This has transformed the parties' electoral campaigns from being labour intensive to capital intensive and undermined the role of the membership even during campaigning periods.

The means of communication the party has at its disposal are a further indication of the changes in its campaigning politics. By the mid-1990s PASOK had abandoned the publication of the party's weekly (*Exormisi*) and closed down the operation of the party's publishing house (Aichmi); these channels of communication were replaced by a monthly publication (*Emphasis*), which is closer to a life-style magazine than to a political one. A recent development in the party's communication channels, in addition to the extensive use of radio and television (interviews, debates, commentaries), has been an emphasis on the use of the internet. This is the result of G. Papandreou's own obsession with this technology rather than the outcome of a realistic plan. In sum, technicians, technocrats and image-makers are the decisive and powerful actors in PASOK campaign politics (Givalos 2005).

Conclusion

Recently, PASOK celebrated 32 years of presence on the Greek political scene. Its contribution to the transition and consolidation of Greece's democratic regime, the numerous reforms it introduced while in power and its instrumental role in the modernizing of the party system are the major axes upon which the Greek socialists can be judged positively. However, their governmental role, which lasted over ten years, has drawn them into a government and state logic that has contributed to a crisis of identity and political orientation.

The long presence of the party in government had three main effects. First, the government party dominated all other aspects of party life: the party's relationship to its social base as well as its internal functions and activities. This resulted in a deepening of the cleavage between the 'old' and the 'new' party. The old PASOK is still committed to some degree to social rhetoric and a more visionary political programme, which aims at the mobilization of mass membership through traditional means. The new party, on the other hand, is committed to the efficient management of governmental affairs and relies primarily on the mobilization of the population at large through modern media and, secondarily, on a party membership loosely defined. The second consequence of PASOK's long incumbency has been the strengthening of a bipolar party system, as competition with ND became PASOK's main concern, leaving little room for changes in its competitive strategy. Third, and as a result of the above effects, when PASOK lost the elections in 2004 and found itself in opposition, it faced the challenge of rebuilding its organization and redrafting its political profile and strategy.

The freshness of G. Papandreou's leadership, with its genuine political liberalism, its efforts to renew the party's political personnel and political agenda through the introduction of themes of the 'post-materialist' agenda and the promotion of liberal values, is far from convincing. To put it differently, the new leadership's novelties are more an expression of the party's uncertainty and indecision than a way out of its crisis and a road to recovery. Of course the latter will depend on the performance of the ND government and its ability to cope with affairs of state and the tasks of governance, while maintaining its lead in popular support. However, recent polls suggest this is becoming increasingly questionable.

Note

[1]　The published works so far have focused only on narrow aspects of the PASOK government. However, it is worth making reference to: Sevastakis (2004); Pantazopoulos (2003; 2004); Loulis (2004); Pappas (2004); Bilios (2005); Verney (2004); Giannitsis (2005); Simitis (2005).

References

Bilios, N. (2005) 'Renewing socialism in Greece: analysing PASOK's modernization paradigm', paper presented at the 55th Annual Conference of the Political Studies Association, Leeds, 4–7 April.

Giannitsis, T. (2005) *Η Ελλάδα και το μέλλον: Πραγματισμός και ψευδαισθήσεις* [Greece and Its Future: Pragmatism and Illusions], Polis, Athens.

Givalos, M. (2005) 'Μετασχηματισμοί και διαφοροποιήσεις του ΠΑΣΟΚ κατά τη δεκαετία 1990–2000' [Transformation and differentiations of PASOK between 1990 and 2000], in *Η κοινή γνώμη στην Ελλάδα 2004* [Public Opinion in Greece 2004], eds Institute VPRC & C. Vernadakis, Savalas, Athens, pp. 86–127.

Kotzaivazoglou, I. & Ikonomou, T. (2005) 'The americanization of Greek politics. The case of the 2004 general election', paper delivered at the 55th Annual Conference of the Political Studies Association, Leeds, 4–7 April.

Loulis, I. (2004) *Το τέλος μιας κυριαρχίας. Πώς και γιατί το Πα.Σο.Κ. έχασε τις εκλογές* [The End of a Domination. How and Why PASOK Lost the Elections], Livanis, Athens.

Mavrogordatos, G. T. (2000) 'Greece', *European Journal of Political Research*, vol. 38, no. 7–8, pp. 397–401.

Nicolacopoulos, I. (2001) *Η καχεκτική Δημοκρατία. Κόμματα και Εκλογές 1946–1967* [The Sickly Democracy. Parties and Elections, 1946–1967], Pattakis, Athens.

Pantazopoulos, A. (2003) *Η Δημοκρατία της Συγκίνησης* [Emotional Democracy], Polis, Athens.

Pantazopoulos, A. (2004) 'Το ΠΑΣΟΚ της νέας Εποχής', [PASOK of the new age], *Sychrona Themata*, vol. 84, pp. 5–10.

Papademitriou, A. C. (1995) 'Αυτοσυγκράτηση ζητεί η Τράπεζα της Ελλάδος' [The Bank of Greece demands self-restraint], *To Vima*, 12 March.

Papandreou, A. (1990) Speech in parliament, Πρακτικά Βουλής [Minutes of Parliament], 14 July.

Papathanassopoulos, S. (2000) 'Election campaigning in the television age: the case of contemporary Greece', *Political Communication*, vol. 17, no. 1, pp. 47–60.

Pappas, T. (2004) *Το ΠΑΣΟΚ του Μέλλοντός τους*, [PASOK of Their Future], Polis, Athens.

Paraskevopoulos, T. (1995) 'Ήπια η έκθεση του ΔΝΤ για την ελληνική οικονομία', [Mild Report of the IMF on Greek Economy], *Epoche*, 21 May.

PASOK. (1989) *Σχέδιο για τις πολιτικές θέσεις και τις βασικές προγραμματικές κατευθύνσεις*, [Plan for the Political Proposals and the Basic Programmatic Orientation], Athens.

PASOK. (2005) *Statutes*, Athens.

Sevastakis, N. (2004) *Κοινότοπη Χώρα. Όψεις του δημοσίου Χώρου και Αντινομίες Αξιών στη Σημερινή Ελλάδα*, [Trivial Country. Facets of Public Space and the Antinomies of Values in Today's Greece], Savalas, Athens.

Seyd, P. (1999) 'New parties/new politics? A case study of the British Labour Party', *Party Politics*, vol. 5, no. 3, pp. 383–405.

Simitis, K. (1998) 'Ομιλία στην Ολομελεια της Βουλής για τον Οικονομικό Προϋπολογισμό του 1999', [Speech at the Plenary Session of the Parliament on the 1998 Budget], 21 December, < www.costas-simitis.gr > .

Simitis, K. (2000) 'Ομιλία στην Ολομέλεια της Βουλής για τον Οικονομικό Προϋπολογισμό του 2001', [Speech at the Plenary Session of the Parliament on the 2001 Budget], 22 December, < www.costas-simitis.gr > .

Simitis, K. (2003a) 'Ομιλία στην παρουσίαση της Χάρτα Σύγκλισης στο Ζάππειο Μέγαρο', [Speech at the presentation of the Convergence Charter], 10 September, < www.costas-simitis.gr > .

Simitis, K. (2003b) 'Ομιλία στο Εθνικό Συμβούλιο του ΠΑΣΟΚ', [Speech at the National Council of PASOK], 9 October, < www.costas-simitis.gr > .

Simitis, K. (2003c) 'Ομιλία στο Ευρωπαϊκό Συμπόσιο με θέμα «Σύγχρονοι Σοσιαλιστές— Νέες Απαντήσεις»', [Speech at the European Symposium on Contemporary Socialists— New Answers], 4 December, < www.costas-simitis.gr > .

Simitis, K. (2005) *Πολιτική για μια δημιουργική Ελλάδα 1996–2004* [Politics for a Creative Greece 1996–2004], Polis, Athens.

Spourdalakis, M. (1988) *The Rise of the Greek Socialist Party*, Routledge, London & New York.

Spourdalakis, M. (ed.) (1998) *ΠΑΣΟΚ. Κόμμα—Κράτος—Κοινωνία*, [PASOK. Party—State— Society], Patakis, Athens.

Van Biezen, I. (2005) 'On the theory and practice of party formation and adaptation in new democracies', *European Journal of Political Research*, no. 44, pp. 147–174.

Verney, S. (2004) 'The end of Socialist hegemony: Europe and the Greek parliamentary election of 7th March 2004', Epern Working Paper no. 15, Sussex European Institute, < http://www. sussex.ac.uk/sei/1-4-2-10.html > .

Voulgaris, G. (2001) *Η Ελλάδα της Μεταπολιτευσης 1974–1990* [Greece in the Metapolitefsi Era 1974–1990], Themelio, Athens.

Party Change and Development in Cyprus (1995–2005)

Christophoros Christophorou

Cyprus is a peculiar case in Southern Europe and the wider European family; it is a divided member-state of the European Union which has developed two separate party systems. The institutional framework of the Republic of Cyprus, established in August 1960, provided for the division of the electorate and elections across community lines. As a result, two party systems emerged, with the ethnic cleavage often invoked in and affecting intra-community politics. Since the collapse of bi-communalism in 1964, a *sui generis* situation has developed. The Greek Cypriots run the government of the Republic of Cyprus and the Turkish Cypriots the areas under their control. In the Republic of Cyprus, under the presidential system, the president can stay in power without formal party support or participation in the exercise of executive power. On the other hand, the non-recognized 'Turkish Republic of Northern Cyprus', self-proclaimed in 1983 in the part occupied by the Turkish army, has a parliamentary system with enhanced powers for the president. On both sides, the present party systems developed after the division of Cyprus in 1974. However, their main features are founded on divisions and social cleavages formed in the 1940s (Christophorou 2006).

Important social, institutional and other developments took place on the island during the 1980s and 1990s, with the course to EU membership being the most influential on both communities. Studies of the parties' electoral programmes and statutes showed that almost all political parties have changed their organization, practices and values. Most of the changes took place after 1995, when the parties attempted to adapt to the new environment and respond to its challenges.

The parties studied in this work are the Greek Cypriot communist Progressive Party of the Working People (Ανορθωτικό Κόμμα Εργαζόμενου Λαού, AKEL) and the right-wing Democratic Rally (Δημοκρατικός Συναγερμός, DISY), as well as the Turkish Cypriot former communist Republican Turkish Party (Cumhuriyetçi Türk Partisi, CTP) and the right-wing National Unity Party (Ulusal Birlik Partisi, UBP). These four cases were selected as representing the two most influential parties within each of the communities, either today or in the period 1995–2005. The work is divided into two parts, the first dealing with the Greek Cypriot parties and the second with the Turkish Cypriot parties. First AKEL and DISY are examined in parallel in four sections. After an overview of the parties' recent history and development, the study focuses on the main characteristics of their programmes and values, on the organizational changes, and on the features of electoral competition and campaigns. The second part follows the same approach for the Turkish Cypriot political parties, the UBP and the CTP. In the concluding section, all four parties are examined together in an effort to discern common features and differences developed within the framework of two separate party systems, in different institutional and social contexts.

Greek Cypriots: The Dominance of Left and Right

The Recent Years: Fragmentation and Stronger Bipolarization

The charismatic figure of Archbishop and President of the Republic Makarios dominated the Cypriot political system from the 1950s, controlling almost everything (Markides 1977). This is why the 1981 parliamentary elections, the first after Makarios's death, marked the starting point of contemporary party politics (Hadjikyriakos & Christophorou 1996). Political development continued throughout the 1980s and 1990s, with the institutionalization of municipal elections (1986) and the creation of new independent non- or semi-governmental authorities and institutions. Institutional development offered additional opportunities for political mobilization (Ierodiakonou 2003, p. 456). Elections became more meaningful and the number of seats in the House of Representatives rose from 35 to 56, while over 2,650 local authority posts became elected offices in 1985 (Press and Information Office 2002). The electoral system for parliamentary elections changed in 1981 from the initial plurality block vote to a reinforced proportional distribution of seats, with a threshold of eight per cent and compulsory voting. A two-round majority system is in force for the election of the president of the Republic. The electoral competition rules changed again in 1995, with the adoption of a system of proportional representation and the threshold set at one 56th of the vote (for the 56-member chamber). The voting age in all elections was changed from 21 to 18 in 1997.

In addition to institutional transformations, the EU accession process has been a major factor for change. Europeanization has played a cohesive role, both in inter-party politics and as an opportunity to unite Cyprus. Europe has been a resource for raising new issues and a fair reason for the parties' organizational changes, enabling the development of their relationships with both the electorate and European institutions (Katsourides 2003). DISY has been a member of the European People's Party since 1994 and AKEL of the United European Left /North European Green Left since 1996. The referendum of April 2004 on a United Nations plan, known as the 'Annan plan' and intended to end the island's division, caused new divisions cutting across party lines and emerged as a factor affecting party politics.

The context and the conditions under which the left-wing Communist Party and the right-wing conservatives started off, and the courses they followed were markedly different.

AKEL was founded in April 1941 under British colonial rule and conditions of political vacuum; through impressive early electoral successes the party gained legitimacy and established its authority as a major political force, which it remains today. AKEL was excluded from the handling of the Cyprus issue and the anti-colonial struggle, and faced legitimacy problems in the transitional period to independence. After testing its influence by opposing Makarios in the first presidential elections (December 1959), the party offered him unconditional support. Later, it offered support to presidential candidates without participating in government. It received in return ministerial portfolios for well-known individuals enjoying its confidence (Table 1). Under the plurality system, AKEL contented itself with a limited number of seats in the house of representatives.

AKEL has consistently sustained its image as a Marxist–Leninist party deeply committed to the communist ideals, though without launching itself into ideological debates or revolutionary positions. It entertained close relations with the Soviet Union and the eastern block, aligning itself to Moscow on all international issues. Locally, it claimed to be the sole representative of the working class and the left-progressive forces. In party discourse, AKEL has identified itself with the people and projected its achievements as people's victories. Without fully extinguishing sparks of ideological fanaticism, the party has since independence displayed moderation and conciliatory approaches (Christophorou 2001a).

The years of perestroika and collapse of the communist world coincided with the death of Ezekias Papaioannou, AKEL secretary-general for 39 years, and an internal crisis, which erupted in 1988, created by ideological differences, personal rivalries and persisting problems from the party's heavy losses in the December 1985 parliamentary elections. The crisis, which continued after the election of a new secretary-general, the 42-year-old Demetris Christofias, ended in 1990 (Hadjikyriakos & Christophorou 1996, pp. 146–151). A large-scale renewal of the leadership took place after dissidents were ousted or resigned, along with a redefinition of the party's values and programme, and some changes in organization.

Table 1 Parliamentary and Presidential Elections in the Republic of Cyprus: Votes, Party Support and Cabinet Composition (1991–2003)

Year	DISY votes (%)	AKEL votes (%)	Presidential party support	President	Inauguration date[†]	Cabinet
1991P	35.8[1]	30.6	AKEL (1988)	G. Vassiliou	(March 1988)	Well-known individuals (three favoured by AKEL)
1993Pr			DISY–DIKO	G. Clerides (DISY)	March 1993	DISY, DIKO
1996P	34.5*	33.0			November 1997	DISY
1998Pr			DISY–EDI–NEO–Liberals	G. Clerides (DISY)	March 1998	DISY,[‡] EDI, EDEK, Liberals
2001P	34	34.7			January 1999	DISY,[‡] EDI, Liberals
2003Pr			AKEL–DIKO–EDEK–others	T. Papadopoulos (DIKO)	March 2003	AKEL, DIKO, EDEK, others

* Alliance with Liberal Party.
[†] Inauguration date refers to either the beginning of the presidential term or a reshuffle of the cabinet.
[‡] Including DIKO dissidents.
Note: P = Parliamentary election and Pr = Presidential election
Source: Christophorou (2001a; 2003).

Voters' loyalty has been very strong for both AKEL and DISY (Table 1), as it was based on the perpetuation of ideological cleavages shaped by the social divisions of the 1940s and reinforced by subsequent events, the latest being the 1974 coup. Sustaining the divisions with the right has remained a focal point in AKEL's politics and electoral strategy. The main axis of this strategy has been to bar the course to DISY and its eventual allies. As a consequence, AKEL has sought alliances with conservative well-known individuals or groups capable of splitting the opponent's camp, labelling them 'the progressive democratic' or 'patriotic democratic forces'. The centre Democratic Party (DIKO) and the socialist Unified Democratic Union of the Centre (EDEK) were the privileged allies. Failure to secure good relations with them resulted in cruel defeats and isolation. This was the case in 1985, when tacit cooperation with DISY in opposing President Spyros Kyprianou's policies on the Cyprus issue caused a reduction in the party's share of more than 16 per cent compared with its 1981 level (Hadjikyriakos & Christophorou 1996, pp. 104–111). Following its electoral recovery in the 1986 municipal elections, AKEL initiated a course of its own by promoting in 1988 the presidential candidacy of businessman Giorgos Vassiliou. It elected him to office, but when he failed to win a second term in 1993 the party was left in relative isolation. With socialist EDEK as its only potential partner, it was not possible to secure a majority vote in any election.

For AKEL, the new environment meant isolation, but also an opportunity not to be missed: it remained the only reliable alternative to the forces in power. DIKO's left-of-centre voters were not happy with the party's alliance with DISY (1993–97) and, together with some EDEK voters, they joined AKEL, the force most likely to counter-balance the right wing's influence.

DISY was founded in 1976 by Glafcos Clerides and cadres from his former Unified Party and the Progressive Front, which collapsed following support by some of their officials for the coup against Makarios in summer 1974. The party faced exclusion and systematic denigration from the day of its inception, as pro-Makarios forces established an 'inner party system', a group of parties and organizations that collaborated and defined the terms of competition so as to exclude their opponents from power (Bosco 2001). They formed an alliance against DISY, which was accused of offering shelter to the perpetrators of the coup and the extreme right. They barred its road to parliament in 1976, despite its 27 per cent share of the vote. With the passage of time, however, DISY emerged as a reliable political force and an alternative to the failing pro-Makarios alliance. DISY's electoral successes in the parliamentary elections of 1981 and, in particular, of 1985, when it became the largest party, gradually opened the road to full legitimacy.

The party contested parliamentary elections alone or in alliances with minor parties and all presidential elections with its chairman as candidate. Minor parties merged with DISY at different times, such as the Democratic National Party in 1976 and the New Democratic Front prior to the February 1988 presidential elections. The Liberal Party merged with DISY in 2003, after successive alliances since 1991. After his defeat in the 1988 presidential elections, Clerides supported the new president Giorgos

Vassiliou's policies on the Cyprus issue, a gesture that was interpreted as proof of conciliatory and moderate political behaviour, and further assisted the party's course to legitimacy.

DISY is a right-wing party, drawing support from traditional conservative forces and appealing to a broad spectrum of voters (Ierodiakonou 2003, p. 305). In the party's founding declaration, democracy and democratic principles were given a prominent place (DISY 1995, pp. 59–69), as a response to the forces attacking the party and its leader for offering shelter to perpetrators of the 1974 coup. In everyday politics, DISY promoted the image of a moderate right-wing and centre-right party. In 1991 it sought rapprochement and electoral cooperation with its major enemy—the pro-Makarios centre party DIKO—claiming that this would unite the entire centre and right-wing front and bar the road to the 'red banners'.

Along with political moderation, DISY used rainbow colours with its light blue logo in 1991, symbols appealing to forces beyond traditional right-wing voters. It also seized a golden opportunity offered by the impasse facing DIKO after it lost power in 1988, and initiated a policy of rapprochement by supporting DIKO's vice chairman as president of parliament in 1991. The formation of a DIKO–DISY alliance in the mayoral elections six months later enabled the party to appeal to a broader base of voters and to break through the inner system. Despite its failure to secure any guarantees for future cooperation in exchange for its generosity to DIKO, it effectively won the latter's enforced support in the second round of the 1993 presidential elections. Clerides won by a margin of only 2,000 votes (0.6 per cent) over the incumbent Vassiliou. In order to succeed, DISY and its leader had reversed their policies on the Cyprus issue and boycotted in late 1992 Vassiliou's efforts for a negotiated solution under the auspices of the United Nations (Hadjikyriakos & Christophorou 1996, p. 185). The policies of Clerides' coalition cabinet, shared equally between DIKO and DISY, shifted to nationalist choices and rhetoric. The common defence doctrine with Greece and the theory of the 'dormant volcano' occupied central stage; failure of the international community to solve the Cyprus issue would cause the volcano to erupt.

Persistence of Old Ideologies versus New Values

AKEL's course on ideological and programmatic choices differed from those of its European counterparts, since it did not change its orientations; it simply reaffirmed its Marxist identity (March & Mudde 2005). The party's positions on the Cyprus issue were almost identical to those of DISY, but it has so far made consistent efforts to deny any affinity with the right-wing party. Its policies on social and other issues have been more moderate than those of the centre parties DIKO and EDEK (Christophorou 2001a).

In 1990 the 17th party congress adopted a manifesto entitled 'Our Concept of Socialism', in which AKEL defined a comprehensive ideological framework. The main idea was that there could be many forms of socialism and choices should take into account not only the 'dramatic changes taking place in the world' but also the 'peculiarities of Cypriot reality' (AKEL 1990a; Ierodiakonou 2003). While paying tribute and affirming commitment to the ideals of Marxist–Leninist theory and the legacy of Engels, the party accepted that the road to socialism would be pursued by democratic means, with respect to pluralism and freedoms.

The 18th congress (November 1995) regretted 'the dissolution of the Soviet Union and the community of socialist countries in East Europe' as a 'negative development for the whole of humanity', and blamed the lack of method and planning in the process of perestroika along with foreign destabilizing interferences. The congress stressed the need to strengthen international solidarity in order to 'tackle the so-called new-order' and called for the active presence of Cyprus within the non-aligned movement, despite its European course (AKEL 1995c, p. 25).

The 18th congress also decided to change the party's negative position on accession to the EU, adopted since the early 1960s. In the light of overall popular support for Europe and in view of the imminent opening of accession negotiations, there was little ground for continuing a negative stance. As explained in the resolution, the party maintained its views about the EU as 'an advanced form of capitalist political and economic integration' and as 'the political extension of the North Atlantic Treaty Organization in Europe'. The latter was summarized in a famous slogan of the 1980s— 'EEC and Nato are the same syndicate'—implying a criminal connotation. The 'radical changes in the objective reality', though, called for an adjustment of position and acceptance of the European course under certain conditions. The main argument was the use of this course to achieve a just solution for the Cyprus issue, while accession should not be at any cost; the Republic of Cyprus as a whole should access the EU and negotiations should be 'substantive and dynamic' (AKEL 1995c, pp. 43–46). The result should not endanger the economic and social achievements of the Cypriot people. As stressed in the resolution, the new stand did not mean that the party's socialist objective for the transformation of society would be abandoned.

On the internal front, the cleavage between right and left, replaced since 1974 by the cleavage of pro- and anti-Makarios forces, re-emerged. AKEL redefined its perception of parties, characterizing the DIKO–DISY coalition government as the 'right and extreme right administration' (AKEL 1995c, p. 11). Thus DIKO was no longer seen as part of the progressive, patriotic, democratic forces. During the same period, and in spite of the failure of its presidential candidate in 1998, AKEL saw new prospects for an alliance with DIKO, which had left the Clerides government in November 1997. It laid the foundations for a comprehensive proposal for a new government in late 2000, some months before the parliamentary election.

This 'proposal for the modernization of our society' constituted a way out of existing policies, which were regarded as serving the interests of big capital, promoting anti-popular measures and 'characterized by a crisis of values, decay and corruption' (AKEL 2000). AKEL's opposition agenda focused on new issues, such as the environment and combating drugs, and on criticisms of the Clerides government for old and newly discovered problems. The whole programme was also a response to the evils caused by the 'new order', globalization and the weaknesses of the EU. In its proposal, which formed the basis of the party's electoral programme in the 2001 parliamentary elections, AKEL stressed the need to 'give vision to and renew the hopes of the people' through modernization of the state and private institutions and changes in the relationship between the administration and the citizens. The party paved the way to the 2003 presidential elections through alliance agreements for the election of the president of the House and mayoral elections in 2001.

After the election of Tassos Papadopoulos to the presidency of the Republic with its support (in 2003), AKEL found itself in trouble on a number of issues and in particular on the Cyprus question. Its rejection of the plan proposed by the UN in April 2004 meant a major divergence from the party's traditional positions both on the solution and on relations with the Turkish Cypriots (Christophorou 2005). On many occasions, its leaders were attempting to defend impossible positions. The combination of the President's views and AKEL's traditional positions of rapprochement with the Turkish Cypriots appeared awkward, causing dissensions within the party.

DISY opted for ideological changes in order to adapt to what its leaders perceived as new realities, both internal and external. In 2005 they appeared even to contemplate an eventual transformation of DISY into a centre party, thus abandoning the right-wing ideology that dominated its policies and strategy of alliances up to Clerides' election to power. Its leadership displayed moderation, while certain groups and cadres often expressed nationalist positions. The second term, won in 1998 with the support of small parties, and the change in the attitude of EDEK, now preaching an end to enmities of the past, led to the formation of a multiparty government. DISY felt the need to break with nationalist positions and escape from introversion, which was limiting its ideological appeal. It needed to change a situation where it focused attention on responding to demands by party members and friends and on dealing with a narrow spectrum of partisan issues. There was also an urgent need to abandon nationalist policies adopted during the coalition government with DIKO and to respond to AKEL's offensive, while at the same time finding a way to keep in touch with centre and right-wing voters. The manifesto on 'Eurodemocracy' of 1998 and the denial of ideological cleavages were an attempt in these directions. Within this frame of reference, DISY was offering itself a way out of an ideological confusion reigning among its supporters[1] due also to the diversity of the groups that had founded the party in 1976. The claim that the terms 'left', 'right' and 'centre' were obsolete and the new identity, defined on the basis of humanistic values, social liberalism and realism, between neo-liberalism and the domination of the state, supported the party's argument that it was 'covering a very broad political spectrum' (DISY 1998).

Under the new orientation, DISY defined itself as a catch-all party, appealing to every citizen. In the 2001 elections, it focused on its pro-European character, in opposition to AKEL's scepticism, and sought the people's vote as a means to reinforce the European perspective. This aimed at shifting attention from AKEL's strong points—opposition to nationalism and focus on internal issues and problems. DISY's main arguments indicated the use of Europe more as a symbolical resource than a set of values. Additionally, the stars of the European flag surrounded the party logo, and rainbow colours replaced the blue of the nationalist period.

DISY did not manage to stay in power. It went into opposition and only months later, at its tenth congress (May 2003), defined its new concept, that of a 'modern dynamic opposition' that would present an alternative proposal for government. In the case of the UN/Annan plan, the leaders of the conservative party reversed traditional roles by saying 'yes', against what appeared in the polls to be the position of two-thirds of its voters. They attempted to explain their positions and achieved relatively good results in the European elections in June 2004.

Party Organization: Strong Leading Coalitions and Empowered Members

Ideological orientations have determined the organizational structure and the relationship of parties with the electorate and their members (Ierodiakonou 2003, pp. 229–235). AKEL adopted democratic centralism and views its members as militants with the duty to be constantly active (AKEL 1995a, pp. 8–10). In theory, membership is open to all and decided at the lowest local level. The superior bodies get involved only in the case of refusal of an application. In practice, AKEL has been following a strict selection and filtering procedure that has resulted in a ceiling in membership figures. This practice protected the party from important membership variations and risks of alteration of its character. Additionally, criteria for candidature and selection procedures for AKEL leadership offices have been a guarantee against dissident candidatures and surprise voting, as well as a safeguard for discipline and guided voting (Ierodiakonou 2003, p. 242).

While no annual data are made public, it appears from figures released sporadically that membership has stagnated since the early 1990s at 14,000 (Table 2). In 2005, more than 90 per cent of the membership paid their dues, but the number of active members is not given with certainty. Party base groups, the local-level units incorporating all members, should meet monthly, but in most cases they hold only three to four meetings a year, with participation below 50 per cent. The party is also interested in 'friends of the party', and in 'supporters', terms that appear in the party 'rules of procedure' and in speeches, but without any definition. Friends can participate in meetings and express their views. Since 1990, they have been given the right to propose names for inclusion on the lists of candidates to local authorities or to the House of Representatives. Selection should ensure a 'balanced ticket, representing the physiognomy of the party, of the popular movement and of the left in general' (AKEL 1995b, p. 21).

The replacement of the splinters, as well as of those who left in response to the 1990 decision that members over 65 years old could not occupy party administrative posts, led to a renewal that was apparent at the 17th congress (1990), in respect of both first-time participants and the age of the delegates. However, with the passage of time the renewal rate has dropped dramatically and that for delegates under the age of 40 fell from 46.2 per cent in 1990 to 21.1 in 2005. In addition, first-time entrants to the central committee dropped from 47 out of 100 in 1990 to only 16 out of 105 in 2005 (AKEL 1990b; 1995c; 2001; *Haravgi*, 22 November 2005).

Table 2 DISY and AKEL Membership, and Ratio of Party Membership to Total Electorate and Party Voters, 1981–2005

Year	Party membership		Members as percentage of electorate		Members as percentage of voters	
	DISY[*]	AKEL	DISY	AKEL	DISY	AKEL
1981	11,000	(13,958)	3.6	4.5	11.8	14.6
1982		13,958[†]				
1984		14,338[†]				
1986	11,000	15,000[†]	3.2	4.3	10.3	17.1
...	...					
1989	13,959					
1990	14,264	15,000[‡]				
1991	15,210	(15,000)	4.0	3.9	12.4	14.3
1992	15,574					
1993	18,402					
1994	21,046					
1995	23,260					
1996	24,515	(14,000)	6.0	3.4	19.2	11.5
1997	26,085					
1998	27,362					
1999	28,774					
2000	29,495					
2001	30,287	(14,000)	6.5	3.0	21.7	9.8
2002	32,951					
2003	34,592					
2004	35,264					
2005	35,502	13,941[§]	7.1	2.8	—	—

Note: Figures in brackets are estimates.
Sources: [*]DISY general director; [†]AKEL 1986, p. 178; [‡]1990a, p. 8; [§]*Haravgi*, 22 November 2005.

It appears that the selection and filtering procedures limit the party's potential for broadening its membership and recruitment of cadres. Another factor is the reluctance of party supporters to become members in a demanding environment, requiring investment in time and effort. The secretary-general reported organizational problems caused by negative phenomena such as 'fatigue, indifference, lack of discipline, tendencies to increase personal influence, and reduced contribution to the practical daily work of the party' (AKEL 1995c, p. 10; AKEL 2001, p. 26). As a result, and despite the increase of both the electorate and the party votes, membership figures have stayed at the same level. This has been achieved through both additional efforts and the registration of about 700 new members before every congress (about five per cent of the total).

The organizational structure of AKEL has not changed substantially. The congress, convened in autumn every five years, remains the highest authority; it elects the 100 members of the central committee (changed to 105 in 2005), which elects the secretary-general and the political bureau. No significant variations in their membership have taken place. In the context of what was perceived as a broadening of internal democracy, the 17th congress (1990) decided that the central committee could transmit its views and minority proposals on important issues for decision by the party base groups, who in 1995 supported European accession (65 per cent), the imposition of value added tax (VAT) and other matters. The base groups also initiate the nomination of delegates to the congress and of candidates to party and to public offices. Consequently, decisions are taken either by special committees or by especially constituted enlarged electoral assemblies, at the level of the body to which the nominations have been made. For example, the lists of candidates to district bodies are finalized at the district level, while the decision about the lists for municipal elections lies with bodies at the municipal level.

Additionally, the party administration was enlarged with special bureaux created to assist the leadership with studies and reports on European affairs (1990), the European Parliament (2004), relations with the Turkish Cypriots, and other issues.

A major asset for AKEL has been the potential of organizations affiliated or linked to it. Collateral organizations, though independent, have been under the influence of the party and have contributed to the establishment of its influence since their creation in the 1940s. This is especially true for the trade unions PEO (Pancyprian Federation of Labour), which in 2000 had 63,500 members, and EKA (Union of Cypriot Peasants), as well as for the party's women's and youth organizations—agents of political socialization. In spite of difficulties and a decline in membership in recent years, trade unions enjoy significant potential for influence, based on historical links and regular contacts with workers and peasants.

Within the framework of AKEL's collective character, it may be assumed that the leader enjoys limited prominence. The conditions under which the present leaders were elected in 1990 resulted in the emergence of a relatively homogeneous group of cadres loyal to the new secretary-general. His re-election since then with 95 per cent of the vote, however, underlines the weight of his authority in the leading coalition, which increased with his election in 2001 to the second most important state office, that of president of the House of Representatives.

Party relations with the executive have changed only since 2003. In the past, and in the light of the limited demands to lend support to Makarios, Kyprianou and Vassiliou, AKEL experienced a malaise when its favourite ministers were ousted from the cabinet by President Kyprianou, or when the executive was promoting decisions in spite of its disagreement. The party took office for the first time in the Papadopoulos government and chose to limit the number of party officials in government, in favour of persons enjoying its confidence. This resulted in limited internal upset. The main problems that emerged from that were linked to potentially differing or opposing views between the government and the party, in particular on the Cyprus issue. Moreover, the party was called upon to solve problems caused by frequent dissensions between the parties in the coalition government.

DISY follows a very simple procedure for registering new members, which is reflected in the growth of its membership. In 2005 the party had 35,502 members, up by 53 per cent from 1995, and by 154 per cent compared with 1989. The membership represented 12 per cent of the party vote in 1991, 19 per cent in 1996 and 22 per cent in 2001 (Table 2). The spectacular growth might be attributed to a variety of reasons: voters felt free to join the party after it gained full legitimacy with Clerides' election, while a number joined it to seek personal favours. The development of the youth and student organizations following the establishment of the University of Cyprus in 1992 might also be another reason. Ierodiakonou (2003, p. 315) stresses the fact that the party reached maturity and instituted procedures that ensured fully functional structures.

The broadening of DISY's ideological appeal and various problems due to rivalries and grievances created the need for more contact with the grassroots. This was felt all the more urgently following the referendum of April 2004 in which, according to exit polls, two-thirds of DISY voters rejected the UN plan officially supported by the party. DISY engaged in practices already tried in 2001, and in late 2004 initiated surveys via the internet and by post, sessions of public dialogue and meetings with citizens. These acted as mobilizing factors for party members and others, enabling them to get closer to the party.

Other measures distinguished DISY's relationship with its members and society in general: after 1995 it set up electoral assemblies at various levels that elected the respective local and district officials, as well as the top leaders (the chairman, the deputy and the three vice chairmen and ten members of the political bureau).[2] These assemblies were broader than the congresses and were further enlarged in 2000 to include all party members at the respective level, a measure put into practice for the election of the leaders in May 2003. District assemblies nominate 'number of seats + 1' candidates to parliamentary elections and the supreme council finalizes the list (DISY 1995; 2003).

Quotas for young people and women in the party's governing bodies and candidate tickets, decided in 2003, were set at 30 per cent for each group as from January 2005. This was in response to the increasing role of young people in strengthening the party, as well as higher female mobilization in politics. The quotas were expected to compensate for competitive disadvantages due to late female mobilization and short party membership life. In the spirit of opening to civil society, the political bureau, the party's executive body, was given the power to enlarge the governing bodies by up to 30 per cent with individuals from outside the party. This was intended to combat the alienation of moderates, who distanced themselves from intra-party competition, considered 'dirty politics'. It also proved a means to change the rules of competition and limit the impact of clientelist and personal influences.

Amendments to the party statute started in 1994 changed the organizational structure and the distribution of power within DISY. Some bodies such as the political committee, an executive body with broad participation, and the extended political bureau ceased to exist, regarded as redundant or not flexible. The supreme council became the deliberative body, with supervisory powers over all party organs, apart from congress, which is the highest party body. The supreme council comprises more than 300 party cadres and representatives. Among them are the 50 members of the political bureau (enlarged since 1999). They are the chairman, the deputy and three vice chairmen and the party's parliamentary spokesman—constituting the executive bureau—ten elected and numerous *ex officio* members, including the parliamentary group. Some elected offices, such as that of the secretary-general and their assistants and others with administrative or organizational duties, were replaced by administrative posts. These and other new posts are reserved for appointed cadres. Since 2000 an administrative council, composed of members of the leadership and administrators, has supervised the functioning of the party's administrative structures (DISY 1995; 1999; 2003). After moving into the opposition, a council of commissioners was created in 2003. Commissioners and, in some cases, assistants were assigned with the task of monitoring the activity of ministers and producing alternative ideas, which was also a way of preparing for eventually assuming office, in the case of returning to power.

It appears from the above that emphasis on administrative aspects responded to the needs for diversification and specialization, while suppression of assumed redundant bodies, enlargement of the political bureau and creation (in 2003) of the executive bureau to deal with day-to-day activities added flexibility, enabling speedy action and decision making (Mair et al. 2004b, p. 266).

Additionally, incompatibilities and limitations opened the road for more members to get involved. Holding party posts is prohibited to public officials, apart from mayors and municipal councillors. Since 2001 the duration of party office has been limited to two four-year terms. The chairman, the deputy and vice chairmen are excluded from the above restrictions. In the case of parliamentary candidates, the party chairman has the right to include up to eight (out of 56) names of his choice. Exceptions to the nominating procedures are possible in the case of alliances, where the power to decide lies with the political bureau, subject to approval by the supreme council (DISY 2003). The candidate for the presidential elections should be chosen on the basis of a proposal by the political bureau to the supreme council, which might transmit its decision to an extraordinary party congress for approval.

Overall, the above changes and innovations have been significant, but one may argue that, to some extent, the main organizational patterns and hierarchy have remained unchanged. In essence, however, the new structure and procedures have changed the internal dynamics, while the efficiency of work has been enhanced through professionalization and stronger administration.

The party had no affiliated organizations in 1976. Conservative trade unions and other groupings were linked and controlled by the forces of the inner system, so DISY initiated the creation of new ones. These are the students' union (Protoporia), the youth organization (Nedisy), the women's organization (Godisy) and the more independent peasants' union (Panagrotikos). Since the establishment of the University of Cyprus in 1992, student and youth mobilization has been particularly high. In addition, the party has in recent years created the Association of Young Scientists and the Association of Senior Citizens, and operated a training school for party cadres and an institute on Eurodemocracy.

DISY has developed a different organizational structure from AKEL. The creation of the six-member executive bureau meant a narrowing of the team running the party affairs on a daily basis, which has ultimately led to an upgrading of the leading coalition. The status of the chairman has acquired prominence, for several reasons. His direct election by the party members, decided in 1999 and first applied in May 2003, has further legitimated and enhanced his authority. This has also been true in connection with his power to nominate or appoint party administrators and candidates to the parliament, as well as to appoint numerous advisors who participate in party meetings without voting rights. Furthermore, the director of the chairman's office acts as the party spokesperson, an additional indirect way of identifying the chairman with the party.

The move of the party chairman to the presidential palace in 1993 has been a source of tensions and conflicts. During Clerides' presidency, problems emerged at various levels linked to the procedures for the replacement of those leaving to take up ministerial portfolios or other offices, the relationship between the party, the President and his ministers and the relationship between the party and the parties or individuals participating in the governmental coalition. A final level of tensions and grievances was caused by members' expectations of personal favours that the party could not meet (Christophorou 2001a; 2003).

The provisions that allowed ministers and other government officials to participate with full rights in the political bureau, introduced in 1999, could contribute to bridging the gap between the party and the government. Experience, though, has shown that participation in meetings was almost non-existent.

Inventive Campaigns Target Centre Voters

The presidential system relegated parliamentary contests to a secondary place, while alliances for the election of the president of the parliament and in mayoral elections have become part of the strategy to win the presidency. The parameters influencing competition have changed following the adoption of the proportional system and the fragmentation of political forces. Forming a majority for supporting a presidential candidate after 2001 required more than two parties. This demanded caution and milder tones between prospective allies in electoral competition. An additional phenomenon was greater flexibility in the dealings especially of large parties seeking cooperation.

While reaffirming its Marxist–Leninist ideology, AKEL tried to broaden its support after 1970 by labelling its ticket of parliamentary and other candidates ΆΚΕΛ—Αριστερά' (AKEL—Left). This changed again in 1991 with the addition of 'Νέες Δυνάμεις' (New Forces), and the inclusion on AKEL's ticket of candidates from outside the party and the left-wing camp. The party's main competitors have been the centre DIKO and EDEK, from which it gained votes following their cooperation with DISY in 1993 and 1998. AKEL's influence increased in the capital and its environs, where both centre parties suffered substantial losses after 1996. AKEL's main target, though, remains DISY. In this way AKEL has the opportunity to play the role of the force that counters the influence of the right. Opinion polls have shown that a small percentage of DISY and AKEL voters could vote for either party, and very few actually did so in 2001 (RAI-MEGA 2001).

The course of events after 1993, with the ascendance to power of the right and AKEL in isolation, forced the party to reconsider its competitive strategy. Experiences of the past led to a change of position on future support for presidential candidates. A short paragraph of the political resolution at the 18th congress epitomized the new concept: 'AKEL contests and demands the share of power that rightly belongs to it and is prepared to undertake the relevant responsibility. AKEL does not simply support candidates but also contests a role and a say in the administration of this country, when and if the candidate it will support wins the presidential elections' (AKEL 1995b, p. 33).

The party failed in the 1998 presidential elections but this did not curtail its capacity to continue growing; by 2001, it had become the largest party (34.7 per cent). It adopted the route plan followed by its opponents, of step-by-step strategic alliances to conquer the executive. In a multistage process AKEL secured a comprehensive agreement with DIKO's leader, Tassos Papadopoulos, in 2001. To achieve its goals, it shifted its focus of attention and the objectives of alliances to power sharing. However, it did not get its fair share because the secondary political forces, DIKO and EDEK, had been making aggressive demands, using blunt words such as 'we will agree to ally forces with the party that will offer us a higher share'. It was clear that programmatic convergence was receiving little credit, while the two major parties were limited in their making of an offer. The crucial element in presidential elections strategy was a high bid and timely agreements, and AKEL achieved executive power only after it accepted this reality.

In parliamentary elections, where each party contests elections alone, AKEL sets up an ad hoc communication group of cadres six months before the elections. They work with the secretariat of the central committee, as well as in cooperation with specialized professionals and agencies, preferably with links to the party. In recent years, AKEL has been cooperating with a communications agency on an informal basis. The role of the professionals is limited to technical issues and to guidance, since the objectives and policies of the campaign are set by the party.

The campaign has been conducted through the use of all means, both traditional and modern, with a *de facto* shift to radio and television. The party's powerful machinery also uses canvassing, since personal contact in Cyprus's small society continues to bear fruit. Additional practices emerged in 2001, with AKEL replacing partisan posters in the streets with paintings of living Cypriot artists, shifting attention from politics to culture. Its leaders visited youth clubs, while open-air music events with famous artists from Greece replaced rallies, and people were called to attend the opening of artistic events. 'We have to be imaginative and creative, to send clear messages,' commented an official. The party has changed its traditional disdain for opinion polls, using them as sources of information about the electorate, for strategic planning and to determine the issues of the campaign. Campaigns have been funded through yearly fundraising, a major means for mobilization, targeting members, friends, followers and businesses. This constituted the main resource for sustaining the party bureaucracy and all party activities, prior to the introduction of a system of state grants to political parties in 1989. State funding has been an important resource for the party because of its electoral size, retained as the criterion for the allocation of public funds.

In the light of the above changes, AKEL can be placed in the early phase of stage two of campaign professionalization, as regards all three dimensions: technology, resources and thematic changes (Farrell & Webb 2000).

The major repercussion of the new situation lies in the contradictions between AKEL's collective character and the exposure gained by party officials in the media. Similarly, limited mobilization for campaigns has increased citizens' disaffection. AKEL is more affected by the new environment, since it used to be almost the sole actor in providing political information, education and guidance to its members. At the same time, this new environment has enabled the party to spread its messages to a larger audience, moving some of the communication barriers and cleavages in traditional societies. An ongoing debate within the party is focusing on whether communication skills or traditional militant activity must or could be the criterion for the promotion of cadres.

From its foundation, DISY faced the enmity of all other forces and fought against all of them. Its competitive strategy in parliamentary elections aimed at gains from the centre parties DIKO and EDEK, targeting also AKEL, not as a potential resource but as an ideological opponent. Promoting polarization proved an efficient strategy for retaining a large part of its voters who were distressed about party policies in 2001. This, however, proved less successful in the capital, Nicosia, where the party suffered heavy losses after 1996 (Christophorou, 2001b).

Facing a tripartite alliance of AKEL, DIKO and the social democrats of KISOS[3] in 2001, the leaders of DISY invented a new concept, 'transcendence', the need to act beyond partisan barriers. They offered support to mayoral candidates of the alliance to downplay an eventual defeat. In late 2002 they proposed the leader of KISOS as presidential candidate against Tassos Papadopoulos, supported by AKEL and DIKO. The trouble in the ranks of the alliance did not last beyond the time of uncertainties linked to EU enlargement and pending efforts to solve the Cyprus issue (Christophorou 2003). When Clerides announced his candidature, in early January 2003, a second candidature split the party, while angry social democrats turned to Papadopoulos, causing the failure of 'transcendental' choices and the loss of the presidency.

DISY's campaigns combined traditional means and, in particular, canvassing as a powerful communication tool, along with new forms of events and activities. The party has, however, come a long way on the path of professionalization started in the early 1980s and with the hiring of consultants from Greece since 1990. The group leading campaigns and setting the agenda used to start work some months before the elections under the leadership of the deputy chairman. The director of communication, other political and administrative officials, and specialists in various fields participated in the work of the group. In reality, a mini-campaign has since the early 1990s been led on a daily basis, on radio and television, as well as in the press. For this work a deputy was nominated as spokesperson, but, as pointed out earlier, often the director of the chairman's office assumed this role. Communication specialists have been hired on a continuous basis, to respond to both short and long-term needs.

The agenda of policy issues depends on the kind of elections, with the Cyprus question and the European course dominating the presidential elections, while internal affairs occupy centre stage in parliamentary elections. However, the distinction has not always been clear.[4] In parliamentary elections, the campaign is not focused on a central figure. The leader's media appearances might receive high ratings, but he has never been the focal point of the campaign. Leaders head the parties and eventually the ticket of candidates in a constituency, needing no votes of preference to be elected. The fact that the Cypriot constitution provides no prime-ministerial post limits drastically any prospects for the presidentialization of parliamentary elections.

Turkish Cypriots in and out of Europe

The present party system developed after all Turkish Cypriots gathered in the northern part of the island, under the effective control of the Turkish army, in summer 1974. The peculiar conditions that have prevailed since the 1940s in Cyprus resulted in a nationalist political establishment (Kaymak 2003), with conservative forces attached to Turkey leading the community.

The CTP is the older formation. It was founded in 1970, 'in order to defend democracy, human rights and inter-communal peace, to oppose the reactionary, chauvinist regime, which was under the influence of the military organizations of that period'.[5] At the time, Turkish Cypriots were living besieged and isolated in enclaves, effectively ruled by Turkish and local military.

Rauf Denktash, along with the influence and control of Turkey, has dominated the political stage since the late 1950s. He represented his community in talks on the Cyprus issue and was its undisputable leader until 2003, when his positions on Cyprus's accession to the EU and on UN proposals for reunification were massively contested by Turkish Cypriots. In 1975 he founded the UBP, which governed until January 2004, and suffered from dissensions and several splits (Dodd 1993; Hatay 2005, pp. 17–18). The left-wing Communal Liberation Party (Toplumcu Kurtuluş Partisi—TKP) founded in 1976 and the communist-oriented CTP have been the main opposition forces. Dissensions and splits caused voter re- and de-alignments, with their best combined result achieved in 1981 (44 per cent) and their worst in 1998 (29 per cent).

Instability has been a principal feature of the party system, with many mergers and splits; there were 20 cabinets in the period from 1976 to 2000 and more than 25 parties contested elections (Table 3). The electoral system changed before each election (Warner 1993, pp. 197–199) to serve the interests of the dominant forces, while splits

Table 3 Turkish Cypriot Election Results, Party Leaders and Cabinets, 1993–2005

| Year | UBP | | CTP | | Party leader | | | Prime minister | Date | Cabinet | |
	Votes	Seats (%)	Votes	Seats (%)	UBP	CTP					
1993	29.9	34.0	25.2	26.0	D. Eroglu	O. Ozgur		H. Atun (DP)	01.01.1994	DP-CTP	majority
								H. Atun (DP)	18.01.1995	DP-CTP	majority
						O. Ozgur		H. Atun (DP)	22.05.1995	DP-CTP	majority
					D. Eroglu	M.A. Talat		H. Atun (DP)	11.12.1995	DP-CTP	majority
								D. Eroglu (UBP)	16.08.1996	UBP-DP	majority
								D. Eroglu (UBP)	16.09.1998	UBP-DP	majority
1998	40.4	48.0	13.4	12.0	D. Eroglu	M.A. Talat		D. Eroglu (UBP)	30.12.1998	UBP-TKP	majority
					D. Eroglu			D. Eroglu (UBP)	08.06.2001	UBP-DP	majority
2003	32.9	36.0	35.2	38.0	D. Eroglu	M.A. Talat		M.A. Talat (CTP)	13.01.2004	CTP-DP	majority
								M.A. Talat (CTP)	09.08.2004	CTP-DP	majority
								M.A. Talat (CTP)	20.10.2004	CTP-DP	minority
2005	31.7	38.0	44.5	48.0	D. Eroglu	M.A. Talat		M.A. Talat (CTP)	10.03.2005	CTP-DP	majority
					D. Eroglu	S.F. Soyer		S.F. Soyer (CTP)	26.04.2005	CTP-DP	Majority

Source: <http://www.cm.gov.nc.tr/cm/kabine/kabban.htm > .

were used to weaken opponents or prevent excessive influence by any political force or leader. A proportional block vote with a five per cent threshold has been in force since 1998. The parliamentary government system with increased powers to the president allowed Rauf Denktash to continue dominating the system.

The party system has developed in a peculiar environment, under the control of and with dependence on Turkey in many fields. The Turkish army maintains more than 30,000 troops and the military control all security issues, including civil defence. The development of political and other institutions suffered significant limitations and constraints, and the political authorities have not so far gained full control over the system.[6] A major part of the budget and investments are funded by Turkey, the official currency is the Turkish lira and the governor of the central bank is from Ankara. Politicians and civilians, including influential journalists, have often faced persecution and threats by nationalists or have been brought before military courts, some on charges of insulting the Turkish military.[7] The role of Turkey at election time has also often been denounced by Turkish Cypriot leaders (Ozsaglam 2003; Hatay 2005).

Changes were made after the Justice and Development Party took office in Ankara, in late 2002: Turkey has kept a low profile in Cyprus, though maintaining its grasp on the community through the economy and an unchanged military presence.

A Course Towards Contrasting Fates

Some of the UBP features might justify its characterization as a 'regime party', since it has remained in power throughout almost its entire existence, identifying itself with the political system. It established its influence through the appeal of its founder and control over the system of power; manipulation of the electoral system and the support it enjoyed from the military and Ankara were further reasons for its dominance. The ambitions of Dervis Eroglu and the clash with Rauf Denktash for power divided the party in 1992 and excluded it from power for about 30 months (Dodd 1993). A new balance emerged with the UBP sharing power with its splinter, the Democratic Party (DP, headed by Denktash's son), from 1996 to 1998 and from 2001 to early 2004.

The monopoly on power and influence was not without problems. Despite the fact that they constituted less than 20 per cent of the population and controlled over 37 per cent of the island's territory, Turkish Cypriots faced serious difficulties. In opinion polls they consistently ranked the economy as their main problem.[8] Grievances about the distribution of Greek Cypriot property, economic problems, corruption, unemployment, dependency on Turkey and immigration from Anatolia and the Black Sea were forcing young people to emigrate. Additionally, lack of international recognition and isolation turned the community into a hostage of the *status quo*.

The UBP share oscillated between 37 per cent (1981) and 55 per cent (1990). With the exception of 1976, in all elections its share among settlers from Turkey was lower than among Turkish Cypriots, though not negligible.

The features of the CTP differed considerably; behind its traditional Marxist–Leninist leadership, a dynamic group of young members, influenced by the leftist ideology of the late 1960s, emerged in 1990 as a driving force for change. They originated in the Youth Federation of (Turkish) Cypriot Students, founded in 1975. At that time, the party was excluded from the inner system and faced persecutions, insults and characterizations such as 'AKEL's agents', 'Greeks' and 'traitors'.[9] In the late 1980s, this dynamic youth group, who had also pioneered the creation of left-wing trade unions, had reached their maturity within the party and were playing a decisive role in changing it. They started in 1990 with organizational issues, partly modifying the party's highly centralized character. In 1992, despite opposition by the old guard, they enshrined in the constitution new ideological features, defining the CTP as a liberal socialist formation accepting the free market and privatization. The party gave its logo a minor face-lift with the replacement of the red background with green. A new era also started with the loosening of the traditionally very close relations with AKEL, while the internationalist approach, rejecting divisions on ethnic criteria, lost its intensity. These major changes allowed the party to break through the inner system and participate as a minor partner in coalition government in 1994. Dissensions on participating in the exercise of power reached a turning point in 1995 and the crisis led to a change in leadership in January 1996. The new leader was Mehmet Ali Talat, a young and ambitious mechanical engineer. He established his own group of cadres and promoted a mediatized image of the leader and the party. The disappointment of the CTP's electorate after 30 months in office, the divisions and split, as well as the bankruptcy of entrepreneurial business activities initiated by the party further contributed to the bad performance and losses (45 per cent) in the elections of December 1998.

Party Programmes: The Impulse of EU Values

The UBP refused to change until it lost power in December 2003. Considering all the changes that had taken place since 2001, such as the UN proposals and the referenda results, the accession of the Republic of Cyprus to the EU, as well as the victory of the CTP and the UBP's loss of power, the party's 15th congress redefined its positions in December 2004, while maintaining its traditional views on substantial issues. The party declared itself in line with liberal democracy and the market economy, and referred to the need to develop various sectors of the economy. Emphasis was put on political issues and the EU (UBP 2004).

In its resolution, the UBP refers to 'Cyprus Turks', meaning simply Turks living in Cyprus and not Turkish Cypriots. This perception is the nationalist approach that denies 'Cypriotism' and has its equivalent among Greek Cypriots. On the Cyprus question, the party changed its position that the problem was solved in 1974 with the division of the island and the instauration of two states. In December 2004 it accepted the need for further negotiations on the Annan plan, formerly rejected by the party, within the framework of the United Nations, 'not the EU'. This implied that the party acknowledged that the issue was not solved in 1974. The UBP also started supporting a European course for Turkish Cypriots, on the assumption that unilateral accession of the Republic of Cyprus was equivalent to union with Greece, the old dream of Greek Cypriots. The 15th congress resolution (December 2004) stressed that accession of Cyprus Turks should proceed separately from the Republic of Cyprus.

The CTP's values continued to change after it gained legitimacy. The coalition with the conservative DP intensified internal debates, focusing on how appropriate and politically correct this cooperation was and on the lack of a common ideological orientation. Frustration at the initial stages and the view of certain officials that 'doing politics with the Democratic Party, under the influence of Turkey, could lead nowhere' eventually led to a *modus vivendi*. The party and its voters faced issues related to private enterprise and relations with Turkey in practice. As they avow today, the coalition experience trained them in the exercise of power and reshaped their values to accept that Turkish interests merited attention.

After the accession negotiations of the Republic of Cyprus with the EU started in 1998, the party promoted a pro-European policy, considering that it would benefit the Turkish Cypriots. It appealed to Rauf Denktash to seize the opportunity and seek a solution that would enable a united Cyprus to join the EU. Solution and Europe were the central themes for the opposition parties, but it was the CTP that capitalized on them. It achieved a spectacular win in the 2002 municipal elections with a programme promoting European values under the slogan 'our open vision' and in 2003 it embraced a large group of NGOs, which it labelled 'united forces', campaigning for the same values. In their common 'declaration for a new Cyprus' in September 2003 they described the procedure and the principles that would allow the accession of a united Cyprus to the EU and facilitate Turkey's EU course.[10]

As leader of his community, taking office after the December 2003 and the February–April 2005 elections, Mehmet Ali Talat tuned his policies with Ankara, especially on issues relating to the Cyprus problem. There was a change in the party's traditional position on 'Cypriotism' of stressing the prevalence of the interests of Cypriots over those of Turkey or Greece and refusing the hegemony of Ankara: Talat stressed the need to consider the interests and concerns of Turkey as well. While speaking in support of a solution, he put the accent on ending the isolation of Turkish Cypriots and defending the non-recognized 'Turkish Republic of Northern Cyprus' (TRNC). The ethnic cleavages between Greeks and Turks appear reinforced in today's policies on both sides on the island.

One should consider that the change of government and the conditions prevailing both in Turkey and in Cyprus have facilitated the new orientations of the CTP; the presence and involvement of Turkey in the north of the island has been less visible than in earlier years and the establishment in Ankara appears less monolithic. However, some have expressed the view that many party voters feel uneasy with the CTP's new role and concerned about the future and tension in relations with the Greek Cypriot side.[11]

Does Good Organization Matter?

When considering the issue of party organization, one should keep in mind the small size of the community and the prohibition on public employees belonging to political organizations. This has led to a situation where a significant number of people are not officially party members but remain active as a kind of shadow members.

The UBP did not deploy any significant efforts to organize; membership was not the source of its power and influence on society. On the other hand, continuous population movements and changes did not allow for a stable electorate or political affiliation. The general policy was to 'leave the people to come to the party'. It was, thus, left to the constituency bodies to act. It seems that no central registry ever existed, while there were indications of a decline both in membership and in general capacity for mobilization. Some officials regretted the fact that the DP was more active, progressing at the expense of the UBP. However, the latter changed in 1999, allowing youth and women's organizations to be represented in district assemblies. They did not allow any central women's organization, which was seen as a denial of power to female party members. Lack of mobilization efforts and the disaffection of young people and dynamic elements in society have changed the party's base. Party officials have stated that election results showed a shift to the right to more conservative positions, which the officials regarded as not representing the party's true character.[12]

As a regime party, the UBP did not develop a sophisticated organizational structure. The congress, its supreme body, convenes every two years and elects 50 members of the party assembly and 13 members of the general directory, which are, respectively, the policy-making and the executive bodies. It also elects the chairman and the secretary-general, who head the assembly and the general directory, respectively. The former appoints five members to the assembly and the latter two members to the general directory. Mayors are *ex officio* members of the assembly. The party structure has not changed in recent years, with the exception of the renaming in 1996 of five vice chairmen as deputy secretaries, their pre-1990 title, and the creation in 2005 of a five-member advisory committee to deal with European affairs. Following an amendment of the party procedural rules in 2003, candidates to elections should be nominated by delegates in district or local electoral assemblies. The general directory should have the final say, with the chairman deploying discretionary powers. However, the implementation of the regulations has not taken place and some have claimed that the chairman made the nominations.[13]

Dervis Eroglu has been the dominant figure in the party since 1983, when he was first elected as its chairman. The many challenges and splits failed to depose him or to weaken his position substantially until he withdrew in early 2006. Exercise of executive power and lack of modern organizational structures have allowed the leader to sustain a network of loyal party officials who have secured his supremacy and re-election for more than 20 years. His discretionary powers such as to veto the inclusion of and rank candidates on party electoral tickets, as well as to nominate candidates to public offices, gave him extraordinary leverage and power over individuals and the party.

The CTP has maintained its organizational character to a great extent, based on democratic centralism and member selection procedures that lead to a kind of *de facto* ceiling in membership figures. Keeping records and the general organization did not reach high levels of efficiency and membership data are lacking. However, high mobilization in election periods has been possible, except during the crisis years after the split caused by the leadership change in 1996, which led to the 1998 electoral debacle.

The CTP's success in the 2002 local elections continued with its 2003 and 2005 ascendance to power, opening a new era for it. The party's membership during good times was estimated at 3,000. If 'good times' means the CTP's 1993 and 2003 elections, 3,000 members corresponded to 12 and six per cent of the party's respective vote and 2.8 and two per cent of the electorate. These figures are relatively high if we consider the fact that the CTP faced up to the early 1990s legitimacy problems and that public employees, who make a significant mass of the electorate, cannot be members of any party. Furthermore, the provision for nominating candidates outside the party membership allowed it to enhance its capacity for mobilization and gaining support. Proposing candidacies for well-known individuals belonging to a variety of organizations campaigning for a solution and accession to EU contributed to enhancing the CTP's appeal in 2003 and 2005, compared with 1998. Recent amendments to the party statutes (July 2003) gave all members the right to participate in district electoral assemblies that nominate candidates to public offices (CTP 2003), a measure implemented neither in December 2003 nor in 2005.

However, the central bodies of the CTP appear similar to those of its Greek Cypriot counterpart, AKEL. Its policy-making body, the assembly, has 55 elected members (increased from 31 in 2003) plus two representatives of the youth and one of the women's organizations. The supreme body is the congress, which elects the assembly and the party chairman. In turn, the assembly elects the secretary-general and the 11-member executive board. The assembly should hold monthly meetings. The executive board deals with day-to-day party affairs. It is assisted by specialized committees established in recent years with the task of drafting policy frameworks on various issues such as the Cyprus problem, education, economy, labour relations, etc. European affairs are handled by the foreign relations committee. At the regional level, district assemblies draft the list of nominees for local and general elections, subject to approval by the central assembly. The district high officials are expected to head the lists. This practice was due to change in accordance with provisions approved in 2003 for the nomination of candidates by all members in electoral assemblies, but the change has not yet been implemented. Furthermore, non-party-members could be nominated after 2003, through special decision of the party congress.

While collective action has been the rule in the functioning of the CTP, following the changes since the early 1990s and the ascendance of Mehmet Ali Talat, the leader has become a central figure. His personality, his service as deputy prime minister and his prospects of heading the government one day have been decisive in this respect. The party structure is not affected when its leaders hold public offices, since the parliamentary group or other public post holders do not sit in the party governing bodies. However, Talat resigned from his post of party chairman because the constitution of the TRNC prohibits the leader of the Turkish Cypriots from being chairman of a political party. The fact that following their taking office in 2003 the CTP leaders shared their time between party and government has exacerbated the party's existing organizational flaws. The party assembly met only three or four times in 2004 and it was expected that the CTP's functioning would be further affected in 2005. It is too early to assess the impact of the above developments.

Success versus Failure without Professional Assistance

Following the split of the UBP in 1992, the party was no longer able to secure a majority of seats and found itself out of office in December 1993. Being the major partner, the UBP had no difficulty in forming coalitions with any of the other parties after its return to power in summer 1996. It formed successive coalitions with the CTP, the DP, the TKP and again the DP until December 2003. The leaders of the CTP and the TKP blamed Denktash and Ankara for the collapse of their coalition with the UBP.[14]

Analysis of election results showed that the UBP support was evenly distributed before 2003, with a higher vote among businessmen and other groups dependent on the administration, as well as older voters. However, the party lost its appeal among those supporting the EU course and a solution to the Cyprus issue. Its main competitors have been the DP but also small nationalist formations and to some extent the CTP. In February 2005 the UBP secured 32 per cent of the vote, and its leader Dervis Eroglu got only 23 per cent in the presidential elections two months later.[15]

The CTP's traditional ally and competitor was the centre-left TKP. After the failure of their common front in 1990, the CTP changed its programmes and values and did not hesitate to form coalition cabinets with the DP. In 2003, it signed a coalition protocol with the Peace and Democracy Movement and the Solution and EU Party, ruling out any cooperation with the UBP or the DP. However, it chose to follow its own strategy: it embraced the NGOs that favoured an EU course and adopted the label 'CTP—United Forces' (Kaymak 2003). Following its success in the 2003 and 2005 elections, it formed coalition governments as the major partner with the DP.

The CTP's main share has been among Turkish Cypriots and, in particular, those who moved to the north of the island in 1974. Its pro-EU and solution policy secured the party a large part of the vote in Nicosia and its environs, a traditional stronghold of conservative forces (Christophorou 2005). The failure of other centre and left-wing forces in 2005 increased the CTP's vote to more than 45 per cent, 13 points ahead of the UBP. With the exception of the 2003 and 2005 elections, the CTP's share among settlers from Turkey has been below ten per cent. This group has consistently voted by more than 80 per cent for the nationalist/conservative parties (Hatay 2005; Christophorou 2001b).

The UBP has not really ever felt the need to develop a competitive strategy and it has used communication professionals only once. The party managed to overcome the blow suffered in the 1992 split but it failed to sense that the need for a solution to the island's division and the European perspective had brought about radical changes to society and the party needed to adjust its policies and practices. Traditional campaigning methods and appearances on television, without any planning or innovation, limited the party's competitive potential. In response to the media era, a media monitoring committee was set up in the mid-1990s on a permanent basis, while the party campaign has been organized by a special committee. Although no candidates should participate in the committee, some affirmed that almost all members of the committee responsible for the 2003 campaign were candidates. The above were combined with lack of financial resources; being away from power, the party might for the first time realize that funds were needed to compensate for organizational flaws, and even fundraising might prove a hard task.

The CTP also conducted campaigns using traditional means, such as street banners and posters, open-air rallies, and distribution of leaflets. Changes in society and the media have reduced their significance to some extent. The end of the power holders' control over the media landscape offered the opposition parties opportunities for media access. Their overall image in the media, coupled with the negative reports by Turkish media received on the island, was rather disheartening, until the turning point in 2000 and 2001, when the media engaged in spreading the message in support of a solution and accession to the EU (Kaymak 2003). Furthermore, professional advice was sought from Istanbul, in 1993, for the drafting of slogans and of the party programme. The designing of the new European image of the party and its leader has been in recent years in the hands of individuals linked to the CTP, working with professionals and a committee established before elections.

The size of the population, the nature of the party and its limited financial resources have not allowed high levels of professionalization, despite the intensive use of broadcasting media. Professionals from Turkey have been viewed with suspicion, as outsiders unaware of the characteristics of the society and parties in north Cyprus. One may argue that the CTP succeeded because flaws and deficiencies in organization were compensated for by changes in the media landscape and the adoption of a positive position by the media towards the CTP, but also by changes in society in general; the fears and concerns of the people were no longer those of the late 1980s, while the potential of the establishment to influence decisions was curtailed by a new environment and lack of programmatic perspective. The *status quo* led to impasses and the CTP's positions and strategy persuaded the community by promising a better future (Christophorou 2005, pp. 102–103).

Conclusions

The main political parties of Cyprus have undergone many different changes, to differing degrees: the Greek Cypriot DISY and the Turkish Cypriot CTP have realized the most extensive changes. DISY has focused more on organizational structures and power sharing, without leaving ideology and values untouched, while the CTP has radically changed its ideology and programmes. With the exception of its position on the EU, AKEL has brought in limited changes, while the Turkish Cypriot UBP has just started modifying its structure and positions.

AKEL opted for an extensive leadership renewal, while remaining loyal to its Marxist–Leninist ideology. The latter's influence remains an exception among the radical left in Europe (March & Mudde 2005). Furthermore, the paradox for AKEL rests in the fact that in 1990 a young leadership achieved a return to the past. Possible explanations for these choices relate to the fact that neither AKEL's policies nor its electoral appeal were based on ideology. The party has based its influence not on the practice of communism but on a variety of factors linked to its role in social and labour battles since the 1940s, its relations with and control of trade unions, and the strong left–right cleavage. The combination of ideological rhetoric and moderate positions on social and other issues has proved successful so far in limiting the potential influence of the centre and other parties, and in maintaining the bipolar features of the system. The adoption of the European course, linked by all to the Cyprus issue, prevented a possible divorce of AKEL from large numbers of its voters and the people, for harming the 'national cause'. Its 'yes, but' position was translated into acceptance of the cohesion function of the EU and unhindered adoption of the harmonization legislation with AKEL's support. However, EU values merited only one reference, with the 'worker's social charter' evoked in the party's modernization proposal of 2000.

The CTP shifted to social democracy, abandoning its communist ideology, before young cadres took office. This proved a necessary step to legitimacy, along with acceptance of Turkey: a communist party leading in the north of the island, opposing Ankara's presence and control, appeared hard to imagine. Additionally, breaking with the past was also asserting the party's independence from 'big brother' AKEL and accusations of treason; the collapse of the Eastern bloc meant less dependence on the latter's help and assistance. Full endorsement of a European course proved to be in line with the aspirations of the Turkish Cypriots and gained the party momentum to power when similar aspirations were gaining ground in Ankara.

DISY followed uncertain ideological course and practices, ranging from extreme right to moderate and centre. While in power, nationalism dominated its policies and the party succumbed to pressures from members and supporters demanding their share of power after years of exclusion. DISY's growth in appeal and membership and the need to leave open doors for future alliances caused a crisis of identity in an already mosaic-like party. It responded with a shift in 1998 to moderate programmatic options defined in the 'Eurodemocracy' document. This option did not solve its problems related to factions and currents of thought, but offered an ideological frame of reference, theoretically at least. Europe has proved a major axis in the party's programmatic proposals since the late 1980s, gaining more significance at the approach of accession. In an environment of increased fragmentation of political forces, DISY combined changes that offered it internal cohesion and extended its potential for electoral influence.

As a regime party, the Turkish Cypriot UBP secured its domination over the years without sensing any pressure for change. Resistance to change was due to characteristics similar to those of parties in the new democracies (Van Biezen 2005), such as oligarchic tendencies and personalization. It is most significant that change was contemplated only after the UBP lost power in early 2004 and the prospects for regaining it soon appeared weak. The extent and the meaning of the changes of values started in late 2004 remain to be seen.

Among the factors that influenced changes in Greek Cypriot party organization, the decentralization of power in the mid-1980s and the parties' pursuit of efficiency occupied a prominent place. In order to avoid failure, parties sought solutions to voter reactions against nomination of candidates to local elections by the central leadership. Empowerment of bodies or base groups, though, did not go so far as to compromise democratic centralism, thus confirming the persistence of AKEL's and the CTP's birth imprint.

DISY's modification of structures and the development of an administration of professionals had many effects. Entrusting organizational and administrative tasks as well as studies and analyses of various issues to technocrats meant, on the one hand, reducing the possibility of political bias and, on the other, saving time for party political personnel to focus more on their political roles and activities in a demanding environment. Efficiency and broadening of internal democracy were also sought with the formation of flexible executive teams along with enlarged deliberative bodies. This enlargement, in particular of the electoral assemblies, had a double effect: the election by the base, by all party members, of the leading coalition has strengthened its legitimacy and authority; at the same time, the new procedures have led to decentralization of decision making on important policy issues, as well as on the nomination of candidates to elected public offices and the election of party officials. The appointment or nomination of individuals beyond the party members to offices or candidatures further weakened the influence of local dignitaries. Overall this achieved cohesion, but did not solve DISY's problems. The nomination of candidates in the 2003 presidential elections and the stance on the referendum of 2004 caused reactions and in the end a split was inevitable.

Government decentralization enhanced the appeal of the Greek Cypriot parties and influenced their alliance strategies. More electoral contests effectively led to greater mobilization. Fragmentation of the political forces encouraged by proportional representation in parliamentary elections made programmatic convergence a harder task than before. In the new environment, parties either minimized or removed the need to agree on programmes of government and focused all their attention and concern on power sharing. This pursuit of power alone made any alliance possible, except between AKEL and DISY, in spite of their converging positions on important issues and moderate politics. The two main parties often succumbed to excessive demands by the smaller formations, even insignificant ones that never contested elections.

The competition strategies adopted in parliamentary elections by all four parties featured a common characteristic—their appeal to candidates for public offices beyond party members—as a means to attract voters beyond their traditional base. In the case of DISY, this appeal also extended to all levels of party offices, both central and peripheral. Moreover, those elected to public offices have been granted *ex officio* rights in party bodies.

The issue of programmatic choices and campaign has been affected by the new media landscape; the media not only set the agenda of political debates, but also imposed a very intensive rhythm in political interventions. This situation made parties more aware of the fact that the image of a party is built not during a campaign but on a day-to-day basis. Additionally, this constantly puts to the test their ability to coordinate daily interventions and be consistent in their views and positions.

Notes

[1] Party officials stated to the author that surveys showed that party supporters had difficulty in defining their identity.

[2] On electoral assemblies that elect the leaders, thus empowering the base, see Mair et al. (2004a, p. 11).

[3] EDEK was renamed KISOS in 2000 and reverted to EDEK in 2003.

[4] Insight on campaigns was provided by party officials interviewed by the author.

[5] Republican Turkish Party, 'Our views on . . .', <http://www.ctpkibris.org/English/history.htm > . For more information on the situation in the 1970s, see Patrick (1976).

[6] Author's interviews with CTP and the Peace and Democracy Movement officials, July 2005.

[7] See Dodd (1993, p. 136) and Reporters Without Borders, 'Reports on Cyprus', <http://www.rsf.org > .

[8] See 'Results of polls', *Halkin Sesi*, 1–4 October 2001 and 'Turkish Cypriot views polled. . .', *Kibris*, 7–12 September 2000.

[9] Author's interviews with CTP officials, July 2005.

[10] See <http://www.ctpkibris.org/basin/basinbildirileri.htm > .

[11] Author's interviews with CTP officials and independent researchers, July 2005.

[12] Author's interviews with UBP officials, July 2005.

[13] Party regulations available at <http://www.ubp-kktc.org/ > .

[14] See *Ortam*, 25 May 2001 and <http://www.ctpkibris.org/English/history.htm > .

[15] See 'Talat, Serdar set to renew partnership', *Cyprus Weekly*, 27 February 2005 and 'New leader, new era', *Kibris*, 18 April 2005.

References

AKEL (1986) *16 Συνέδριο—Έκθεση Δράσης της Κ.Ε. του ΑΚΕΛ* [16th Congress—Activity Report of the CC of AKEL], Nicosia.

AKEL (1990a) *Our Concept of Socialism*, Nicosia.

AKEL (1990b) *Political Resolution and Other Material*, Nicosia.

AKEL (1995a) *Καταστατικό του ΑΚΕΛ* [Statutes of AKEL], Nicosia.

AKEL (1995b) *Καινωνισμοί λειτουργίας του ΑΚΕΛ* [Rules of Procedure of AKEL], Nicosia.

AKEL (1995c) *AKEL 18th Congress—Material and Other Documents*, Nicosia.

AKEL (2000) *Proposal for the Modernization of Our Society*, Nicosia.

AKEL (2001) *Αποφάσεις και άλλα ντοκουμέντα 19^{ου} συνεδρίου ΑΚΕΛ—7–10 Δεκεμβρίου 2000* [Resolutions and Other Documents of the 19th Congress of AKEL—7–10 December 2000], Nicosia.

Bosco, A. (2001) 'Four actors in search of a role. The Southern European communist parties', in *Parties, Politics and Democracy in the New Southern Europe*, eds P. N. Diamandouros & R. Gunther, Johns Hopkins University Press, Baltimore and London, pp. 329–387.

Christophorou, C. (2001a) 'Consolidation and continuity through change: parliamentary elections in Cyprus, May 2001', *South European Society & Politics*, vol. 6, no. 2, pp. 97–118.

Christophorou, C. (2001b) *Πληθυσμός και πολιτική στην κατεχόμενη Κύπρο* [Population and Politics in Occupied Cyprus], Hellenic Association of Political Science, Athens.

Christophorou, C. (2003) 'A European course with a communist party: the presidential election in the Republic of Cyprus, February 2003', *South European Society & Politics*, vol. 8, no. 3, pp. 94–118.

Christophorou, C. (2005) 'The vote for a united Cyprus deepens divisions—the 24 April 2004 referenda in Cyprus, April 2005', *South European Society & Politics*, vol. 10, no. 1, pp. 85–104.

Christophorou, C. (2006) 'The emergence of modern politics in Cyprus (1940–1959)', in *Britain in Cyprus. Colonialism and Post-colonialism 1878–2006*, eds H. Faustmann & N. Peristianis, Bibliopolis, Mannheim.

CTP (2003) 'CTP Tüzüğü', [CTP Statutes], < http://www.ctpkibris.org/tuzuk/ftuzuk.htm > .

DISY (1995) *Δημοκρατικός Συναγερμός—Καταστατικό* [Democratic Rally—Statutes], Nicosia.

DISY (1998) *Η πρότασή μας για τον 21ο αιώνα* [Eurodemocracy: Our Proposal for the 21st Century], Nicosia, < http://www.disy.org.cy/articles/diakirixeis/diak_2.htm > .

DISY (1999) *Δημοκρατικός Συναγερμός—Καταστατικό* [Democratic Rally—Statutes], Nicosia.

DISY (2003) *Δημοκρατικός Συναγερμός—Καταστατικό* [Democratic Rally—Statutes], Nicosia.

Dodd, C. H. (1993) 'The ascendancy of the right, 1985–1993', in *The Political Social and Economic Development of Northern Cyprus*, ed. C. H. Dodd, Eothen, London, pp. 136–166.

Farrell, D. M. & Webb, P. (2000) 'Political parties as campaign organizations', in *Parties without Partisans. Political Change in Advanced Industrial Democracies*, eds R. J. Dalton & M. P. Wattenberg, Oxford University Press, Oxford, pp. 102–128.

Hadjikyriakos, A. & Christophorou, C. (1996) *Βουλευτικές, Ιστορία Αριθμοί, Ανάλυση* [Parliamentary Elections, History, Figures, Analysis], Intercollege Press, Nicosia.

Hatay, M. (2005) *Beyond Numbers—an Inquiry into the Political Integration of the Turkish 'Settlers' in Northern Cyprus*, Peace Research Institute of Oslo, Nicosia.

Ierodiakonou, L. (2003) *Τεθλασμένη Πορεία—Κύπρος 1959–2003, Πολιτικό Σύστημα, Πολιτικοί Θεσμοί, Διαδρομή Εκδημοκρατισμού* [A Zigzag Course—Cyprus 1959–2003, Political System, Political Institutions, Democratization Process], Alithia, Nicosia.

Katsourides, I. (2003) 'Europeanization and political parties in accession countries: the political parties of Cyprus', paper delivered at the EpsNet 2003 Plenary Conference, Paris, 13–14 June, < http://www.pedz.uni-mannheim.de/daten/edz-k/gde/03/Katsourides.pdf > .

Kaymak, E. (2003) 'December's parliamentary elections in Northern Cyprus: before and after', < http://www.erpic.org/perihelion/wps/northcyprus.htm > .

Mair, P., Müller, W. C. & Plasser, F. (2004a) 'Electoral challenges and party responses', in *Political Parties and Electoral Change. Party Responses to Electoral Markets*, eds P. Mair, W. C. Müller & F. Plasser, Sage, London, pp. 1–19.

Mair, P., Müller, W. C. & Plasser, F. (2004b) 'Political parties in changing electoral markets', in *Political Parties and Electoral Change. Party Responses to Electoral Markets*, eds P. Mair, W. C. Müller & F. Plasser, Sage, London, pp. 264–274.

March, L. & Mudde, C. (2005) 'What's left of the radical left? The European radical left after 1989: decline *and* mutation', *Comparative European Politics*, vol. 3, no. 1, pp. 23–49.

Markides, K. (1977) *The Rise and Fall of the Cyprus Republic*, Yale University, New Haven and London.

Ozsaglam, M. (2003) 'The role of Turkey in 14th December elections in Northern Cyprus', < http://www.erpic.org/perihelion/articles2003/december/turkey.htm > .

Patrick, A. R. (1976) *Political Geography and the Cyprus Conflict (1963–1971)*, University of Waterloo, Waterloo.

Press and Information Office. (2002) *Αποτελέσματα δημοτικόν εκλογόν Δεκεμβρίου 2001* [Results of the December 2001 Municipal Elections], Nicosia.

RAI-MEGA (2001) *Δημοσκόπηση Μάιος 2001* [Opinion Poll May 2001], Nicosia.

UBP (2004) *'İlerleme ve Gelişim için Siyasal Vizyon'* [Political Vision for Progress and Development], Nicosia.

Van Biezen, I. (2005) 'On the theory and practice of party formation and adaptation in new democracies', *European Journal of Political Research*, vol. 44, pp. 147–174.

Warner, J. (1993) 'Parliamentary and presidential elections', in *The Political Social and Economic Development of Northern Cyprus*, ed. C. H. Dodd, Eothen, London, pp. 193–217.

From Political Islam to Conservative Democracy: The Case of the Justice and Development Party in Turkey

Ergun Özbudun

Introduction

If one of the most interesting characteristics of the Turkish party system in the 1990s was the rapid rise of political Islam under the banner of the Welfare Party (RP), an equally, perhaps, even more, noteworthy development in the early 2000s is its transformation under the Justice and Development Party (Adalet ve Kalkınma Partisi, AKP) leadership into a moderate conservative democratic party. The AKP won the 3 November 2002 parliamentary elections with 34.3 per cent of the vote and almost two-thirds (363) of the assembly seats. Various aspects of this transformation will be the central focus of this essay. In the first section dealing with recent party history, the AKP will be studied in the context of the earlier Islamist parties, since the AKP itself is a very new party (established on 14 August 2001) and only such comparison can give an idea of the extent of this transformation. In the second section, party values and programme will be examined in greater detail, especially in comparison with those of the previous Islamist parties. It will be argued that the AKP has less in common with them than with the mainstream centre-right parties in Turkey. In the following section on party organization, again some comparisons will be made with the predecessor parties. In the section on competitive strategy and campaign tactics, the emphasis will be on the AKP's dilemma between maintaining the loyalty of its religious-conservative voters and keeping its appeal to a much broader centre-right sector of the Turkish electorate.

Recent Party History

In the history of the Turkish Republic, the first party with clear Islamist credentials was the National Order Party (MNP) established in 1970 under the leadership of Necmettin Erbakan, an independent deputy from Konya and a former professor at Istanbul Technical University. The party was closed down by the constitutional court following the military intervention of 1971, and was replaced by the National Salvation Party (MSP) in 1973 under the same leadership. The MSP remained a medium-size party in the 1970s and its national vote share never exceeded 12 per cent. However, it played an important role in coalition politics between 1973 and 1980, because of the peculiarities of the parliamentary arithmetic. Mr Erbakan served as deputy prime minister in both the Bülent Ecevit (centre-left) and Süleyman Demirel (centre-right) governments.[1] The party was closed down again after the military intervention of 1980, and reorganized in 1983 under the name of the Welfare Party. After a modest restart in the local elections of 1984, its vote percentage rose to 7.2 in the 1987 national elections, and to 16.9 in 1991 (in alliance with the Nationalist Action Party and the Reformist Democracy Party). In the 1990s, the RP vote rose rapidly. In the 1994 local elections it captured the mayoralties of the two largest cities of Turkey (Istanbul and Ankara), as well as those of many other provincial centres, with over 19 per cent of the national vote. The 21.4 per cent of the national vote and 158 parliamentary seats it won in the December 1995 parliamentary elections represented the party's best national showing ever, making it the largest party in parliament (see Table 1).

Opinions vary about the nature of the challenge the RP represented. The party combined religious and nonreligious appeals, as seen in its emphasis on industrialization, social justice, honest government, and the restoration of Turkey's former grandeur. It is unclear whether the RP seriously intended to establish an Islamic state based on *sharia* (Islamic law) or would be satisfied with certain, mostly symbolic, Islamic acts in some areas of social life. The party's statements on these issues were vague and contradictory, lending themselves to more than a single interpretation.

Ambivalence also marked the RP's views toward democracy. The party's 1995 campaign platform called the present Turkish system a 'fraud', a 'guided democracy', and a 'dark-room regime' and announced the RP's intention to establish a 'real pluralistic democracy'. However, apart from promises to enhance freedom of conscience and to make greater use of referenda and popular councils, real democracy was never defined. In the party's view, freedom of conscience implied the 'right to live

Table 1 Percentage of Votes of Islamist Parties in Parliamentary and General Local Elections (1973–2004)

Year	Party	Votes (%)
1973	(parliamentary): National Salvation Party (MSP)	11.8
1977	(parliamentary): MSP	8.6
1984	(local): Welfare Party (RP)	4.4
1987	(parliamentary): RP	7.2
1989	(local): RP	9.8
1991	(parliamentary): RP (in coalition with the MHP and IDP)[*]	16.9
1994	(local): RP	19.1
1995	(parliamentary): RP	21.4
1999	(parliamentary): Virtue Party (FP)	15.4
2002	(parliamentary): Justice and Development Party (AKP)	34.3
2004	(local): AKP	41.2

[*]MHP stands for the Nationalist Action Party and IDP for the Reformist Democracy Party.

according to one's beliefs', a concept bound to create conflicts with Turkey's secular legal system.

The RP prudently refrained from challenging the basic premises of democracy and stated that elections constitute the only route to political power. One gets the impression, however, that the version of democracy it envisaged was more majoritarian than liberal or pluralistic. Erbakan and other party spokesmen stated that democracy was not the aim, but only a means; the aim was to establish the 'order of happiness', apparently a reference to the time of Prophet Muhammad, usually called the age of happiness (*asr-ı saadet*) in Islamic writings. Ruşen Çakır, a leading Turkish student of the RP, concluded that 'the RP is neither pro-*Sharia* nor democrat, because it is both pro-*Sharia* and democrat in its own way' (Çakır 1994, pp. 128–129).[2]

In the field of the economy, the RP proposed an Islamic-inspired 'just order' (*adil düzen*) that it conceived of as a third way, different from and superior to both capitalism and socialism. Although the party claimed the just order was the 'true private enterprise regime', its implementation—even if it were possible—would have required heavy state controls. In foreign policy, the RP advocated an essentially third-worldist policy, much closer relations with other Islamic countries, an Islamic common market, an Islamic NATO, an Islamic UNESCO, and an Islamic monetary unit. The RP's foreign policy discourse often contained anti-American, anti-European, anti-Zionist, and even anti-Semitic elements. The RP was strongly opposed to Turkey's accession to the European Union, which it described as a 'Christian club'.

The RP came to power in 1996 in coalition with the centre-right True Path Party (DYP) under the premiership of Mr Erbakan. The RP–DYP government's policies soon created serious frictions with the military, the secular state establishment, and most of the leading civil society organizations. The process that started with the dramatic meeting of 28 February 1997 of the National Security Council, at which military commanders strongly criticized the government and demanded strict measures against religious reaction, led to the resignation of the Erbakan government, and eventually to the prohibition of the RP by the Constitutional Court in 1998, for having violated the secularist principles of the Turkish constitution. The Constitutional Court's decision was also upheld by the European Court of Human Rights.

The RP was replaced by the Virtue Party (FP) led by Recai Kutan, Erbakan's close associate. Erbakan himself had been barred from politics for five years by the decision of the Constitutional Court. However, the Constitutional Court also closed down the FP in 2001, which led to a split in the Islamist ranks. The group that called themselves 'innovationists' (*yenilikçiler*) established the AKP under the leadership of Recep Tayyip Erdoğan, former mayor of Istanbul, on 14 August 2001, while the 'traditionalists' (*gelenekçiler*) organized under the name of the Felicity Party (SP) led by Recai Kutan, the former leader of the dissolved FP. In the 3 November 2002 parliamentary elections, the AKP came to power with 34.3 per cent of the vote and almost two-thirds of parliamentary seats, while the SP remained a minor party with only 2.5 per cent of the vote. The subsequent AKP government was the first single-party government since 1991, when the Motherland Party (ANAP) lost its parliamentary majority.

Analyses of the voter base of the AKP demonstrated that the party is not a direct descendant of any of the older parties; nor do the party leaders claim such lineage. A 2002 pre-election survey showed that only 27.4 per cent of the AKP voters had voted for the FP in 1999; a surprisingly high 21.9 per cent had voted for the ultra-nationalist Nationalist Action Party (MHP), 9.2 per cent for the centre-right ANAP, 7.3 per cent for the centre-right True Path Party (DYP), and 6.9 per cent for the centre-left Democratic Left Party (DSP). Similarly, 57 per cent of former FP voters, 30.5 per cent of former MHP voters, 16.8 per cent of former DYP voters, 16.7 per cent of former ANAP voters, and 10.8 per cent of former DSP voters expressed their intention to vote for the AKP in the 2002 elections (Foundation for Social, Economic and Political Research [TÜSES] 2002, pp. 70–71). These findings are corroborated by those of two other survey research organizations, ANAR and SAM, in surveys carried out in October 2002.[3] Thus, the AKP seems to have received substantial support from the former voters of the two centre-right parties (ANAP and DYP) and those of the ultra-nationalist MHP, in addition to more than half of the former Islamist FP voters. The rest of the latter seem to have remained loyal to the Erbakan tradition now represented by the SP, which received only 2.5 per cent of the vote in the 2002 elections. Surprisingly, some 10 per cent of former voters of the leftist DSP also indicated their intention to vote for the AKP.

On the basis of these findings, it may be concluded that the AKP appears to have successfully rebuilt the Özal ANAP coalition, bringing together former centre-right voters, moderate Islamists, moderate nationalists, and even a certain segment of the former centre-left. Indeed, ANAP maintained this coalition for two legislative terms (1983–91), when it formed a single-party government and played a vital role in developing a free market economy open to international competition and in normalizing politics following a period (1980–83) of stern military rule. The ANAP coalition started to weaken in the 1990s for reasons beyond the scope of this work, and today the party is reduced to a clearly minor party status. Sociologically speaking, the AKP coalition is based on the support of much of the rural population, artisans and small traders in the cities, urban slum-dwellers, and the rapidly rising Islamist bourgeoisie. A Turkish scholar describes the AKP as 'the political representative of the new middle class' comprising provincial artisans and traders, small and mid-range entrepreneurs, and young business executives, although he adds that the AKP also received votes from a good portion of the working class (İnsel 2003, pp. 297–299). Obviously, this is a rather heterogeneous coalition, socially and politically. Only time will tell if the AKP will be able to maintain it in the long run, a formidable task which the ANAP failed to accomplish. If the AKP fails in this task, it may well follow the route of the ANAP to become a minor party based essentially on Islamist votes.

The ideological differences between the AKP and its predecessor Islamist parties will be dealt with in the next section. Suffice it to say here that the differences are real and profound. Such a radical transformation may be due to a number of factors. However, in explaining it, one should not neglect the effect of the '28 February process' and the consequent prohibition of the RP and the FP by the Constitutional Court. Indeed, the Turkish constitution is strongly committed to secularism, and parties that are found to be violating these secularist principles run the serious risk of being closed down. As a result of the closure of the RP and FP, a group of former Islamist politicians seems to have reached the conclusion that challenging the secular state in Turkey is a dead-end. The AKP represents the transformation of political Islam into a moderate conservative democratic party, reconciled to the secular principles of the constitution.

The AKP Programme and Values

The AKP's constitution describes the Republic 'as the most important acquisition of the Turkish nation' and asserts that 'the will of the nation is the only determinant power'. The party 'considers the will of the nation, the rule of law, reason, science, experience, democracy, the fundamental rights and freedoms, and morality as the main references of its conception of government'. The AKP 'acknowledges and respects all the birthrights of people, such as having different beliefs, ideas, races, languages, the right of expression, the right of association, and the right to live. It considers that diversity is not (a source of) differentiation, but our cultural richness that reinforces our solidarity.' The AKP believes that national will can be sovereign only when political rights are freely exercised, and, in turn, free exercise of political rights can only be realized in a pluralist and participatory democratic society. The AKP emphasizes the freedom of expression for everybody and the right to live according to one's beliefs. The state should not favour or oppose any belief or thought, and the guarantee of this understanding are the constitutional principles regarding secularism and equality before the law. In the field of the economy, the AKP aims to establish a free market economy with all its institutions and rules and recognizes the role of the state in the economy only in a regulatory and supervisory capacity (AKP 2002b, art. 4).

Similarly, the AKP's 'Development and Democratization Programme' strongly emphasizes democracy, human rights, and the rule of law. Thus, it is asserted that 'freedoms constitute the foundation of democracy' and that respect for individual rights and freedoms is the basic condition for the establishment of social peace and well-being, as well as for the acceptance of a democratic political regime by the people. It promises to bring human rights standards in Turkey to the level envisaged by the Universal Declaration of Human Rights, the European Convention of Human Rights, the Paris Charter, and the Helsinki Final Act. It specifically mentions freedom of thought and expression, the right to information, the right to seek justice, and the right to a fair trial. The AKP's notion of democracy is more pluralistic than majoritarian. The importance of tolerance, dialogue, and respect for minority rights is constantly emphasized.

The AKP programme much more clearly supports secularism than did the former Islamist parties. Thus, it is stated that while religion is one of the most important institutions of humanity, secularism is a *sine qua non* condition for democracy, and the guarantee of freedom of religion and conscience. 'Secularism allows people of all religions and beliefs to practise their religion in peace, to express their religious convictions and to live accordingly, but also allows people with no religious beliefs to organize their lives in their own direction. Therefore, secularism is a principle of freedom and social peace' (AKP 2002a). Last but not least, the AKP regards Atatürk's principles and reforms as the most important vehicle for raising Turkish society above the level of contemporary civilization and considers them an element of social peace.

The programme's section on the economy declares the party's commitment to a functioning free market economy with all its rules and institutions, and aims to limit the state's role in the economy to a merely regulatory and supervisory function. The programme supports privatization and the encouragement of foreign investment in Turkey.

On foreign policy, the programme emphasizes the importance of Turkey's ties with the United States, European countries and the European Union, NATO, and the Central Asian Turkic republics. The programme also states that the AKP attributes a special importance to Turkey's relations with Islamic countries (AKP 2002a).

On the basis of its programme, the AKP seems hardly distinguishable from a liberal or conservative democratic party. Although the party describes itself as 'conservative democrat', there is very little emphasis on conservative values in the programme, except for the passages supporting family values and emphasizing the need to strengthen the family. The party's views on conservative democracy are more clearly elaborated in a document entitled *Conservative Democracy* (Akdoğan 2003), prepared and distributed by the central headquarters of the party. In his introduction to this document, the party leader Recep Tayyip Erdoğan states the AKP's opposition to the notion of 'political community which radicalizes politics', a clear reference to the practice of the older Islamist parties. Erdoğan also criticizes a second type of political party which he terms 'political corporations', namely parties that lack any political principles and aim at the distribution of public rent among its supporters. Erdoğan claims that the AKP has become 'the undisputable single force of the centre-right'. He also made it clear that the AKP's understanding of conservatism was not against change, but that it advocated change 'in the sense of development and progress'. 'The AKP emphasizes a modern conservatism open to innovation, in place of the conservatism of the past which was built on the status quo. The AKP advocates change based on an evolutionary, gradual, and natural societal transformation.'[4]

The AKP's conservatism can best be described as an attitude in favour of natural and evolutionary change, and a posture against social engineering. Erdoğan makes this clear when he states that 'all efforts that impose or order certain principles and aim at a homogeneous society, or are based on social engineering are obstacles to a healthy democratic system ... Our identity as conservative democrats makes us oppose all kinds of social and political engineering' (AKP 2004a, p. 9). In his speech at the first general congress of the AKP on 12 October 2003, Erdoğan also gave certain clues as to the party's understanding of conservative democracy. He claimed that the AKP substituted a notion of politics based on compromise and reconciliation in place of a politics based on conflict, and described the AKP's democratic conservatism as representing the 'societal centre'. Thus, he sees democratic conservatism as a means of bridging the gap between the state and society, to unite the centre with the periphery. In his view, there is no conflict between republican and democratic values, and he points to Kemal Atatürk as the source of republican values, which should remain 'as our firmest foundations'. Finally, he repudiates religious, ethnic, and regional nationalism as the 'red lines' of the AKP (AKP 2004b, pp. 4–7).

It may be argued that party statutes, programmes, and other official documents are of limited value in understanding the true nature of a party, since it is always possible that such documents may hide its real intentions. Thus, some radical secularists in Turkey view the AKP with suspicion and suspect that the party's real intention is to establish an Islamic republic. However, the party's performance in government does not lend support to such gloomy predictions. The AKP government has so far followed moderate policies, accomplished significant constitutional and legislative reforms to raise democratic standards in Turkey to the level required by the Copenhagen criteria, accepted Turkey's accession to the EU as one of its most important priorities, and prudently refrained from policies (such as lifting the ban on wearing headscarves at universities) that would have caused frictions with the secular state establishment. During its three years in power, the AKP majority in parliament adopted two constitutional amendments (those of 2002 and 2004) and six 'harmonization packages' designed to harmonize Turkish legislation with EU standards. Particularly significant were the constitutional amendments of 2004 which, among other things, repealed the death penalty for all crimes, abolished the controversial state security courts, recognized the supremacy of international agreements over domestic legislation in the field of human rights, and gave a stronger wording to the article on gender equality. Furthermore, the AKP sought and obtained the support of the major opposition party, the Republican People's Party (CHP), for both the constitutional amendments and the harmonization packages (Özbudun & Yazıcı 2004). It is a well-known fact that Turkish voters do not normally base their voting choices on parties' abstract ideologies and political identities, but mostly on their performance, image, and the personal characteristics of their leaders. In this sense, the AKP's conservative democrat image may well be intended more for the consumption of intellectuals, the state establishment, and foreign policy-makers than as an ideology that will effectively mobilize its voter base (Fedayi 2004; Yıldız 2004, p. 46). A Turkish political scientist describes the AKP as 'Islamic in name, liberal in practice, democrat in attitude, and westernist in direction'.[5]

Party Organization

The Turkish political parties law, adopted in 1983 by the then military regime, is probably the most detailed of its kind in Europe. It contains not only party prohibitions, but also extremely detailed regulations on party organization, registration, membership, nominations, discipline, and party finance. Consequently, all Turkish parties have very similar organizational structures imposed upon them by the law. Thus, at all levels, the presidents and executive committees are elected by their respective congresses composed of delegates chosen by registered members. The central organs are the grand (general) congress, the party president (leader), the central executive committee, and the central disciplinary committee. The grand congress is the highest decision-making body; it elects the party president, the central executive committee, and the central disciplinary committee. Local organizations consist of province, sub-province (county), and municipality organizations (all settlements with a minimum of 2,000 inhabitants are entitled to have a municipal organization). The law does not permit party organization below the sub-province or municipality level. There are therefore no legal organizational units at the village or urban neighbourhood level. However, parties usually get around this prohibition by appointing informal party representatives, or even representative committees at the village or urban neighbourhood levels. At the province and sub-province levels, party presidents and the executive committees are elected by the province and sub-province congresses, respectively.

As regards the nomination of parliamentary candidates, article 37 of the law leaves the choice of candidate selection method to party statutes. However, if a party decides to hold primary elections to select its candidates, such elections are to be held under judicial supervision. The current practice in almost all parties is to have candidates selected by the central executive committee, where the influence of the party leader is paramount. The political parties law also contains certain provisions concerning the parties' parliamentary groups. Under article 27 of the law, parliamentary groups may take binding group decisions. Article 28 stipulates that the decisions concerning a vote of confidence or no confidence in a minister or the council of ministers can be taken only by the party's parliamentary group. Thus, although legally speaking the parties' central executive committees do not have the power to take binding decisions on matters of vote of confidence, in practice both organs work together closely and both are dominated to a large extent by the party leader. The AKP is no exception in this regard.

The AKP's organizational structure closely conforms to this overall design (AKP 2002b). The party's highest decision-making body is the grand congress, which is composed of delegates chosen by provincial congresses and *ex officio* delegates. *Ex officio* delegates comprise the party leader, members of the central decision-making and executive committee, the president and members of the central disciplinary committee, founding members, and ministers and deputies who are party members (AKP 2002b, art. 62). The congress is authorized to elect the party leader, the central decision-making and executive committee, the central disciplinary committee, and the members of the intra-party democracy arbitration committee. It has also the power to change the party's statute and programme, to take binding or non-binding decisions on public issues and party policies, and to decide on the dissolution of the party (AKP 2002b, art. 61). The grand congress meets not more often than every two years, and at least every three years (AKP 2002b, art. 63).

The central decision-making and executive committee is the second-highest authority in the party. It is composed of 50 members (and 25 substitutes) elected by the grand congress by secret vote. It is chaired by the party leader and meets at least once a month (AKP 2002b, art. 73). It is authorized to make decisions on party policies and all organizational matters including decisions to form a government or to leave a coalition government (AKP 2002b, art. 148). However, as in all Turkish political parties, the party leader exercises a paramount influence within this committee. As regards party leadership, the AKP's statute introduces a novelty by limiting the tenure of the leader to four ordinary terms (that is, 12 years at most) (AKP 2002b, art. 75). Within the central decision-making and executive committee, a smaller body called the central executive committee ensures the daily functioning of the party. It is composed of the party president, vice-presidents (at the moment there are 11 vice-presidents), the secretary-general, and the president and the vice-president of the party parliamentary group (AKP 2002b, arts 79–82). It may be concluded that, together with the party leader, the central executive committee is the most powerful body in the party. Theoretically speaking, one may expect frictions between the central executive committee and the council of ministers when the party is in power. There are no legal obstacles to ministers also serving as members of the central executive committee. In practice, however, these posts are generally separated. Bearing in mind the dominant influence of the party leader, the chances for such frictions developing between the two bodies are negligible.

Another novelty of the AKP's statute which is not found in other parties is the establishment of intra-party democracy and arbitration committees at the central and provincial levels. These committees are authorized to find amicable settlements to conflicts among party members or party organs arising out of their party functions (AKP 2002b, arts 98–102).

At the local level, the AKP's organization consists of municipal, sub-provincial, and provincial congresses and executive committees. The smallest unit is the municipal organization, consisting of the municipal congress, the municipal president, and the municipal executive committee, all elected by the municipal congress (AKP 2002b, arts 21–27). Below the municipal level, however, informal party representatives or representative committees can be appointed at the urban neighbourhood, village, and polling district levels. Polling district committees are composed of one president and nine members, three of whom are from the main party organization, and three each from the women's and youth organizations. Polling district presidents also serve as election observers on the voting day. In addition, provincial executive committees may establish electoral committees to conduct electoral activities within the constituency (AKP 2002b, art. 19). Sub-provincial and provincial party organizations are organized along the same lines, consisting of a delegates' congress, a president, and an executive committee elected by the congress. The AKP, like most of the other Turkish parties, also has youth and women's organizations at all organizational levels. Again as with most other Turkish political parties, the AKP has a highly centralized and hierarchical organization. This is partly a function of the political parties law, and partly one of Turkish political culture, which encourages strong central and personalistic leadership. Thus, although local organizations cannot be dismissed as mere appendages of limited usefulness, they are largely dominated by the central bodies.

As was pointed out above, this organizational model, largely imposed by the political parties law, is more or less standard for all Turkish political parties. What distinguishes one party from the others is, therefore, not its formal organizational features, but its organizational culture. I have argued elsewhere that most Turkish political parties combine certain characteristics of cadre, catch-all, and cartel parties, with strong clientelistic features. The only Turkish political party that deviated from this pattern and approached the characteristics of a mass party was the RP, one of the predecessors of the AKP. What distinguished the RP from the others was the strong ideological and emotional attachment of its members (a 'devotee party' in Duverger's terminology) and the party's intense efforts at indoctrination, mobilization, and intra-party education (Özbudun 2000, pp. 92–3). A pertinent question is whether the AKP maintains the same organizational culture. The AKP's vice-president, interviewed by the author, indicated that this was not the case and that the AKP members do not have quite the same ideological and emotional motivations. In any case, according to his estimate, only 12–15 per cent of the AKP members were previously RP or FP members.[6]

If one criterion for a mass party is the number of members, the AKP can still be said to be approaching the mass party model. As of mid-July 2005, the AKP reportedly had 2,362,857 members, an approximately 21.9 per cent member/AKP voter ratio and about 5.5 per cent member/registered voters ratio. This is a very high membership (members/voters) ratio compared with most European standards. Earlier research had shown, however, that membership ratio is generally high for all Turkish parties. Thus, a 1996 survey had found that 12.1 per cent of all voters were members of a political party (TÜSES 1996, p. 93). Such inflated figures may raise doubts about their accuracy. However, nowadays party membership registers are also kept by the prosecutor general of the Court of Cassation, which should increase their reliability. Another explanation may lie in the clientelistic nature of Turkish political parties. A majority of party members see their membership as a means to obtain personal, sometimes quite small, sometimes very substantial, benefits from their parties, particularly when they happen to be in government. A good example is the ANAP, which was the government party between 1983 and 1991, and still seems to have more than six million registered members, although it received only five per cent of the vote in the 2002 elections (about one-fifth of the number of its registered members). A third factor is the efforts by the local party officials to register their friends and members of families in order to augment their delegate base. But perhaps a more convincing explanation is that most Turkish party members do not clearly distinguish between being a party member and being a mere supporter. Party membership in Turkey entails certain rights, but almost no obligations to the party, including paying membership dues. Thus, in all Turkish parties only a very small proportion of party income comes from membership dues, and the AKP is no exception in this regard.

Still, the AKP's membership figure of more than two million does not seem to be unrealistic. Party officials state that about 300,000 of them perform some active party duty, such as being deputies, mayors, city councillors, members of the provincial general assemblies, members of the executive committees at the central, provincial, sub-provincial, and municipal levels; village, neighbourhood, and polling district representatives; members of the executive committees of women's and youth organizations at all levels, etc. This figure indicates a highly active and vibrant party life, and it does not include ordinary militants who have no official public or party positions.

Another characteristic that brings the AKP close to a mass party model is the emphasis given to intra-party education and indoctrination. For example, in 2005 two-day education seminars were organized in 17 different localities, and a national education seminar was convened in Ankara in September 2005, in which three members from each province participated. Its purpose was to educate the educators, and the ultimate aim was to educate 300,000 active-duty members. The seminars addressed such subjects as party organization, election processes, party ideology, economy, and foreign policy. In addition, during election times, seminars on electoral matters are organized for polling station observers.

Communications between the central bodies and the local organizations seem to be highly effective. The party officials claim that the AKP makes the most efficient use of computer facilities of all Turkish parties. A good example of the use of computers, as well as of the AKP's efforts to maintain close contacts with its members and supporters, is the AKP communication centre (Akim). The centre receives complaints and requests from members and non-members, on party and governmental matters, processes them, transmits them to relevant authorities, and informs the petitioners of the outcome. The fully computerized Akim has been functioning for two-and-a-half years, and has so far received some 217,000 applications; the monthly average is about 9,000–11,000 applications, some 60 per cent of which are processed and answered. Akim centres are also established in all 81 provinces, and in some of the major sub-provinces.

Competitive Strategy and Campaign Politics

The AKP's main competitive strategy seems to be based on capturing and maintaining the centre-right votes. Centre-right parties have always dominated Turkish politics since the transition to a multi-party system in 1946–50. The erosion of the two once-powerful centre-right parties (ANAP and DYP) for a number of reasons gave the AKP a golden opportunity to capture that space. That explains the party leaders' statements that the AKP has become the singular force on the centre-right and that it represents the societal centre. The AKP leadership seems to have realistically concluded that relying on hard-core Islamist votes would never make them a majority party. Certainly, the party's 34.3 per cent vote share in the parliamentary elections of 2002 and its even better showing in the general local elections of 2004 (over 41 per cent) far exceed the potential of the earlier Islamist parties. The AKP leadership gives every indication that it will follow the same competitive strategy in the coming elections. In this race, its main competitors would be the ANAP and the DYP and the ultra-nationalist MHP. Given the extreme volatility of Turkish voters, it will not be an easy task for the AKP to maintain the dominant position it now enjoys on the centre-right.

As in most other democratic countries, election campaigns in Turkey have centred around the personality and personal characteristics of the party leader in recent years. This is particularly the case for the AKP, where Erdoğan's powerful charismatic personality and 'man of the people' image contributed substantially to the party's electoral success. Another recent general trend is the increasing professionalization of electoral campaigns and the growing importance of television. Nowadays, each party conducts its electoral campaign with the help of professional public relations experts and pollsters. The RP was probably the only Turkish party in modern times to appreciate the value of traditional door-to-door canvassing methods while not neglecting more modern campaign techniques. Reliance on such face-to-face personal contacts seems to have paid off handsomely in the RP case.

Like all other parties, the AKP attributes special importance to the organization of electoral campaigns. A booklet called *Guide to Elections* prepared by the central office of the party is intended to inform all campaign workers of the intricacies of the highly detailed Turkish election laws (AKP 2002c). Another guide prepared for the 2004 local elections gives more practical advice on how to organize the campaign. Thus, it is emphasized that only the standard campaign materials prepared by the central office of the party can be used by local organizations, hinting at the highly centralized character of the campaign. Campaign workers are also advised to wear proper attire, to display a warm and friendly attitude toward voters, to refrain from unnecessary debates with voters, to refrain from demeaning other parties or candidates, to employ different discourses for different categories of voters, and to maintain close contacts with local non-governmental organizations. Campaign workers are warned against expressing their own personal opinions instead of those of the party (AKP 2004c). In addition to the activities of local campaign workers, the party leadership, particularly Mr Erdoğan, was very active both in the 2002 parliamentary and the 2004 local election campaigns.

Conclusion

As stated at the outset, the transformation of Turkish political Islam, once considered a serious threat to the stability of democracy, into a moderate conservative democratic party is a development of paramount importance in Turkish politics. This development can be seen as a significant step toward bridging the age-old deep cleavage between secularists and Islamists, thus contributing to the consolidation of democracy in Turkey.[7] The success or failure of the AKP experience is likely to have repercussions beyond Turkey's borders and in the entire Islamic world. This radical change from the practice of older Islamist parties seems to have been a function of the realization by a wing of the former Islamist parties (RP and FP) that challenging the secular character of the state in Turkey would be futile. Thus, the formation of the AKP was triggered by the closure of the FP by the Constitutional Court. Furthermore, the leaders of the 'innovationist' faction realized that relying essentially on hard-core Islamist votes would condemn the party forever to a minority (if not a minor party) status—hence, the AKP's effort to broaden its appeal to the centre-right of the political spectrum. This new approach has contributed significantly to diminishing the importance of the secularist–Islamist cleavage in Turkish politics.

The most serious risk facing the AKP stems from its coalitional character. Despite strong disclaimers from the party leadership, there is little doubt about this coalitional nature. The AKP brings together moderate Islamists, moderate nationalists, secular but socially conservative centre-right voters, and a sizable number of liberal intellectuals. The similarity to Turgut Özal's ANAP coalition is striking. However, the ANAP was not able to maintain this coalition for a long time, and today it has been reduced to a minor party. It is not certain that the AKP will succeed where the ANAP failed. A second danger is the extreme volatility of Turkish voters, who generally base their voting decisions on short-term calculations of gains and losses. Turkish parties generally lack deep and lasting roots in society, and their performance in government becomes the main criterion in voters' choice. It should be borne in mind that none of the three parties that formed a coalition government between 1999 and 2002 is now represented in parliament. A third danger may arise from Erdoğan's plans, if he so decides, to become the president of the Republic in 2007, in which case he will have to leave the party leadership and resign from his party. His powerful charismatic authority has certainly been an important factor that has kept together the disparate elements within the AKP. It is not certain that a new leader will have the same kind of moral authority. A fourth danger may arise if Turkey's EU accession negotiations are interrupted or fail to produce the expected results. This may lead to ultra-nationalist and isolationist reactions and may put the AKP into a difficult corner as the party most strongly associated with the objective of full EU membership. In short, there are still many unknowns. What is certain, however, is that the AKP's performance will continue to have profound implications for the future of Turkish politics.

Notes

[1] On the MSP period see Landau (1976); Toprak (1981); Sarıbay (1985); and Özbudun (1987).

[2] These paragraphs on the RP draw on my book (Özbudun 2000, pp. 87–88).

[3] Akyol (2002). See also Esmer (2002): Esmer estimates that a quarter of the former DSP voters voted for the AKP in 2002.

[4] Akdoğan (2003). Quotations from Erdoğan's 'Introduction' are from the enlarged version of the document on the website of the AKP: < www.AKParti.org.tr/Muhafaz.doc > ; Erdoğan's views are also repeated in AKP (2004a, pp. 1–12).

[5] Ali Yaşar Sarıbay, 'AKP Kimliksizliğe Mahkum' [The AKP is bound to lack an identity], quoted by Yıldız (2004, p. 47).

[6] I gratefully acknowledge the information provided by Mr Dengir Mir Mehmet Fırat, Vice-President of the AKP, in an interview that took place on 13 July 2005. The information presented here is based on this interview unless indicated otherwise.

[7] Several years ago, I described the rise of Islamic fundamentalism and ethnic Kurdish nationalism as the chief obstacles to the consolidation of democracy. See Özbudun (2000, pp. 141–145).

References

Akdoğan, Y. (2003) *Muhafazakar Demokrasi* [Conservative Democracy], AK Parti Yayınları, Ankara.

AKP (2002a) *AK Parti Kalkınma ve Demokratiklesme Programı* [The AKP Development and Democratization Program], AK Parti Yayınları, Ankara.

AKP (2002b) *AK Parti Tüzüğü* [The Constitution of the AKP], AK Parti Yayınları, Ankara.

AKP (2002c) *Seçim Rehberi* [Guide to Elections], AK Parti Yayınları, Ankara.

AKP (2004a) *International Symposium on Conservatism and Democracy*, AK Parti Publication, Ankara.

AKP (2004b) *AK Parti 1. Olağan Büyük Kongresi, Genel Başkan R.Tayyip Erdoğan'in Konuşması* [The First Regular Grand Congress of the AKP, the Speech by the Party Chairman R. Tayyip Erdogan], AK Parti Yayınları, Ankara.

AKP (2004c) *28 Mart 2004 Yerel Seçim Kılavuzu* [Guide to the Local Elections of 28 March 2004], AK Parti Yayınları, Ankara.

Akyol, T. (2002) 'AKP'nin Arkasında Ne Var?' [What is behind the AKP?], *Milliyet*, 19 October.

Çakır, R. (1994) *Ne Şeriat, Ne Demokrasi: Refah Partisini Anlamak* [Neither the Sharia nor Democracy: Understanding the Welfare Party], Metis, Istanbul.

Esmer, Y. (2002) '3 Kasım Analizi' [The Analysis of 3 November], *Milliyet*, 18 November.

Fedayi, C. (2004) 'AKP'nin Siyasal Kimliği Üzerine: Kimlik Arkadan Gelsin' [On the political identity of the AKP: let identity come from behind], *Muhafazakar Düşünce*, vol. 1, no. 1, pp. 149–163.

İnsel, A. (2003) 'The AKP and normalizing democracy in Turkey', *South Atlantic Quarterly*, vol. 102, no. 2–3, pp. 293–308.

Landau, J. M. (1976) 'The National Salvation Party in Turkey', *Asian and African Studies*, vol. 11, no. 1, pp. 1–57.

Özbudun, E. (1987) 'Islam and politics in modern Turkey: the case of the National Salvation Party', in *The Islamic Impulse*, ed. B. Stowasser, Croom Helm, London, pp. 142–156.

Özbudun, E. (2000) *Contemporary Turkish Politics: Challenges to Democratic Consolidation*, Lynne Rienner, Boulder and London.

Özbudun, E & Yazıcı, S (2004) *Democratization Reforms in Turkey (1993–2004)*, TESEV, Istanbul.

Sarıbay, A. Y. (1985) *Türkiye'de Modernleşme, Din ve Parti Politikası: MSP Örnek Olayi* [Modernization, Religion, and Party Politics in Turkey: A Case Study of the MSP], Alan, Istanbul.

Toprak, B. (1981) *Islam and Political Development in Turkey*, E. J. Brill, Leiden.

TÜSES (1996) *Türkiye'de Siyasi Parti Seçmenlerinin Nitelikleri, Kimlikleri ve Eğilimleri* [Characteristics, Identities, and Tendencies of Political Party Voters in Turkey], Ankara.

TÜSES. (2002) *Türkiye'de Siyasi Partilerin Yandaş/Seçmen Profili (1994–2002)* [The Supporter/Voter Profiles of Political Parties in Turkey], Istanbul.

Yıldız, A. (2004) 'AK Parti'nin 'Yeni Muhafazakar Demokratlığı' [The new conservative democracy of the AKP], *Liberal Dusunce*, vol. 9, no. 34, pp. 41–48.

Old Soldiers Never Die: The Republican People's Party of Turkey

Ilter Turan

Introduction

Turkish political parties and the party system have undergone major changes during recent decades. While pressures created by rapid socio-economic change have promoted this transformation, military interventions that have led to the closing of political parties have interjected an element of discontinuity into the picture. The Republican People's Party (Cumhuriyet Halk Partisi, CHP) in this context constitutes a remarkable contrast to others, having a history that goes back to 1923. Like others, the party was closed after the 1980 military coup. But, unlike many others, it reconstituted itself shortly after its reopening became a possibility and today the CHP has become the major opposition party. The next sections examine the party's history, values, organization, competitive strategy and electoral campaign politics.

From the Party of the Original Intent to the Born Again Republicans

The CHP was established in 1923, days before the declaration of the republic by Kemal Atatürk. Since that time, with an interlude between 1981 and 1992, the party has been one of the major actors on the Turkish political scene. The CHP had gone through four stages of evolution until 1981, when it was closed down by the military junta along with all pre-1980 political parties.

The Single Party Period (1923–46)

Until 1946, the CHP ruled as a single party, leading the formulation and implementation of cultural modernization policies known as the Kemalist reforms.

The First Democratic Experiment (1946–60)

In 1946, stimulated by changes in the world system, the party opened Turkey's politics to competition, losing power to the Democratic Party in 1950. In opposition for the next ten years, the CHP stood as the defender of republican reforms, often perceived by voters as the defence of bureaucratic domination. The first democratic experiment was terminated by a military intervention which had been encouraged by the CHP alleging that the rules of the democratic game had been subverted by the governing Democratic Party.

The Transformation (1961–73)

After the restoration of civilian politics in 1961, the CHP continued its electoral decline, which stimulated a search for a new ideology and larger constituencies. After much intra-party strife, an imprecise 'left of centre' ideology was adopted, aiming to attract the support of workers, low-income groups in the cities, and peasants. This turn toward a mass party led to the departure of the octogenarian leader İsmet İnönü, who was replaced by Bülent Ecevit.

The Mass Party (1973–81)

The attempts to become a mass party paid off. Though failing to win a majority of seats in the parliament, the CHP won more seats than any other party in the 1973 and 1977 elections. During this time Turkey's politics were becoming increasingly polarized, with the government and opposition failing to end extensive violence and economic decline. The military intervened again in 1980 and closed down all existing political parties.

The generals who ruled Turkey during 1980–83 thought that a stable political system should have only two parties—a moderate left-wing party and a moderate right party. Toward that end, they abolished all pre-1980 parties, banned their leading cadres from active politics for five to ten years (Turan 2004, p. 125) and tried to build a new system by allowing only three new parties to participate in the 1983 parliamentary elections (Turan 2003, p. 155; Tachau 2000, p. 139). A gradual restoration of party life began with the 1984 local elections, in which all the parties banned in the 1983 elections could participate. The Social Democratic Party (SODEP), representing in part the CHP cadres and traditions, scored some victories while the Populist Party (PP), backed by the military, scored none. The anomaly of a parliamentary party with no popular backing—the PP—and one without parliamentary representation but electoral support—the SODEP—presented a situation in which both parties stood to gain from uniting as they did in late 1985, forming the Social Democratic Populist Party (SHP). In the meantime, the pre-1980 president of the CHP, Bülent Ecevit, had asked his spouse to establish the Democratic Left Party (DSP), planning to attract the votes of his former party (Sayarı 2002). Mr Ecevit dissociated himself from the CHP and the new parties that tried to build on that heritage, and chose to pursue an independent path.

Until 1992 the old CHP cadres worked within the SHP. When in 1987 the ban on the pre-1980 party leaders was repealed through a constitutional referendum, many of them joined the SHP as the representative of the CHP tradition. In the 1987 elections the SHP came in second with 24.8 per cent of the vote. In the 1989 local elections, it became the most successful party. Such electoral achievement did not prevent an intra-party leadership struggle between Erdal İnönü, the SHP's president since its founding, and Deniz Baykal, who had served in pre-1980 governments. Between 1987 and 1992, Baykal tried no less than three times to take over the presidency of the party, failing each time.

In 1992, with the ban on pre-1980 parties repealed, Baykal and 21 followers left to re-establish the CHP. In September, the (re)opening convention was held, electing Mr Baykal president. The return of the CHP meant that now three political parties (SHP, DSP and the new CHP) shared the legacy of the pre-1980 Republican People's Party. As the local elections of 1994 showed, such fragmentation weakened all. Since the DSP dissociated itself from the CHP tradition, the other two groups began to discuss the possibility of uniting (İnönü 1999). After hesitation and the postponing of the unification, the process was finally completed in February 1995, under the compromise leadership of Hikmet Çetin (Bila 1999). However, Çetin's tenure proved to be temporary, since Baykal captured the CHP's presidency at the party national convention in September 1995.

When Baykal became the CHP's leader, the party was the junior partner in Mrs Çiller's coalition government. The new CHP chief made some immediate demands of Professor Çiller. When they were not met, he withdrew his support and brought the government down (Bila 1999, p. 406). The same coalition was reconstituted within two months, agreeing on early elections for December 1995 (Table 1).

Baykal may have hoped to improve his party's electoral position through early elections, but its share declined to 10.7 per cent, barely above the national ten per cent threshold. During 1995–99, the CHP remained out of government. This was a period of political turmoil. The major partner in the initial coalition government was the religiously oriented Welfare Party, whose actions were often unacceptable to the National Security Council, whose military members were sensitive about the strict laicist republican tradition. The government was forced to resign. The Motherland (ANAP) and True Path (DYP) parties established a minority coalition supported by the CHP in return for a promise to move the elections ahead (Bila 1999). Judging that

Table 1 CHP Electoral and Governmental Performance (1950–2002)

Year	Votes (%)	CHP seats (total no. of seats)	CHP government and opposition role
1950	39.4	69 (487)	Main opposition party
1954	35.4	31 (541)	Main opposition party
1957	41.1	178 (610)	Main opposition party
1961	36.7	158 (450)	Major party in three cabinets and opposition party afterwards
1965	28.7	134 (450)	Main opposition party
1969	27.4	143 (450)	Main opposition party; after 1971 the party supports national unity cabinets under military pressure
1973	33.3	185 (450)	Major party in one cabinet and main opposition party afterwards
1977	41.4	213 (450)	Main opposition party; major party in one cabinet; major opposition party afterwards
1987	(SHP) 24.8	99 (450)	Main opposition party
1991	(SHP/CHP) 20.8	88 (450)	Minor party in four cabinets
1995	10.7	49 (550)	Main opposition party
1999	8.7	—	—
2002	19.4	178 (550)	Main opposition party

Source: Based on Tuncer (2003).

his electoral fortunes were improving, and growing impatient, Mr Baykal supported a motion of censure to bring the government down. A minority government, headed by Mr Ecevit of the rival DSP, led the country to early elections.

The 1999 elections spelled disaster for the CHP, which failed to achieve the electoral threshold (it had received only 8.7 per cent) and acquire parliamentary representation. Painfully, its rival sister the DSP had come in first with 22.5 per cent of the vote. There were calls for Baykal's resignation. After days of indecision, he obliged, opening the way to factional battles. He chose not to attend the party convention, alleging that none of the candidates appealed to all segments of the party (Bila 1999, p. 431). Altan Öymen, an experienced senior member with a long parliamentary and ministerial career in the pre-1980 period, won in the third round. Evidence of irregularities in the elections for the party assembly culminated in the resignation of its newly elected members *in toto*. An extraordinary convention was held three months later in order to elect a new assembly. Baykal loyalists captured a majority of the seats.

Öymen, a mild-mannered person with a conciliatory approach, judged that the party reconstruction should start with the updating of the membership lists. The local organizations, however, perceived this effort as a device to undermine their power. Many had achieved their position during Baykal's reign and, encouraged by Baykal himself, refused to cooperate with the national headquarters. Local organizations received support from the party assembly in which Baykal supporters prevailed (*Milliyet*, 26 September 2000). As Öymen's multiple efforts to implement his programme were thwarted by the party assembly and the executive committee, he decided to call an extraordinary convention to redress the situation. The party convention (September 2000) ended in a complete victory for Baykal; 16 months after resigning, he was back in command. With his return in 2002, a group of parliamentarians left the party to re-establish the SHP.

Between the 1999 and 2002 elections, a three-party coalition (ANAP, DSP and MHP, that is, the Nationalist Action Party) ruled Turkey with dwindling support. With no credible alternative in sight, the government decided to call early elections in October 2002. Following a pattern that had emerged since 1991, the parties in power fared poorly. In fact, they fared so poorly in the 2002 elections that, owing to the electoral threshold, none gained parliamentary seats. The winner with 34.5 per cent was the newly established Justice and Development Party (AKP), a recent offshoot from the religiously oriented Felicity Party. The CHP, also benefiting from having been away from power, came in second with 19.4 per cent of the vote.

The CHP was initially the only parliamentary opposition. After three years, 24 deputies had left it for other parties or to become independent (*Hürriyet*, 20 November 2005). Opinion polls suggest that the CHP support had declined to around ten per cent (*Sabah*, 20 November 2005). Deniz Baykal had not tolerated challenges to his leadership and had ousted challengers and their supporters from the party, charging them with party discipline violations. After having rebuffed a call earlier in the year for an extraordinary convention, earning a scolding from the courts for having failed to observe party laws, on 20 November 2005 he held a convention in which he ran unopposed, receiving more than 90 per cent of the delegates' votes.

The CHP will likely continue to be riddled with internal tensions and quarrels. While this may partly derive from the authoritarian proclivities of its leader, it should be remembered that the recent history of the CHP cannot be understood independently of what has been happening in the Turkish political parties and the party system in general. Since 1991, the party system has been characterized by the 'erosion of two party dominance and the rise of political fragmentation, increased electoral volatility and the decline of party identification among voters, the fractionalization and the weakening of centrist parties' (Sayarı 2002, p. 9). The CHP has not been spared these tendencies.

The True Believer Faces New Realities: Values, Ideologies And Programmes

The CHP ideology represents an uneasy combination of legacies that still need to form a coherent whole. The first legacy is that of the modernizing single party that led the liberation effort from foreign occupation. Noting that this tradition had led the party to stand for the values of the centre, Kalaycıoğlu has argued that 'it propagate(s) a nationalist, centralist, laicist and populist political platform. It has always stood for a mixed economy with a statist component' (1994, p. 408). Modernization, which usually means Westernization, is also a part of this legacy. The second legacy is that of democracy. It was under the CHP's leadership that competitive politics had been introduced. While the party takes pride in having led Turkey to democratic rule, it harbours a distrust of rival politicians for fear they would compromise the achievements of the Kemalist revolution. This generates a tendency within the CHP to side with the bureaucratic and military elite in state versus society conflicts. The third legacy is the social democracy adopted by the party in the late 1960s. The social democratic connection has encouraged the party to link up with the international social democratic movements, become a member of the Socialist International (1976) and the Party of European Socialism (1999) and develop a more universal outlook in politics.

The three legacies are far from having been integrated into a coherent whole. Rather, depending on the circumstances, specific events and developments, party leaders adopt positions that are more in line with one or another of these legacies. Such ideological flexibility causes confusion even among party ranks, as shown by the words of Tarhan Erdem, who was secretary-general in 2000: 'in the CHP everybody says we are social democrats, but this is just a shell. Nobody knows what is inside. Therefore, there is no consistency of ideas, members are occupied mainly with internal bickering' (2001, p. 39). Similar complaints are also made by other observers. According to Tosun, for example, 'the party does not have identifiable positions on many matters of import such as identity politics' (2003, p. 356), while Ayata observes that the CHP has failed to develop a new vision, since 'it never discussed the role of Turkey in Europe, within its own region, or what kind of integration with the EU was appropriate. The CHP lacks a clear view on globalization. The ideas of the leadership oscillate in a range from xenophobic perspectives to full integration with the globe, even abolishing borders of the nation state' (2002, p. 119).

The absence of a coherent outlook compounds another weakness, the inability to develop practicable programmes and policy alternatives to those implemented by governments. The inability to offer credible alternatives directs the CHP to elevate the debate to the level of the symbolic and ideological. Thus, incoherent pronouncements and rhetoric rather than policy characterize the way the party operates in day-to-day politics (Sakallıoğlu 1999, p. 20). Are we then to conclude that predictability is totally lacking? Rather than saying yes or no, it may be better to identify some critical axes and examine the general line of party thinking on these. I will choose four such major axes: secularism versus confessionalism, state-dominated versus market economy, pro- versus anti-globalization and pro- versus anti-EU.

If one were asked to describe the CHP with a single label, that label would be 'secularism'. The party is an uncompromising defender of secularism, which it sees as the most important achievement of the republic. The adamant stance of the party on this principle finds extensive support among social and political groups such as the bureaucracy, the military and the modern, educated, urban elites that have historically supported the party. In a comparison of the ideology of Turkish political parties, Esmer has found that the CHP ranks high on secularism, low on religiosity, traditions and moral values (2002, p. 102). This corroborates earlier evidence that those supporting social democratic parties display lower levels of religiosity (Kalaycıoğlu 1994, p. 420). The fact that right-wing parties, which attach greater importance to religion and nationalism, have done better at the polls has resulted in occasional impulses to reconsider the CHP's hard-line secularism, but these have been quickly rejected. Since the current government party—the AKP—is seen as strong in religious orientation, the CHP offers itself as the defender of the secular republican tradition. No significant changes in this orientation are expected.

As regards economics, the CHP has consistently displayed reservations about the market system, a stance deriving from two distinct but related traditions. Historically, the party initiated the development of state industries and later supported the introduction of economic planning. The party mentality still harbours an autarchical bent. The adoption of social democratic ideas in the late 1960s entrenched further the proclivity to favour the state in economic affairs. The CHP version of social democracy favoured precepts that were on their way out in Western Europe, including state-led industrialization and planned economic development. The rapid growth of the Turkish economy driven by private enterprise and its integration into the world economic system has transformed the situation in ways that render the CHP approach somewhat removed from current developments.

Before the elections of 2002, Kemal Derviş, the architect of the recent economic reforms, joined the party. The leadership created the impression that he would contribute to the transformation of the party's socio-economic philosophy so as to achieve greater harmony with those that were prevalent in Western Europe. Some prominent businessmen were also placed on tickets. However, it soon became clear that no major shift in the statist approach would be made. Those who would bring fresh economic thinking were pushed aside. Derviş himself accepted the leadership of the United Nations Development Programme, finding an honourable exit. The party returned to its classical ideological mould. Contemporary manifestations of the CHP's statist ideology include opposing the privatization of state enterprises, criticizing the International Monetary Fund (IMF) approved economic stabilization and restructuring programmes, the protection of small businesses against 'unfair' competition and favouring state subsidies to agriculture.

The notion of the independent unitary nation state is deeply entrenched in the CHP ideology. This produces an ambivalent mindset about relations with the outside world. On the one hand, it is recognized that Turkey has to interact with it for its security and prosperity. On the other hand, because the country has been liberated from the occupation of western imperialist powers, there is suspicion and hesitation in relating to the outside world. Such mistrust is reinforced by a view of external economic actors as always ready to exploit Turkey. The party has not reflected in a systematic way on globalization. Mr Baykal produces piecemeal reactions, generally critical of the global economic system. Globalization does not constitute a central concern, if judged by the scant attention it receives in the leader's pronouncements.

Of greater interest are Turkey's relations with the European Union, currently at the stage of accession negotiations. Here again, the ambivalence concerning globalization comes into play. There is added impetus in favour of a stronger European relationship, however, deriving from the republic's pro-Western orientation from its inception and the extensive support it has received from the public. The result is the approval of the relationship with Europe at the general level, but harsh criticism of the government for giving in too much to EU demands on specific issue areas such as Cyprus. Despite the critical rhetoric, the CHP has not subverted, but rather supported, Turkey's EU relationship at all critical junctures.

In conclusion, the CHP has been slow in transforming its ideology and programmes to address the rapid changes that Turkish society and economy have experienced. The original centre of educated, urban, modern, bureaucratic elites has become larger, more differentiated and heterogeneous. A satisfactory corresponding change in the CHP's outlook and programmes has not materialized (Çarkoğlu et al. 2000, p. 51). Consequently, the party has failed to enhance its electoral base. Even those who have professed voting for the CHP in the 1999 elections have indicated that members of the parliament are not familiar with the needs and wants of the people (Esmer 2002, p. 108; Turan 2004, p. 174). Occasional urges to change have been quickly abandoned when challenged by the traditional, dwindling party loyalists (Ayata 2002, p. 111). The CHP has continued to interpret social democracy in light of its own historically formed cognitive map, shaped not by struggles between social classes, but by conflict between those subscribing to the secularist modern culture and those with more traditional values. For example, the party programme devotes much attention to standard social services provided by the state (free education, social security, basic health services) but policies on pressing contemporary problems such as the eradication of poverty in urban squatter settlements and the correction of disparities in income and growing unemployment, all natural topics for a social democratic party, have been absent (Sakallıoğlu cited in Turan 2004, p. 178).

'Organized Complexity': The CHP as Organization

The current political parties law, promulgated by the military leadership in 1983 to avoid the problems of the pre-1980 era, prescribes a single organizational model for all Turkish parties. It regulates in detail all aspects of party life. Almost every one of its provisions involves a restriction of some kind (Çarkoğlu et al. 2000, p. 104). Although a few changes have been introduced since its promulgation, these have not modified its basic restrictive nature.

Organized Troops or a Motley Crowd: The Membership

Turkish political parties are not mass organizations with large memberships (Turan 2003, p. 157). Records would suggest that a respectable percentage of the population are party members, but numbers lose their significance if one asks whether members pay dues or have elementary familiarity with party doctrine (Özbudun 2000, p. 80). Membership lists are not well kept: at party conventions and election times, frequent complaints are heard about their unreliability. The CHP does not have a more impressive history than others concerning membership records, but has improved considerably during recent years. Local CHP leaders are notorious for filling up the lists with friends, relatives, children and dead parents to appear to have strong backing and maintain their power (Ayata 1992, p. 97). Some so-called members may not even know the address of the local party headquarters (Tunçay n.d., p. 180).

Table 2 shows growth of party membership during recent years. After the party was re-established in 1992, its membership rose to a modest 115,111 members in 1993. A sudden rise occurred when the CHP and SHP united in 1996. In 2000, under Altan Öymen, the old lists became invalid and everyone was asked to reregister. Numbers went down to a mere 170,000 from almost two million. The redrawing of the membership lists has not discouraged the local leaders from incorporating their kin and friends as members. In early June 2005, it was reported that some provincial organizations had been filling lists with friends, relatives and others who had little to do with the party. Discontented members had taken local organizations to court, alleging fraud.[1]

The Leviathan: Power Relations between Local Organizations and the National Leadership

The quarrel over membership registration creates the impression that membership constitutes a local power base that the national leadership has to take into serious consideration in planning and implementing its activities. If this may have been true during the earlier history of the party, it does not appear to be the case now. Subjugation of the local organization to the national headquarters is assured both by

Table 2 CHP Membership, and Ratio of Party Membership to Party Voters and Total Electorate, 1993–2005

Year	CHP membership	CHP members as percentage of CHP voters	CHP members as percentage of electorate
1993	115,111		
1994	131,022		
1995	163,540	5.4	0.82
1996	1,707,761		
1997	1,787,393		
1998	1,833,975		
1999	1,850,657	7.8	4.94
2000	170,000		
2001	240,922		
2002	288,830	4.7	0.70
2003	454,602		
2004	502,879		
2005	561,041		

Sources: The pre-1999 figures were kindly provided by my colleague Ömer Faruk Gençkaya of Bilkent University. The post-1999 figures were furnished by the CHP through the courtesy of Algan Hacaloğlu, deputy secretary-general of the party. Erol Tuncer, the president of TESAV Foundation, a political research think-tank, secured records held at the office of the Attorney of the Republic for the entire period covered.

the social features of the local leadership and the availability of mechanisms that help the central headquarters to keep local organizations under control, preventing them from developing horizontal links to challenge its domination.

At its founding stages, the CHP represented a nationalist coalition comprising bureaucrats, military officers and local notables, who included landowners, merchants and religious dignitaries. Until the party's closing down in 1981, the remnants of the local elite continued to identify with the party with a sense of *noblesse oblige*, although the CHP no longer represented their small business and agricultural interests. These local notables, who vanished with the 1981 party closure, had strong power bases that enabled them to mobilize electoral support for the party. When the CHP was reopened, the old elite was replaced by individuals who acted as brokers between the national headquarters and local constituencies. Many came from bureaucratic backgrounds or the liberal professions. This new type of leader could be replaced by the centre without the risk of suffering serious local losses. Furthermore, since winning a majority was not a realistic expectation, the CHP leadership did not feel constrained by the possibility that dealing with non-submissive local leaders might cost votes to the party.

More important than the sociology of local leadership are the instruments available to the party's national leadership in eliciting not only compliance but often submission of local party leaders to its policies, decisions and preferences. In Turkey all parties subscribe to the same organizational model prescribed by law that holds the national headquarters responsible for all party actions and activities and gives it extensive powers vis-à-vis local organizations. Most critically, the national headquarters is free to abolish local organizations, to remove their officers and replace them with people of their own choice. For example, in 2000, 52 of the 80 presidents of provincial party organizations were appointed by the national leadership rather than elected in a local convention (Erdem 2001, p. 216). Generally speaking, the party's leadership does not hesitate to remove the heads of provincial organizations who support potential challengers to Deniz Baykal. This was most recently evidenced in the case of Mustafa Sarıgül, who put up his candidacy against the party leader at the 2005 extraordinary national convention. Nearly all the provincial leaders who backed him have been removed, while half a dozen deputies who announced their sympathy for Mr Baykal's rival have felt compelled to leave their party.

The second mechanism the party leadership employs to keep members and local organizations in line is the centralization of candidate designation. The law stipulates that candidates for any electoral office may be named either by an intra-party primary or by appointment by the national party bodies. The lawmakers had anticipated that primary elections would be the rule and appointment the exception, but the latter has become the preferred practice. Since its return in 1992, the CHP has never used primaries as the basic way to name its candidates. Candidates have generally been selected by national leadership while local organizations have been consulted only summarily if at all. This practice not only leads the potential candidates (including incumbents) to ingratiate themselves with the party leader rather than with provincial organizations, but also reduces the influence of local organizations within the party. The dependence on the party president to become a candidate is exacerbated by the fact that a significant number of incumbents are chosen for their national prominence or for their expertise, but they lack strong constituency ties. For example, in the 2002 elections, well-known businessmen such as Ersin Arıoğlu, Muharrem Eskiyapan and Memduh Hacıoğlu, the union leader Bayram Meral, actor Berhan Şimsek and singer-intellectual Zülfü Livaneli were made candidates and won. While the choice of these individuals might have brought in new talent to the party, it would have been difficult for them to get on the ticket if a primary election had been held. Such a reliance on the backing of national leaders makes the parliamentary group their ally vis-à-vis challengers.

The third instrument is financial. Extending public financial support to political parties to reduce their reliance on private donors, who might try to advance their private interests, has been in operation since 1965. It was also included in the 1982 constitution, stipulating that this should be in sufficient quantity and equitably distributed. Since membership dues are not collected regularly and other sources of income are modest (becoming even more meagre when the party is out of power), parties have come to rely on public funding. Even in the case of the CHP, which came into the possession of the substantial movable and immovable wealth of the pre-1980 CHP, government grants occupy a prominent place in the budget. From 1999 to 2004, the share of transfers from the public treasury to the party coffers on average constituted 42 per cent of the CHP budget.[2] Local organizations are often dependent on support from the national headquarters for their activities and such financial dependency works to strengthen the central party against local organizations.

The Labyrinths of Power: The Organizational Structure of the Party

The preceding discussion has dealt with the relations between two pillars of the party, the local and the national organization. In fact, the statute of the party identifies the central organs, the provincial organs and the party groups of the elected. The central organs include the national convention, the presidency, the party assembly, the national executive committee and the high disciplinary committee. To some extent parallel to the national organization, the provincial organs include the provincial convention, the president of the provincial organization, the assembly and the disciplinary committee. This model is replicated once again at the level of the subprovince. The party groups, on the other hand, comprise all members of the party in an elected body such as the national parliament and the provincial and municipal assemblies.[3]

In appearance, a grassroots electoral model is employed to determine the officeholders at each level. In precincts (*mahallle*),[4] the registered members of the party elect delegates to represent them at the subprovincial convention. The number of delegates to be elected for the subprovincial convention, no more than 400, is determined by the national executive committee. The precincts are allocated delegates in proportion to their share of the vote in the most recent national election. The subprovincial convention engages in a similar exercise to choose delegates to the provincial convention (no more than 600) and the latter to the national party convention. In addition to the party president, the members of the party assembly, the party's deputies in the parliament, the members of the high disciplinary committee and honorary members, the national convention includes 1,100 elected delegates from the provincial organizations.

The grassroots democratic model does not fully operate in practice. The fact that the party's national leadership can remove leaders and disband the elected committees of local organizations not only undermines the interest of the rank and file in party affairs, but also renders being an elected officer somewhat less significant than it might appear. Upon examination, it is not difficult to conclude that the electoral process tends to work in reverse of how it is supposed to operate. The subprovincial and provincial leaders name delegates who will represent them at the next higher-level convention, making sure that they are elected (Tunçay n.d., p. 200). Even the type of ballot used is carefully selected to ensure the desired outcome. For example, rival tickets—rather than an open list of candidates (where the delegates can mark their choices)—are preferred, so that those disapproved by party leaders do not get elected. The national leadership expects the provincial organizations to bring in delegates who will conform to the choices of the party's dominant coalition. They are not interested in input from delegates.

The unchallenged prevalence of the national leadership over local organizations is also replicated in its relationship with the parliamentary group. As already noted, many of the members owe their parliamentary post to the party's national leaders, usually the party president. He expects loyalty, not challenges to his rule. Since challenging the leader on his ideas or policies is considered a violation of party discipline and processed by a disciplinary committee fiercely loyal to the party president, the meetings of the parliamentary group are often uninteresting events where the party leader speaks and the others listen and applaud. There is little discussion. To the extent it occurs, it is dominated by those who display their loyalty to the party chief. The lack of opportunity of the parliamentary group to give major input into the political process is sometimes found to be frustrating and disillusioning by deputies. As a consequence, since 2002 24 MPs have left the CHP, to become independents or more usually to join another parliamentary party. [5]

Who Is in Charge Around Here? The Leader-Dominated Party

The party leader has a powerful position in all Turkish political parties. With weak links to society and reliance on patronage to hold it together, parties attempt to reach the electorate through the party leader, which, in turn, enhances the power of the leader vis-à-vis other parts of the organization (Turan 2003, p. 157; Çarkoğlu et al. 2000, p. 53). Nevertheless, the degree of the leader's power in relation to other party organs varies among parties. In the CHP, as Tosun has noted, 'the absolute power of the leader has been institutionalized' (2003, p. 358). This has been possible in part because at the time of the party's reopening, all provincial and subprovincial leaders were appointed by Deniz Baykal, probably on the basis of personal loyalty to him (Tunçay n.d., p. 173). The brief interlude after the 1999 election disaster, when he left the presidency, did not prove long enough to disentrench the loyalists. Particularly after his return to the leadership, Baykal has tightened his reign on the party, emphasizing unqualified personal loyalty to him. Persons whose loyalty has been suspect have been removed either by dismissal or by not being nominated to party positions at national conventions. Any challenge to his leadership, however weak or unlikely to succeed, has been met with strong reactions.

When the Mayor of the Istanbul's Şişli borough, Mr Sarıgül, put up his candidacy for party presidency in January 2005 and lost in a quarrelsome extraordinary convention, he was thrown out of the party for disciplinary violations, returning only after a court ordered him reinstated. Members of the high disciplinary committee who felt that the Mayor had not committed disciplinary violations also ended up losing their positions. This reflects a pattern of thinking which regards criticizing or challenging the national and (by emulation) local leaders as a violation of party discipline. Expulsion is the standard punishment (Erdem 2001, p. 155). Bending of the rules or simply ignoring them in order to avert challenges to the absolute power of leadership is also employed. For example, in 2005 a petition by intra-party opposition groups calling for an extraordinary convention and bearing the required signatures was simply ignored and earned an embarrassing reprimand from the courts (Erdem 2005).

The party leader is elected by secret ballot by a majority of delegates attending the national party convention. Since the loyalty and therefore the votes of a sufficient number of delegates are already secured through their pre-selection at subprovincial and provincial conventions, the re-election of the party leader is assured. In the case of the CHP, even major failures in electoral performance have not produced challenges to Baykal's leadership. Mr Baykal appears assured of tenure unless he decides to leave the position. This might happen if his party were to fail to achieve parliamentary representation at the next elections.

The predominance of the leader in party politics has produced a situation that resembles politics in absolutist monarchies. Persons, groups and factions compete to get the attention and earn the favour of the party leader. The same relationship is replicated, but more moderately, at local levels. This basic feature has made the party an inward-looking organization absorbed in internal bickering with little influence in national politics and unimpressive electoral achievements. Such a state of affairs may appear to be all the more surprising in view of the personal background of Mr Baykal, which one would expect to be more liberal, democratic and universalistic.[6]

It should not be surprising that in a leader-dominated party, policy decisions are often pronouncements of the leader on this or that issue. Whether he consults others is judgmental, not a political necessity. He conducts 'reactive' politics in part because the party has not been able to review its ideology to render it coherent and more in tune with contemporary Turkish society, in part because the fragmented nature of the party's support has stood in the way of achieving a consensus on policy proposals, and, finally, in part because of Mr Baykal's own proclivity to rhetoric. Rather than registering a coherent response to the actions and policies of the government party and formulating and propagating its own policy goals among the electorate, he limits himself to criticism of what the government does, without even being aware that such criticism might contradict earlier party positions, programmes and the tenets of social democracy.

Even on matters of major import such as taking part in government or leaving it, Mr Baykal appears to have been the sole decision maker. This appears to have been the case in 1995 when he assumed the party's presidency. Upon taking office, he asked Premier Çiller, the CHP's coalition partner, to dismiss the Minister of the Interior because he had received a report alleging that many governors under the minister held anti-secular tendencies (Bila 1999). The minister's credentials did not justify such an allegation, but the show of force Mr Baykal initiated ended by bringing the government down. The same parties proceeded a few weeks later to establish a new coalition. During the entire affair, there is little evidence that the appropriate organs of the party were involved in the shaping of decisions. Some discussion may have taken place among the inner circle of advisors congregated around him.

Unidirectional Flows: Intra-party communication

The leader-dominated party does not provide many opportunities for members, local officials or deputies to communicate their views, expectations or demands to the leadership. The leader meets the parliamentary party group regularly. These meetings, however, do not provide opportunities for deputies to communicate their views. The leader arrives after everyone has been seated. Everyone rises and applauds him. He addresses the group. Deputies may take the floor to extol the virtues of the party and its leaders. More typically, deputies may communicate personal and district problems and requests through officers of the parliamentary group. The dependence of deputies on the party leader for renomination weakens both the individual deputy and the parliamentary group vis-à-vis the leader. It also reduces ties between the local organizations and representatives.

Communication between national headquarters, provincial organizations and members is sporadic and unsystematic. The highest forum for communication is the biannual national convention. Extraordinary conventions are also frequent. Since the reopening of the party in 1992, five regular and five extraordinary conventions have been held. The president may call mini-conventions comprising the provincial party presidents or he may invite some for consultations. These instruments are used occasionally, especially before elections to name candidates. Though less frequently nowadays, the party leader goes to provincial and subprovincial centres for mass rallies. He may occasionally choose to attend a provincial convention. These provide opportunities for provincial and national leaders to interact.

Routine communications dealing with rules, procedures, budgets and complaints are handled by the party bureaucracy headed by the secretary-general, who is chosen from among the members of the executive committee by a majority vote of the party assembly. The secretary-general then appoints assistant secretary-generals from among members of the executive committee, who are subject to the approval of the party president. The secretariat is a bureaucratic centre, not an autonomous power centre. The secretary-general is in regular contact with the rank and file and gets to know local leaders personally. Particularly in times of crisis, these resources have rendered him influential.

It is interesting that electronic communications are not used to their full potential, although such services are available throughout the country and used efficiently by others. A visit to the party's poorly designed and uninformative website is rather discouraging. Not user friendly, it gives the impression of an amateur's work. The volume of intra-party communications is modest, mostly carrying information from national headquarters to local organizations. The weakness of intra-party communications leads to frustration and alienation among both local organizations and members. These produce occasional rebellions that are met with disciplinary action. Some deputies and members then leave the party.

Treading on Thin Ice: Sources of Support and Competitive Strategies

Classical analyses of Turkish politics have identified the centre–periphery cleavage as basic in shaping Turkish politics (Özbudun 2000, p. 81; Kalaycıoğlu 1999). After the CHP in the late 1960s began to describe itself as a left-of-centre party, what was a centre–periphery alignment came to be named and perceived as a left–right alignment. The post-1983 political parties that inherited the CHP legacy are nowadays generally referred to as parties of the left. The mobility of votes between parties during the recent elections suggests that the salience of this cleavage may be declining. In the elections of 1987 the centre-left parties (DSP and SHP) claimed 33.3 per cent of the vote. The sum went down to 31.6 per cent in 1991. In 1995, when the reconstituted CHP, united with the SHP, entered its first election, the CHP–DSP total (10.7 per cent and 14.6 per cent, respectively) was no more than 25.3 per cent. The DSP landslide in 1999 raised the total to 30.9 per cent, but the CHP, with only 8.7 per cent of the vote, remained outside the parliament. In 2002, the CHP reached 19.4 per cent, but the CHP–DSP total was only 20.6 per cent.

The intense electoral volatility during recent years has worked at the expense of the centre-left. CHP voters appear to be shifting to the centre and extreme right (Esmer 2002, p. 98). Furthermore, voters are increasingly willing to favour different parties at each election, dropping partisan identifications (Çarkoğlu et al. 2000, pp. 41–43). Even the Virtue Party (now Felicity) of the religious right has been a beneficiary of the dispersal of the CHP votes (Ayata 2002, p. 106). More typically, votes have gone back and forth between the two parties of the centre-left. According to survey data, 21 per cent of those who voted for the CHP in 1995, voted for the DSP in 2001 (Turan 2004, p. 170).

Although partisan identity (68 per cent), the party voted in previous election (57 per cent) and secularism (secular versus religious, 54 per cent), rather than socio-economic differences, continue to account for party preferences (Akgün 2002, p. 76), inter-party mobility both within the same block and between blocks has been rising.

Discerning attributes of the CHP voters is still possible: the CHP voter is likely to be an older, whitecollar or retired, educated person living in an urban centre (Foundation for Social, Economic and Political Research of Turkey [TÜSES] 2002, p. 79; Turan 2004, p. 239; Ayata 2002, p. 107; Esmer 2002, p. 79). Working women also tend to support the CHP in greater numbers, although their preferences are becoming diversified (Ayata & Ayata 2002, p. 147).

The volatile electoral environment has forced the party to try different competitive strategies. Against the parties in the same camp, there are invitations to unite under the CHP roof, the natural address. The DSP has rejected such suggestions adamantly. At the level of the voters, this strategy may be somewhat appealing, since voters of the centre-left have moved between these parties. Against parties in the opposing camp, a strategy of polarization is pursued. The religious parties including the current government party are depicted as the negation of the secular, modern society the CHP has stood for since its birth. As regards the other parties, such as the Nationalist Action and the True Path, the party has begun to pursue an increasingly nationalist line, hoping that it might arrest losses in that direction and persuade some voters from those quarters to cross over.

The party pictures itself as the exclusive defender of the secular, modern tradition of the republic, raising the spectre of a return to a religious order if it is not supported. This has not worked to convince the voters in earlier elections. It may have had some positive effect on the party's electoral performance in 2002, but it is not clear whether the same can be repeated in future elections.

The Unholy War: Campaign Politics

Although elections are to be held every five years, all elections after 1983 have been brought forward by the parliament. This has led the campaigns to be short, three months or often less, including a month or more for candidate designation. Once the parliament has decided on early elections, the party assembly appoints a five-person committee from among its members and those of the parliamentary group, led by the party chief. Each member assumes responsibility for one of the five areas of activity: communication, propaganda, research, organization and finance. The committee plans the party's campaign strategy, including activities (a) intended to influence the public directly and requiring professional consulting, and (b) that reach the voters through the intermediation of local organizations, requiring the mobilization of party activists.

Before the campaign is launched, a study is conducted by professional consultants to identify possible major campaign themes. The final choice is made by the party assembly with the party head having the determining role. The effort is directed toward matching the expectations of the public with party ideology in a way that can easily be accepted and popularized by party workers. In 1999, Atatürk, republicanism and secularism were chosen as the major themes. This ideological approach was not rewarded by the voters. In 2002, 'Human beings come first' was the slogan preferred to address the discontent the strict economic reform policies had generated. A complementary theme was 'struggle against poverty and corruption'. Once chosen, the general theme cannot be changed; only adjustments may be made. The party hires professional consultants to monitor the campaign and examine how electoral support is faring and which slogans produce greater impact.

As is also the case with other parties, the campaign is leader centred. Television commercials are not allowed but each party is given free time on the state television channel, TRT-1, for several speeches. Private channels organize debates. In the CHP's case, TRT-1 broadcasts have been used exclusively by Mr Baykal. Other methods of directly reaching the public such as newspaper ads, outdoor posters, electronic and regular mailings, distribution of flyers, and party badges have also been used frequently during recent elections. This has been the result of more money becoming available through state funding, doubled during election years. These activities do not require large numbers of party activists and are easy to administer.

The other part of the campaign, comprising mass meetings and rallies, involves the participation of local party organizations. During the 1999 and 2002 campaigns, approximately 50 rallies were held in different parts of the country. These bring members of local organizations into the picture, boost their morale and give them opportunities to mobilize crowds, showing off to their opponents. They receive national TV coverage, motivating the organizers to work hard to make the event a success. As planes and helicopters are used nowadays, several events are scheduled in different centres on the same day. To finance the increasingly capital-intensive campaigns, those aspiring to candidacy are asked to make contributions. Those who are designated candidates are expected to provide a considerable amount of their own funding. [7]

Conclusion: Dying a Slow Death or Living a Miserable Life?

During its renewed existence from 1992 onwards, the CHP has been influenced by forces that have affected all Turkish political parties: the decline of party identification, the fragmentation of parties and the volatility of electoral outcomes. Like others, voter support for the CHP has fluctuated, but has persistently been below pre-1980 levels. The party's inability to develop ideas and programmes responsive to the new needs and the failure to appeal to new constituencies have weakened its ties with the electorate, producing a party controlled by a narrowly based group of activists who hold on to their positions by submitting to the authority of the party leader. This has made it possible for the leader to maintain his position irrespective of his performance. Without credible ideas, programmes or policy proposals and lacking broadly based constituencies, the party relies on ideology to mobilize support among the dwindling number of Kemalists and nowadays traditional nationalists.

The party has not been able to liberate itself from its past and to address major questions such as globalization, relations with the EU, how the state should relate to the market economy and what course Turkey's democratization should take. The uncertain voter support it enjoys and the fear of losing votes to its right and left have led the CHP to settle for a role as a weak opposition party in a multi-party system rather than as the main opposition in a two-party system. Understandably, the two-party system the 2002 elections produced is seen as a temporary result of the ten per cent national threshold. Apart from its brief tenure at the time of its re-establishment, the party has been in opposition or out of parliament, leading some to question whether the party has had any serious interest in some day becoming the government. An uncertain fate awaits the CHP. Most observers and opinion polls predict that the party will lose votes in the next elections though acquiring modest parliamentary representation. Do old soldiers ever die? There seems to be no reason to foresee that the party will transform itself successfully and become a major actor in the politics of the new Turkey that is in the process of emerging.

Notes

[1] See *Vatan* (1 and 5 June); *Sabah* (3 June); and *Milliyet* (3 June).

[2] The 1999–2004 budgets were made available by Algan Hacaloglu, CHP deputy secretary-general and MP from Istanbul. I am indebted to him for his help.

[3] All Turkish political parties are compelled to subscribe to a basic organizational model that is depicted in Political Parties Law (*Siyasi Partiler Kanunu*, no. 2820, 24 April 1983). Section III, articles 13–35 are devoted to party organization. The statute of the CHP, Sections III, IV and VI define party organization, mainly repeating what is depicted in the law.

[4] Precinct (*mahalle*) is the smallest administrative unit in any residential area. It is run by an elected headman and a five-man council of elders. The office is non-partisan and candidates cannot run for office bearing party labels.

[5] It is not uncommon that deputies elected under the label of one party leave their party during the legislative term and join another. See Turan (1985) and Turan et al. (2005).

[6] Mr Baykal was born in 1937 in the coastal town of Antalya and graduated from the Law School of Ankara University, becoming a graduate assistant at the Faculty of Political Sciences in political sociology. He had been active in politics since his student days. He was one of the members of the inner circle of Mr Bülent Ecevit when the party went through a major transformation, adopting left-of-centre ideology. He served as the minister of energy and natural resources in the first Ecevit government in 1973–74. Re-elected in 1977, he served as the minister of public finance in the second Ecevit government in 1978–79. When in 1981 the CHP was closed down, he practised law until his return to politics. Soon after resuming political activity,

he tried to get elected as president of the SHP but three times failed in his bid. He became the president of the CHP after it was re-established and united with the SHP.

[7] This section relies on the accounts of a CHP deputy, Bülent Tanla. As a pollster and strategic consultant by profession, he was involved in the preparation of both the 1999 and 2002 campaigns. I had a long telephone interview with Mr Tanla on 6 September 2005.

References

Akgün, B. (2002) *Türkiye'de Seçmen Davranışı, Partiler Sistemi ve Siyasal Güven* [Voting Behavior, Party System and Political Trust in Turkey], Güven, Ankara.

Ayata, A. G. (1992) *CHP: Örgüt ve İdeoloji* [CHP: Organization and Ideology], Gündoğan, Ankara.

Ayata, A. G. (2002) 'The Republican People's Party', in *Political Parties in Turkey*, eds B. Rubin & M. Heper, Frank Cass, London, pp. 102–121.

Ayata, A. G. & Ayata, S. (2002) 'Ethnic and religious bases of voting', in *Politics, Parties and Elections in Turkey*, eds S. Sayari & Y. Esmer, Lynne Rienner, Boulder, CO, pp. 137–156.

Bila, H. (1999) *CHP 1919–1999*, Doğan, Istanbul.

Çarkoğlu, A., Erdem, T. & Kabasakal, M. (2000) 'Türkiye'de yeni bir parti sistemine doğru' [Toward a new party system in Turkey], in *Siyasi Partilerde Reform* [The Reform of Political Parties], ed. A. Çarkoğlu, Tesev, Istanbul, pp. 29–129.

Erdem, T. (2001) *Tıkanan Siyaset*, [Politics at Impasse], Sel, Istanbul.

Erdem, T. (2005) 'İhtar Ne Yazar!' [A reprimand: who cares!], *Radikal*, 26 July, p. 11.

Esmer, Y. (2002) 'At the ballot box: the determinants of voting behavior', in *Politics, Parties and Elections in Turkey*, eds S. Sayari & Y. Esmer, Lynne Rienner, Boulder, CO, pp. 91–114.

İnönü, E. (1999) *Anılar ve Düşünceler I*, [Memories and Thoughts], Yorum, Istanbul.

Kalaycıoğlu, E. (1994) 'Elections and party preferences in Turkey', *Comparative Political Studies*, vol. 27, no. 8, pp. 402–424.

Kalaycıoğlu, E. (1999) 'The shaping of party preferences in Turkey: coping with the post Cold War era', *New Perspectives on Turkey*, no. 24, pp. 47–76.

Özbudun, E. (2000) *Contemporary Turkish Politics: Challenges to Democratic Consolidation*, Lynne Rienner, Boulder, CO.

Sakallıoğlu, Ü. (1999) 'Türkiye 1999: Tatbikat'ten harekete', [Turkey in 1999: from military exercise to action], *Birikim*, no. 122, pp. 16–22.

Sayarı, S. (2002) 'The changing party system', in *Politics, Parties and Elections in Turkey*, eds S. Sayari & Y. Esmer, Lynne Rienner, Boulder, CO, pp. 9–32.

Tachau, F. (2000) 'Turkish political parties and elections: half a century of multi-party democracy', *Turkish Studies*, vol. 1, no. 1, pp. 128–148.

Tosun, T. (2003) *Siyasette Yeniden Mevzilenmeler* [Taking New Positions in Politics], Büke, Istanbul.

Tunçay, S. (n.d.) *Parti İçi Demokrasi ve Türkiye* [Intra-party Democracy and Turkey], Gündoğan, Ankara.

Tuncer, E. (2003) *Osmanlı'dan Günümüze Seçimler* [Elections from Ottoman Times to Today], TESAV, Ankara.

Turan, A. E. (2004) *Türkiye'de Seçmen Davranışı: Önceki Kırılmalar ve 2002 Seçimi* [Voting Behavior in Turkey: Previous Discontinuities and the Elections of 2002], Bilgi Üniversitesi, Istanbul.

Turan, I. (1985) 'Changing horses in midstream: party changers in the Turkish Grand National Assembly', *Legislative Studies Quarterly*, vol. 10, no. 1, pp. 21–34.

Turan, I. (2003) 'Volatility in politics, stability in parliament: an impossible dream? The Turkish Grand National Assembly during the last two decades', *Journal of Legislative Studies*, vol. 9, no. 2, pp. 151–176.

Turan, I., İba, S. & Zarakol, A. (2005) 'Inter-party mobility in the Turkish Grand National Assembly: curse or blessing?', *European Journal of Turkish Studies, thematic issue on 'Being an MP in Contemporary Turkey'*, vol. 3, <http://www.ejts.org/document400.html>.

TÜSES. (2002) *Türkiye'de Siyasi Partilerin Yandaş/Seçmen Profili (1994–2002)* [The Supporter/Voter Profiles of Political Parties in Turkey], Istanbul.

Notes on Contributors

Javier Astudillo is an Associate Lecturer in the Department of Political and Social Sciences of the Universitat Pompeu Fabra (Barcelona) and doctor-member of the Juan March Institute of Studies and Research (Madrid). Between 1998 and 2000 he was a Fulbright Scholar in the Center for European Studies of Harvard University. He is the author of *Los Recursos del Socialismo: las Cambiantes Relaciones entre el PSOE y la UGT (1982–1993)* (1998).

Anna Bosco is Associate Professor of Political Parties and Interest Groups at the University of Trieste. She has carried out research on party change in Italy, Spain, Portugal, Greece and East-Central Europe. Among her most recent publications is *Da Franco a Zapatero. La Spagna dalla periferia al cuore dell'Europa* (2005) and *Partiti ed elettori nel Sud Europa* (as editor, 2006). She is assistant editor of *South European Society & Politics*.

Christophoros Christophorou (PhD, University of Lille) is a Council of Europe expert on media and elections and was the first director of the Cyprus Radio and Television Authority. He teaches communication at Intercollege in Nicosia. He is the creator of the only existing database on Cyprus elections (< we3 www.eklektor.org>) and has published books on electoral behaviour.

Elias Dinas is a PhD student in the University of Macedonia, where he also works as a researcher. His research interests include partisanship, leadership evaluations, electoral behaviour, and religious values.

Elena García-Guereta is an Associate Lecturer in the Department of Political Science of the Universidad Complutense (Madrid) and doctor-member of the Juan March Institute of Studies and Research (Madrid). She is the author of *Factores Externos e Internos en la Transformación de los Partidos Políticos: el Caso de AP-PP* (2001).

Daniela Giannetti is an Associate Professor in the Faculty of Political Science, University of Bologna. She has published in the fields of rational choice theory, political parties, and coalition governments. Among her most recent publications is *Teoria politica positiva. L' approccio razionale alla politica* (2003).

Carlos Jalali is an Assistant Professor in the Autonomous Section of Social, Juridical and Political Sciences, University of Aveiro, and a researcher in the Centre for the Study of Governance and Public Policy (University of Aveiro). Recent publications include 'A Yellow Card for the Government, Offside for European Issues? The European Elections of 2004 in Portugal', in *Campaigning for Europe: Campaigns, Mass*

Media and the European Parliamentary Elections of 2004 (eds M. Maier & J. Tenscher, 2006).

Marco Lisi is a doctoral candidate at the University of Florence. He has done research principally on the Portuguese political parties and the democratization of the Portuguese political system.

Mónica Méndez Lago is Lecturer in Political Science at the University of Murcia. She is currently on leave, working as technical advisor at the Centro de Investigaciones Sociológicas, in Madrid. She is the author of *La Estrategia Organizativa del Partido Socialista Obrero Español (1975–1996)* (2000).

Leonardo Morlino is Professor of Political Science at the Istituto di Scienze Umane (Florence). His most recent books include *Assessing the Quality of Democracy* (as co-editor and co-author, 2005) and *Democracias y Democratizaciones* (2006). His research interests are focused on the analysis of the 'qualities' of democracy in Europe and on the rule of law and democratic transitions in the new neighbours of the European Union.

Rosa Mulé is an Associate Professor at the Faculty of Political Science 'Roberto Ruffilli', University of Bologna. She has published in the fields of political parties, political participation, and the welfare state. She is the author of *Political Parties, Games and Redistribution* (2001).

Ergun Özbudun is Professor of Political Science and Constitutional Law at Bilkent University in Ankara. Formerly, he was a research fellow at Harvard University and a Visiting Professor at Columbia, Princeton, and Paris (Sorbonne) Universities. His publications include *Social Change and Political Participation in Turkey* (1976) and *Contemporary Turkish Politics: Challenges to Democratic Consolidation* (2000).

Takis S. Pappas is an Assistant Professor in the Department of Balkan, Slavic, and Oriental Studies of the University of Macedonia, Thessaloniki. He is the author of *Making Party Democracy in Greece* (1999) and many articles, the most recent of which is 'Shared Culture, Individual Strategy and Collective Action: Explaining Slobodan Milošević's Charismatic Rise to Power', in *Southeast European and Black Sea Studies* (2005). Currently, he is working on a book about the emergence of the Greek Socialist Party (PASOK) in the mid-1970s.

Francesco Raniolo is Professor of Political Science at the University of Calabria. His research interests include democracy and participation, political parties, and the relationship between politics and bureaucracy. He is the author of *I partiti conservatori in Europa occidentale* (2000) and *La partecipazione politica* (2002).

Michalis Spourdalakis is a Professor in the Department of Political Science and Public Administration at the University of Athens. He teaches Political Sociology and Greek Politics. He is the author of *The Rise of the Greek Socialist Party* (1988) and *On the Theory and the Study of Political Parties* (1990, in Greek).

Chrisanthos Tassis is a PhD candidate in the Department of Political Science and Public Administration at the University of Athens.

Ilter Turan is Professor of Political Science at Bilgi University, Istanbul. His research and writing have mainly been on Turkish political institutions and behaviour. He has also written occasionally on Turkish foreign policy and the domestic and international politics of water.

INDEX